WALES

Simon Jenkins

WALES

Churches, Houses, Castles

ALLEN LANE
an imprint of
PENGUIN BOOKS

ALLEN LANE

Published by the Penguin Group

Penguin Books Ltd, 80 Strand, London WC2R 0RL, England

Penguin Group (USA) Inc., 375 Hudson Street, New York, New York 10014, USA

Penguin Group (Canada), 90 Eglinton Avenue East, Suite 700, Toronto, Ontario,
Canada M4P 2Y3 (a division of Pearson Canada Inc.)

Penguin Ireland, 25 St Stephen's Green, Dublin 2, Ireland (a division of Penguin Books Ltd)

Penguin Group (Australia), 250 Camberwell Road, Camberwell, Victoria 3124,
Australia (a division of Pearson Australia Group Pty Ltd)

Penguin Books India Pvt Ltd, 11 Community Centre,
Panchsheel Park, New Dehli – 110 017, India

Penguin Group (NZ), 67 Apollo Drive, North Shore 0632, New Zealand
(a division of Pearson New Zealand Ltd)

Penguin Books (South Africa) (Pty) Ltd, 24 Sturdee Avenue,
Rosebank 2196, South Africa

Penguin Books Ltd, Registered Offices: 80 Strand, London WC2R 0RL, England

www.penguin.com

First published 2008

1

Copyright © Simon Jenkins, 2008

The moral right of the author has been asserted

Designed by Andrew Barker
Typeset in 8.769/10.964 pt Adobe Minion
Printed and bound in Italy by Printer Trento s.r.l.

ISBN: 978-0-713-99893-1

Illustration on page ii: *Tudor ascendancy – Plas Mawr, Conwy*

To the memory of Daniel Jenkins

Contents

Preface

This is a book about Wales, a territory which for the past five centuries has been constitutionally conjoined with England. So what is Wales?

We all have our sense of a place, a composite of its geography, its history and our own fragmentary acquaintance. I should lay my cards on the table. I have known Wales all my life but never as a native or permanent resident. The son of a Welsh father and an English mother, I have always lived in England but spent virtually every holiday in Wales, where my parents are buried in the village of Pennal in Merioneth, now Gwynedd.

My self-description is therefore careful: I am half-Welsh. Since the Welsh are famously sensitive to any comment on their affairs, especially by outsiders, I have discovered that this 'half-ness' confers only the most limited licence. But then sub-divisions of states in every European country are becoming ever more proud of their status and jealous of their culture in the face of so-called globalization. In this they are supported by a swelling army of incomers, whether with or without family links, who find comfort and a sense of identity in small places.

I have travelled to every corner of Wales and have grown aware of it as a distinctive place, apart from England, not just with its own language and devolved National Assembly, but also with a separate human geography. Even where they do not speak the Welsh language, as a majority do not, the Welsh speak English with a specific, euphonious accent rooted in the cadences of that tongue. They acknowledge a distinctive history and culture, worship distinctive heroes and see their identity in distinctive buildings.

This separateness is remarkable given Wales's long border with England and its nearness to English centres of population – nearer than its one-time Celtic cousins, Cornwall and Northumbria. The attempt of English colonizers and rulers from the Normans to the Tudors to eliminate Wales as a political entity has been counter-productive. It bred what the Englishman-turned-Welshman, John Cowper Powys, called a 'proud humility … within a harmless, patient, unfathomable, evasive soul'.

The English are starkly ignorant of Wales. They are taught about their own country and, to an extent, about Scotland and Ireland. Yet to them the story of Wales is a closed book. The celebrities of Welsh history, Rhodri Fawr, Hywel Dda, Nest ap Rhys, Gerald of Wales, Llywelyn the Great and Owain Glyndŵr inhabit a historical mist, alongside druids, Merlin, King Arthur and his round table. The sound of the triple harp and the penillion, glories of British music, lie in the same obscurity as does the sound of Welsh, a supposedly 'foreign' tongue within the shores of the British Isles. As for the crucial significance of Welsh politics to the story of England for four centuries after the Norman conquest, it is a blank, as I discuss in the introduction.

Whether or not Wales is a land, a country, a nation or a state is a perennial source of debate. In modern Europe, territorial sovereignty is qualified by tiers of allegiance, from parish to county, province to region, nation to 'supra-nation'. While governmental power has a tendency to centralize, democracy fights to decentralize, to return power to the geographical building-blocks of self-rule.

Over the past half-century, the story of European public administration has generally been one of power moving upwards to the European Union and downwards to devolved group assemblies, to Basques, Catalans, Bretons, Bavarians, Sicilians and Scots. In 2000 Wales shared in this latter shift and is struggling to secure a wider range of subsidiary powers. Hence for the first time since the defeat of Owain Glyndŵr, Wales has its own political institutions and national leadership.

The new Welsh Assembly sounds Welsh, thinks Welsh and legislates for Wales. In the 1860s Matthew Arnold could deplore Welsh distinctiveness since 'the fusion of all the inhabitants of these islands into one homogeneous English-speaking whole … the swallowing up of separate provincial nationalities, is a consummation towards which the natural course of things irresistibly tends.' Such an intolerant statement is inconceivable today.

I believe that devolution to Wales will strengthen over time, and the Welsh will feel more of a coherent people within a coherent country in the process. They will not be independent – no European state is truly that – but they will take on ever more 'nationalist' colouring. They will have an opportunity to heal the age-old rift between north and south, and to entrench their language and culture in their institutions. I hope this book is an aid to that process.

My exploration of Welsh buildings follows similar explorations of the churches and houses of England. The experience has been markedly different. England seemed merely the sum of its parts while Wales is far more. Its most notable buildings are interlinked with its history by the paradox that the majority were the work of an invading and occupying power, England. As a result, any exploration of the Welsh landscape throbs with self-consciousness and renders the concept of the 'Welshness' in a building peculiarly challenging, a challenge to which I return in the introduction and to which this entire book is a response.

I must thank many who made my travels and researches in Wales so enjoyable. They include the Welsh historic buildings agency, Cadw, for help with pictures and for its admirable publications (quite the best of any of the genre in Britain). Help with pictures has also come from the National Trust, Country Life and the Friends of Friendless Churches, who have been most dogged in Wales. Credit is due to such organizations as the chapel-based Welsh Religious Buildings Trust and the Diocese of Bangor, who have made real efforts to keep their buildings open to public view.

Personal thanks for help, advice and hospitality are due to Jan and Elizabeth Morris, Auriol Linlithgow, Peter Lord, Miles Wynn-Cato, Peter Welford and Judy Corbett, Mark Baker, Lindsay Evans, Brooke Boothby, John Mack, Marilyn Lewis and Christine Kenyon (both of Cadw), and Fiona Reynolds of the National Trust. Peter Lord, Jan Morris and Peter Welford read and commented on the typescript, in whole or in part. My editor, Stuart Proffitt, took an unflinching interest in the project. Notification of mistakes to the publisher will be most welcome.

Introduction

Aros mae'r mynyddau mawr,
Rhuo trostynt mae y gwynt;
Clywir eto gyda'r wawr
*Gân bugeiliaid megis cynt.**

The rugged summit of Aran Fawddwy in mid-Wales offers a panorama without equal in the British Isles. North lie the majestic peaks of Snowdonia. East are the soft hills and dales towards the River Severn and England. To the south the reclining humps of the Brecon Beacons guard the steep valleys of Gwent and Glamorgan. West is the sea and the glorious sweep of Cardigan Bay, from Llŷn and Bardsey Island down to the intimate coves of Pembrokeshire.

All Wales is embraced by this view. No place in Europe offers such an encompassing vista of one country. From this vantage point there is no obvious sign of human settlement. There is only landscape, rolling and soaring, with the imagination free to ponder the history and genius of the place. For whatever else Wales may or may not be, it is unquestionably one place.

Ten miles down the Dyfi valley from Aran Fawddwy is a spot where I have often stood, amidst the oldest built thing I know, a small stone circle on the deserted hillside of Tarren Hendre. I have wondered what its creators hoped or feared in devising this strange device.† Wales has some 140 recorded structures like this – henges, cromlechs, huts and barrows, best evoked at the Bryn Celli Ddu burial mound on Anglesey. All knowledge of their occupants has gone, leaving only a sense of wonderment at their ability to quarry and move stone. These are the people who transported bluestones from the Preseli mountains of Pembrokeshire to Stonehenge, one of Europe's most extraordinary works of prehistoric engineering.

Stones are the stuff of Wales. From stone mountains to stones engraved with mystic Celtic patterns, from stone forts erected by Wales's conquerors to stone

---

* The mighty hills unchanging stand,
Tireless the winds across them blow;
The shepherd's song across the land
Sounds with the dawn as long ago.
(John Ceiriog Hughes)
† Above Pant-yr-onn.

Plas Newydd: Llangollen tranquillity

villages, stone churches and the stone from which the Welsh have always dug their wealth. This is not a land of soft earth or chalk or shifting sands. It is a land of unyielding stoniness. Even the poem which adorns the lowering cornice of Cardiff's new opera house declares, 'In these stones horizons sing.' It is as if Wales were a nation trapped in its own intractable geological fact.

Whoever arranged my stone circle did so two millennia before the arrival in the 5th century BC of invading Celts, Indo-European-speaking tribes from the mainland of Europe. Of them we again know little, except that they divided into two groups, roughly identified by their language. The Irish and Scots spoke Goidelic (Gaelic) and the Britons a tongue called Brythonic, found initially across England, Wales and lowland Scotland and evolving into Cornish, Welsh and Breton.

Tacitus records a tantalizing glimpse of the ancient Welsh people, massed for war on the shores of Anglesey, probably in AD 61, and terrifying the Roman legionaries by the curses their druids and women hurled across the Menai Straits. These were the same druids, Tacitus later wrote, whom acolytes from France joined to study the animism of the woods and winds, who 'smeared their altars with blood from their prisoners and sought the will of the gods by exploring the entrails of men'.

We know that when the invading Romans first crossed the Severn in AD 47 (after landing in Britain in 43) they found a hard land to master. It took thirty years to defeat the Ordovices in the north and the Silures and Demetae in the south. The eventual conquest, in AD 79, was commanded from Chester and Caerleon outside Newport, the latter one of the largest Roman camps extant in Britain.

To subjugate this land required, at one point, a garrison of 30,000 troops. A network of Roman roads, forts and villas was built across Wales and survived for three centuries of colonization. The Roman presence was most intense in Gwent and Glamorgan, where the ever-observant 12th-century monk Gerald of Wales (see Manorbier, Dyfed) recorded 'immense palaces ... hot baths, the remains of temples and an amphitheatre', and wondered at the sophistication of such people. The surviving amphitheatre at Caerleon is calculated to have seated 6,000 people. Roman sites are still being discovered, including one in 2008 outside Dolgellau, and a Mithraic temple near Caernarfon, the Roman Segontium.

With the colonists eventually came Christianity, though how far it penetrated into the Welsh population is unknown. Nor do we know what survived after the Romans left, when Magnus Maximus retreated from Britain in AD 383 to attempt to seize the imperial throne and rescue the Roman empire. This

Bryn Celli Ddu: mystic prehistory

ignorance is particularly regrettable since, while many inhabitants may have reverted to paganism, the new faith must have put down such firm roots that, barely a century after the Roman departure, a Christian movement appears to have swept the country, more remarkable than any recorded in Europe, the so-called age of saints. It was in the two centuries after the retreat of Rome that this region emerged as distinctively Welsh, yet we know almost nothing about its development.

Scholars believe that the 5th-century *clas* or teaching monastery at Llantwit Major in Glamorgan may have been founded at least within living memory of a Roman presence. There is a Roman villa here and the founder of Llantwit, Illtud, made it a centre of Christian study, sending missions to Ireland, Cornwall and Brittany. Illtud was believed to have been taught by Germanus of Auxerre in Gaul, one of the few known characters to have visited Britain in the immediate aftermath of the Roman retreat, in AD 429. There appear to have been many Roman patricians still resident. Archaeology records villas still in occupation well into the 5th century.

We assume that the remaining Romans (like the Britons in 20th-century India) did not abandon their habits or their religion. By then men of charisma and zeal were forming *clasau* (plural of *clas*) throughout Wales. St Samson passed from Llantwit to Caldey (Dyfed) and Cornwall. The patron saint of Irish Christianity, Patrick, is said to have come from Llantwit, or at least studied there. There were *clasau* at Llanbadarn, Tywyn, Meifod and at least thirty other sites. The one founded by Deiniol at Bangor in 525 claims to be the oldest cathedral in Britain. St David, the devout son of a Dyfed king, founded a *clas* in his native Pembrokeshire in the mid-6th century which became a centre of Celtic Christianity for 500 years.

Wales in other words was almost certainly not 're-Christianised' by Irish missionaries, as was once thought, but shared in a continuous post-Roman Christian culture that inspired and united the coastal peoples of the Irish Sea in the 5th and 6th centuries, a time when England was preoccupied with invasions of pagan Angles, Saxons and, later, Scandinavians.

The Anglo-Saxon occupation of England was protracted and terrible. The newcomers slaughtered or evicted the British and drove them north and west, evidenced by the almost complete supplanting of the Brythonic language in England, and the probable driving of some Britons to settle with their language in Brittany. It was this process that created Wales, secure in its mountains where lowland Saxons were loathe to venture. When the 6th-century missionary, Beuno, heard Anglo-Saxon being spoken on the far side of the Severn, he was disturbed by such 'strange-tongued men whose voice I heard across the river' and vowed to go no farther. These people, he prophesied, 'will obtain possession of this place, and it will be theirs and they will hold it for themselves.'

The survival of a continuous Brythonic culture in Wales is the only sensible explanation for the vigour of Christianity at this time. Yet for a book primarily about buildings it is a baffling period. The departure of the Romans led to an abrupt halt in the archaeological record of building activity. As the Welsh historian John Davies points out, 'The ethos which had sprung from the Greeks and which had been spread by the Romans vanished … With the long sunset came an age of myth and fantasy almost devoid of historical certainties.'

Myth and fantasy dominate what evidence we have. The writings in Latin about Wales of the 6th-century Gildas and the 9th-century Nennius tended to treat history as the stuff of sermons and diatribes. To Gildas the Saxon invasion was a straightforward punishment of the Britons for their sins. Nennius admitted that he based his writings on 'a heap of legends' and, where checkable, displays what Davies calls a 'monumental ignorance'. To him we owe the origins of the Arthur myth.

The paramount source on the British church in the Dark Ages, the Venerable Bede, used Gildas as a source and was hopelessly anti-Welsh (and pro-Irish). The Welsh, he wrote, had 'a natural hatred for the English and uphold their own bad customs against the true Easter of the Catholic church: nevertheless they are opposed by the power of God and man alike.' The best that can be said for these sources is that they validate the existence of an active religious culture in Wales back to the 5th century, one that was worthy of their critical attention.

There were as yet no towns to replace those abandoned by the Romans and we are bereft of evidence as to how the Welsh lived in the Dark Ages. It is assumed that they continued to inhabit such enclosures as Tre'r Ceiri (Gwynedd), the 'Welsh Machu Picchu' on the mountains of the Llŷn, or the stone huts at Din Llugwy (Anglesey). Other buildings, which would have been of wood and thatch, have long vanished.

The structure of government in the three centuries after the Roman departure is equally obscure. An Irish king, Nial, plundered west Wales in 405 and Irish influences are detectable in the south-west, notably an Irish script known as ogham, which occurs on standing stones only in this region. Brecon owes its name to an Irish king. A north Briton from the present Cumbria, Cunedda, invaded Anglesey some time after the Roman departure, some claim in order to drive out migrant Irish at the behest of the remaining Romans.

Here it was Cunedda's sons who founded the royal house of Gwynedd and were to claim sovereignty over it for some seven centuries. Cunedda represented a link between north Wales and Brythonic-speaking Northumbria, where his people were being pushed northwards by the Anglo-Saxons. His court, moving between Northumbria and north Wales, produced the earliest Welsh poets, including Aneirin and Taliesin. The former told of battles against the Saxons by the 'old northerners' as far south as Yorkshire, where 'Although they were being slain, they slew;/ To the world's end they will be honoured.'

Aneirin's 'northern' Welsh was widely spoken in the Scots border country and lives on in such place names such as Penrith, Lanercost and Cumbria, similar to the Welsh word for Wales, Cymru. If his 9th-century copyists were accurate, Aneirin's tongue was remarkably pure and explains Gerald of Wales's remark in the 12th century that north Welsh was a richer language than that in the south, because its speakers were 'less intermixed with foreigners' (presumably Irish and Normans).

In his new introduction to the great Welsh epic, the Mabinogion, Will Parker points out that north Welsh culture in the Dark Ages was in large part that of refugees, dreaming of their lost lands in north Britain and forging a vigorous identity that was to colour and fracture Welsh politics for almost a millennium.

The descendents of Cunedda, such as Maelgwn Gwynedd and Cadwaladr, ruled Gwynedd through most of the Dark Ages. Powys, along the mid-Welsh border, was ruled by Eliseg, Cyngen and Rhodri Mawr, until the Cadwgans became its ancestral princes. South Wales was more divided, between Dyfed and Ceredigion (Pembroke and Cardigan) in the west and Brycheiniog (Brecon), Glywysing (Glamorgan) and Gwent in the east. But records were sparse and subsequent attacks by Vikings tended to eradicate archaeological evidence. John Davies's diagram of the royal houses of Wales in the Dark Ages is as complicated as the map of the London Underground.

Meanwhile the Welsh church was evolving from the age of the *clasau* to a more Roman coherence of episcopal spheres of influence, represented eventually by dioceses at Llandaff, St David's and Bangor. Here at last we have evidence of sorts, in stone crosses, place names and the outline of sacred enclosures. Wales starts to emerge from legend into fact.

The crosses are most vivid. While churches of wood and turf were rising and falling, crosses survived with their decoration and inscriptions intact, whether in Roman or Irish ogham script. Two stones in the churchyard at Nevern (Dyfed) mark the beginning and the end of this period, one to the Latin-named Vitalianus, possibly of the 5th century, the other, the great Nevern Cross, an abstract design of the 11th. They straddle an astonishing six centuries of British history.

Like those displayed in the collection at Margam (Glamorgan) the Nevern Cross displays a remarkable craftsmanship. To Jan Morris, ever the sardonic observer, 'the notorious deviousness of the Welsh finds its exact imagery in the convoluted art forms of the Celts, which depended upon illusory circles, disturbing knots and bafflingly inconclusive squiggles.' Yet they were works of great skill. As Nora Chadwick writes (in *The Celts*), 'A single false step, a slip of the tool, and the entire cross would have been ruined. But we do not find false cuts. The whole is of an almost mechanical perfection.' The crosses bear witness to the earliest known Welsh art, flourishing for some five centuries before the Norman conquest.

Interpreting sacred enclosures is more complex. The sites took their names from the founder of a church, who might be a hermit, monk, chief or son of a king. Many early 'saints' appear to have enjoyed hereditary authority and their monasteries were de facto centres of civil as well as religious life. David was al-legedly the son of a king of Dyfed, Tysilio of a prince of Powys and Cadoc of a prince of Glamorgan. The prefix for a sacred place, *llan*, might be applied to the name of a local chief as well as a holy man. Hence Llangybi might be just the sacred enclosure of Cybi's clan.

Traces of these structures remain in their often circular plans and groves of yews, which later builders tended to respect even as they rebuilt walls and roofs. Short and with no architectural division between nave and chancel, Celtic churches had square-ended chancels (as opposed to the Norman apses) and no towers. A sense of these places can be had at Llandrillo (Clwyd) and St Govan (Dyfed). By the 11th and 12th centuries more were of stone. Some so-called 'Norman' churches, possibly Tywyn (Gwynedd) and Penmon (Anglesey), may have nothing to do with the Normans and more with the Irish/Welsh culture of the period. The surviving rounded arch at Strata Florida (Dyfed) post-dates the conquest but is clearly not Norman.

The ghosts of these Celtic churches flit across Wales's lonely beaches, moun-tains and deserted valleys, evoking the Dark Ages more forcefully than anywhere else I know in Europe. Their worship remained independent of Canterbury and Rome and was still under the guidance of the *clasau* into the 12th century. A remarkable priest at Llanbadarn (Dyfed), Rhygyfarch, author of a life of St David and of the Llanbadarn Psalter (now in Trinity College, Dublin), lament-ed the decline of the old church: 'One vile Norman intimidates one hundred natives with his command/ And terrifies them with his look./ You, Wales … your beard droops and your eye is sad.' It has been the cry of the Welsh down the ages.

By the 9th century more concerted attempts were being made to assert national unity in the face of the Saxon and Viking menace. Evidence is the 170-mile dyke constructed by the Mercian king Offa to delineate the Welsh/ English border in 784. By the middle of the next century, Rhodri Mawr of Powys had conquered and ruled most of Wales. His grandson, Hywel Dda, through judicious marriage, governed Gwynedd, Powys and Deheubarth (Dyfed and the present Breconshire) and negotiated a peace with the English earls.

In the 940s Hywel formulated a Welsh legal code whose emphasis on the folk-law of kinship (and the rights of women and children) rather than the law of regal and ecclesiastic authority survived in parts of Wales into the 16th century. It is regarded as among the most liberal codes in Europe at the time, even laying down the three grades of bard, the lowest being minstrel. The 'laws of Hywel Dda' gave early substance to Welsh cultural self-awareness. They were a seminal document of national consciousness.

A century after Hywel's death in 950, Gruffudd ap Llywelyn, king of Gwynedd, conquered Powys, Deheubarth and Morgannwg (Glamorgan and Gwent) and thus achieved the Welsh Encyclopedia's accolade of being 'the sole ruler in the history of Wales to have authority over the whole country.' But in 1062 Gruffudd fell foul of the powerful English earl Harold Godwinesson and was murdered by a Welsh rival.

Wales thus contrived to fall apart when it most needed to stand together, just three years before the Norman conquest. A century later, Wales's most remarkable commentator, the monk Gerald of Wales (see Manorbier, Dyfed), son of a Norman father and a Welsh mother, was to reflect on this core weakness of the Welsh. They were, he wrote, 'as easy to subdue in battle as they are difficult to subdue in war … If only they could be inseparable, they would be insuperable.' But they were not inseparable. Wales was never conquered by the Saxons but its feuds and political fissures, its internal belligerence, ill-prepared it for the whirlwind that arrived on its borders at the end of the 11th century.

THE NORMAN CONQUEST

The Normans were the new Romans. While it took them three years to subdue England, it took them three centuries to subdue Wales. English historians, their tunnel vision fixed on wars with Scotland and France, grossly underrate the effort and expense that medieval English kings were forced to devote to holding Wales in thrall. Its strategic position on the route to Ireland and adjacent to the Midlands meant that control over it was both crucial and unreliable.

Wales was to demand a prodigious political and military enterprise, involving periodic wars and strategic marriages, the building of costly castles, monasteries and colonies, and the creation of an extraordinary class of Marcher lords, whose potency was to cause English kings constant trouble. When a devastating civil war, the Wars of the Roses, eventually engulfed England, Wales

St David's Cathedral: effigy of the Lord Rhys

and the Tudor dynasty could alone offer salvation and settlement at Bosworth in 1485.

After the conquest, William realized that the Welsh border was his most exposed. He paid the Welsh the compliment of granting the Marcher earldoms to his most trusted courtiers, Hugh Lupus in Cheshire, the Mortimers and Montgomerys in Shropshire and the FitzOsberns in Hereford. These fighting commanders had come to England and were ready to settle Wales, usually through local warlords, on the assumption that it meant loot.

Initially William sought peace with the princes of Wales, going on pilgrimage to St David's in their honour and forming an alliance with the king of Deheubarth, Rhys ap Tewdwr. William's son, William Rufus, was less secure and less astute, permitting the Marcher lords to raid across the border and visit rape and pillage on the Welsh.

These men were descendants of the Norse 'north-men' who had colonized France from Scandinavia. They cared little for politics and rarely settled down. Their troops were near unstoppable. To Vaughan-Thomas, 'The concentrated impact of a band of trained (and mailed) knights was the Norman equivalent of a Panzer division.' An undisciplined mob of sword-waving Celtic warriors, however brave, was no match for them.

After the death of the Conqueror in 1087, Marcher lords poured into Wales. Hugh of Chester struck north across Clwyd, Roger of Montgomery and his son battled through Powys and down the coast to Pembroke, FitzOsbern made for Brecon from his base at Chepstow. On their way they would demand tribute or fealty from Welsh princes or forge devious alliances of one against another, each side seeking security or personal gain. In Pembroke, Montgomery set the warrior Gerald of Windsor in command of his castle. Robert of Gloucester took command of Cardiff.

Within their domains these rulers enjoyed an autonomy beyond any that would be tolerated in England. As in Normandy, so in Wales, English kings could hold territory only through the agency of these barons. As a result the title of Marcher lord was eagerly sought by the leading Norman families in England, extending from the Montgomerys and Mortimers to the de Barris, de Clares, Bohuns and Broases. This independence, initially required for the governance of Wales, was asserted by all barons against King John in Magna Carta in 1215. Welsh resistance can take some credit for that.

Only the mountain fastness of Gwynedd remained largely immune to the Normans. In 1188 when Gerald of Wales and Archbishop Baldwin took their promotion of the Third Crusade from south to north, Baldwin was too frightened to cross the Dyfi into territory that no Norman could safely enter. Gerald,

The moated bastions of Caerphilly Castle

relying on his half-Welshness, travelled on alone. Gwynedd remained 'Pura Walia' throughout the Middle Ages, and retains a self-styled purity to this day. Cardiff politicians humorously refer to it as 'Taliban country' (some not so humorously).

With the Normans, the buildings of Wales come into focus. They do so primarily in the network of castles built by the conquerors to a density and splendour rare in Europe. The remains of some 600 early medieval fortresses have been detected in Wales and the Marches. The mightiest, at Chepstow, was begun by FitzOsbern just a year after the battle of Hastings and was built of stone from the start.

Within two decades, some 80 wooden motte and bailey forts had been erected across south Wales to protect the land route to Ireland and contain Welsh resistance to the north. These structures were later rebuilt in stone, increasingly round rather than square to resist missile attack. Such warrior knights as William Marshall constructed a great keep at Pembroke in 1204, the most awesome symbol of Norman power in Britain.

Adjacent to these castles, the Normans created some 70 fortified colonies, laid out on the rectangular Romano-French plan. Settlers from France or England, or in south Pembrokeshire from Flanders, were granted mercantile privileges in return for helping to defend the castle. Long, thin burgage plots concentrated houses on narrow streets while gardens stretched out to the walls, a pattern still visible in Pembroke. The Welsh were excluded from such settlements and farmers were driven from the fields adjacent to the walls.

The conquest of Wales was a thorough business. Norman families were expected to settle there and intermarry with local royalty. Henry I gave his mistress, Princess Nest, daughter of Rhys, the last king of Deheubarth, in marriage to the constable of Pembroke, Gerald of Windsor. Her story (see Cilgerran Castle, Dyfedd) was one of constant toing-and-froing between Norman and Welsh authority. Her grandson, the aforementioned Gerald of Wales, was perpetually torn in his loyalty, boasting both Marcher lordship and Welsh royal blood. He claimed that such half-breeds 'inherit our courage from the Welsh and our skill in battle from the Normans', yet he was always aware that neither side fully trusted him.

Norman voices, Norman justice and Norman culture now mingled with Welsh in the great halls that represented medieval power in Wales, whether military or ecclesiastical. But there was no fusion of cultures as in England, where the Anglo-Saxon and Norman languages merged into one tongue (unlike the earlier Anglo-Saxon and Brythonic). The writings of Gerald at the end of the 12th century depict Wales as still Welsh and the Normans as still interlopers.

This was due in large part to the exclusivity of the borough settlements. Privileges needed to persuade Norman colonists to settle in this hostile country ensured its continued hostility. In south Pembrokeshire the Welsh were 'cleansed' altogether and Flemish migrants introduced as a mass settlement. Welsh place names vanished and an enclave formed that became known as 'little England beyond Wales'. That was the case nowhere else.

Religious conquest was considered as crucial as military. Early Norman churches were built at Chepstow and Newport (Gwent). Eager to bring Celtic Christianity under the authority of Canterbury and Rome, the Normans brought Augustinians and Benedictines to settle Llanthony, Ewenni, Brecon and elsewhere, in monasteries of a size and splendour never before seen in the British Isles. They rebuilt the cathedral at St David's, the last major romanesque structure in Britain, with twenty-two different varieties of chevron ornament. By the end of the Middle Ages nowhere in Wales was said to be more than an hour's ride from a monastery.

Nor was the monastic invasion purely a Norman affair. The arrival of the ascetic Cistercians in the 12th century was widely sponsored by local princes, such as Lord Rhys at Strata Florida (Dyfed), eager for a more distinctively Welsh

Cistercian elegance: Tintern Abbey

monasticism. Most of Wales's great churches were to be of this order, Tintern, Valle Crucis, Abbey-cwm-hir and Margam. Elsewhere Celtic chapels of wood and thatch were reconstructed of stone.

Hardly a structure in this book does not have some fragment of Norman work buried in its walls. But while the style might be that of the invader and while the monasteries might speak in tongues of French and Latin, parochial religion persisted as Welsh. Through to the days of Glyndŵr in the 1400s, Welsh clerics could dream of re-founding a national church separate from the 'degenerate' English. It was a dream to which the evangelists of the Tudor reformation deftly appealed.

English castles were built in Wales for almost three centuries because Welsh national aspirations never evaporated. Across the span of the 13th century the two Llywelyns, ap Iorwerth 'the Great' (1173–1240) and his grandson, ap Gruffudd (?–1282), sallied forth from their ancestral base in Gwynedd, briefly to succeed where earlier Welsh kings had mostly failed, in uniting Wales against the English.

The Llywelyns won sufficient ascendancy for ap Iorwerth to marry King John's daughter, Joan (buried in Anglesey), and have his sovereignty recognized in Magna Carta. He married all his daughters to Marcher families, formed a court and an administration, raising taxes and issuing edicts under a privy seal. In 1267, ap Gruffudd was acknowledged by the English as Prince of Wales under the Treaty of Montgomery, when Henry III was hard-pressed by Simon de Montfort. Wales came nearer to being united than at any time since the Conquest. Ap Gruffudd was engaged to de Montfort's daughter and his confidence was reflected in the setting up of Welsh market towns to rival those of the Norman English, such as Llanidloes, Machynlleth and Newtown in mid-Wales.

The Llywelyns copied the Normans in building castles, at Cricieth, Castell y Bere and wild Dolwyddelan, guarding the Gwynedd coast and the passes through Snowdonia. Powis was originally a Welsh castle, as was Dinefwr in Dyfed. But the glory did not last. The Marcher lords, the Mortimers and de Clares, were not ready to see their domains in central and south Wales endangered either by weak English kings or by Welsh nationalists. In 1268 Gilbert de Clare built himself a mighty fortress that still stands at Caerphilly (Glamorgan), basing its design on his study of the siege of Kenilworth. Henry III's warrior son, Edward I, declared Llywelyn ap Gruffudd 'a rebel and a disturber of the peace'.

Between 1277 and 1283 Edward waged the most concerted military campaign seen on mainland Britain since the Norman invasion. The Marcher lords were charged with regaining territory lost to Llywelyn in the south and Edward

Cwmyoy: tumbling tower beneath a Norman sky

himself marched into Gwynedd. He isolated the rebel bread-basket of Anglesey and drove Llywelyn deep into Snowdonia. The last Welsh ruler to be acknowledged by the English eventually died in a skirmish near Builth Wells.

The defeat was total, signalled by Edward's Treaty of Rhuddlan of 1284, under which 'Divine Providence ... has now wholly and entirely transferred under our proper dominion the land of Wales with its inhabitants.' This formally ended Welsh law and divided Wales into English shires. Llywelyn's brother, Dafydd, was horribly executed. Edward spent three years in Wales and crowned his heir prince, a custom that has continued to today. The Welsh poet Gruffudd ab yr Ynad Coch composed the celebrated lament,

Och hyd atat-ti, Dduw, na ddaw – môr dros dir!
Pa beth y'n gedir i ohiriaw?*

Welsh architecture now evolved from merely awesome to spectacular. Nothing signalled the seriousness of Edward's Welsh campaign as did his castles. Seventeen were built in all, of which ten were wholly new and of the first rank. Three, Conwy, Caernarfon and Harlech, were begun in 1283 and the most sophisticated, Beaumaris, in 1295. To Vaughan-Thomas they were 'the finest system of mutually-supporting castles created in medieval Europe ... not only fortifications but genuine masterpieces.'

The designer of twelve of the Welsh castles was the Savoyard architect Master James of St George (*c.* 1230–1309). Little is known of his background, other than his authorship of the fortress of St George d'Esperanche in Savoy. He studied, as did Edward, the castles built by the crusaders in the Levant and understood the importance of site and access, as well as the technology of modern sieges. Each of his castles was unique to its location, concentric at Beaumaris (Anglesey) and Harlech, and elongated with inner and outer wards at Conwy and Caernarfon (all Gwynedd). The latter, with its octagonal towers and patterned stonework, was a conscious imitation of the fortification of Constantinople. 'On a strait at the western edge of Europe,' wrote John Davies, 'it created something of the splendour which had existed for centuries on a strait at the eastern edge.'

The cost was prodigious, justified by St George to the king on the grounds that 'Welshmen are Welshmen'. By 1283, 3,000 English masons were reputedly working on royal works in north Wales. Caernarfon cost the then huge sum of £27,000 and Beaumaris £15,000. Nor were these just castles. They were asser-

* O God, why does not the sea cover the land!
Why are we left to linger?

tions of political supremacy, palaces to receive the king and house his constables and focus of a network of exclusively English colonial towns.

These fortified 'bastides' are visible today at Rhuddlan, Conwy, Caernarfon and Beaumaris. The Welsh were firmly excluded, meaning that in the 14th century, three centuries after the Conquest, almost everywhere in Wales that could be termed a town was still owned and occupied by the English. Nothing did more to keep alive the flame of Welsh national consciousness.

Edward's castles proved a mixed blessing. The cost of sustaining them was exorbitant and their garrisons dwindled to a few dozen soldiers. The borough monopolies meant that Welsh traders began to bypass them. Welsh Wales was still largely rural, divided into cantrefs, or collections of farms under clan chiefs. They were near impossible to bring to heel. As for the castles, a century later when Glyndŵr rose in revolt, they proved as useful to the rebels as to the king.

Even fear of rebellion did not halt the English mania for church-building. Monasteries and Marcher lords alike sent masons, trained in France or England, to add aisles and traceried windows to the churches of which they were patrons. The Early Gothic style, spreading west from Wells, appeared in the west front at Llandaff, the chancel at Brecon and the beautiful arcades at St Mary, Haverfordwest. Many town churches, having been rebuilt by the Normans, were rebuilt again in the Gothic style by the Plantagenets.

English kings were intermittently careful to appoint Welsh-speaking clergy to Wales, some of whom, like the monastic abbots, sided with the Welsh in times of rebellion. The greatest figure of the Welsh church in the Middle Ages, Bishop Henry de Gower (d. 1347), may have been himself a Welshman and rose to become chancellor of Oxford and builder of one of the most splendid palaces in Britain, at St David's. It boasts not one great hall but two. Its façade is studded with 'marble' jewelling.

Nowhere in Britain was the tradition of pilgrimage stronger than in Wales, notably to the shrine of St David's and the monastery of Enlli on Bardsey, off the Llŷn peninsula. In 1190, to aid the late Henry II's pacification programme, the papacy allegedly declared that two pilgrimages to St David's or two to Bardsey equalled one to Rome. Three supposedly equalled one to Jerusalem. This declaration put the two shrines on a par with Santiago de Compostela and offered a dramatic boost to Welsh tourism and church-building.

The main pilgrim routes were from Chepstow to St David's and from the Dee to Bardsey. The latter possibly included the shrine to St Winefride at Holywell, where Henry V went to give thanks for his victory at Agincourt (aided by Welsh archers). The more adventurous would combine the two sites, travelling up the coast of Cardigan Bay via Strata Florida. For the many who died on the way, coastal chapels such as Llandanwg (Gwynedd) offered an embarkation point for coffins to Bardsey.

To a country accustomed only to the life and lore of the local valley, pilgrimage must have brought a window on the world. Strangers poured through Wales from England, carrying news and learning, money and disease. Late medieval churches such as Clynnog Fawr and Llanengan on the Llŷn grew rich on the proceeds. Wales's ubiquitous upland churches have meaning only if we see them offering weary travellers physical and spiritual sustenance. The isolated Conwy church of Llangelynnin, hidden within a high mountain enclosure, retains its old well and the ruin of a hostel and stable. Its mud-floored transept is believed to have been meant to keep strangers away from regular worshippers in the nave. Llangelynnin is a supremely evocative relic of Christianity in Britain.

THE GLYNDŴR REVOLT

The Black Death in 1348 and the turmoil of the Peasants' Revolt in 1381 disturbed the settled order of Plantagenet England. In Wales this took dramatic form. The spirit of Llywelyn's glory was rekindled by the charismatic figure of Owain Glyndŵr. He was no peasant champion but a member of the *uchelwyr*, or emergent Welsh middle class, who accumulated capital and were increasingly essential to the English administration of Wales.

Glyndŵr claimed royal descent from the princes of both Powys and Deheubarth (as could hundreds of Welshmen) yet he was also a London lawyer who had fought under the banner of Richard II. His revolt began in 1400 over a legal dispute concerning land with Lord Grey of Ruthin, a dispute which a stable English regime would have been able to settle by means short of war.

England was not stable. Richard II had been deposed the previous year and subsequently murdered, and the throne usurped by Henry Bolingbroke, now Henry IV. The opportunity for rebellion was apparent and a spark had taken flame. In 1400 Glyndŵr had himself declared Prince of Wales at Corwen and soon the revolt spread across almost the whole principality.

For a brief period Wales (other than Pembroke and Gwent) took on the semblance of an independent kingdom, as it had under Gruffudd and the Llywelyns. Its new ruler held parliaments at Harlech, Dolgellau and Machynlleth, issuing proclamations under a Great Seal and appointing bishops. He sought alliances against England with France and the Avignon pope. From the latter he sought an independent Welsh church, securing the support of Cistercians in this venture. He proposed two Welsh universities to match England's. Glyndŵr was, to

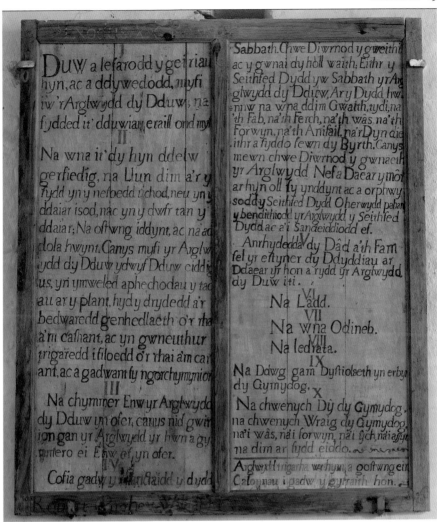

Llangelynnin: Reformation commandments

Shakespeare in *Henry IV*, 'in faith a worthy gentleman, exceedingly well-read and profited in strange concealments, valiant as a lion'.

As in the 11th and 13th centuries, neither an English king nor the Marcher lords could tolerate such separatism for long. In 1405 Glyndŵr formed an alliance with the prominent Marcher, Mortimer, to whom he married his daughter, and with another rebel against Henry's rule, Henry Percy of Northumberland. This coalition was a potentially lethal threat to the English crown.

The great castles built by Edward I at Caernarfon, Rhuddlan and Chepstow held for the king. Prince Henry, the future Henry V, summoned his new cannons from the royal arsenal and laid siege to Glyndŵr's bases at Aberystwyth and Harlech. In 1409 they fell. The rebellion had lasted barely a decade. The Welsh monarch disappeared into the hills crying (to the King of France) that 'my nation has been trodden underfoot by the fury of the barbarous Saxons.'

The land Glyndŵr left behind was ruined, as much by his own warmongering as by that of the English. In his Jacobean history of Gwydir, Sir John Wynn remarked that 'it was Glyndŵr's policy to bring all things to waste, that the English should not find strength nor resting place in the country.' The revolt, he said, 'brought such desolation that green grass grew in the market place ... and deer fed in the churchyard'.

In defeating Glyndŵr the English might have created a wilderness and called it peace, but the Welsh had emphatically lost. Henry IV savagely forbade the Welsh to assemble, marry the English, trade in the English boroughs or hold public office. Glyndŵr, in the manner of his disappearance, contrived at least to give defeat an aura of mystery. As his most recent biographer, Rees Davies, wrote, Wales at last had 'a leader who combined the bravery of a Hector, the wizardry of a Merlin and the elusiveness of a Scarlet Pimpernel.' His burial place is unknown and 'reappearances' on mountainsides were often rumoured. Glyndŵr's banner still flutters over Welsh buildings and remains a nationalist rallying point.

Within a generation of this defeat the Wars of the Roses brought more anguish to Wales. The Marcher lords now included such magnates as the Mortimers, Nevilles and Percys, sucking Wales into a contest in which it had no part. Wales was mostly for Lancaster, and the Yorkist Earl of Pembroke lost his head for it. Harlech was the last Lancastrian fortress to surrender to the eventually triumphant Yorkists, yielding the song 'Men of Harlech'.

Yet it was the alliance of the exiled Henry Tudor to the Lancastrian Earl of Stanley, husband of Henry's widowed mother, Margaret Beaufort, that toppled Richard III at Bosworth in 1485. That alliance placed a quarter-Welshman on the throne of England and brought the two countries into a legislative union that was to last half a millennium. The Tudor ascendancy was, for Wales, a glorious liberation, a making and yet a sort of breaking.

THE TUDOR ASCENDANCY

Ask most Britons the nationality of the Tudors and they will reply 'English' – indeed the very word embodies Englishness. Yet Henry VII was born in Pembroke Castle. His father, Edmund Tudor, was son of Owain ap Maredudd, who took the name of his grandfather of the Tewdwr line, descendants of

Cadwaladr the Great. His marriage in 1452 to Margaret Beaufort, a descendant of Edward III's third son, John of Gaunt, by his third wife, was a dubious basis for claiming the throne. He went for safe-keeping to Brittany during the final stages of the Wars of the Roses.

At the battle of Bosworth in 1485 a land snatched by the sword from its ancestral princes was snatched back in like fashion. To cement his tenuous hold on power, Henry married Elizabeth of York, daughter of Edward IV and sister of the murdered 'princes in the tower'. He subsequently and obsessively hired genealogists to prove his legitimacy, and named his eldest son Arthur in honour of the legendary Celtic king. Legitimacy was to obsess the Tudors and gave rise to the tendentious portrayal of Richard III by Shakespeare as a king so utterly evil that any usurpation was justified.

The Venetian ambassador duly reported home that 'the Welsh may be said to have recovered their independence'. It was an incorrect gloss. There was no independence embedded in Henry's triumph, though there was at least a liberation from oppression. The Tudors rewarded Welshmen but not Wales. When Henry's son, Henry VIII, formally united 'England and Wales' in an Act of Union in 1536 he declared, among other things, that: 'No person or persons that use the Welsh speech or language shall have or enjoy any manor, office or fees with the realm of England, Wales or other of the king's dominions ... unless they use the speech and language of English.'

The power of the Marcher lords went into decline. Land-ownership was dispersed and Welshmen rushed to London for patronage. The *uchelwyr* saw their moment. The English settlement boroughs were thrown open to Welsh trade. Unlike some parts of England, and certainly Scotland and Ireland, Wales was generally prosperous in the late Middle Ages, benefiting from its proximity to the English markets for livestock and wool. Writing in 1603, George Owen remarked that 'No country in England so flourished in one hundred years as Wales has done since the government of Henry VII ... the people changed in heart within and the land altered in hue without, from evil to good.'

This was reflected in the ownership of property. Welsh castles and houses passed into the hands of a new Anglo-Welsh aristocracy: Herberts (Powis, Raglan, Chepstow), Tudors (Pembroke), Rhyses (Carew, Weobley), Myddeltons (Chirk) and Wynns (Gwydir). Buildings which for three centuries were needed for military repression fell into disuse or were converted into spacious, often ostentatious, residences. Sir Rhys ap Thomas had lived in exile in Bruges during the Wars of the Roses and brought to his rebuilt castle at Carew the late-medieval splendour of a Continental court, staging in 1507 a tournament reputedly finer than any yet seen in Britain. Carew, Raglan and Powis emerged in new habits, with great halls, high chambers and family parlours adorned with overmantels, tapestries, paintings and manuscripts. Wales was ready to play its part in the new European renaissance.

Almost all of this is gone, reduced to shattered walls and gaunt windows, testifying only to the Regency (and later the 20th-century) obsession with ruins. More evocative are the houses of the new bourgeoisie. The finest Tudor town house in Britain is Robert Wynn's Plas Mawr in Conwy (Gwynedd) of 1576, a hall house later converted into a mini-palazzo, its reception rooms dripping in new-rich heraldry. At Llanvihangel Court (Gwent) the front was redesigned in 1559 to remove the screens passage and give the house a balanced façade. At St Fagans outside Cardiff a medieval hall plan within is concealed behind a symmetrical exterior.

Nor was such grandiosity confined to the rich. Most yeoman houses were drastically modernized in the course of the 16th century. The dominant domestic structure was the long house or, for those who could afford it, the hall house. The former, often now a barn, can be seen on many a Welsh hillside or in the open-air museum at St Fagans. Hall houses were given fireplaces, and chimneys replaced open hearths. Chambers were inserted into the upper half of the hall, reached by proper staircases, and solars extended into family quarters. This modernization can be seen extensively at Gwydir (Gwynedd) and more modestly at Tretower (Powys). New houses might retain the hall plan, but were fitted from the start with upstairs chambers, as at Llancaeach Fawr (Glamorgan). Only in materials was there much regional variation, with half-timbering appearing along the English borders and stone dominant elsewhere.

Welsh churches benefited from the rebuilding on a scale not seen since the Norman Conquest. Hardly one was left untouched. In Clwyd and Powys Henry VII's mother, Lady Margaret Beaufort (widowed and married to Lord Stanley in 1482), commissioned the most extensive programme of 15th-century patronage in Britain. These 'Stanley churches', including Mold, Wrexham and Gresford, rank with the best of East Anglia and have been dubbed one of the seven wonders of Wales. Meanwhile lesser parish churches, even hilltop chapels, saw thatched roofs replaced with slates, windows punched into thick walls and porches added.

Above all, in well-wooded Wales the carpenters came into their own. Magnificent roofs can be seen at St David's, Tenby and Llangollen. Finer still were the rood screens and lofts. Welsh screens form a supreme collection of British medieval craftsmanship. They originated in the division of the early church between clergy and laity, often by means of a pulpitum wall. By the 15th century, liturgical practice replaced such exclusivity with the softer division of a wooden screen – as in many Eastern Orthodox churches. This carried the rood (or cross) and often a loft for musicians. While the roods were mostly destroyed in the Reformation, many screens and lofts survived.

In his *Medieval Screens of the Southern Marches*, Richard Wheeler seeks to imagine 'the teeming splendour that was the late medieval church interior, alive with colour and gilding, imagery and carvings, awakened by the dance of candlelight'. In the half-century from the Tudor ascendancy to the Reformation (*c*.1485–1536), screens were the focus of Christian worship. They embraced not just religious iconography but a secular gallery of humans, animals, snakes, monsters and trails of vine, oak, water-leaf and hawthorn.

The masterpieces at Llanegryn and Llananno illustrate a peculiarly Welsh style of screen in which the panel patterns of screen and loft are variegated. At Llaneleu and Betws Newydd tympanums survive, in the latter case with the most complete set of screen, loft and tympanum anywhere. We can enter a dozen Welsh churches and see decoration worthy of London's Victoria and Albert Museum (to which so much English church furniture disappeared). The historian Glanmore Williams noted that 'the poets of Wales ranked carpenters alongside themselves as artists ... likening their own use of words to the carpenters' carving of wood'. Church screens were as distinctive a feature of Welsh art as the ancient Celtic crosses.

The dissolution of Welsh monastic houses passed almost without a murmur. In the 1530s, Caldey (Dyfed) had just one monk left. The Cistercians' Tintern, Strata Florida and Cwm-hir had been of international repute yet had withered into insignificance. Noting how rarely historians refer to them, Williams concludes that 'they can hardly be said to have been making any profound impression on contemporary piety and devotion'. Their final contribution was in supplying fittings to houses and parish churches. Gwydir's walls are alive with fragments of Maenan, the arcades in Llanidloes came from Cwm-hir and the screen and loft at Llanegryn were reputed to have been carried from Cymer.

During the Reformation, Wales supplied no Pilgrimage of Grace or armed rebellion against the new prayer book. The authority represented by the formal church had been long associated with English oppression, and the Tudor monarchs (or their clerical advisers) shrewdly presented the Reformation as a return to a truly British Christianity, in which Wales had played so prominent a part. According to Marcus Tanner, Matthew Parker, one of Elizabeth's archbishops of Canterbury, proclaimed a return 'to the purity and traditions of the Early Church before the arrival of the popish St Augustine'.

Iconoclasm swept Wales, as it did England, and the destruction must have

Borders rococo: the Chirk gates

been dreadful. What was lost is conveyed by the fragment of the monumental Jesse tree in St Mary, Abergavenny (Gwent). But apart from the destruction of statuary and stained glass, what is remarkable is how much survived. Some screens were taken down and stored, murals were overpainted and glass hidden, such as the window at Llanrhaeadr. The greatest iconoclast of the British church was to be 17th- and 18th-century neglect and decay.

In 1563 the Bible and Prayer Book were commanded to be translated into Welsh, given that otherwise Elizabeth's 'most loving and obedient subjects … are therefore utterly destituted of God's holy word'. Partial translations by Richard Davies and William Salesbury were consolidated by William Morgan of St Asaph (see Tŷ Mawr, Gwynedd). Morgan's 1588 translation, predating England's King James Bible, was so popular that it was not to be updated until the 20th century. The original version, reprinted into great leather-bound volumes, still gathers dust on lecterns across Wales. Its ubiquity was one of the many proclaimed reasons for the survival of the Welsh language.

By the end of Elizabeth's reign, Welsh buildings comprised a patchwork. There were the Norman and Edwardian castles and market towns, in which

Welshmen could now live and trade freely. Fortresses such as Powis, Raglan, Carew and Manorbier were adapted from old castles into renaissance mansions. Hall houses were modernized and extended. No longer did landowners sit by open fires in smoky halls with open rafters. Even their churches were light and comfortable, rebuilt and lit by Perpendicular windows.

How far Wales emerged into the modern age with a distinctive architecture of its own is a much-debated topic. To me it is neither here nor there. Buildings in Wales were Welsh buildings, their architecture dictated by convenience and technology. In so far as castles and churches were built by English invaders and their styles were alien, this was no different from what England borrowed from France, and France from points south and east. The Victorian antiquarian Thomas Rickman dubbed as 'Early English' that most French of innovations, the pointed arch, which must make Brecon cathedral 'Early Welsh'. I use the term 'Early Gothic' in this book. The buildings introduced into Wales by the English were and remain intrinsic to its history and culture. I return to this subject at the end of the introduction.

STUARTS TO VICTORIANS

After the euphoria of the Tudor ascendancy, Welsh building did not flourish. The Tudors were succeeded by the ascendancies of the Scottish Stuarts and the German Hanoverians. Many great Welsh families drifted to England, the Pembrokes to Wilton, the Cecils (formerly the Seisylls) to Hatfield, and the Beauforts to Badminton, which was adorned with fittings stripped from Raglan.

A few new houses were spectacular. Plas Teg (Clwyd) was built *c.* 1610 for the Trevors with an appearance half-fortress, half-palace. Later in the same century, a handful of Welsh Royalists returned at the Restoration to re-create what they had seen in Paris and the Hague. Interiors at Erddig (Clwyd) and Powis (Powys) and the whole of Tredegar (Gwent) date from this time. William Morgan's Gilt Room at Tredegar and Wynn's panelling at Gwydir are flourishes of a rare but spectacular Welsh baroque.

The houses of the Georgian era were those of a comfortable gentry rather than an ancestral aristocracy. Thomas Lloyd, in his survey of Welsh mansions for *The Lost Houses of Wales*, points out that many were not big and changed hands frequently. Most that survive do not qualify for this book as they are still privately occupied. Yet rarely do we encounter anything on a par with the English works of Vanbrugh, Kent, Gibbs, Chambers, Smith of Warwick or Robert Adam. The names of leading British architects are seldom heard in Wales.

Of accessible houses of the period we are left with such sober façades as Trevor (Clwyd), Nanteos (Dyfed) and Abercamlais (Powys). We can admire the fine reception rooms of Picton (Dyfed), possibly by Gibbs, and of Chirk, and the fine Orangery at Margam. There is rococo work at Fonmon (Glamorgan), Nanteos (Dyfed) and Cresselly (Dyfed), and in the iron gates of Robert and John Davies of Wrexham. The best survivor of Regency gothick is Plas Newydd by James Wyatt on Anglesey, dramatically located over the Menai Straits. Though John Nash worked extensively in Carmarthen and Cardigan before going to London, his one accessible work is the demure Llanerchaeron (Dyfed).

The Georgian and Regency eras offered Wales one starring role in the story of British art. This lay in its blessed legacy, scenery. Wales's appeal to the Romantic movement was intense, beginning with the Welsh-born Richard Wilson (1713–82) and his pupil, Thomas Jones. In the 1770s William Gilpin blazed a picturesque trail with his *Observations on the River Wye* and Sir Watkin Williams-Wynn introduced Paul Sandby to Snowdonia. They in turn attracted the Romantic poets, Gray and Wordsworth. Turner's first Royal Academy picture in 1802 was a dramatic portrayal of Dolbadarn Castle. Domestic tourism, prevented by the Napoleonic Wars from crossing the Continent, turned upland Wales into a Celtic Arcadia.

This was nowhere more vividly demonstrated than by Thomas Johnes in creating Wales's most glorious contribution to the Picturesque movement, his Regency house and landscape at Hafod outside Aberystwyth, embellished by Nash. To the indefatigable English traveller in Wales, George Borrow, Hafod was 'a truly fairy place... beautiful but fantastic'. Cardiganshire council allowed it to be dynamited and sown with conifers in 1962.

Elsewhere the remains of a renaissance garden can be seen at Powis, as can landscapes at Margam (Glamorgan) and Plas Newydd (Anglesey), where Humphrey Repton makes a rare Welsh appearance. Capability Brown confined his work to Cardiff Castle (and a park at Wynnstay). Follies survive in abundance, as at Clytha, Paxton's Tower and the Kymin outside Monmouth.

Searchers after Welsh 18th-century architecture do better to wander through the Georgianized boroughs of the Norman and Edwardian settlements, such as Pembroke, Monmouth, Conwy and Beaumaris. They are among the pleasantest small towns in Britain. I have illustrated them with Monmouth's Shire Hall, Presteigne's Judge's Lodgings, Beaumaris's Old Courthouse and walled Conwy, once medieval but now mostly Georgian. In their footsteps were such 'model towns' as the copper-works estate of Morriston outside Swansea (1768), Milford Haven (1790), Aberaeron (1807) and W. A. Madock's Tremadog (1810).

The Plough Chapel, Brecon

The revival of the Welsh Church under the Tudors lost momentum in the 17th and 18th centuries. In his *Last of the Celts*, Marcus Tanner writes that 'the process of rot was so gentle that few noticed its slow advance … Devoid of instruction, the mass of people clung to a jumble of half-remembered Catholic practices and semi-pagan beliefs.' They went on pilgrimages of a sort, notably to the spring at Holywell, much to the anger of the Protestant authorities. Catholic recusancy was not widespread, as it was in the adjacent Midlands, but some remained true to the Old Religion, both in the environs of Brecon (Powys) and in the privacy of their estates: with chapels for William Salusbury at Rug (1637) and Sir Richard Wynn at Gwydir (1673). The only new Georgian church of note in Wales was built in 1736 at Worthenbury (Clwyd).

Wales was ripe for Methodist picking. Wesley himself was nervous of preaching there because he did not speak the language, but he visited extensively, especially the English-speaking south. In the event it was not Wesleyanism but a more fundamentalist Calvinism that took fire in Wales. Preceding Wesley's conversion in 1738 came that of Howel Harris, three years earlier, and of Daniel Rowland. These men preached in Welsh and travelled hundreds of miles, founding new Welsh 'circulating schools' and bringing cheap Bibles into every village.

Rowland could preach for six hours and draw crowds a day's journey to hear him. The fervour of these preachers' oratory – building to a sing-song crescendo or *hwyl* – brought them a celebrity like that of modern American evangelists. Theirs was a salvationist religion of miracles, confessions and the driving out of Satan. It devastated the Established Church in Wales. The formal Methodist secession from Anglicanism at the start of the 19th century was a crucial stimulus to a distinctively Welsh religious consciousness.

The Nonconformists offered what Anglicans had ceased offering since the Middle Ages: emotional enthusiasm, charity and education. By the 1840s, there were estimated to be as many Calvinists in Wales as Anglicans (200,000 each in a population of 900,000). There were a further 175,000 Independents and 100,000 Baptists, along with Wesleyans, Congregationalists, Presbyterians and various sub-divisions. Roman Catholicism also flourished, particularly with the immigration of miners from Ireland and Spain.

The Rhondda alone had 150 chapels in the 19th century. A local minister, the Reverend William Jones, was said to have designed 200 of the 1,600 chapels in Glamorgan. Nor were these buildings solely in the industrial south. Nonconformity was as strong in the rural and smaller mining areas of the north. Merioneth boasted 273 chapels with a capacity of 75,000 seats at the turn of the 20th century, against just 34 Anglican churches. There were more chapel seats than population.

These chapels were paid for out of the wealth generated by Wales's industrial revolution: coal, iron and shipping in the south; slate, minerals and agriculture in the north. Their elders were farmers, teachers, lawyers, merchants and their language was Welsh. Ninety per cent of Methodist schools were Welsh-speaking, an important factor in the survival of the Welsh language.

To some, this explosion of Welsh faith was reminiscent of the age of saints. It depended on peripatetic preachers and on the chapel as a centre of civic as well as religious life. Nonconformist buildings evolved to match. Dissenters had originally worshipped in the open air or in barns, like those at Maesyronnen (1697) and Dolobran (1700). These simple preaching boxes have great charm, furnished to focus attention on the Word, 'Y Gair', rather than the altar – though Peter Sager, that astute German observer of 20th-century Wales, concluded, if Welsh religion 'is based on the word, never have God's houses been so parsimonious in their language'.

By the 19th century, builders had acquired a new confidence, begun by Peniel Chapel in Tremadog (Gwynedd). Dissent adopted classicism, as had the American and French revolutionaries, as a gesture of opposition to the gothic of the Anglican revival. As the Victorian era progressed, this classicism evolved into a bastardized baroque. At Morriston and Maesteg in Glamorgan, two so-called 'cathedrals of Dissent' towered over the surrounding houses, much as English churches did over their villages. Congregations moved into what were grand auditoriums to hear and sing the word of God. The sound of their choirs burst out over the coal-smoke and the terraces, and Sunday schools and friendly societies dominated Welsh social life.

Nor was this just what the architectural historian John Hilling called 'mad façadism'. Internal furnishings were often of high quality, those at the Plough in Brecon copying Wren's St James, Piccadilly, in London. The pulpit, the organ and the choir pews achieved an architectural apotheosis. Some chapels even adopted the once-hated gothic. In the resort of Aberdyfi in Gwynedd, two of the local chapels are classical and two gothic, the former being Welsh foundations, the latter English. Whether this distinction was deliberate or fortuitous I have been unable to discern. Either way, to the chapel historian Anthony Jones they were 'without question the national architecture of Wales. These virile expressions of the national genius … were physical symbols of a driven evangelical mission, a faith that captured the hearts and minds of the Welsh.'

Chapels dot Wales's towns, fields and hillsides, wherever a local farmer or quarry owner wished to spare his workers a long walk to prayer or wherever another chapel decided on a 'missionary' outpost. They make every Welsh settlement instantly recognizable as such, in a religious pluralism replicated in no other community in Europe. They recall Wales's Celtic religiosity, though they are a reminder also of another Welsh tradition, a disputatiousness that split communities and even families.

In all histories of the Welsh chapel, this factionalism is the great unmentionable. Social gradations and subtle snobberies would turn on matters of abstruse dogma. My childhood village of Pennal (Gwynedd) had both a Wesleyan and a Calvinist chapel, probably related to some distant rivalry between farmers and quarrymen. Husbands and wives might divide in prayer on a Sunday, depending on some inherited loyalty. Even today many of these Welsh congregations prefer to see their chapels die than admit a merger. Gerald's remark in the 12th century still applies, that if only the Welsh could be inseparable they would be insuperable.

The Established Church was slow to meet the Nonconformist challenge. Lady Charlotte Guest of Dowlais wrote in her diary in 1834 of 'the Dissenters who, to our shame, have done more for religion in Wales than our Church has ever attempted'. But attempt it eventually did. As in England, from the 1830s onwards there was a concerted mission to revive Anglicanism through restoring church buildings and propagating church schools, though almost all taught in English. The restorations were often drastic, careless of what went before. Walls, roofs and fittings, most of them untouched since at least the 15th century, were destroyed and replaced, rarely with much concern to salvage what might be saved from the past. The task and the cost were prodigious.

The Victorian Anglican revival in Wales benefited from the best of both Welsh and English architects and was often of a higher quality than in England. Sir George Gilbert Scott was summoned to restore all the cathedrals other than Llandaff. He and contemporaries such as G. E. Street and John Seddon are encountered everywhere. Of new churches, William Butterfield designed Penarth, J. D. Sedding Llanfair Cilgedin, and J. L. Pearson Llangasty. Henry Wilson created the remarkable Art Nouveau Brithdir outside Dolgellau. Of Welsh architects, John Douglas was prominent in the north and John Prichard in the south, notably at Llandaff. Charles Barry's assistant, John Gibson, produced the 'marble church' at Bodelwyddan. Most prolific of all was the ever-sensitive 20th-century restorer W. D. Caröe. His works are too numerous to cite but will be found throughout this book, from tiny Patrisio to grand Llandaff.

Today only a small portion of Wales's colossal inventory of churches and chapels are in religious use. Many have been demolished and more stand empty and redundant or re-used as shops, warehouses and domestic properties. The sensitive re-use of these buildings is one of the great challenges to Welsh town planning. For whatever their denomination their distinction and ubiquity renders them an intrinsic part of the Welsh story.

Meanwhile at least some of the money realized from Wales's mineral wealth (and from adjacent Merseyside) leaked into Victorian and Edwardian building. Unlike in the 18th century, Welsh Victorian mansions could rival the best of England. In Cardiff the 3rd Marquess of Bute, his family having married Herbert money, commissioned William Burges to create the astonishing Wagnerian fantasies of Cardiff Castle and Castell Coch. At Penrhyn Castle near his Bethesda slate mine, George Dawkins-Pennant in c.1820 had Thomas Hopper design one of the greatest neo-Norman palaces in Britain, reputedly on the site of a palace of Rhodri Mawr. It is a triumph of National Trust restoration.

As grandiose were Gwrych Castle overlooking Colwyn Bay, built by the Lancashire Heskeths, and the Williams-Wynn castle at Bodelwyddan. The Clwyd hinterland sprouted remarkable houses, Eden Nesfield's Dutch revivals at Kinmel and Bodrhydden, and Sir Gilbert Scott's Hafodunos. In the 1860s the eccentric Lord Sudeley erected one of the first concrete houses at Gregynog (Powys) and went on to create an entire estate of the material. Bute's Glamorganshire contemporaries, the Crawshays and Guests of Merthyr and the

Victorian escapism: Castell Coch

Talbots of Port Talbot, were less extravagant. Victorian Margam and Cyfarthfa were not great houses, despite their owners being among the richest in Britain.

A nobler legacy was offered by the Mostyns of North Wales, who laid out Llandudno as a graceful resort with an aspect that the Victorians boasted was 'worthy of the Bay of Naples'. That title is perhaps more appropriate to architecture's other contribution to the Welsh shoreline, Clough Williams-Ellis's village of Portmeirion, its popularity rebutting the disapproval of modernist critics.

Welsh industrialists had to provide houses for their workers within the difficult topography of the Glamorgan valleys. The town of Rhondda Fawr was nine miles long and just over half a mile wide. While this involved long walks to pithead and chapel, the layouts offered easy access to the clear air of the mountains immediately behind. John Hilling points out that Wales's two-storey terrace cottages were 'usually neat and soundly built and, according to the standards of the day, well designed with entrances at back and front … The noisome back-to-back terraces and miserable tenement courts found in so many of the English industrial towns were rarely built in Wales.' My father, born in the Merthyr suburb of Dowlais, often recalled this proximity to nature as exhilarating, and compared it favourably with his experience of working-class England and Scotland. Examples of such houses are preserved at Blaenafon and St Fagans museum in Cardiff.

The Welsh industrial boom had one final and spectacular manifestation, and that was civic. Cardiff's town hall in Cathays Park was the most lavish in Britain and unashamedly nationalist in its iconography, assuming that the wealth of King Coal was inexhaustible. When Wales did finally receive devolved government at the start of the 21st century, it was sad that these buildings were not adapted to that purpose. Cardiff was cut in two, with the historic dignities of its nationhood stranded two miles from the new centre of government on Cardiff Bay.

TODAY AND TOMORROW

To say that Welsh architecture degenerated in the 20th century would be an understatement. The phenomenal growth in domestic, civic and religious building of the final decades of the Victorian era ceased and the economy began a long period of slow decline interrupted only by wartime booms. New town halls in Swansea and Newport, in a vaguely Art Deco revivalism, reflected the earlier confidence of Cardiff. But by the middle of the century the story of Welsh buildings is of a country that appeared to have lost identity and heart.

Clough Williams-Ellis and Frank Lloyd Wright at Portmeirion

The authors of the new Pevsner architectural guides to Wales (published 1979–2009) found depressingly few buildings of the period to include, mostly box-like schools, universities and municipal offices commissioned by a public sector bereft of money and imagination. Town and country planning seemed to collapse. Council houses were not concentrated in planned communities but sprawled over hillsides. Stained concrete blocks and towers intruded even on such sensitive settings as Harlech Castle and Bodelwyddan. Car parks sprawled round the castle footings at Beaumaris and an elevated road gashed through

Caernarfon. The uplands of mid-Wales were defaced with wind turbines and the coast with caravan parks.

Across much of Wales, chapels fell silent and the tradition of tidy, compact stone-built villages was replaced by car-reliant bungalow estates. Writers, even the adopted Welshman John Cowper Powys, offered Welsh villages no moral support. He wrote that 'their prevailing slate roofs, ugly chapels, their austere, unpicturesque and melancholy architecture have nothing of that old-world warmth and glow and atmospheric welcome that such places have in England'. Dylan Thomas portrayed what came to be regarded as the iconic Welsh community, Llareggub in *Under Milk Wood*, as a 'black shadow' from which the soul had been drained, leaving behind only a mean obsession with gossip.

This collapse in self-confidence led to Welsh buildings receiving scant official protection. It was difficult to stir interest in, let alone raise money for, rescuing buildings at risk comparable with that galvanized in England by the Victoria and Albert Museum's 1974 'Lost Houses' exhibition. Thomas Lloyd's *Lost Houses of Wales* records the disappearance, mostly in the second half of the 20th century, of some 400 country houses. At the time of writing the catalogue of large Welsh houses awaiting rescue includes Edwinsford, Piercefield, Ruperra, Troy and two included in this book, Hafodunos and Kinmel (both Clwyd).

Much of this was experienced elsewhere in the British Isles. In his polemic on *Britain's Lost Cities* the architectural historian Gavin Stamp writes of a demolition psychosis of the 1950s and 1960s that seemed to echo wartime bombardment. 'Particularly in the large cities of the north of England and Scotland there was a sense of shame about the industrial past, a visceral and blinkered rejection of the dark but substantial legacy of the Victorians – fuelled in part by a crude Socialist vision – that could amount to little more than civic self-hatred.' Stamp's hyperbolic strictures apply with force in Glamorganshire, in the unimaginative renewal of Swansea and Newport docks and the failure to link Cardiff Bay to its city centre. The story of Welsh conservation in the 20th century was not a happy one.

At this point we enter the sensitive realm of generalization, unavoidable in discussing a nation's cultural outlook. The Welsh are commonly accused – and accuse themselves – of lacking a 'public eye'. Their culture, so rich in music, speech and literature, is said to lack a tradition of painting and architecture. In *The Artist in Wales* (1957) the art historian David Bell notoriously wrote: 'At no time since the Norman conquest has the Welshman had any visual artistic tradition.' Donald Moore added in 'Art in a Small Nation' that the Welsh see their surroundings in a sort of childish mist. He asked, 'Is the indifference to visual experience a matter of inheritance or simply of arrested development?'

This presumed inadequacy is variously attributed to Wales lacking a tradition of wealthy artistic patronage, to Nonconformist chapel culture and to Welsh architecture having, for centuries, been a manifestation of English oppression. The Welsh are said to be 'hard-wired' to aesthetic defeatism, if not to visual philistinism. Even where it produces an artist of quality, such as Kyffin Williams, he writes of travelling in sunnier climes but missing 'the seam of melancholy that is in most Welshmen and that derives from the dark hills, the heavy clouds and the enveloping sea mists'.

Wales is the world capital of the self-deprecating remark. Meic Stephens' admirable collection of Welsh quotations has 1,071 of them, the overwhelming majority pessimistic. R. S. Thomas cries, 'Where can I go, then, from the smell / Of decay, from the putrefying of a dead / Nation?' Elsewhere, though a Protestant parson, he writes of:

Protestantism, the adroit castrator
Of art, the bitter negation
Of song and dance, and the heart's innocent joy –
You have botched our flesh and left us only the soul's
Terrible impotence in a warm world.

Yet Wales is not a philistine country and has long enjoyed a cultural life more than a match for regions of a similar size in Britain or the rest of Europe. It has produced artists aplenty, from Richard Wilson and Hugh Hughes to Augustus John, Ceri Richards and Kyffin Williams. It opened its arms to newcomers such as David Cox and Eric Gill, who founded artists' colonies at Betws-y-coed and Capel-y-ffin. There were craftsmen such as the Davies brothers, sculptors such as Goscombe John and architects from John Nash and John Prichard to Clough Williams-Ellis. There is a regular battle to give the visual arts a more prominent place in the National Eisteddfod.

As for blaming Nonconformity, John Harvey has written eloquently in defence of the aesthetics of chapel culture. Calvin specifically distinguished religious iconography from secular art, which he admired. Quite apart from their rich musical life, Welsh chapels were handsome works of architecture, filled with carving in line of descent from Welsh 16th-century screens. Nonconformity was also, as Harvey points out, serviced by 'a veritable industry of commercial religious suppliers' for home and hearth.

The 'oppressive neighbour' syndrome to explain official Wales's unconcern with its historic architecture may be an explanation but it is not an excuse. I have tried in this book to rebut the claim that Wales lacks an aesthetic sense. It is a land of intense scenic beauty, 'Switzerland without the mountain tops' one visitor remarked. If the Welsh eye is dull to such beauty it must be dulled by familiarity. Almost everywhere beyond the south-eastern strip is a feast for the eye. The mountains of the north, as Coleridge observed, 'with all their terrors and all their glories, are pictures to the blind and music to the deaf'. There is still an abundance of such beauty in Wales.

This brings us back to the question of architecture. Jan Morris holds that the only authentically Welsh building is the farm, designed, in Frank Lloyd Wright's words, 'genially to improve the hill on which it sits'. Such structures, perched on their mountainsides with low roofs, long profiles, slate flagstones and dark dressers, are to Morris the only buildings that are quintessentially Wales. But the farmhouse is a universal form. If it is peculiarly Welsh, so too is the slate village nestling against a mighty spoil tip, or the terraced cottage of the Glamorgan valley. So is the rendered chapel, the black-and-white Powys farm or the stuccoed Ruthin townhouse. Building materials are always special to a place and thus help define it, stone in the south, wood and brick in the borders and slate in the north, but materials are not national possessions.

When we move from materials to style, all architecture is vulnerable to outside influence. In his *The Englishness of English Art*, the historian Nikolaus Pevsner remarked that 'none of the other nations of Europe has so abject an inferiority about its own aesthetic capabilities as England'. But England embraces this cosmopolitanism rather than moans about it. Certainly many of the buildings in this book were constructed by non-Welshmen, as were buildings in most countries. The Normans brought their architecture to England as to Wales. So did later waves of French, Flemish, Dutch and Germans. It is absurd to dismiss as alien the styles that took root in centuries of Welsh building. Long after the English boroughs had been de-Anglicized, they were being rebuilt by and for the Welsh in Georgian and Victorian vernacular.

Those who study the domestic architecture of Scotland and Ireland should also note that Wales was, for the most part, more prosperous and the generality of its buildings more distinguished than in these other 'colonial' extremities, at least since the Tudor ascendancy. I have often compared the townscapes of Llanidloes or Tremadog or Meifod with similar Scots or Irish settlements, which appear mean in comparison. Welsh Victorian buildings, even workers' cottages, were more substantial and on less congested sites than their equivalents in England. Wales's inclination to sell itself short does its history a disservice.

Welsh farms and industrial valleys were poor in times of recession – and their poverty is the stuff of Welsh history – but they were not poor all the time, and not so as to drive millions across the Atlantic. The story of Welsh emigration is often colourful, but it was not a mass phenomenon, if only because the wealth of the Glamorgan valleys held it back. That visual philistinism should be a Welsh response to an English-imposed poverty does not ring true.

No one reading Peter Lord's seminal trilogy, *The Visual Culture of Wales*, can be left in any doubt of the vigour of the tale it tells. One strand is the 'folk art' championed by a founder of St Fagans museum, Cyril Fox, who in 1934 argued that cultural awareness lay in 'a more widespread understanding of native and traditional design and technique in arts and crafts, especially in that of building'. This understanding would, he said, 'save western peoples from the worst vulgarities in construction and decoration of the present day'. St Fagans is today an exhibition of this aspect of Welshness.

But as Lord demonstrates, Welsh visual sensibility has no need to boast either the folksiness of St Fagans or the imported 'high art' on the walls of the National Museum of Wales. It is present in the totality of visual images, pictorial and architectural, that contribute to any nation's historical record and its sense of identity. A Celtic cross, a Norman castle, a Tudor townhouse, a Calvinist chapel, a tycoon's palace are all 'Welsh'. I see no reason to seek any deeper definition of 'the Welshness of Welsh architecture'.

I came to Welsh buildings in the belief that comprehending them is vital to understanding Wales's present and thus to guiding its future. This commitment is more urgent as relics of the past, especially the recent industrial past, swiftly vanish. But the conclusion is not pessimistic. Most of my chosen buildings are intact, in themselves if not in their surroundings. The rate of destruction has diminished and the standard of conservation in Wales is higher than ever.

As I frequently mention in the text, I would like to see more forceful intervention in reinstating old buildings that have been allowed to decline into ruin. There are simply too many ruins in Wales. The most visually rewarding Welsh buildings are those, like St David's and Llandaff Cathedrals or Powis and Chirk Castles, which have been regularly adapted to new requirements. The Victorian conservers and restorers, the Butes in Glamorgan and the Philippses in Pembrokeshire, had a vision that should be revived, obviously with appropriate scholarship. This is largely a matter of confidence.

I see Welsh buildings as far more than a public museum. The oldest ones are probably safe for all time, forming the historical backdrop against which a re-invigorated Welsh culture will display its wares in the 21st century. Acting as their custodians offers the Welsh a way of participating in that display and appreciating those wares. Thus can a newly confident country handle its pains and glories, its past humiliations and its future triumphs. Thus can Wales progress.

Criteria, Access, Sources

I have visited all the buildings in this book. Houses and churches closed to the general public are therefore not included, though they may be mentioned in passing. Churches included are accessible after a reasonable effort in obtaining a key, except in very few cases where the inside can be seen through clear windows. I regret that this has meant omitting some good town churches, and many chapels, that are open only for services. I have also omitted houses open only on rare occasions and to groups, not least out of respect for the privacy of the owners.

My criterion for inclusion is the pleasure derived from a visit. I emphasize that the stars refer not to the quality or even importance of a building but to the enjoyment of seeing it, including its setting and ease of access. Though I normally treat a building as a structure some part of which is roofed, I have embraced some burial mounds and ruins for their importance to the story of Welsh buildings. On the vexed question of Wales's innumerable castles (over 100 in a recognizable state) I have omitted many that are simply crumbling walls or whose presence is diminished by surrounding development. This will seem arbitrary to those whose favourites I have missed, and to them I apologize. I have not included opening times since these change from year to year and can be found on the web and from the annual *Hudsons Historic Houses and Gardens*.

Finding a Welsh building is often a challenge, especially churches and chapels in deserted places. Many are badly signed or not signed at all, a matter for the Welsh tourist authority. I have assumed that most visitors have maps or, increasingly, web or satellite-based locators. In addition to the maps, I have therefore given rough indications of where a particular building is sited, for purpose of map-reading convenience. The distances are 'as the crow flies'.

My chief sources are listed in the bibliography at the end of the book. Most useful have been the histories of Wales by the scholarly John Davies and the more popular Wynford Vaughan-Thomas. I have also drawn heavily on John Hilling's *The Historic Architecture of Wales* and Peter Lord's trilogy, *The Visual Culture of Wales*. Jan Morris's *The Matter of Wales* is my constant companion, while the best guidebooks are the *Blue Guide* and Peter Sager's lively and literary Pallas Guide, by a German who fell in love with Wales.

The nearly completed *Buildings of Wales* series from Yale (the final volume is to be published in 2009) is masterful and all the better for being only just in the process of completion (I declare an interest as chairman of the series). The volumes are referred to in the text by the relevant author or authors as 'in Pevsner'. Information on individual buildings comes chiefly from literature found on site. The Cadw guides are, in my view, better than their English equivalents. Tim Hughes's recent *Wales's Best One Hundred Churches* is admirable. The Welsh Academy's idiosyncratic *Encyclopaedia of Wales* I found indispensable. Cross-references in the text to English houses and churches with their counties in brackets are to entries in my books on England's 'Thousand Best'.

Welsh spellings are a constant conundrum. The drive to re-establish the language has been reflected in widespread renaming and translation of signs. My policy, followed by other guides, has been to use Welsh spellings where identification to English-speakers is clear, but not where they will be confusing: hence I have used Dyfi for Dovey or Caernarfon for Carnarvon but stayed with Cardiff, Swansea and Montgomery. This cannot hope to be consistent. Even many Welsh spellings are uncertain. Eglwys Gymyn can be spelled Cynin, Cymyn, Cummin, Cymin, Gummin and the Irish, Chummein. I have tried to respect the Welsh language, but this is a book written in English. I would love it if a Welsh version could be prepared.

The following abbreviations are used in the headings to house and castle entries:

Cadw: Welsh Assembly historic buildings agency (Welsh for 'to keep')
NT: National Trust
Priv: privately owned
Mus: museum, usually in local-council ownership
H: hotel

Wales's Top Thirty Buildings
(the Four Stars)

Anglesey
PENMON CHURCH
PLAS NEWYDD

Clwyd
BODELWYDDAN CHURCH
CHIRK CASTLE
ERDDIG
GRESFORD CHURCH
PLAS TEG
WREXHAM CHURCH

Dyfed
ST DAVID'S CATHEDRAL

Glamorgan
CAERPHILLY CASTLE
CARDIFF CASTLE
CARDIFF CITY HALL
CASTELL COCH
LLANDAFF CATHEDRAL

Gwent
CHEPSTOW CASTLE
NEWPORT CATHEDRAL
RAGLAN CASTLE
TREDEGAR HOUSE

Gwynedd
BRITHDIR CHURCH
CAERNARFON CASTLE
CLYNNOG FAWR CHURCH
CONWY CASTLE
GWYDIR
HARLECH CASTLE
PENRHYN CASTLE
PLAS MAWR
PORTMEIRION

Powys
BRECON CATHEDRAL
PATRISIO CHURCH
POWIS CASTLE

Anglesey

Anglesey, or Ynys Môn, is steeped in the relics and romance of Wales's pre-history, meriting the title of 'Mam Cymru', mother of Wales. Pre-Celtic remains dot the landscape, as in the tomb at Bryn-celli-ddu. Later the island was known as a centre of druidic worship. Tacitus relates that acolytes were sent from France to study the lore of the woods and winds. Here, he said, 'Natives smeared their altars with blood from their prisoners and sought the will of the gods by exploring the entrails of men.' This was the last place in Wales to defy the Romans, whose fort at Holyhead is still visible round St Cybi's church.

At Din Llugwy hut village pre-history merges into the Celtic era. At Llangadwaladr a stone of King Cadfan dates from the 7th century. Both Penmon and Llaneilian are Celtic saints' shrines, the former still with its original well, a remarkable survival of the romanesque in Wales, stylistically Irish and distinct from that of the Anglo-Normans.

Anglesey was the redoubt of the Llywelyns, princes of Gwynedd and of Wales, its cornfields supplying Welsh armies in their fight against the English throughout the Middle Ages. In response, Edward I settled one of his most impressive castles and boroughs at Beaumaris, today a charming small town of picturesque Georgian buildings.

Since then the island has kept quietly to itself. The only accessible house of note is Plas Newydd, gothick in style and beautifully situated on the Menai Straits, notable for its mural by Rex Whistler.

Houses and Castles

Beaumaris:
  Castle ∗∗∗
  Old Gaol ∗∗
  Old Courthouse ∗
Bryn Celli Ddu ∗
Din Llugwy ∗∗
Plas Newydd ∗∗∗∗

Churches

Amlwch ∗
Beaumaris ∗∗
Holyhead ∗∗
Llandysilio ∗
Llaneilian ∗∗∗
Llanfigel ∗
Llangadwaladr ∗∗
Llangwyfan ∗
Penmon ∗∗∗∗

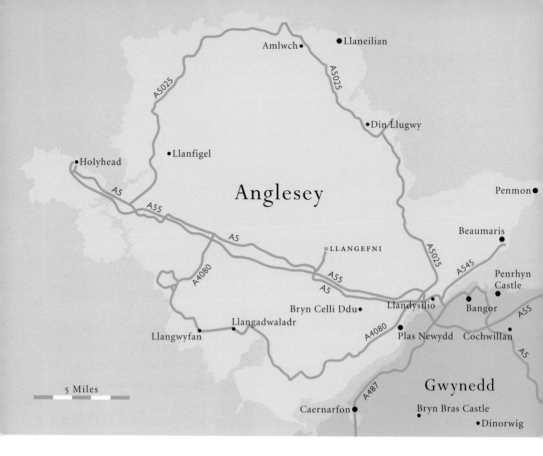

Houses and Castles

BEAUMARIS

The town of Beaumaris is little adulterated by modern development and has surely the loveliest location in Wales, looking over the Menai Straits with Snowdonia for a backdrop. It was founded by Edward I after the death of Llywelyn and became the centre of his administration and later the county town of Anglesey. Named 'beautiful marsh' (from the same root as Paris's Marais) to attract sceptical Norman settlers, it has the atmosphere of a Kent Cinque Port. A handsome high street is lined with coaching inns and houses used by island gentry during the assize. The county courthouse and prison survive, restored, and are open to the public. The moated castle is cosily located at one end of the street.

CASTLE ★★★
Moated St George fortress unfinished
but in good repair (Cadw)

Beaumaris Castle is no great fortress. It is the undamaged, though unfinished, climax to the great works undertaken in Wales by Edward I's master-builder, James of St George. Like Bodiam in Sussex, everything suggests a building for comfort and show rather than defence. This was to be a secure headquarters of the English occupation of the Principality, to accommodate the king and his retinue of soldiers, judges and administrators. Suites of rooms were to be constructed here, protected not from a main force but from native insurgency.

The castle was begun in 1295, the inhabitants of the former Welsh town of Llan-faes being moved to the duly named Newborough. Though devoid of natural advantages, the site shows James of St George at his most sophisticated, with concentric rings of a moat, supplied from

Beaumaris Castle with Snowdonia backdrop

the sea, an outer wall, an outer ward and a massive inner wall. Attackers entering by the seagate would have had to run the gauntlet of a barbican and a south gate with ten obstacles. They need have no fear today. In a display of Welsh contempt for English occupation, a children's playground has been defiantly sited in place of the seaward moat. The effect is from some angles to reduce Beaumaris to a doll's house.

The castle walls are of a deep russet sandstone with occasional white chequer-boarding. The inner ward is spacious and has the appearance more of a fortified palace than a castle. The walls bear the relics of old fireplaces, while on the far side, in the northern gatehouse, were to be domestic apartments. This gatehouse palace was a feature of St George's plans – there is another at Harlech. Here it was never completed. Five great windows look down on the ward, with an upper stage unbuilt.

The castle walls are a maze of passages, sleeping chambers and latrines, the mod cons of a medieval fortress. Inside one of the towers is a charming small chapel built of limestone with polygonal apse, graceful ribbing and trefoil arcading. Thoroughly restored it makes one long for similar restoration elsewhere on the site.

OLD GAOL ✱✱✱
Fully equipped Victorian prison with factory and condemned cell

Occupying a complete block in the old town, the walls of Beaumaris gaol rise impressively over the surrounding streets, far more terrifying than the castle. This was the prison not just for the borough but for the whole island and was the result of Robert Peel's 1823 Gaol Act, laying down conditions that would be considered spacious in a prison today.

Previous prisons had been mostly medieval in every sense, corrupt in their management, their cells rat-infested and prisoners manacled to prevent escape. Among other improvements, the inmates were now to be weighed on admission and discharge to ensure they had been well fed, and given work and wages. Exact quantities of food and clothing were stipulated, for men and women separately.

The design of the building was by a Yorkshireman, Hansom (of cab fame), and included a separate 'house of correction' for lesser offenders such as vagrants. When prisons were transferred to the Home Office in 1877, Beaumaris had fewer than a dozen prisoners, who were transferred to Caernarfon. The gaol was then used as a police station and lock-up.

It is kept now as on the day it closed, demonstrating a Victorian revolution in social reform, treating humans with a measure of dignity. The community clearly set itself to try to help transgressors to rehabilitate themselves in the context of the town. In this it appears less soul-destroying than any modern equivalent.

The prison is of forty rooms on two floors, shaped as a T with exercise and work yards at the back. There was a gibbet for public hangings, so they could be seen from the street. The condemned cell was twice the size of ordinary ones and had its own fireplace. That said, only two executions ever took place, one of a man bitterly protesting his innocence. He cursed the church clock opposite, which is said never to have kept the right time since.

Other facilities include a chapel with a fireplace and admonitory verses on the walls, reminding inmates of the justice of God (though not His forgiveness). There are an infirmary, laundry, washroom, kitchen, women's workroom and connecting nursery. At the rear is the only treadmill left in a British prison. The users worked a water pump, ten minutes on and ten minutes off for eight hours. As a result, all cells had the rare luxury of running water.

OLD COURTHOUSE *
Original chamber, jury and robing rooms
still in use

Beaumaris is blessed not just with castle, church and prison but with its courthouse, still used as such until 1996. Magistrates still sit here on occasions, but mostly they are replaced by wax figures of judge, barristers and an onlooker in the gallery. There are robes and a black cap (for capital sentences) in the robing room.

The building was erected in 1614 and the main courtroom is of this date, including a fine open roof with original hammerbeams and trusses. The windows and pitch-pine panelling and fittings are later, and give the room the appearance of a severe Methodist chapel. Separate booths and benches are allocated to accused, witnesses and lawyers, as well as to the mayor and council. Behind is the grand jury room, where citizens met to decide whether a case merited hearing or was frivolous. This process is now delegated to lawyers, with a resulting explosion of litigation. Not all reform is progressive.

BRYN CELLI DDU *

BURIAL MOUND
Llanfair P.G.
Ancient site with interior shrine
and standing stone (Cadw)

Who were these people? We know only that they probably came from the south and that the sea, rather than the land, was their chief means of dispersal. They predated the Celts, who arrived in Wales about 500 BC.

The two most celebrated burial sites on Anglesey date from c.2000 BC, at Barclodiad y Gawres and Bryn Celli Ddu. The former is located dramatically on a headland north of Aberffraw and contains rare drawings scratched on the wall. But it looks like a camouflaged bomb shelter. Bryn Celli Ddu has a more authentic atmosphere.

It is reached over the fields from a side road, along paths lined with streams, hawthorn and sloes, and is encircled with a low rampart and ring of standing stones. The chamber itself emerges from a narrow covered passage into the mound. The room is (now) utterly plain, with ledges and a stone pillar in the middle. Visitors inspired by its *genius loci* lay offerings of wild flowers, shells and stones on a shelf.

Outside the mound is a standing stone, copy

Pre-Celtic grandeur: Bryn Celli Ddu

of an original now in the National Museum of Wales. It has a meandering decoration, art at its oldest and most simple.

DIN LLUGWY **

Llanallgo
Stone huts in defended enclosure (Cadw)

This is the most evocative Romano-British settlement in Britain. Visitors must walk for half a mile across the fields before climbing to a clearing amid trees, immediately recognizable as an encampment. The place is thought to have been occupied in the late-Roman period, and presumably afterwards. Excavation has revealed 4th-century pottery and coins and evidence of ironworking.

The walls of two round huts and a number of rectangular ones survive, as do surrounding walls of considerable thickness. Since such villages would normally be of wood and daub, the scale of these buildings suggests a prosperous community. The walls rise waist-high and door lintels are still standing.

With the trees dancing in the wind and a complete absence of modern buildings near the site the druidical past is made present. Here priests and bards incited their audience to remember their ancestors. Here Tacitus had the Romans determined to stamp out druidism, 'felling the groves dedicated to savage superstition', and thus ensuring the passage of druidism into Welsh myth.

PLAS NEWYDD ****

Gothick house in beautiful location, Whistler mural (NT)

Everything in the Marquess of Anglesey's house on the Menai Straits is subordinate to its setting. Where others have an approach avenue, Plas Newydd has an exotic descent through beeches, limes and sub-tropical vegetation. Where others have terraces overlooking lakes, Plas Newydd has the rushing strait. Where others might have a hill in the distance, Plas Newydd has the massed majesty of Snowdon.

Plas Newydd: domesticated gothick

The medieval house belonged to the Griffiths of Penrhyn in the 1470s, descending through the Bayly family to the present marquess via the titles of Lord Paget and the Earl of Uxbridge. It was Sir Henry Bayly who, in the 1780s and 1790s, began the rebuilding of the house in a style variously gothic revival (usually termed gothick) and neo-classical, principally to the designs of James Wyatt. There is also a Repton Red Book for the layout of the grounds, dated 1799. The exterior was 'un-gothicked' in the 1930s when the interior was reordered for a grand mural by Rex Whistler.

Though owned by the National Trust, Plas Newydd is still occupied and cared for by the 7th Marquess of Anglesey, who succeeded to the title in 1947. He is the descendant of the 1st Marquess, who was head of Wellington's cavalry, lost his leg at Waterloo and is commemorated in a Nelsonian column on the hill behind the house.

On first view, the exterior is an anticlimax. The style is over-altered and in gunmetal grey render, which looks good neither in sun nor in rain. Its virtue is that, unlike Penrhyn, it does not try to be what it is not.

The approach is past a field in the middle of which is a large cromlech. There are too many trees shrouding the first glimpses of the house and a visit is best begun on the terrace where we can see what Wyatt was seeking to exploit. The wooded land across the strait opposite, that of the Vaynol estate, has been bought by the National Trust to protect the view.

The entrance is into Wyatt's so-called Gothick Hall, spare and chapel-like but with a lierne and fan plaster vault and delicate gallery at the far end. The chamber is naked but was once crammed with pennants, banners, armour, chinoiserie and a stuffed bear. It needs them.

Next is the Music Room, Wyatt's Plas Newydd masterpiece, though the execution was by Joseph Potter of Lichfield. The delicate fan vault perfectly matches the proportions of the windows. A conversation piece by Rex Whistler shows the family in 1938 (including the present marquess painting), all looking rather bored. A swaggering Lawrence of the 1st Marquess in full Hussar rig hangs on the wall.

The staircase hall is austerely Doric, adorned with military portraits and landscapes and leading to the upper floor. This is conventionally domestic, though Lord Anglesey's bedroom contains a state bed, covered in exquisite Chinese silk with flower patterns, repeated in the pelmet over the windows. This and adjacent rooms are full of sea pictures, appropriate to the view from the windows.

The ground-floor rooms on the 'view' side have been much reorganized and are of interest chiefly for the homely arrangement of pictures and furniture. Light floods them all. Large landscape pictures suit the marriage of architecture and outlook that is a feature here.

The enfilade culminates in two rooms dedicated to Whistler, a friend of the family who stayed often at Plas Newydd, where he painted his last and one of his greatest capriccios (rivalling that of Port Lympne in Kent). It is of canvas glued to the plaster and fills the wall of what was the dining room. It depicts a series of famous buildings – Windsor Castle, St Martin-in-the-Fields, Trajan's Column – as if they were outside the window of Plas Newydd. Overhead are billowing clouds and in the foreground symbolic objects, such as Poseidon's trident, the family dog and Whistler himself as a gardener.

Churches

AMLWCH

OUR LADY, STAR OF THE SEA ✶
Modernist church by Italian architect

Twentieth-century churches in Wales are a rarity. Since this church is closed and at risk, its inclusion breaks my accessibility rule, but it is worth a visit even for the exterior. The Roman Catholic foundation was designed in 1933 by an Italian, Giuseppe Rinvolucri, who lived in Conwy and was apparently conversant with European Modernism. He also designed churches at Porthmadog and Abergele, employing local workers and using mostly concrete, which is now deteriorating.

The style is set by sweeping parabolic arches, perhaps inspired by airship hangars or by upturned boats in Amlwch harbour. The nave-cum-chancel is set on a white single-storey plinth with porthole windows. The parabola shape was much favoured by Arts and Crafts church architects, such as Lethaby at Brockhampton (Herefs). The west end has a bold gable with sloping sides and a west door on a double flight of steps.

The interior concrete walls, again parabolic, are divided by six ribs and lit by arches of glass set as bands of white and blue light supplemented by stars in the east wall. The blue and white is apparently made of old milk of magnesia bottles. A large east end mural Crucifixion against a landscape of sea and sky is by Gordon Wallace in 1963. This church must be saved.

BEAUMARIS

ST MARY AND ST NICHOLAS ✶✶
Rich 'colony' church, 15th-century tomb

The church of Edward I's new borough is appropriately substantial, with a defensive west tower. It nestles in the centre of the lovely old town (see above), with one side overlooked by almshouse dormers. The exterior is predominantly Perpendicular and the porch large enough to hold the effigy of Princess Joan, wife of Llywelyn the Great and illegitimate daughter of King John. The marriage was one of many Norman attempts to tame the Welsh through matrimony. She died in 1237.

The interior is spaciously civic, the four-bay arcades and aisles in 13th-century Decorated gothic, the nave walls rudely scraped to the stone. A later roof, contemporary with the Perpendicular chancel, is panelled and has coloured bosses. A rear organ loft gazes down the length of the church. All this is rendered gloomy both by the scraping and by Victorian glass of variable quality.

The interior is rich in contents. The chancel misericords are among the finest in Wales, probably brought from the friary at Llan-faes, founded in honour of Princess Joan. Most are of women carrying wheat and ale or balancing a bucket on the head. Above on the north side is a rare Trinitarian brass of c.1530. Another brass near the nave lectern records charitable donations in 1743, including one for six shillings from 'Tabora the Black', a former slave in the town.

The church's treasure is the Bulkeley tomb at its west end, of William Bulkeley (d. c.1490), deputy constable of the castle, and of his wife, and made of Midlands alabaster. He is armoured and the couple are supported round the sides of the tomb by bishops and saints as weepers. It reminds me of the memorials to be seen in Calcutta, later imperial tombs in some distant colony.

HOLYHEAD

ST CYBI **
Perpendicular church with stone carvings
and Burne-Jones window

Since Roman times the town and port looking out over the sea to Ireland have been important strategically and commercially. Holyhead possessed a Roman fort and 6th-century Celtic *clas* and was well endowed by the Normans in the 12th century. It was a college with twelve clergy on its dissolution in 1547. The church is sited within visible Roman walls overlooking the harbour. A chapel in the churchyard was an *eglwys y bedd*, or shrine, later a school.

The present church, heavily restored by Scott in 1877, dates from a comprehensive 15th-century rebuilding and is thus late Perpendicular, wide and low with boldly battlemented roofs. A buttressed porch indicates the many uses – legal, social and commercial – to which such structures were put. The strange south transept has a modest window but intricate and unusual abstract carvings beneath the ornamented battlement.

The south door carries a rare sculpted tympanum of Christ crucified with the head of God overlooking him, apparently 15th century. Two saints are in panels on either side. The interior is dark, with a three-bay nave and an alarmingly wide crossing arch. The east window has reticulated tracery earlier than the rest of the church, presumably surviving from a 13th-century chancel. A William Morris window includes figures by Burne-Jones.

LLANDYSILIO *

Menai Bridge
Island church in Menai straits

Llandysilio and its churchyard occupy an ideal site on an island in the Swellies, the mile of turbulent water between the two Menai bridges. There is no better position from which to view these two masterpieces of early engineering: Robert Stephenson's box-girder Britannia railway bridge (marred by an upper road deck in 1980) and Thomas Telford's 1826 suspension bridge. Steep banks of green rise on either side of the straits, here dotted with islands amid the dangerous tides.

Tysilio was reputedly son of a 6th-century king of Powys and a celebrity of the age of saints. He studied under Gwyddfarch, the first abbot of Meifod (Powys). While there are many churches dedicated to him, this appears to have been a personal foundation, before he returned to Meifod. An inscription over the door declares that 'St Tysilio built this church, 630 AD'. The island is popular for burials and rises to a cenotaph, surrounded by pines.

The building is of limited interest inside. A tiny single chamber was probably constructed on old foundations in the 15th century and rebuilt by the Victorians. The roof re-uses medieval trusses and collar beams. The 19th-century fittings are rich, as if to compensate for the destruction of whatever was before. There is no electricity, just a candelabra and pedal organ.

LLANEILIAN ***

Saint's shrine, screen with loft and
painted musicians

This exquisite church lies due east of the heights of Parys Mountain, whose vast open-cast mine is one of the wonders of Wales. The site was reputedly awarded to Eilian as a result of his curing the blindness of King Cadwallon (see Llangadwaladr below). The present church is mostly 15th-century. An earlier preaching cross survives in the churchyard, as do the remains of an ossuary, supposedly filled with the bones of shipwrecked sailors.

Llaneilian lies on a mound looking out to sea, a stumpy Norman tower with pyramid spire presumably serving as a navigation beacon. The interior retains a firmly pre-Victorian atmosphere and layout, with the nave and chancel divided by a large screen into what are virtually two rooms. The iconoclasts were clearly kind here.

The treasure is the screen, rudimentary in execution compared to mainland survivals but assertive in design and with the deepest coving I can recall. It must jut a full 3 feet over the nave to accommodate the singers and musicians at the Easter festival. The panels are bordered in customary vine- and ivy-leaf carving. A grim reaper hovers over the central arch forming a rather lugubrious chancel entrance. The blade of his scythe says, 'The Sting of Death is Sin'.

The importance of music to the late-medieval church is suggested not just by the screen gallery but by four delightful musicians on the roof corbels of the chancel, matching three apostles and the Virgin in the nave. They are all playing wind instruments, one a bagpipe, a rare depiction of an instrument often banned in churches as supposedly sinful.

An opening on the right of the chancel leads down an enclosed passage to St Eilian's chapel, a most unusual structure. It was built in the 14th century, possibly over his tomb. Like the church it has resisted Victorian restoration and retains its old, gnarled woodwork in doors, seats and panelling. A polygonal altar once had two panels removed, legend holding that a sick person crawling through would be cured by the saint.

LLANFIGEL *

Restored church with Georgian fittings

There are so many churches on Anglesey like Llanfigel that it is hard to choose between them. This tiny church was derelict in the 18th cen-

tury but restored by the Morris family, with a complete set of Georgian furnishings. So many families needed their own grade of pew opposite the pulpit that the redundant altar had to be squeezed under the east window behind a small railing. Lesser mortals sat on benches, and paupers on the floor at the back. There is a 14th-century font and ancient tiled floor. The lighting is by candles set in metal candelabra.

The church was closed in 1994 but a campaign to keep it open was launched, money raised and the building is now with the Friends of Friendless Churches. An annual service is said to be so crowded that visitors have to listen from outside. The Georgian vicarage, Plas Llanfigel to the north of the church, is larger by far.

LLANGADWALADR **

Kingly church with Royalist chapel

In so far as we know anything of the early kings and saints of Wales, we know that Cadwaladr was son of Cadwallon, son of Cadfan, all kings of Gwynedd. Cadwaladr died c.664 and was canonized by Pope Sergius in 689 as 'blessed king and sovereign of Britain', to the best of my knowledge the only Welsh saint other than David to be so honoured.

The church itself was a place of worship for the monarchs of Gwynedd, whose Anglesey court was held at neighbouring Aberffraw. Cadwaladr's most lasting act of filial piety was to have a memorial to his grandfather, Cadfan, carved and placed in the church, where it today adorns the north wall, and is believed to be the earliest tomb to carry the Celtic cross and thus indicate that the early Welsh kings were already Christians. The inscription in Latin refers to 'Cadfan wisest and most renowned of kings'.

The present church is a chunky, friendly place, despite the hardness of the Victorian restoration. The ghost of a romanesque arch can be seen in the north wall. The chief features of the exterior are the north and south chapels, the former for the local Meyrick family and the latter for the Owens of Bodowen. Both were added in the 17th century.

The Bodowen chapel is remarkable both out-

Hierarchical seating at Llanfigel

side and inside. Dated 1661 it is lit by large Perpendicular windows and further emphasized by two angled buttresses. Next to the west door of the chapel is a leper's window, supposedly so lepers could watch the service from outside.

The chapel interior is linked to the chancel by a wide arch that looks ready to dip in the middle. This 17th-century gothic survival, like Rug (Clwyd), was normally a sign of High Church sympathies. Hugh Owen, for whom the chapel was built by his widow, was an ardent Royalist, dying in 1659. His great-uncle, Owen Lewis, was a Catholic priest and founder of the English College in Rome. There was once a painting of Charles I in the east window. The chapel also contains a charming Jacobean memorial to Hugh with his wife, Ann, kneeling at prayer.

The church's chief treasure, other than the Cadfan stone, is the 15th-century east window of the chancel. It ranks with the later work at Llanrhaeadr (Clwyd) as a masterpiece of Per-

pendicular glazing, and was saved from iconoclasts by being removed and hidden at the Reformation. It was probably commissioned in thanksgiving for the safe return of a Meyrick offspring, Meurig ap Llywelyn, from the battle of Bosworth.

The window is of the Crucifixion with St Mary and St John on either side. Christ's figure is depicted with his skeleton in the glass. Also shown are St Cadwaladr, splendidly attired and with orb and sceptre, and the donors, Meurig and his wife, Marged. Their son, Owain, is in battle dress with his wife, Elin. The window is believed to have been resited in 1661.

LLANGWYFAN *

Aberffraw
Church on beach islet lost in mists of Irish Sea

The church is probably locked and the interior is plain. But of all island churches – reachable on a causeway except at high tide – this is the

most inviting. It sits on a solitary rock above the sea-wrack of a bay near Aberffraw, looking out across the sweep of Caernarfon Bay to the Rivals.

The church is a mile from the nearest parking place. Sadly it is not a mile from the motor-bike racing circuit on the cliffs immediately to the north, blighting beach and church alike with a continuous roar of engines.

The church, much of it apparently romanesque, must have lost its north aisle (or nave). A crude three-bay arcade can be seen ghost-like in the exterior wall. The interior, furnished with chairs and a later pulpit, is devoid of architectural features yet still evokes the simple faith of these poor island people. With the sea swirling round the little churchyard, the sand, sky and birds are architecture enough. It is very easy to see why so many people are still being buried on the island. The grass is thick and as soft as a feather bed. Were it not for the motorbikes, this would be the most serene resting place in all Wales.

PENMON

ST SEIRIOL ★★★★
Romanesque priory, early carvings,
wild location with holy well

Penmon is the most rewarding church on Anglesey. It was the hermitage of a late-6th-century monk, St Seiriol, who, so legend holds, would converse with the island's other great man of the time, St Cybi of Holyhead, somewhere between the two places. Since the journey was east–west Seiriol walked against the sun and Cybi into it, earning them the epithets Seiriol the Pale and Cybi the Golden.

Since no self-respecting hermit was without an island, Seiriol's cell was said to be on the present Puffin Island, or Priestholm, a mile beyond the priory at the easternmost point of Anglesey. Monastic ruins survive on the island. The walk from Penmon to the windswept point of Anglesey, with beach, lighthouse and coffee bar, is gloriously wild with a view on a clear day

LEFT: *Llangwyfan, alone with the sea*   ABOVE: *Anglesey romanesque at Penmon*

across the straits to Puffin Island and beyond, to Conwy Sands and Snowdonia.

The original church was burned by the Danes in 971 and rebuilt by the Welsh in c.1140. Today it sits beyond its village behind a wall and surrounded by scrub and moor, in appearance little changed over a millennium. The romanesque nave and tower still stand, the latter with its original pyramidal stone roof. The priory house, now a private residence, and the ruins of the 13th-century refectory complete a three-sided court, originally the cloister.

Though the old chancel was rebuilt as the parish church by the Victorians, romanesque doors and the old nave and transept remain remarkably preserved. The tower arch is particularly fine, tripartite with chequer, zigzag and chevron decoration. On the left capital appear to be two versions of a man shouting, on the right a dancer. An exterior doorway also has chequer-work. A blind arcade in the south transept is adorned with more chevron decoration, and a deep-set window contains fragments of medieval glass. Also in the transept is an ex-plicit sheela-na-gig of a woman holding open her vagina.

Penmon is full of treasures. The font was originally the base of a cross, incised with a continuous knot pattern to symbolize eternity. Another cross was shorn of one arm to enable its use in a window, while a third was found nearby and, despite defacing, depicts a man on a horse with demons and Danish interlacing. Set into the wall of the nave is a particularly lovely Limoges enamel of the 13th century showing Jesus in a red nimbus. Penmon is wrapped in the sort of peace, as Peter Sager says, 'that one always hopes to find at the end of all roads and all journeys'.

Across the yard is a post-Reformation dovecote of c.1600. In the undergrowth nearby are the remains of a 6th-century cell and holy well, a rare survival. It is arched, roofed and retains its old seating. The whole site is a remarkable evocation of medieval Christianity, the more so as deriving not from the Norman invasion but from indigenous Welsh builders, drawing inspiration from Irish and Norse styles.

Clwyd
[Denbighshire, Flintshire]

Clwyd has been dubbed the Welsh Tuscany for its rolling hills and secret valleys – and perhaps for its appeal to the rich of Cheshire. This has always been border country, assigned by the Normans to the earls of Chester. Since the Tudors its Maelor Saesneg has dug deep into Shropshire east of Wrexham, no government having had the courage to put this floating part of Flintshire into England.

The Normans erected motte-and-bailey forts at Rhuddlan and elsewhere, but did not have to defend the territory as they did in points west and south. Through the Middle Ages the country saw armies march back and forth to wars in Gwynedd to the west. Edward I left new castles at Ruthin, Rhuddlan and Denbigh and the Mortimers built a mighty fortress at Chirk.

The region's loyalty to the Welsh cause was always in some doubt. Only under Glyndŵr, a member of the Flint gentry, did it display a true Welshness. But Glyndŵr was married to a Mortimer and operating in the turbulent age of Richard II and Henry IV, when no one's allegiance was sure.

Clwyd's early churches were of little distinction, except in the isolated serenity

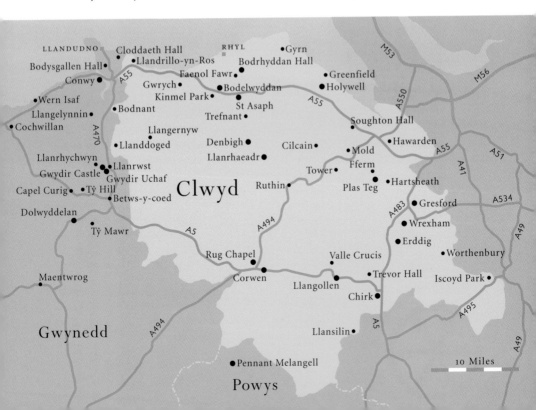

of Cilcain. St Asaph is a lovable but unimpressive cathedral. By contrast, the Tudor ascendancy was peculiarly favourable, bringing money to existing foundations under the patronage of Henry VII's mother, Lady Margaret Beaufort (later Stanley). Her 'Stanley' churches stand comparison with those of East Anglia, and include Mold, Gresford, the tower at Wrexham and the shrine at Holywell. Other benefactors yielded the great Jesse window at Llanrhaeadr, the angel roof at Cilcain and the painted ceiling at Ruthin.

The Elizabethans built houses at Faenol and Fferm, the Jacobeans were spectacular at Plas Teg and fine memorials survive in churches at Gresford and Denbigh. The 17th century also contributed Rug Chapel, an exercise in decorative if discreet Catholic recusancy.

Domestic building in the 17th century was triumphantly epitomized by Erddig, now immaculately presented by the National Trust. To the Georgians Clwyd owes little that is visible, other than some interiors at Chirk with its Davies gates and the 'Ladies of Llangollen' at eccentric Plas Newydd. The charming church of Worthenbury is a rare Welsh ecclesiastical building of the period.

In the 19th century Clwyd found its stride on the strength of English wealth. Castellated Regency was at its most extraordinary at Bodelwyddan and Gwrych Castle. Sir Gilbert Scott brought High Gothic to Hafodunos and Eden Nesfield brought Queen Anne revival to Kinmel and his charming additions to Bodrhyddan Hall. Victorian church builders created the 'marble church' of Bodelwyddan and adorned Gladstone's Hawarden with the finest Burne-Jones windows.

Houses and Castles

BODELWYDDAN ***

Castellated mansion with portrait gallery and Arts and Crafts interiors (Mus)

Considering the troubled history of the North-Welsh Williams family it is a miracle that anything survives of Bodelwyddan. Yet survive it does, nobly set on a rolling slope above the Vale of Clwyd, cocking a snook at an ugly hospital below. The land passed from the ancient Humphrey (or Wmffre) family to Sir William Williams in the 1690s. The latter had been a controversial Speaker of the Commons under Charles II and his eldest son founded the Williams-Wynn dynasty, owner of extensive estates across North Wales.

An old house on the site went through various transformations, including neo-classical remodelling in 1800–1808. It was then rebuilt in the 1830s in castellated gothic by Hansom and Welch. The estate remained heavily in debt until rescued by a Williams daughter, Lady Margaret Willoughby de Broke, who returned to Wales on her husband's death in 1852. She brought his money with her and earned from her in-laws the nickname 'the Welsh robber'. Her 'marble church' at Bodelwyddan is described below.

By the time of the Great War the house and estate were again 'embarrassed' and passed to the army. This experience was predictably unhappy, the neighbouring camp of Kinmel being scene in 1919 of the Kinmel Mutiny against

Houses and Castles

Bodelwyddan ✶✶✶
Bodnant ✶
Bodrhyddan Hall ✶✶✶
Chirk ✶✶✶✶
Erddig ✶✶✶✶
Faenol Fawr ✶
Fferm ✶
Greenfield ✶

Gwrych Castle ✶✶
Gyrn ✶
Hafodunos ✶
Hartsheath ✶
Iscoyd Park ✶✶
Kinmel Park ✶✶
Llangollen:
    Plas Newydd ✶✶✶

Plas Teg ✶✶✶✶
Ruthin:
    Castle ✶✶
    Nantclwyd House ✶✶
Soughton Hall ✶✶
Tower ✶
Trevor Hall ✶✶

Churches

Bodelwyddan ✶✶✶✶
Cilcain ✶
Corwen:
    Rug Chapel ✶✶✶
Denbigh:
    Llanfarchell ✶✶✶
Gresford ✶✶✶✶
Hawarden ✶✶

Holywell ✶✶✶
Llanddoged ✶
Llandrillo-yn-Rhos ✶
Llangar ✶✶
Llangernyw ✶
Llangollen:
    St Collen ✶
    Valle Crucis ✶✶

Llanrhaeadr ✶✶✶
Llansilin ✶✶
Mold ✶
Ruthin ✶✶
St Asaph ✶✶✶
Trefnant ✶
Worthenbury ✶✶
Wrexham ✶✶✶✶

poor living conditions. The house later became Lowther College for Girls until it closed, again heavily indebted, in 1982.

Bodelwyddan was rescued by Clwyd County Council with a consortium of Warner low-cost hotels, saviour of a dozen English houses, and in collaboration with the National Portrait Gallery. The castle is now a mix of gallery, museum, hotel, park, shops and café, clinging dramatically to the hillside amid its formal gardens.

The Council's redecoration of the main rooms in the 1980s, under the direction of Roderick Gradidge of the Art Workers Guild, is a bravura work of Victorian revivalism. The rooms have been given furniture as well as paintings and thus seem warmer and more lived-in than most museums. Given the loss of decorative plans of the old house, Gradidge had a free hand to re-create an Arts and Crafts interior and left his masterpiece.

Paintings inevitably dominate the interior. A corridor is devoted to portraits by G. F. Watts. The billiard room is lined with Spy cartoons.

A fine portrait of Lady Dilke, 'art historian and feminist', hangs in the dining room. Most dramatic of all, the gothic drawing room has a Thomas Lawrence portrait of Sophia Coutts. Signage and education are kept firmly in the background.

BODNANT ✶

Tudorbethan mansion amid
celebrated garden (NT)

Bodnant is for gardeners, with reputedly the finest collection of rhododendron, azalea and other exotics in Britain. The estate is perched on the side of the Conwy valley with deep ravines cutting down to the river and Snowdonia in the distance. In spring it is a landscape ablaze. The gardens belong to the National Trust, while the house is private and belongs to the Aberconway family. Since the house exterior dominates the gardens and is seen by all, I have included it in my list.

The house was rebuilt from a Georgian

predecessor in 1881 by Henry Pochin in a 'Tudorbethan' style. The two main façades are asymmetric, with wings, turrets and gables distributed almost at will. The lower floors are of stone, the upper ones black-and-white timbered – a blown up version of Aberconwy House in Conwy. There is a conservatory to one side and a staircase tower rising to a prominent lantern. I am told it is lovely inside.

In the grounds is a charming folly called the Pin Mill at the end of a canal lake. The building came from Woodchester in Gloucestershire where, at one point, it was used for making pins. It was bought as derelict by the 2nd Lord Aberconway in 1938 and transported to adorn his expanding garden. Like most such water follies (as at Frampton, Gloucs) it demonstrates a happy fusion of architecture and nature.

BODRHYDDAN HALL ***

1 mile east of Rhuddlan
William-and-Mary/Victorian mansion of Conwy family, baroque chimneypieces (Priv)

Every Welsh county should have a Bodrhyddan, a mansion in the custodianship of the family that built it, cares for it and accepts its role in the community. Though open only infrequently in the summer, both house and garden are a monument to the Conwys, who arrived with Edward I as constables of his fortress at neighbouring Rhuddlan and have stayed ever since.

Visitors down the long drive are greeted by a theatrical Victorian frontispiece in Anglo-Dutch revival by Eden Nesfield. It was designed in 1872 when he was working on the more substantial Kinmel along the coast. The character of the house derives from the relationship of this façade to the two earlier houses on the site. One was Sir Richard Conwy's hall house of *c.*1450, walling of which can be seen at the back, and the other a William and Mary building of 1696 which forms the central bays of the south front.

The Nesfield façade is strongly vertical, of three storeys with an attic just five bays wide. A pedimented front door rises to a balconied second storey on huge brackets with matching pilas-

ters above and a dormer crowned by the family crest, a pelican. It might be a townhouse in The Hague. This feature is balanced by single-storey wings for a billiard room and conservatory on either side.

Moving to the south front we see Nesfield neatly enclosing the five bays of the 17th-century house in a forest of mansards, dormers and chimneys. It is composed like a family portrait of relatives round a pair of ageing parents. In front is a parterre with stern yews designed by Nesfield's father, W. A. Nesfield, replacing what was the entrance drive to the earlier house.

The interior was substantially rearranged by Nesfield and is enjoyably crammed with family memorabilia and pictures. The entrance hall has an armoury of weapons, with an Egyptian museum to one side. This contains a mummy collected by a Conwy on her honeymoon in 1836. Beyond is the old Great Hall, still so called, with a medieval dining table and family portraits on the walls. Nesfield refashioned the old fireplace into an Art Nouveau inglenook.

A staircase leads to the spacious drawing room, formed of the chamber over the hall with the wings of the William and Mary house incorporated as alcoves. It is flooded with light, enhanced by the repainting in white and gold of two chimneypieces, probably imported by an antiquarian family member, William Shipley. He also revived the Conwy name which had been lost through female descent.

Shipley's chimneypieces, probably of Continental origin, are the most remarkable feature of the house. They were probably bought, like many church fittings, during a boom in the European antiques market that followed Napoleon's depredations. They are in high baroque, displaying acanthus swirling and enclosing panels of biblical and other scenes. These panels were allegedly looted from an Armada ship wrecked off Anglesey, in which case they must have been inserted into later frames. A similar chimneypiece dominates the so-called Dean's dining room downstairs, but here in its original black, heavy and gloomy.

Bodrhyddan deserves to be better known. Its grounds, laid out by Nesfield and embellished by Clough Williams-Ellis, include redwoods, a

Arts and crafts at Bodelwyddan

Chirk Castle: Pugin medievalism

new summer house and an ancient well whose spring never dries. Its wellhead is attributed to Inigo Jones in 1612.

CHIRK ****

8 miles south of Wrexham
Marcher castle with medieval and Georgian state rooms, hall by Pugin (NT)

I first saw Chirk as the ancients would, looming out of the mist on a wild rainy day across surrounding meadows. It looked as implacable as once it was impregnable. The visitor must walk up from the car park, fighting the elements in bad weather and arriving at the great gate like a Welsh interloper assaulting a Marcher lord.

The castle was Roger Mortimer's contribution to Edward I's conquest of Wales, built between 1295 and 1310. Like most border castles it passed through many hands and lost many heads until the arrival of more settled Tudor times. It was bought by a successful Denbigh merchant, Thomas Myddelton, who went on to

be a founder-member of the East India Company and Lord Mayor of London. His brother, Hugh, created London's water supply, the New River Company in Islington, where he is recalled in Myddelton Square.

Myddelton's son fortified Chirk for Parliament in the Civil War but saw it seized by local Royalists. He was forced to lay siege to his own house, which he was understandably reluctant to damage. Like many Welshmen, Myddelton changed sides to become a Royalist late in the day and was duly besieged in Chirk by a Parliamentary force. He contrived to hold on until the Restoration, and remained secure in his ownership thereafter.

Subsequent Myddeltons added to the Tudor state rooms round the courtyard with 18th- and 19th-century insertions and alterations. The castle was rented in 1911 to Lord Howard de Walden, a medievalist eager for a proper castle. He staged jousts and falconry fairs in the grounds and filled the rooms with armour and weapons. On one such occasion a guest came down to breakfast to find his lordship reading *The Times* in full chain mail. It is said that when the Myddeltons resumed occupancy after the

Second World War, the younger de Waldens were unaware that they did not own the place. Myddeltons departed only recently.

The exterior is as built in the 14th century, with only the insertion of Tudor windows to suggest domesticity. The courtyard retains its medieval appearance, one of few British castles to do so (cf. Berkeley, Gloucs, and Skipton, N. Yorks). The entrance is through the Cromwell Hall, a re-creation by Pugin from what would have been Myddelton's great hall. It is appropriately rich in panelling, weaponry and heraldry. Coats of arms are of Myddeltons down the ages. On the screen hangs a picture of Chirk made of bog oak inlaid with bone.

The hall leads via a screens passage to the main staircase, a bold classical insertion of 1778 hacked out of the medieval walls. It appears to herald a suite of Georgian state rooms but does so only briefly. The state dining room is Adam in style by a Chester mason, Joseph Turner, laid out for dinner under the gaze of a boulle clock by Balthazar. The saloon has been plunged in National Trust gloom to protect its Mortlake tapestries, rendering Turner's ceiling and a set of school-of-Lely portraits near invisible. An exquisite Shudi harpsichord carries accomplished marquetry. On a wet day the whole room might be under water.

The small drawing room turns the corner to the long gallery, an earlier Restoration room with an oak floor big enough to make a good indoor cricket pitch. Here stands Chirk's glory, the ebony cabinet given by Charles II to Myddelton as a reward for turning Royalist in the Civil War. It is beautifully inlaid, with ivory and tortoiseshell framing scenes from the life of Christ. The windows here offer views over the park to the surrounding countryside. The yew hedges in the formal garden are immaculate.

Off the gallery is the king's bedroom with a bed in which Charles I is improbably said to have slept. (Did he lie in a hundred such beds for distribution to faithful courtiers?) Across the courtyard the servants' hall is dark and austere, as if awaiting a Cromwellian sermon. On the wall hang portraits of castle servants. Adam's Tower is a survivor of a medieval residential tower, sadly denuded of furnishings.

Chirk's park gates (see p. 24) are a delightful surprise. They are the masterpieces of the Welsh ironsmiths the Davies brothers, designed in c.1719. In a wild Welsh rococo, they echo Tijou's gates at Hampton Court, a swirling tableau of foliage and birds round the Myddeltons' wolf motif, forming an elegant welcome to a supposedly grim fortress.

ERDDIG ****

2 miles south of Wrexham
Restoration house unaltered since the 19th century. State bedroom, gallery and estate offices preserved (NT)

Erddig is the jewel in the crown of Welsh country houses. It may lack the punch of Powis or the fireworks of Cardiff Castle, but it has a depth of character, a sense of habitation blessed by age, of few houses in Britain. Erddig is impossible not to love. As restored by the National Trust, it evokes the lives of all who have resided within its walls, rich and poor.

The opening line of the guide applies to so many houses: 'In 1682 Joshua Edisbury was appointed High Sheriff of Denbighshire: it was to be the making of Erddig and the unmaking of Edisbury.' He set about building himself a mansion in the Restoration style of Roger Pratt, to designs by Thomas Webb of Cheshire. It had a basement and a hipped roof and was furnished as well as money could buy.

Within ten years Edisbury was hopelessly in debt. He turned for help to Elihu Yale, later of New England (see Wrexham Church), and to a wealthy brother, but to no avail. He died in London in disgrace and the house passed to Sir John Trevor, Master of the Rolls, and then in 1716 to another Chancery lawyer, John Mellor.

Mellor was a tight-fisted bachelor 'not very agreeable to the country' but he saved Erddig. He built wings to the original house and turned what had been the home of a local landowner into the residence of a London grandee. In 1724 his steward wrote to him that, since his last visit, 'There have been four coaches full of gentry … who admired the Hall and furniture mitily.' The house passed to Mellor's nephew, Simon Yorke, in whose family it remained to the end.

Of all the tales of the triumphs and woes of British country houses few equal that of the Yorkes of Erddig. Never grand or attaining high office and often desperately poor, they held to one principle, that the house and contents were the family and held the genius of the place. They must not be touched, let alone sold.

Towards the end of the family's ownership in the late 1960s, Philip Yorke could be found camping in his own freezing room, the walls subsiding into coal workings, rain pouring on to the state bed, wallpaper peeling and calor gas bills piling up. He struggled to make a living as a prep schoolmaster, security guard and tour operator with his own minibus. Still nothing was touched. After three years of negotiation, Erddig passed to the National Trust in 1973, virtually as it was in the 18th century.

Externally the main body of the house is undistinguished. The nine-bay east front to the garden lost its balance with the addition of wings, while its frontispiece is modest. The west front was refaced in 1772 and is dull.

The excitement is inside. The main rooms remained mostly as they had been in the 17th century. Domestic offices fill the lower ground floor, giving the estate a sense of oneness with the family. Here are the agent's offices, housekeeper's room, butler's pantry and servants' hall, all embracing domestic and estate management. The hall is hung with portraits of servants, a family tradition under the Yorkes and justly celebrated. They include the carpenter, woodman, butcher, 'housemaid and spider-brusher' and even a black coach boy with a horn.

The ground floor was altered by the Yorkes in the 18th century when the state bedroom was moved upstairs and replaced in 1827 by a neoclassical dining room by Thomas Hopper. It is filled with portraits of Yorkes and the family into which they married in 1770, the Custs of Belton in Lincolnshire. The saloon dates from the 17th-century house and looks out over the formal garden. It has rich panelling and excellent furniture, much of it dating from Mellor's acquisition. There is a boulle bureau veneered in brass and tortoiseshell. Mellor was fascinat-

ed by mirrors and collected fine pier-glasses.

The tapestry room is hung with Soho works, again commissioned by Mellor. In the centre is a Delft vase made for William and Mary and reputedly a gift from Queen Anne. The Chinese room is filled with porcelain. The library contains a set of drawings illustrating 'the Royal Tribes of Wales' by Joseph Allen. The old entrance hall, now music room, has an enjoyable collection of 'after Lelys and Knellers'. The private chapel was created by Mellor, the social gradations of the house replicated in the pew arrangements, with a classical reredos of 1663. The window glass includes 15th-century fragments.

Upstairs at Erddig is now all bedrooms, cluttered with furniture and, in the case of the nursery, toys and a doll's house. The showpiece is the State Bedroom and its early 18th-century bed, hung with precious silks and with a counterpane of peacocks. The room displays an exquisite japanned bureau and lacquered Chinese screen, surrounded by green Chinese wallpaper. Much was given to the family by Yale, then a governor in India.

The two ends of the bedroom floor are divided by a charming gallery running east–west. Apart from a collection of Dutch and other pictures it displays two models, one of the Chinese Pagoda at Kew and another of the Temple at Palmyra. The Blue Bedroom includes a set of mezzotints by Thomas Frye in an expressively mannerist style. The attic floor is filled with junk, temporary exhibitions and conservation in progress. Erddig is never still.

The outbuildings survive intact, demonstrating the self-sufficiency (we would now call it sustainability) of a pre-20th-century estate. We see joiner's shop, sawmill, wagon shed, smithy, stables, dairy, laundry, bakehouse and kitchen with large Venetian window. The habit of the Yorkes of composing doggerel about Erddig is everywhere on display. Hence a laundress 'though by duty of her post, / She is less often seen than most, / Her tuneful song in accents clear, / Is heard within our Chapel here.'

The formal garden is a triumph of dignified conservation, never having been overwhelmed by Georgian Picturesque or naturalism. The woods were home to a Victorian nightingale so

Erddig library: Restoration learning

celebrated that, reports the guide, 'half Wrexham would be in the wood until a late hour of the night … several unpropitious matches as well as a considerable augmentation of the population, to be provided for from the parish rates, were the result of the amorous power of his soft lay.'

FAENOL FAWR *

1 mile north of Bodelwyddan
Elizabethan pub/restaurant with gabled façade and interiors (H)

Those recovering from the visual horrors of Glan Clwyd hospital, under the shadows of Bodelwyddan Castle, should repair to the bar at Faenol Fawr. This hotel/restaurant occupies an Elizabethan H-plan house with interiors only mildly abused by their present use. The hotel has been well restored after a serious fire to the upper storey in 1984.

The house was built in 1597 by the Lloyd family. Its façade is an extreme example of Dutch step-gabling, covering not just the main façade gables but the side dormer windows as well. It appears to be unaltered. Not so the interior, though the components of a 16th-century hall house appear to have been rearranged rather than destroyed. The hall is divided from the bar to the right, with what appears to be the original kitchen fireplace and a stretch of original screen. A Jacobean staircase rises from the hall.

To the left of the entrance, the restaurant is the old parlour with a fireplace dated 1597, adorned with scrolls and heraldry, presumably of the Lloyd family. The panelled staircase is of 1725, when the entrance was moved to this side of the hall. The stair has bulbous balusters and sweeping handrail. Two upstairs floors, their timbering restored after the fire, have been opened out and have the character of long galleries. Faenol Fawr is an authentic Tudor mansion.

FFERM *

Hope, 3 miles south-east of Mold
Hall house surviving as family home (Priv)

This miniature manor is on the Hartsheath estate (see below), apparently dated c.1585 and not the emphatic 1506 over the porch. The house is of a conventional late-Elizabeth hall plan, with fireplace and chimney built in, not added later. One wing of the original H-plan has vanished, leaving just a hall with service wing rising two storeys to an attic.

The interior is charming, a home occupied by tenants proud to show visitors round (by appointment). The tiny hall is divided from the entrance passage by its original screen with moulded uprights. Flagstones cover the floor and heavy beams fill the ceilings, especially in the rear kitchen, which retains its fireplace and bread oven.

The staircase is appropriately cramped, lined with portraits of the Jones family of Hartsheath. Everywhere are sudden steps, beams and ancient cupboards. In one bedroom there appears to be an ancient oratory, if not priest's hole. The house is flanked by a medieval brewhouse and a courtyard of buildings of the same date as the manor, a delightful group.

GREENFIELD *

1 mile north of Holywell
ABBEY FARM MUSEUM,
PENTRE FARMHOUSE
Welsh longhouse restored to
17th-century state (Mus)

Wales is well endowed with old farmhouses but few are accessible. Thanks are therefore due to open-air museums such as St Fagans in the south and the more modest Abbey Farm at Greenfield in the north. Part of the Greenfield Valley Heritage Park, it stands next to Norman Basingwerk Abbey, of which a few walls remain stabilized in a meadow down the road from Holywell. Adjacent was an old farm and it is this that formed the basis of what is now a small museum.

Pentre Farmhouse was moved to the museum in 1983 from the slopes of Moel Famau some six miles inland. It is a simple hall house dating from the 16th century but altered an estimated eight times since, of which the fourth period (in the 17th century) was chosen for the rebuilding. This was when a byre and hall with dais were converted into a two-storey house with staircase tower and upstairs bedroom. The byre thus remains in place downstairs and the hall is supplemented by a parlour, a typical Welsh longhouse. Windows have both stone and wood mullions.

The house is presented in the current 'country life' style, with whitewash and flagstones and a pair of waxwork figures. The rooms are furnished in the 17th-century style. Health and safety is not too intrusive, apart from a ludicrous burglar alarm on the wall (of a longhouse!).

A second (Victorian) farm, Cwm Llydan, has been reconstructed near by, illustrating a further two centuries of housing development. The improvements seem limited.

GWRYCH CASTLE **

1 mile west of Abergele
Giant fantasy castle on hillside
awaiting restoration (Priv)

Even as a ruin Gwrych merits two stars. Restored it would merit four. It ranks with Hafodunos and Kinmel among the most shocking ruins in Wales, all within a few miles of each other. Until the 1990s this was an intact Victorian castle/mansion clinging to the mountainside of Cefn yr Ogof, overlooking the Irish Sea. The Hesketh family, creators of Gwrych, famously compared the view to the Bay of Naples. When the sun shines and the towers of Liverpool can be seen in the far distance, the comparison is apt.

Gwrych (pronounced 'greech') is the finest relic, perhaps in all Britain, of the Romantic

Clwyd romanticism: Gwrych Castle

gothic revival of the early 19th century, of a nostalgia for medieval chivalry and a conscious aversion to the industrial revolution on whose wealth it was built. It was created on his wife's land by Lloyd Hesketh Bamford-Hesketh, among the richest of Lancashire grandees. On coming into his inheritance in 1816, Hesketh commissioned Charles Busby (co-planner of Regency Brighton) to build his ideal of a fantasy castle. Hesketh had been helped by the antiquarian Thomas Rickman, the classifier of periods of gothic architecture.

The structure was to be a Welsh Windsor, with state rooms and private apartments behind a façade of castellated towers, turrets, outhouses and conservatories. The irregular outline curved round the hillside with deliberate theatricality, producing reputedly the longest built façade in Britain. It was not completed until 1853, by which time Rickman's gothic windows were made of cast iron.

The castle enjoyed barely a century of glory, chiefly under Hesketh's Welsh-speaking daughter Winifred, Countess of Dundonald, who died in 1924. Estranged from her husband, she left the house to sons whose interests lay in London and Scotland. It was used to house Jewish refugee children from Germany during the Second World War and was sold by the family in 1945.

Gwrych endured a steady decline, first as a private house of the Salt family, then a hotel (at which the boxer Randolph Turpin trained), then a zoo, then private apartments and in the 1980s a bar and nightclub. In 1964 the park between the castle and the seashore became a golf club. A succession of entrepreneurs bought the castle to use its land for caravans and chalets. By 1990 few could find out who owned the place and from 1994 onwards 'travellers' squatted the property and the interior was destroyed by fires, apparently to the satisfaction of unknown American owners.

The disaster enveloping the house caught

the attention of a local teenager, Mark Baker, who sent letters to anyone he could find, including the Prince of Wales. He set up a website, wrote a book and formed a trust 'to preserve Gwrych'. He was phenomenally successful. At the time of writing, Gwrych has been acquired by a Yorkshire hotel group, Clayton Hotels, who seem determined to rebuild and restore it to its former glory.

Visitors can walk round the outside and admire the battlements rising high against the forest. They can poke about its extravagant outbuildings. Seen from below, from left to right, the vista is of a garden temple, a melon and pineapple house, a French garden, the Conwy fly-tower, the outdoor theatre (of which there are two), the chapel and then the bulk of the main house. This is followed by the bothy, stables and brewhouse, a gigantic icehouse and a further lookout tower. To the rear are the extensive service buildings of a Victorian mansion, including kennels cut into the hillside. Shattered windows offer glimpses inside, of great halls and stairways full of fallen rubble.

The thick forest, fast encroaching on the house, hides relics of the great days, including a miniature railway and a temple composed of a magic yew circle with a holm oak in its centre. From Gwrych's terraces the view east towards the Wirral can still evoke Italian fantasies, but the foreground is not Naples but Pompeii.

GYRN *

Llanasa, 3 miles east of Prestatyn
Victorian mansion to be revived
as gallery (Priv)

Gyrn is another of the Victorian mansions along the North Welsh coast owned by Mersey tycoons keeping an eye on their wealth from a distance. The castellated villa was built for a Flintshire cotton manufacturer on Mostyn land. In the 1850s it was bought and extended by Sir Edward Bates, a Liverpool shipowner and is now being restored by an enterprising businessman, David Howard, as a conference centre and art gallery.

The chief asset of the house is the view,

looking out over the Dee and the Wirral to the Mersey in the distance. The architecture of the original wing is of little interest but the extension includes a baronial wing with tower, oriel window and giant picture gallery. The tower was said to enable Bates to watch his ships through his telescope as they passed the mouth of the Dee. This gave him time to race to the shore and take his launch to Liverpool in time to welcome his captains ashore.

The house has a spectacular ravine to one side whose wild vegetation awaits an eager taming hand.

HAFODUNOS *

Llangernyw, 8 miles south-west of Abergele
Ruined Victorian mansion by Gilbert Scott
with sculpted reliefs (Priv)

Hafodunos is another Welsh tragedy, included only in the hope that, like Gwrych, it finds a saviour. Wales is rich in romantic valleys and lush settings for great houses, yet poor in surviving examples of the latter.

Sir Gilbert Scott was an architect normally associated with churches and official buildings. He must have been exhilarated when asked by Henry Sandbach, son of a rich Liverpool trading family, to replace old Hafodunos on its steep hillside overlooking the river Gallen. While it does not rank with St Pancras or the Foreign Office, it certainly compares with his other great house at Kelham (Notts).

The house was begun in 1859 and decorated in collaboration with Margaret Sandbach's favourite sculptor, John Gibson, who supplied reliefs for the interior. The spectacular sloping grounds were laid out by Hooker. Like so many Victorian houses, Hafodunos enjoyed barely two generations of glory before a succession of deaths left the estate in the hands of a daughter, who was finally forced to sell it in 1934.

It then endured a descent all too familiar with British houses in the mid-20th century, successively a girls' school, accountancy college, old people's home, hostel for the homeless and mental hospice. The building was closed as unfit in 1993 and plunged into the purgatory of planning permission for caravans and chalets. Its grade one status, which should be a spur to salvation, became an excuse for inaction and decay.

As dry and wet rot spread, the house was steadily vandalized until, in 2004, two arsonists set it ablaze. Hafodunos is currently a gaunt, roofless ruin, Gibson's plaques staring out over collapsed stairs and gaping windows. Yet Scott's gables, chimneys and clock-tower stand. The polychrome walls and traceried windows still display their mottos. The brick and stone are robust and those bold enough to trespass through the surrounding jungle can sense the spirit of the place.

As for the grounds, thick with specimens brought back from Bhutan and Sikkim, they remind me of Ankor Wat. At Hafodunos nature is seizing back the works of man.

HARTSHEATH *

Hope, 3 miles south-east of Mold
Regency family home with original furnishings (Priv)

This is a typically dignified mansion built for the new rich of the Regency. Its date is 1825 and its owner was the manager of a local mine, which appears not to have lasted long. The architect, a young man name Charles Mathews was, according to Hubbard in Pevsner, 'better remembered as an actor'. We must take his word.

The building might be a lesser work by John Nash, a classical box of five bays by five bays, of stone rather than Nash's brick and stucco, and with an ascetic Doric porch. The last has been glazed to keep the draught from the hall. The internal arrangement is as expected, with a staircase rising four flights to a roof lantern, demonstrating how simply a fine staircase can transform a plain house into a grand one.

The plasterwork throughout appears to be contemporary with the building, as are excellent marble chimneypieces. The drawing room retains its Regency furniture, with wallpaper dating from 1841 according to graffiti in one corner. The house is furnished with portraits, watercolours and swords, in keeping with the

style of the building. The current owner is an art historian and Oxford women's rugby blue. Hartsheath is in safe hands.

ISCOYD PARK **

2 miles west of Nr Whitchurch
Georgian house fronting earlier building with rococo library (Priv)

I warm to any house with a cricket field on its front lawn. Iscoyd, once the seat of the Godsal family with 2,000 acres, looks out across the flat country of Maelor Saesneg. This is the detached part of Flintshire east of the Dee, English in character.

The house is of three periods. The original was built *c.*1700, but this was overwhelmed by a new formal block built towards the park in 1743, at right angles to the old one. This is of two storeys across five bays and faces the present drive. A front portico and dining room were added to this in 1843. Stern Georgian windows with white keystones knit the composition together, except at the back where a surviving Venetian window hints at something more dramatic.

The interior is a busy family home, with a Georgian-style print room entirely filled with prints of dogs. What makes Iscoyd extraordinary is the wide rear staircase which links the later and earlier parts of the house. Decorated with a mural of the park, it leads to an architectural *coup de théâtre*, a library lying axially from front to back of the old building. This rises the equivalent of two storeys with a grand rococo fireplace as its centrepiece, a breathtaking space.

Iscoyd retains a set of Stuart, Georgian and Victorian stables and farm buildings to the rear, including a delightful dovecote.

KINMEL PARK **

3 miles south-east of Abergele
Nesfield mansion in Wren/Dutch renaissance style with baroque stables (Priv)

This is another house suspended between dereliction and, hopefully, restoration, currently viewable only from the outside. Kinmel is a major work of Eden Nesfield (see Bodrhyddan Hall, above), a chateau on a hill overlooking the Vale of Clwyd. The estate belonged to the Hughes family, owners of the giant opencast Parys mine on Anglesey.

Successive houses on the site were either burned or demolished, until Hugh Robert Hughes visited Hampton Court with Nesfield in 1868. He calmly told him to build something much the same in Wales. Hughes' initials (HRH) apparently gave him ambitions of royal grandeur.

Kinmel is one of the earliest manifestations of the Queen Anne or 'Wrenaissance' revival, later brought to full realization by Nesfield's pupil, Richard Norman Shaw. It is thus important architecturally and historically and should never be demolished.

The house emerges round a bend in a spectacular drive, uphill across an open park. Woods loom above, accompanied by earlier stables in a neo-baroque style by William Burn, splendid enough to be a mansion in their own right. The effect is supremely theatrical, enhanced by an open gravel forecourt big enough to troop the colour. The gates, also by Nesfield, recall Tijou's at Hampton Court.

The main façade is a balanced, symmetrical composition of nineteen bays. The central pavilion breaks the rhythm in an architectural syncopation, narrowing the fenestration and thrusting the eye upwards to a steep roof with dormers and a lofty chimney. The effect is similar to that later created by Norman Shaw at Bryanston (Dorset). The walls are of red brick with pilasters and stone dressings, the windows and dormers white with close glazing bars.

The unrestored interior includes a two-storey ballroom and a 60ft library and drawing room. After serving as an army billet during the war the house became a girls' school, Clarendon, and later a hotel/bar. A fire gutted the upper floor in 1975, also destroying the chapel.

On the main A55 is Nesfield's entrance lodge, the Golden Lodge, an exquisite work encrusted with Arts and Crafts motifs and renaissance detail. It is a major work of architecture, finer even than Nesfield's similar essays in this style at Kew.

PLAS NEWYDD ***

Llangollen
Eccentric monument to Lesbian love
and Georgian serendipity (Mus)

Sarah Ponsonby and Eleanor Butler were of Irish parentage. They met in Kilkenny in 1768, when Sarah was 13 and Eleanor 29, and fell in love, whatever that means to a 13-year-old. Despite desperate efforts by their parents, which had one sent to a convent and the other into marriage, ten years later they ran away together. They were intercepted at Waterford in Ireland dressed as men. Sarah was armed with a pistol and swore 'to live and die with Miss Butler'.

Later that year their families relented and the ladies went to Wales, where they found Llangollen 'the beautifullest country in the world'. In 1780 they resolved to live there 'a life of sweet and delicious retirement', which they did for fifty years. Unlike male homosexuals, who were imprisoned, they were regarded as eccentric, even admirable in their selfless devotion to each other.

The Ladies of Llangollen, as they became known, were famed for their lively company. Living on the route through Wales to Snowdonia, Holyhead and Dublin, a visit to 'the ladies' became a feature of early Welsh tourism, assisted by their gift for letter-writing and their accumulation of passing gossip. They corresponded with Byron, Canning, Burke and Castlereagh, and were visited by the Duke of Wellington, the Duke of Gloucester, Wordsworth, Scott, Sheridan and Wedgwood. Wordsworth wrote of 'Sisters in love, a love allowed to climb/ Even on this earth, above the reach of time!'

The ladies rarely left Llangollen. They dressed like parsons, their hair swept back and powdered, with top hats, cravats, petticoats and black coats. Eleanor wore various noble orders round her neck, giving her the look of an elder statesman. Their servant, Mary Carryl, came from Ireland and had a famous temper, which the ladies loved. The library contained thousands of books and the household was erudite, humorous, mischievous and extrovert, an engaging Enlightenment backwater.

Plas Newydd: the Ladies of Llangollen

The house was originally a farm cottage. The ladies extended it and added the gothick oriel windows and porches. It was a later owner who gave the exterior its present black-and-white appearance, by applying ornamental battens to the walls. The porch, including pieces donated by the Duke of Wellington, is as decorated as an Italian baptistery. The house, seen across a lush lawn and with the surrounding hills as backdrop, is most picturesque.

The interior is almost beyond description. The rooms have been much altered but remain true to the spirit of the ladies' occupation. Their particular love was wood carving, and visitors were expected always to bring some item of wood to decorate the house. Hence every inch is encrusted with works from all over Europe, gothic and renaissance, religious and secular, together with ancient books and medieval glass fragments.

Upstairs is a 'state bedchamber' or spare bedroom, opposite the ladies' own bedroom. Downstairs are the oak room, hung with gilded leather, the dining room and the library. As at A La Ronde (Devon), also created by two ladies, the atmosphere is of Georgian curiosity, full of the thrill of new discoveries before the onset of Victorian heaviness.

Plas Newydd was acquired in 1876 by General John Yorke of Erddig (see above). He had known the ladies in his youth and turned the house into a museum in their honour, thus saving it for posterity. It was bought by the council in 1932 and has been well restored, given that it was sold and cleared many times after Sarah's death in 1831. It is a place of delight and a monument to love.

PLAS TEG ★★★★

4 miles south-east of Mold
Jacobean pile restored and refurnished with parrots and Old Master copies (Priv)

Plas Teg, ancestral seat of the Trevor family, is the most enjoyable early Jacobean house in Wales. This is largely due to its recent rescue by Cornelia Bayley. The house might easily have gone the way of Hafodunos and Gwrych, given

local authority disregard. Instead it is eccentric and safe.

Plas Teg was built *c.*1610 and shares an English renaissance plan with such contemporaries as Hardwick (Derbys) and Charlton (London, Greenwich). It was built for Sir John Trevor, an Elizabethan courtier/adventurer who became surveyor of the navy in 1598 and navy secretary under James I. Later, accused of fraud, he withdrew to his Welsh estate and erected a house in the style of an English grandee. Later Trevors and Trevor-Ropers recovered their fortunes and acquired Glynde House in Sussex. Plas Teg was never a principal residence and was thus untouched by the 18th and 19th centuries.

The house was requisitioned in the war and eventually sold in 1944, to find its fate as a furniture store. In 1957 the owner applied for demolition, at a time when such houses were vanishing at the rate of one a month. This stung a prosperous Trevor descendant, Patrick Trevor-Roper, to step forward and buy the house, stabilizing it and passing it on to two historic-building enthusiasts. They were defeated by the cost of its upkeep, and it was regularly vandalized and burgled.

The house reverted to dereliction until the arrival, in 1986, of Mrs Bayley, an indomitable and mildly hippie antique dealer. Her first night was spent on the floor of the only room then watertight. She brought those essential prerequisites for country house salvation, an obsession, a little money and, in her case, a large number of parrots. She has turned it into a haunt of ghosts, paranormal investigators, artists and enthusiasts.

The house stands grey and forbidding, overlooking the Mold–Wrexham road. The façade is symmetrical, four corner towers flanking three recessed and gabled bays. The design is complex, suggesting a plan by Robert Smythson. The hall runs front to back, Hardwick style, not sideways, with a great chamber directly above it on what is the principal floor.

The inside runs riot. Bayley's patronage of China's new trade in reproduction Western art accords (if only just) with the Jacobean flamboyance of the place. The grand hall, previously divided, was restored to its full size and given

Plas Teg: Jacobean eccentricity

flagstones, an open fireplace and copies of large works by Veronese and Rubens.

The ground floor has recovered its dining room (hung with 'Lelys') and a parlour/drawing room, with French Empire furniture. Behind various curtains are concealed the kitchens and basements, crammed with Bayley's scourings of antique and car-boot sales the length of the land. One room is devoted entirely to live parrots, who appear to be eating it.

The staircase has robust Jacobean balusters with, on the landing, a painted cloth in place of a tapestry. The great chamber has been restored with hand-stitched silk wall-hangings. Most remarkable for a house of this size, every bedroom – even on the second floor – has been refurnished, with four-poster beds, paintings and sculptures.

Bathrooms contain Bayley's collection of early plumbing. Some baths look like instru-ments of torture – one has a brazier directly underneath to heat its water. Every corner of Plas Teg is occupied by busts, faded prints, fans, rocking chairs, ornamental candles, artificial flowers, seashells and ghosts. It is a house resuscitated, joyfully celebrated by Mark Baker in his admirable history of the place.

RUTHIN

CASTLE **
Exotic conversion of Edwardian fortress
into hotel (H)

Ruthin is the most charming small town in Wales, a match for England's Rye, Broadway or Lavenham. Every prospect pleases. Seventeenth-century and earlier private houses survive and the central square has an informal elegance. To crown everything, Ruthin Castle is not another Denbigh or Rhuddlan, a benighted mound of stone like so many handed down by the old Ministry of Works. The Victorians were ahead of the game and transformed the empty ruin. It is now a thriving hotel and the town is the better for it.

Ruthin was awarded by Edward I to Reginald de Grey, Baron of Wilton, in 1282 as reward for help in his Welsh campaigns. Its location where the Vale of Clwyd is at its most lovely must have contrasted with the Anglo-Norman image of Wales as a place of savage wilderness. None the less, Grey had to defend his holding against insurgency. Walls, a bridge, a chapel dedicated to St Peter (see below) and a castle were built to protect the small community of English colonists. The castle was designed by Master James of St George.

A century later it was a feud between de Grey and Glyndŵr that sparked the latter's rebellion. The town was sacked in 1400, de Grey being captured by Glyndŵr and held to ransom, the payment of which ruined the family and helped finance Glyndŵr's revolt. None the less, de Greys remained at Ruthin until 1508 when the castle was sold to the monarch and, in 1632, to the Myddeltons of Chirk. It was fortified for the king in the Civil War, thereafter being slighted and supplying stone to rebuild the town. It was a Myddelton, Maria West, who in 1826 decided to rebuild the castle as a house, linked by a picturesque bridge to the old ruin.

In 1849 this structure was extended by Maria's son to plans by Henry Clutton, in vivid red sandstone. Regency restraint became Victorian ostentation. The earlier white limestone was given red dressings. A long wall was built round the site with a neo-Perpendicular gate to the town. Wings, towers, graceful oriels and chimneys dart in every direction. Magnificent trees decorate the grounds. It is a successful work of Picturesque, with fragments of the old castle looming out of the vegetation or incorporated into the structure. Two large dragons flank the entrance.

The interior has been much abused since the house was sold in 1920 to become a clinic and in 1963 a hotel. It needs the flair of a Bodelwyddan. Yet the old swagger remains. There are antlers in the entrance hall, and the grand salon has a carved wooden fireplace displayed at the Great Exhibition.

NANTCLWYD HOUSE ✶✶
Medieval town house restored to
eight periods of occupation (Mus)

In a side street off Ruthin's main square is a timber-frame house which ring-dating puts at 1435. The guidebook pleads the case for a 1314 original on the site. It was owned or built by a local weaver, Gronw ap Madoc, and later used as a girls' school, an Edwardian rectory and the judge's lodging for the town. It was in private hands until the 1980s and was eventually bought by the county council.

The restored house reflects these various uses. Rather than re-create what would have been an ersatz medieval interior, different rooms have been reinstated to demonstrate their appearance successively in 1435, 1620, 1690, 1740, 1891, 1916 and 1942. This is a remarkable museological feat.

The house exterior is black-and-white timbered with two prominent gable wings jettied forward to the road. The interior is inevitably an oddity, given the intention to reflect so many 'pasts'. The hall is decorated for 1942 and the rector's study for 1916, with mild touches of Art Deco.

The schoolroom is claimed for 1891 and the well-panelled Georgian bedroom for 1740, hung with Chinese wallpaper. A Jacobean 1620s room has yellow and purple painted fabrics and looks as if brand new (which once it was). The 1690s Restoration room, or 'cabinet', is brightly painted and decorated with Kidderminster-stuff hangings. After this the medieval chamber is almost an anticlimax.

SOUGHTON HALL ✶✶
Northop, 2 miles north of Mold
Bankes mansion Victorianized and converted into hotel, original interiors (H)

Soughton Hall is one of the oddest houses in North Wales. From a distance down the magnificent lime drive it might be the product of a Victorian nightmare. On closer view it looks more friendly, perhaps a French railway terminus. The façade was designed in 1867 by the architect John Douglas, and it is now a hotel.

The house was built in about 1714 and acquired in 1732 by the bishop of Bath and Wells, formerly of St Asaph. His daughter married a Bankes, of Kingston Lacy in Dorset, and the house has been in the family ever since. The present structure was mostly built by a later William Bankes, antiquarian, roué and creator of the present Kingston Lacy. When he came into the ownership of Soughton in the 1820s he had his architect, Charles Barry, give it a new splendour, as Barry also did Kingston. In 1841 Bankes had to flee prosecution for homosexuality and never returned to Britain.

Bankes's house was again altered in the 1860s by his nephew with the aid of Douglas. This removed whatever Georgian effect the exterior might have retained, replacing it with much red stone and brick. Windows were altered, the porch was made heavier and a cupola was replaced by a spiky turret.

The interior, however, retains ghosts of various stages in the house's history. These include fittings, doors and fireplaces of the early 18th and early 19th centuries. The downstairs hall is clearly Georgian. A superb staircase sweeps up to a suite of state rooms, including saloon and dining room. The former has a Tudor-style beamed and stencilled ceiling, the latter is described by Hubbard in Pevsner as 'looking like a progeny of the Brighton Pavilion'.

TOWER *

Nercwys, 1 mile south of Mold
Medieval tower with puzzling dates (Priv)

Tower is hard to find on the southern outskirts of Mold. Charles Wynne-Eyton, whose family have owned it for 500 years, has restored it, tends its garden and invites all-comers to see and even stay (on selected days).

The house needs a detective rather than a historian. It appears to be a rare survival of a fortified farm on the Welsh side of the border. An original hall house has all but disappeared under later gentrification, but a late-medieval residential tower survives, with semi-circular stair turret. Records show it as built by the splendidly named Rheinallt Gruffydd ap Bleddyn in the 14th century. Legend has the English mayor of Chester hanged in its vaulted chamber in 1465.

This chamber forms the present dining hall, while the old hall above it has been divided into two large bedrooms. Their windows, seen from outside, are remarkable. They must be 16th-century since for most of its subsequent life the house was a farm. No less odd are the magnificent gargoyles which crown the tower, beneath what is clearly a late-Georgian parapet. The interior panelling and furnishings are Victorian.

The house is very much a home, full of family paraphernalia. There are county maps, fans, old swords and an impressive breastplate with two bullet holes in it. Visiting doctors argue over which would have caused death. Though the house is modest, the gates to the road are worthy of a Chatsworth, brought from the grounds of a neighbouring Eyton property, Leeswood. They may be by the Davies brothers, whose finest work is at Chirk.

TREVOR HALL **

Nr Cefn-mawr, 2 miles east of Llangollen
Georgian mansion on hill, restored with pop art (Priv)

The redbrick mansion is well sited overlooking the Dee, the Shropshire Union Canal and the A5, as they approach Llangollen. It was a seat of the prolific Trevors and was owned by their descendants until the Second World War. The house was rented to the Edwards family in the 19th century and sold in 1956 to a local timber merchant, who was allowed to fell the trees and applied for permission to demolish the house. This was refused in 1961, but the house survived just two more years before being gutted by fire, an all-too-familiar occurrence. A farmer then roofed it for his cattle.

This ruin was acquired by a historic buildings enthusiast and saviour of many Welsh houses, Michael Tree, in 1987. He demolished the Victorian accretions, restored seventy-three sash windows and sold it to a record producer, Louis Parker, in the 1990s. Since his death it has been decorated and opened for weekend hire by his widow, Louise. The furnishings are themed, wild, eccentric, kitsch and fun.

The house appears to be based on an early hall house, with lateral fireplace, off-centre entrance and side wings. This was rebuilt c.1742 with a grand façade nine bays wide and a pedimented doorcase up a flight of stairs. The generous proportions are deceptive since the house, with a corridor at the back, is just one room deep, enabling all rooms to enjoy the view.

Tree carefully restored the interior to its Georgian proportions, including a central hall with large classical fireplace and stair rising the full height of the house. The decoration is idiosyncratic. It includes mementos of rock groups promoted by Parker, a serious collection of 1960s and 1970s memorabilia. For the present a great house has come back to life.

Churches

BODELWYDDAN

ST MARGARET ★★★★
Victorian swagger church, rich marble interiors and carvings

The justly celebrated 'marble church' is a Victorian wow. Dazzling silver limestone leaps across green lawns as if defying the passing traffic to a wrestling match. Though brutally separated from its castle and estate by the A55, Bodelwyddan makes neighbouring St Asaph's cathedral look like a proprietary chapel.

A Williams daughter, Lady Willoughby de Broke, returned to the Vale of Clwyd in 1852 and spent her husband's fortune, partly on rescuing the house and estate (see above), a forlorn venture, and partly on building a new parish church in his honour, a resounding success. The design was entrusted, or perhaps encrusted, to John Gibson, pupil of the fashionable builder of the Palace of Westminster, Sir Charles Barry. The style is neo-Decorated with trimmings.

The stone was quarried in Anglesey and has a luminous whiteness that seems to radiate even through rain. The 200-foot spire is of the Northamptonshire type, with double pinnacles and flying buttresses at the base of the steeple. This in turn has bands and slight entasis to emphasize its height. Two further pinnacles adorn the nave roof. The surrounding grass, with gravestones moved to the east end, is over-cropped. The graves include those of 83 Canadians who died at Kinmel (see above) in the flu epidemic of 1919.

The interior displays every penny of its then astronomical cost of £60,000. The upward thrust of the exterior is replaced with an almost squat luxuriance. Quatrefoil Belgian marble piers rise to chamfered Decorated arches, a tiny clerestory and heavy oak roof. No nails were used in the construction, only wooden pegs. The pier capitals have deeply cut stiff-leaf carvings, each one a harvest festival in itself. The corbels in the arch spandrels are also carved foliage, concealing the initials of the Willoughby family names.

The chancel is episcopal in appearance, lined with ogee-arched canopies above stalls and reredos. The marble here is from Dorset and the Languedoc. I have never seen ogees 'nod' so vigorously, as if the priests were in continuous argument. Those flanking the altar seem to take off and fly. Even the floor is marble.

The furnishings are similarly rich. The eagle on the lectern (by T. H. Kendall of Warwick) does not listen but appears, like the ogees, to disagree with what is being read. The apostle pulpit is by Thomas Earp. The font, by Peter Hollins, is in the form of a marble shell being held by two daughters of the donor, an epitome of Victorian sentimentality. The stained glass, mostly by O'Connor and T. F. Curtis, seems insipid even for this venue, and the one window by Burne-Jones is not much better.

CILCAIN

2 miles west of Mold
ST MARY ★
Spectacular angel roof

Cilcain is a village long engulfed by the Clwydian hills as they tumble over each other to escape the coastal crowds, a place of sudden, sodden

Marble ostentation at Bodelwyddan

valleys and brief vistas, through which Offa's Dyke plods a tough but rewarding path.

The old limestone church is besieged by herbaceousness. The double nave has been halved by the regrettable glazing of the four-bay arcade, but this is no matter as the roof is all, one of the most thrilling in Wales. Every member is dressed and decorated. The alternate arched-braced and hammerbeam trusses carry four astonishing angels, apparently imported and so big that they must have been intended for an altogether loftier position. They have folded wings and carry instruments of the Passion. The faces are well carved, some with personal expressions. Are these portraits of late-medieval maidens? Grotesque carvings decorate the adjacent trusses.

At the back of the church are brass pew name-plates giving the owners of farms in the area. There is also an excellent 16th-century Crucifixion in the east window depicting Christ with the Virgin, St John, St George and St Peter. Each is set amid rolling hills that might be those of Clwyd outside. The porch gates came from Mold church and are attributed to Robert Davies.

CORWEN

RUG CHAPEL ★★★★
High-church interior, painted decoration

The chapel sits in a garden of Welsh delights, a bouquet of lavender, herbs and roses in the care of Cadw. The exterior is Victorian, the inside a jewel of mid-17th-century decoration.

Rug was built in 1637 by a Royalist colonel, William Salusbury (1580–1660). He was born under Elizabeth and survived many ecclesiastical vicissitudes to see the House of Stuart restored before he died. Devoted to the Old Religion he built a private chapel in which Catholic rituals could be discreetly maintained, though he was not a formal recusant. Naturalist decoration, the use of Welsh and a Lord's Prayer on the pulpit indicate a respect for Reformation worship. A similar chapel, built half a century later, is at Gwydir (Gwynedd).

The single-chamber interior was left un-

altered in a mid-Victorian restoration. The original roof is in place resting on five painted trusses, its panels painted with swirls of green. On the hammerbeams are painted, cut-out angels of doll-like charm. Behind them a painted frieze runs the length of the roof.

The chancel contains two magnificent canopied pews, richly decorated, together with a credence table, chair and 17th-century altar rail. The 19th-century screen is broken at its northern end by surviving panels from the old pulpit. Box pews form the first two ranks of seating and benches the rest, joined by a continuous base carved with beasts above a floral scroll. The whole church appears the product of one naive but delightful imagination, a fusion of nature and belief.

On the north wall is a *memento mori*, elaborately classical with inscriptions in Latin and Welsh. A skull peeps over the side of a dinner table, set with hour-glass and candles. The Victorian stained glass is by Westlake. Rug delighted the young Edwin Lutyens and he claimed it as inspiration for some of his work in Delhi, though I cannot imagine where.

DENBIGH

ST MARCELLA'S, LLANFARCHELL
(WHITCHURCH) ★★★
Double-nave with painted roof frieze,
Salusbury monuments

The parish church of Denbigh is in the country a mile to the east of the town, whitewashed and prominent on a mound in the Vale of Clwyd. Here Hopkins described the 'meal-drift as melting across skies' filled with 'silk-sack clouds'. The site predated the English settlement at Denbigh, which the Normans located on a more defensible site. Such is the holiness of place – or the meanness of the English – that until the 19th century citizens had to trek out of town for worship.

The church is a comprehensive Perpendicular rebuild, big and double-naved with a fine five-bay arcade running down the middle and with no architectural divide between naves and chancels. The roof has lost its hammerbeam an-

Simple piety at Rug

gels but the frieze carries brightly painted carvings of animals and boys doing country things, such as pulling a donkey's tail. The screen is modern.

St Marcella's is a place for monuments, one of the richest collections in Wales. Pride of place goes to the magnificent chest tomb of Sir John Salusbury (d. 1578) and his wife, Dame Joan. The effigies are of alabaster in Elizabethan garb and retain some colour. The copious weepers are nine sons and four daughters similarly attired, with two dead infants in swaddling clothes.

Salusbury was known as 'John of the Thumbs', either because of his immense strength or because he was said to have had two thumbs on each hand, and four big toes.

This monument, still medieval in form, compares with that in the north chapel to Humphrey Lloyd (d. 1568), which appears to be twenty years earlier. This is in the form of a wall aedicule with the kneeling figure enveloped by renaissance architecture, Lloyd being a noted antiquary. More voluptuous is the monument in the chancel to the Salusbury family of 1715, all baroque flourish. The motto declares that 'time will these letters wear away and marble moulder as t'were day. Yet

Medieval jollity at Gresford

nothing shall annoy the just their virtues.' This is surely a rare use of the verb annoy.

Along the north wall is a fine set of memorial brasses of all periods, while the west wall carries hatchments. A tablet at the back of the church commemorates a local man, Twm o'r Nant (d. 1810), a Welsh literary hero who rose from labouring origins to write 'interludes' and songs, some bawdy, some poignant. He was dubbed the Welsh Shakespeare.

GRESFORD

ALL SOULS ✴✴✴✴
Stanley church with medieval glass and misericords, Victorian monuments

The church is in the old village on the outskirts of an ugly settlement along the main road. Its Perpendicular is worthy of East Anglia, with the added glory of much medieval glass. The church is the best of the Stanley group, patronized by Henry VII's mother, Lady Stanley, though it also benefited from a sacred relic, of which all trace vanished after the Reformation. Its ghost survives in a curious passage behind the altar.

Most of the building is late 15th-century, with an all-through aisled nave and chancel, flat-roofed and battlemented. Parts of a former church remain at the west end and in the un-adorned bottom half of the tower. At the west of the south aisle is a flamboyant window of the Decorated period with swirling tracery. The external string courses carry gurning grotesques, with a Virgin on the south porch in a pretty ogival niche. Though the church was built on the profits of coal, the stone is of a lovely golden colour.

Gresford's interior is architecturally plain, in the manner of late-medieval hall churches. Slender arcades carry a generous clerestory, uninterrupted from west to east beneath a roof enriched with angels with spread wings and brightly painted bosses. The volume is punctuated by fine two-decker Georgian chandeliers as if in the drawing room of a rich Tudor palace.

The entrance to the chancel is marked only by a modest screen. The lights are open except for filigree tracery in the arches, where some uprights are cast iron. The loft platform is shallow with a lovely fan vault in its coving.

The original choir stalls and misericords remain in the chancel, decorated with angels and a menagerie of beasts, mythical and genuine. The raised sanctuary has a crypt that must once have concealed the vanished relic, reached by pilgrims along a passage behind the present altar.

Both of Gresford's aisles are treasure troves. The north chapel has a window of 1498 almost as fine as that of Llanrhaeadr, despite damage caused by cleaning in 1966. It portrays the life of the Virgin in a series of naturalistic panels, its survival remarkable given the Reformation's aversion to her picture. The Annunciation is exquisite, a gem of medieval art to find in a village church. At the window's foot is the donor, John ap Madog Vaughan, and his family.

The south aisle windows depict the execution of John the Baptist, and of St Apollonia, patron saint of toothache, complete with pincers. A Jacobean monument in the chapel is to John Trevor (d. 1589) in the bizarre form of a reclining effigy cut in half by its epitaph panel. On the chapel's north wall a semi-circular tablet commemorates the Gresford mine disaster of 1934, when 266 local men died.

A well-preserved, elongated medieval effigy to Madog ap Llywelyn lies in the aisle, near a curious Romano-British stone depicting Atropos, the Fate who cut the thread of life with her shears (hence atrophy). Gresford has memorials by Chantrey and Westmacott and glass by the Victorians, Hardman, Kempe, and Clayton and Bell, a composite museum of the Victorian glazier's art.

The tower contains a celebrated ring of eight bells, declared one of the 'wonders of Wales'. No less wonderful is the ancient yew by the southeast gate, 1,600 years old.

HAWARDEN

ST DEINIOL ✶✶
Gladstone memorial chapel,
Pre-Raphaelite stained glass

Hawarden and Gladstone are synonymous in these parts. The great man came into the Hawarden estate by marrying Catherine, sister of Sir Stephen Glynne, whose ineptitude brought it close to ruin. Glynnes had held Hawarden since the 17th century.

They live there still but under the name of Gladstone. The church, where both Glynnes

and Gladstones were rectors, is the resting place of one of Britain's two greatest prime ministers buried in Wales (the other is that of Lloyd George, at Llanystumdwy).

The building is entirely Victorian. No sooner had a former church been restored in 1856 than it burned almost to the ground, to be rebuilt by Sir Gilbert Scott – heavy, indeed ponderous. A visit is rather like a Gladstone speech, a worthy and pious thud on the head.

No sooner is the heart sinking in the gloom than the Gladstone memorial chapel erupts into view. Designed by John Douglas, it is an Arts and Crafts masterpiece, charmingly out of character with its subject. Gladstone and his wife lie asleep holding a large cross, as if in the prow of the ship of life braving a huge wave. This curls over their heads, where it is transformed into the outstretched wings of an angel.

The designer of the tomb, William Blake Richmond, had been much impressed by meeting Gladstone in Rome in 1866, where the latter had said of a spectacular sunset that he would 'have given up five years of my life rather than miss that! How near the Creator is and what a world of beauty'. Gladstone then began reciting Dante 'in a dramatic voice and faultless Italian'. Small wonder Richard was an admirer.

The tomb chest is attended by weepers depicting not the family, in medieval fashion, but Dante, Homer, Aristotle and King David, men 'whose genius was forever the study of his spare hours' and whom he regarded as 'his master spirits'. Those were the days.

Hawarden church is enlivened by its glass, mostly by Burne-Jones and his associates, who were friends of the Gladstones. The great west window was to be Burne-Jones's last work, a memorial to Gladstone and his wife, depicting Ascensiontide. The church is filled also with works by such master glaziers as Holiday, Powell and Wailes, making Hawarden a place of pilgrimage for stained-glass enthusiasts as well as Gladstonians.

The rector's stall survived the fire. It is Perpendicular, adorned with flamboyant tracery and the coat of arms of the Pool family of 1505. It displays the Tudor vigour from which the Victorians took such inspiration.

HOLYWELL

ST WINEFRIDE'S WELL ✳✳✳
Late-gothic wellhead, spring with
magic properties

Holywell unashamedly proclaims itself the Welsh Lourdes. The well is said to date from St Beuno's day in the 7th century and was already celebrated in the 11th, probably linked with the Cistercian abbey at neighbouring Basingwerk, on the coast.

The dedication to Beuno's neice, Winefride, must be later. She was decapitated by a Welsh chieftain for resisting his advances. Where her head fell, her blood turned into a spring of pure water. Beuno, being to hand and a saint, replaced her head on her shoulders, leaving only a white scar. The story is depicted in a pendant in the crypt vault, though barely decipherable. Winefride's niche has been given a new statue, complete with a neck scar. I am indebted to the guidebook for its assurance that, while 'her sanctity is unquestioned … the story of her head being cut off is … inherently unlikely'.

The well was popular throughout the Middle Ages and afterwards. Henry V made a pilgrimage to the shrine, as did Edward IV and Richard III. The present vault is a relic of the lofty piety of the late Middle Ages and was probably built by Lady Margaret Beaufort, later Stanley (see Introduction, p. 22). A boss in the well vault is said to depict Margaret and her (Stanley) husband.

After the Reformation, government officials were ordered to prevent recusants visiting the shrine. Reports tell of secret masses at the well and in back rooms in the town. Any visitor came to be viewed with suspicion. Yet it remained so popular – and profitable to local innkeepers – that suppression proved near impossible. The statue of the saint herself was not destroyed until the Civil War.

Following the Restoration, the Catholic James II visited the well in 1686 to pray for a son for his wife, Mary of Modena. The saint was credited with the birth of a boy and Holywell was ecstatic, but a Catholic heir precipitated the invasion of William of Orange and James's expulsion in 1688. Holywell has much for which to answer.

The Jesuits who guarded the well were regularly persecuted, but ten years later Celia Fiennes found the well still crowded with pilgrims, all proclaiming illnesses cured by Winefride's intercessions. Holywell's two main inns, the Star and the Cross Keys, were raided for holding secret masses and possessing religious items. The Protestant bishop of St Asaph constantly pleaded with the authorities to halt the flow of visitors, who came mostly by sea from Lancashire and Ireland. Defoe noted its popularity in 1724 and Dr Johnson was shocked by the nakedness of the bathers.

The chapel was eventually turned into a school and by the end of the 18th century visits diminished. They revived following Catholic emancipation in the 19th century, the Cross Keys becoming a convent. Jesuits formally rented the well from the local council in 1873. In 1917 came catastrophe when a local mine caused the spring to run dry and 'the over-simple faith of some pilgrims was sorely tested'. Water was diverted from another spring some distance away.

The well is set into the side of a wooded hill on the road towards the coast. It would be picturesque were it not for a modern block permitted immediately above it. Below are a gift shop and museum dedicated to the miraculous power of the water. There is a rack of discarded wooden crutches to prove it.

The bathing pool is set in a lawn adjacent to the wellhead. There are candles and tents in which bathers desiring total immersion can change. On my visit a set of wet footprints on the flagstones seemed mysteriously to lead nowhere at all, as if the owner had experienced sudden ascension.

The wellhead itself is a lovely structure, the water bubbling up into a cistern beneath a late-Perpendicular stellar vault. This is filled with murky bosses and carvings of figures and animals, one of the most accomplished late-gothic works in Wales. The chapel above is accessible (key in the well shop), a perfect Perpendicular chamber with more carvings and an embossed stone roof. Spacious windows look down on the bathers below.

Miraculous perpendicular at Holywell

LLANDDOGED

2 miles north of Llanrwst
ST DOGED *
Regency fixtures and fittings

The church looks out from its circular church-yard over the Conwy valley. It was rebuilt in 1839 by the rector, Thomas Davies, reordering the double nave, box pews and other fittings in the style of a Dissenter chapel. Though Victorian, it is more a Georgian re-creation, the external bargeboards a touch of Regency flamboyance. The naves are divided by a five-bay gothic arcade.

Some pews are named and the *plas* pew is upholstered. Seating at the west end is tiered in the style of a theatre, marked for boys and girls. The arrangement of the east end is Puritan, with the altar pushed to one side and the pulpit prominent against the north wall. It has a clerk's desk and, on the wall behind it, large murals in Welsh exhorting, 'Preach the Gospel' ('Pregethwch yr Efengyl') and 'Honour the Monarch' ('Anrhydeddwch y Brenin'). Davies was eager to mimic chapel culture while honouring his church's loyalty to the queen.

The royal arms are incorrect: supposedly of Queen Victoria, they are in fact Hanoverian. The 18th-century memorials are to the local Kyffin family.

LLANDRILLO-YN-RHOS

CAPEL TRILLO *
Tiny cell chapel on beach

The busy esplanade of Colwyn Bay stretches towards the Little Orme and Llandudno without so much as a sign pointing towards the tiniest religious building in Wales (smaller even than St Govan's, Dyfed). The beehive cell is tucked into the undercliff opposite an Art Deco house called St Michael's. Why these places were on the beach is a mystery, though the shore would have been a centre of community activity – as in south India today.

The original cell would have had a steeper pitched roof and the two windows would have been open. It was restored inaccurately with a shallower roof in the 19th century and the insertion of windows dedicated to St Trillo and St Elian by Morris and Co. Otherwise there is just room for six chairs on the pebble floor. Lavender and arbutus flourish outside. The place would be more evocative if the promenade had stopped short and the chapel restored to the beach and the elements.

LLANGAR **

1 mile south of Corwen
Complete set of wall-paintings, newly restored

What Welsh churches may lack in grandeur nature happily supplies. Llangar sits on the bank of the upper Dee as it curves towards Bala between the Berwyn and Arennig mountains. Wild fruit trees line the path from the road while yew and ash guard a churchyard casually littered with picturesque headstones and chests. The restored church, single-chamber with bellcote and porch, is dazzlingly lime-washed and in the care of Cadw, which makes it hard to access (key and guide from the distant Rug visitor centre).

The church was abandoned in 1856 in favour of a new one at Cynwyd, to which most of its monuments were transferred, but the Georgian furnishings were preserved. In 1991 came the discovery of wall-paintings beneath later over-painting, one of the most extensive sets in Wales. They are now restored, gazing down on flagstones, 17th-century windows and 18th-century furnishings amid sunlight shafts of white and brown.

The pew arrangement is unusual in that the triple-decker pulpit is located by a south window in the middle of the nave while the box pews are arranged opposite along the north wall. There is a rectory pew inside the chancel area. Two of the pews carry the names of their owners. The rest of the seating consists of open benches which, combined with the need to turn to see the preacher, must have been most uncomfortable.

Llangar's wall-paintings are severely damaged and indistinct. They are most remarkable for their painted frames, as if to emphasize their

Dee valley Puritan: Llangar

educational purpose. A few are 15th-century but most are from the 17th and even 18th century. They include biblical scenes, church celebrities, texts and written verses, as if a teacher were using the walls as a blackboard. Some panels tell stories from the Bible while others list the seven deadly sins, with a pig for gluttony and a lion for pride. A bishop's throne is just distinguishable.

This is another place where I would set aside archaeological fastidiousness and do what the original painter of these murals would have done, touching them up to restore their coherence. As it is, what we see is quaint and atmospheric rather than meaningful.

LLANGERNYW

8 miles south-west of Abergele
ST DIGAIN ✶
Stone circle, oldest tree, Victorian glass

There is much mystery to Llangernyw. Incised stones stand outside the south wall, apparent survivors of concentric prehistoric rings which the church builders dared not remove. Yet one has a Christian cross, probably of the 6th century. Is this an early Christian 'borrowing' of pagan site furniture?

To the north of the churchyard stands a yew of truly amazing antiquity. It is not just the oldest recorded in Britain but the Tree Council claims it as 'one of the oldest living things in the world', ring-dated to over 4,000 years ago by its ground-level girth of 41 feet. This mound among the tumbling hills of the Gallen valley is truly a place of ancient ghosts.

The church is rare in Wales in being cruciform, its exterior picturesque with whitewash. It was heavily restored in the 1840s, including the 15th-century roof, but the restoration is happy and warm, the pulpit unthreatening, the pews welcoming. Only the rood, a clumsy 1930s insert, is out of place.

The church has excellent 19th-century glass, in reproduction Decorated and Perpendicular windows. The east window, dedicated to the Lloyds of neighbouring Hafodunos Hall, is by Charles Clutterbuck (*c.*1830). The window in the south transept is dedicated to the wife of a later owner of the hall, H. R. Sandbach (d. 1852). She died of breast cancer and the window shows four virtues, that on the right reputedly Margaret as a buxom young woman and on the left as afflicted, with her hands across her chest.

LLANGOLLEN

ST COLLEN ✶
Spectacular roof carvings, memorial to 'Ladies of Llangollen'

The one reason for seeking this hard-to-access church (and in a tourist town!) is one of the finest roofs in Wales. The church is mostly Victorian restoration, but contains a memorial to the Ladies of Llangollen, Eleanor Butler and Sarah Ponsonby (see Plas Newydd, above). This was erected in 1937 by a feminist follower of Jung, Mary Gordon, with herself and the sculptor, Violet Labouchere, as models.

The roofs, to what were originally the nave and south aisle, reflect the flowering of Welsh carpentry at the end of the Middle Ages and are attributed to workers at the adjacent monastery of Valle Crucis. The structure is hammerbeam, carrying a gallery of naturalistic and religious imagery, with particular enrichment over the former sanctuary. The frieze between the beams carries trailing vegetation.

The carvers display extraordinary imagination. Subjects embrace Celtic knots and swirls, early-medieval leaf and flower patterns, angels and depictions of Jesus, the Virgin and St Peter. These are enhanced by images of men and women, jokers and grotesques, drunks and rabbits. To Tim Hughes, 'This pell-mell vision is our own Sistine ceiling, what we got in Wales while Michelangelo was working in Rome.'

LLANGOLLEN

VALLE CRUCIS ✶✶
Cistercian relic languishing among caravans

Valle Crucis was a monument to Welsh ecclesiastical patronage. It was founded as a Cistercian house in 1201 by Madog ap Gruffudd Maelor and served briefly as the centre of his borders

Cistercian serenity at Valle Crucis

principality, semi-independent of Powys. Here he was buried and his heirs alongside him on a site supposedly chosen for the stone cross in the valley erected in honour of an ancient Powys prince, Eliseg.

The site at present is rather a memorial to official philistinism. The abbey is exquisitely sited by a stream north of Llangollen. Much of the ruin still stands and some of the domestic quarters are still roofed. Yet caravans have been led up to the walls. This so disgusted Peter Sager on his visit that he immediately returned to Llangollen and I came close to doing likewise. Every visitor records the same outrage, yet the caravans remain.

Of the great abbey church the east and west walls rise to their full height. The former is Early Gothic, with three lovely windows separated by pilasters that rise to embrace the windows

above. The latter shows early tracery, including a Decorated rose window. The west door is a rich composition of deep mouldings and stiff-leaf capitals, with dogtooth decorating the pointed arch above. Inside are traces of vaulting, stiff-leaf, an altar and a piscina.

The east range of conventual buildings survives in reroofed form, notably the lovely chapter house. This has Decorated windows with reticulated tracery and piers whose moulding rises from floor to arch apex with no capitals. Above is the dorter or sleeping area, later adapted to be the abbot's hall and lodgings. It now contains the burial stones of Madog's descendants.

Valle Crucis lapsed from strict Cistercian rule, and poets such as Iolo Goch and Gutyn Owain related the sumptuous hospitality to be had at its table before the Dissolution. One feast reputedly included a thousand apples and gifts to guests of swords and bucklers.

Llanrhaeadr: the Jesse window

LLANRHAEADR

2 miles south of Denbigh
ST DYFNOG ✱✱✱
Best medieval glass in Wales

The names are confusing, sometimes Llanrhae-adr Dyffryn Clwyd and sometimes Llanrhae-adr-yng-Nghinmeirch, fiendishly difficult for an English tongue and ear. (Rhaeadr is Welsh for waterfall.) The small church, heavily restored, is happily bypassed by the road and sits picturesquely in its churchyard. The carving in its porch suggests previous use on a rood screen. Inside is a typically Clwydian double nave, with a roof carrying angels on hammerbeams. There is a wagon ceiling over the sanctuary.

The glory of Llanrhaeadr is its intact Jesse window, dated 1533. For size and completeness

it is a unique depiction of Christ's biblical ancestors to survive from the Middle Ages, owing to its removal into hiding during the Civil War. Even so, its preservation from decay (which took a worse toll on British medieval glass than any iconoclast) is remarkable.

The window depicts Jesse lying at the bottom, customarily on his side and looking pleased with himself. The branches of the tree of his descendants swirl upwards past David, Solomon and other kings and prophets to Christ above. The characters are truncated by the divisions in the glass but this appears to be original. The whole is set in a forest of leaves, a glorious tableau of colour. An inscription attributes the insertion of the window to Robert Jones.

A west window is also filled with medieval glass, but this is a jumbled kaleidoscope of a century earlier, found in a heap in a local cottage. It was reinserted in the 19th century in the customary random order. There must be a way of

reassembling these jigsaw puzzles. In the south nave is a monument of 1702 to Maurice Jones of Llanrhaeadr Hall, a sophisticated work with classical columns beneath a curved canopy and with relevant heraldry, drapery and weeping putti.

Llanrhaeadr is a charming village, with hall, vicarage, almshouses and holy well with stone bridges in the wood above the church. The well was supposedly once paved with marble.

LLANSILIN

5 miles west of Oswestry
ST SILIN **
Clutter of Georgian and Victorian furnishings

Llansilin wins the prize for openness, its lights still ablaze and welcoming on a cold autumn evening. With its grove of yews it seems lost amid rolling Denbighshire hills close to the English border, with Shropshire just half a mile away. The church is surrounded by an inner bailey of cottages and an outer bailey of bosomy hillsides, a delicious place.

The exterior is puzzling, a mix of 13th-century and 15th-century work, best seen in the contrasting lancet and squared Perpendicular windows. The south door proudly displays bullet holes reputedly from the Civil War. The interior is that of a large hall church with nave and parallel aisle. A spectacular roof has king-posts but is ceiled over the chancel. The arcades have enjoyable if crude foliated capitals.

The pleasure of Llansilin is its ancient clutter, of a sort unique to British churches. The north aisle includes bits of old private pews, a bier, pew name-brasses and a benefactions board of 1740, painted to look like marble. Here the Maurice family and others bequeathed welfare to be dispensed, so they insisted, 'for ever'. A Georgian memorial in the vestry is to David Maurice (d. 1719) with a rococo ironwork base. A brass candelabra hovers low over the nave.

The rear gallery looks suitably battered and dingy, with a painting of the Ten Commandments on its wall. Two windows commemorate Huw Morys, a local bard made good. He was later known as 'the nightingale of Ceiriog' for singing the praises of the Royalists in the Civil War, which may explain the bullet holes in the south door.

MOLD

ST MARY *
Rich Stanley church, carved animals

The location is splendid, on a mound overlooking the market in the centre of this rather dull town. Mold is a Perpendicular church enlarged under Margaret Stanley's benefaction. Work continued well into the Reformation period, while the tower was not built until the 18th century. With a Victorian Perpendicular chancel by Scott, the story is of continuous rebuilding in the old style.

Restoration has given the exterior a hardness that exaggerates its Perpendicular tedium, but it is enlivened by animals decorating its friezes. Children can be left to count them for an hour. The interior is enriched, like other Stanley churches, with emblems of the founder's kin. The arcades are especially fine, likened by Hubbard in Pevsner to those at Lavenham, shafted and chamfered and with carved angels in the spandrels. Above are panels carved with Tudor roses, foliage and, where the sculptor is lost for inspiration, more animals.

The aisle windows are many-lighted, the clerestory modest. Mold suggests the Perpendicular style near exhaustion. The chancel is entirely by Scott. The grave of the Welsh landscape artist Richard Wilson is in the churchyard by the east wall.

RUTHIN

ST PETER **
Tudor panelled roofs, gentry brasses

Tucked off the main square of Ruthin is the chapel built by the de Greys on becoming lords of Ruthin under Edward I. It became both a parish church and an Augustinian priory, the remains of whose cloister are incorporated in a private house to the rear. With the old grammar school and Christ's Hospital almshouse, the

St Asaph: episcopal filigree

group is a rare survival of a pre-Reformation close (like Abingdon in Oxfordshire). The vicar is still known as the warden.

Much of the church is 18th century and Victorian, with fierce resetting, repointing and retooling. Two naves have become a nave and a north aisle, obstructed by a large organ case on which are painted fake panels. The vestry was once the choir. Of the 14th-century church little survives apart from the Decorated arcades, whose capitals and corbels comprise a minor gallery of gothic art. One corbel appears to depict a negro.

As so often in well-wooded Clwyd it is the 16th-century roofs that catch the eye, with, in this case, no fewer than 408 carved panels. The north aisle roof is the finer, more delicately patterned than the nave, indicating a probable reversal of roles. Some bosses depict the leading families of the neighbourhood, allowing it to be dated to the early years of the Tudor ascendancy.

Charming small brasses are displayed on the north wall, including to the Goodman family, founders of the adjacent almshouses after the Dissolution. The clearance of box pews in the 19th century would nowadays be deplored, but the guide records a visitor in 1855 fulminating that 'the proprietors of the odious boxes which disfigure the church appear positively to glory in their shame'. He was shocked by the 'menagerie' of carved animals adorning them, while the heraldry was a display of ostentation worthy of a 'Burke or Debrett to the local dignitaries'.

ST ASAPH

CATHEDRAL ✳✳✳
Scott restoration of Decorated interior, translators' chapel

The diocese is an ancient one, dating from 1143 and dedicated to a 6th-century saint. The church was spoken of as 'a poverty stricken little cathedral' and suffered sorely in the Edwardian wars.

The cathedral was rebuilt in the Decorated style in the 14th century but remains architecturally a parish church, and a heavily restored one.

The restoration gives the exterior a picturesquely random selection of building materials, as if the masons were encouraged to use whatever came to hand, provided it was different. Hence the white, red and grey limestone, the rough and smooth ashlar dressings and a west wall so chequer-boarded one could play chess on it. The windows are unexciting, with geometrical tracery in the aisles and reticulated tracery elsewhere. The west door has a graceful Decorated arch.

The character of the interior is set by plain arcades, free of pier capitals, the moulding running uniform from floor to apex and back to floor. This Decorated feature undulates powerfully the length of the nave, over the crossing and into the chancel. For the rest, the building is largely the work of Scott. He rebuilt the chancel and reroofed and retiled the floors throughout.

It now looks handsome but spanking new. Even the seats have been upholstered. The roof has a complex pattern of trusses carrying brightly painted bosses. The Perpendicular canopied choir stalls are original, the bishop's throne and dean's stall Scott at his most earnest.

The north transept contains the 'translators' chapel' dedicated to the Welsh divines who rendered the Bible into Welsh in the 16th century (see Tŷ Mawr, Gwynedd). The presiding genius, William Morgan, was bishop of St Asaph. A charming painted cloth depicting the Tree of Life by a Haitian artist hangs in the south transept.

TREFNANT

3 miles south of St Asaph
HOLY TRINITY *
Victorian memorial church by Scott

The small church was built with no expense spared by Sir Gilbert Scott in 1855 as a memorial to Colonel and Mrs Salusbury by their daughters. It forms part of a typical Victorian group, of church, parsonage and school. While lacking the patina of age it is an excellent example of what the Victorians could do when not struggling to rebuild an existing structure.

The style is florid Early Gothic, richly observed in the nave arcades of polished Anglesey marble and in the lush foliage of the capitals and chancel arch. According to Hubbard in Pevsner a local Denbigh carver studied French 13th-century carving in an architectural museum in London under Scott's direction. He 'arranged every group of leaves from natural specimens gathered as they were needed from the woods and hedges round'.

All is luxuriant, the pulpit with marble stairs to it, the font and the choir stalls, all from the Scott office. The stained glass is by Wailes in the west window and the rest mostly by Powell. The overall effect is extremely dark.

WORTHENBURY

ST DEINIOL **
Georgian church with box pews and strange Lord's Prayer

The church is an evening beacon across the flat border landscape. It is Georgian and splendidly so, an earlier church having been replaced in 1736 by the local Puleston family. This may have been to celebrate Sir Roger Puleston's success in getting an Act of Parliament to separate the parish from the see of Bangor. The architect was Richard Trubshaw.

The exterior is early Georgian, brick with stone-dressed, arched windows and the Wrennish flourish of a balustrade with baroque finials on the tower. The interior has a coved roof and an apsidal chancel with pilasters and fine railings. There is a graceful gallery at the west end.

Worthenbury retains its original furnishings, including its box pews. The pulpit with tester is three-decker and surrounded by a maze of pews reflecting the status of their owners. There are two squires' pews in the chancel, each with a fireplace and one with a private door. Another squire's pew faces it, while in the nave nine other pews are in subtle gradations of prominence and comfort, most of them owned by the Pulestons and given or let to tenants and staff.

On the vexed question of how to reuse private pews, where there is a will there is a way. One is set aside for private prayer, another for a crèche/nursery, another for a small exhibition. The window glass is a jumble, some painted, some stained, some ancient, some modern. The medieval fragments are reputed to have come from a Jesse window in Winchester college. In the gallery is a Lord's Prayer, inscribed in a curious and mysterious shape.

WREXHAM

ST GILES ★★★★
Finest Welsh tower, medieval carvings,
Yale tomb, Burne-Jones window

The church dominates this dejected and devastated town. Everything about the church, from the Davies gates to the mighty tower and rich interior, marks it out as the glory of the Marches. Rebuilt in the Decorated style in the 14th century it was burned in the mid-15th century and rebuilt piecemeal until Margaret Stanley (formerly Beaufort) arrived with her patronage after Bosworth in 1485.

The tower is one of the best Perpendicular designs in Britain. It soars through seven principal stages, each panelled, with niches, ogival windows, fluted corner pilasters and, at the top, four hexagonal corner pavilions in the Somerset manner. Most unusual is the survival of the niche statues, giving the façade a richness rare in any medieval church. The only, rectifiable, shortcoming is that this tower needs cleaning. The differential staining of the sandstone makes the features and recesses unnecessarily heavy. It should be a shimmering golden masterpiece.

The interior is intriguing because the customary 'Stanley Perpendicular' of Mold and Gresford is absent. Instead we are confronted by two heavy Decorated arcades beneath solid walls pierced by clerestory windows. Between the arches are large corbels, three of them carrying Victorian statues.

This heaviness is relieved by the roof, which is almost flat and decorated with sixteen open-winged angels, brightly painted and playing instruments, including lutes, bagpipes and harps. They are like exotic birds hiding aloft. The trusses sit on corbels taken from all periods in the church's history. One has a mermaid combing her hair. Another is said to depict Margaret Beaufort and her last husband, Stanley, Earl of Derby, for some reason with donkey's ears.

To the east, the Tudor period is dominant but in strange fashion. The former east window has become the arch of a new chancel, with fragments of its tracery jutting like jagged saw teeth. Above the arch is a 16th-century wall-painting of the Day of Judgment. At the bases of the arch, pretty gothic canopies survive, serving no purpose but to defer to the rococo iron gates below. These are the work of the Davies brothers and were given in 1707 by a scion of Wrexham, Elihu Yale. Though born in America, Yale came to live in his family home at the end of his life: his tomb is beneath the tower.

The chancel is flooded with light from Perpendicular chancel windows. It contains 14th-century sedilia with green men in their canopies. The reredos relief in Arts and Crafts style is of 1914.

The north aisle forms the Royal Welch Fusiliers chapel and has a simple Burne-Jones window of expressive saints set against a monochrome background. Next to it is an extravagantly baroque memorial to Mary Myddleton (d. 1747) by Roubiliac. It shows an angel blowing a trumpet at the lady in question, causing her obelisk to shatter and her body to leap naked from the coffin beneath. In the south aisle are windows by Kempe. The Victorian restoration by Ferrey sits light on the stones of Wrexham.

The 'Discover' project, a scheme for opening and interpreting churches in Wrexham, is admirable and should be a model for every diocese.

Perpendicular might at Wrexham

Dyfed
[Carmarthenshire, Pembrokeshire, Cardiganshire]

The ancient Welsh kingdom of Deheubarth evolved from the kingdom of Dyfed in the 10th century and spread over most of south-west Wales. By the time of William the Conqueror's visit to the shrine of St David in 1081, it was an established Christian society some five centuries old, evoked by the crosses in the churchyard at Nevern. St David's and the great *clas* of Llanbadarn outside modern Aberystwyth drew adherents from Wales and Ireland. The region seemed relatively free of the political turbulence of the rest of Wales, so much so that William reached an understanding of autonomy with the king of Deheubarth, Rhys ap Tewdwr, whose capital was at Dinefwr.

Only under William's son, William Rufus, was this understanding breached. In 1190 the Montgomerys swept south from Ludlow through Powys and Ceredigion to the coast at Pembroke. Castles were built and English and Flemish colonists imported. The southern strip of Pembrokeshire was so thoroughly 'cleansed' of Welsh as to be known as 'little England beyond Wales', its language and place names English to this day.

The castles of the Norman conquest guarded the route to Ireland and were second only to those of Gwynedd in scale. Pembroke's great keep was built by the Norman knight, William Marshall, in the early 12th century. There followed Carreg Cennen, Cilgerran, Kidwelly, Carew, Laugharne and Manorbier, the last being the birthplace of Gerald of Wales, vivid chronicler of Wales in the late 12th and early 13th centuries.

Normans and Welsh lived in uneasy proximity across Deheubarth for two centuries, culminating in the brief re-establishment of the kingdom by the Lord Rhys at the end of the 12th century. The Welsh Cistercian monastery at Strata Florida became a burial site for the later princes and it was there that Llywelyn the Great summoned his supporters in 1238 to do homage to his son.

In part to assert their authority, the Normans rebuilt the cathedral at St David's, the last great romanesque building in Britain. Lesser Celtic churches were rebuilt to service the pilgrimage routes to St David's and north to Bardsey, the most evocative being at Mwnt and Nevern. Later gothic builders created the great colonists' church of St Mary's, Haverfordwest, and the 14th-century bishop's palace at St David's, under Bishop Gower one of the most splendid medieval houses in Britain.

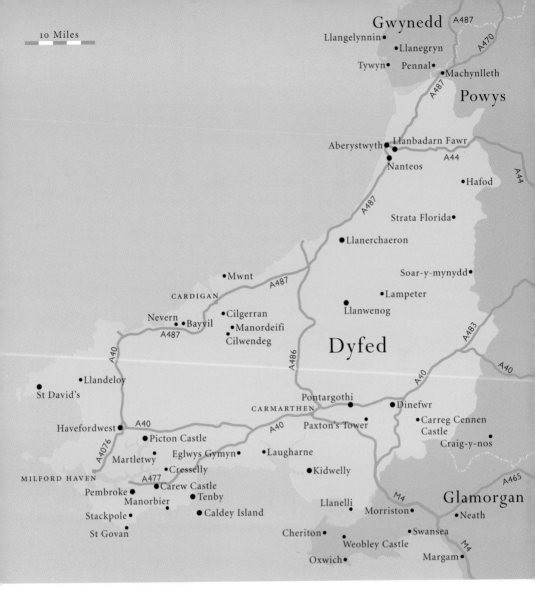

Gwynedd A487
Llangelynnin•
•Llanegryn
Tywyn• Pennal•
•Machynlleth
A487
Powys
A470

Aberystwyth• •Llanbadarn Fawr
•
Nanteos A44

•Hafod
A44

A487

Strata Florida•

•Llanerchaeron

Soar-y-mynydd•

•Mwnt A487
CARDIGAN •Lampeter
•Cilgerran Llanwenog
Nevern •Bayvil •Manordeifi
A487 Cilwendeg
Dyfed A483

A40 A486 A40

•Llandeloy
St David's Pontargothi
CARMARTHEN •Dinefwr
Havefordwest• A40 •Carreg Cennen
A40 Paxton's Tower Castle
•Picton Castle Craig-y-nos
Martletwy Eglwys Gymyn• •Laugharne
A4076 •Cresselly
MILFORD HAVEN A477 •Kidwelly
Pembroke• •Carew Castle Glamorgan
Manorbier •Tenby Llanelli M4 A465
Stackpole• •Caldey Island Morriston• •Neath
St Govan• Cheriton• •Swansea
Weobley Castle M4
Oxwich• Margam•

The Tudor ascendancy favoured Pembrokeshire, Henry Tudor having been born and raised in Pembroke Castle and his father buried at St David's. Courtiers converted Carew and Manorbier as sumptuous Elizabethan houses. The church memorials and merchant's house at Tenby recall wealthy Tudor entrepreneurs.

In the 17th and 18th centuries the coastal settlements of Carmarthenshire and Pembrokeshire developed prosperous farming communities, notably in the Tywi and Teifi valleys. The Georgians left comfortable houses at Dinefwr, at Nash's Llanerchaeron and in the stylish conversion of Picton Castle, to designs reputedly by Gibbs. Good rococo interiors can be found at Cresselly and Nanteos.

The industrial prosperity of Glamorgan and the accessibility of North Wales were not available to Dyfed, which retains a Cornish seclusion to this day. Its most prominent Victorian relic was the hotel constructed in 1864 by Seddon on the front at Aberystwyth, later converted into the new University of Wales. To the south, Pontargothi chapel is a remarkable work of gothic revival.

Houses and Castles

Aberystwyth, The Old College ★★★
Carew Castle ★★★
Carreg Cennen Castle ★★
Cilgerran Castle ★★
Cilwendeg Shell House ★
Cresselly ★★
Dinefwr, Newton House ★★★

Kidwelly Castle ★★
Lampeter, St David's College ★★
Laugharne:
  Castle ★★
  Dylan Thomas House ★★
Llanelli House ★
Llanerchaeron ★★★

Manorbier Castle ★★
Nanteos ★★★
Paxton's Tower ★
Pembroke Castle ★★★
Picton Castle ★★★
St David's, Bishop's Palace ★★
Tenby, Tudor Merchant's House ★★

Churches

Bayvil ★
Caldey Island ★★★
Eglwys Gymyn ★★
Hafod ★
Haverfordwest ★★★
Kidwelly ★★★
Llanbadarn Fawr ★★★
Llandeloy ★

Llanwenog ★★★
Manorbier ★
Manordeifi ★★
Martletwy ★
Mwnt ★
Nevern ★★
Pontargothi ★★★

St David's Cathedral ★★★★
St Govan ★★
Soar-y-mynydd ★★
Stackpole ★★
Strata Florida ★
Tenby ★★★

Houses and Castles

ABERYSTWYTH

THE OLD COLLEGE ★★★
Seaside fantasy hotel by Seddon converted into university (Priv)

Aberystwyth has long been a lost soul among Welsh resorts. Today, with a booming university community and a reviving leisure industry, it is acquiring a new personality. How appropriate that its most distinguished building should be a hotel turned college, dominating the sea-front next to the ruins of the old castle.

The site was that of a house built by John Nash (his first) for Uvedale Price as part of a project to turn Aberystwyth into a Regency resort, a Welsh Brighton. The hotel was intended to take this ambition forward into the railway age and in 1864 a design was commissioned from the neo-gothic architect J. P. Seddon. It was intended to rank with Scott's at St Pancras and Broderick's at Scarborough.

Within a year the hotel was bankrupt and the building was bought for £10,000 by a committee to found a national University of Wales (first mooted by Glyndŵr). There followed three decades of arguing about money,

Carew Castle: fort turned palace

with Seddon struggling to convert his design into a university and always on the brink of dismissal.

Seddon's original design is confined to the central block, entered on the landward side by an eccentric triangular *porte-cochère*, a homage to the old Nash house on the site, which was triangular. Both front and rear façades look like crosses between a Welsh castle and a French chateau, billowing with towers, battlements, arcades and windows of every shape and style. The nine-storey towers echo the castle next door. Built of soft Bath stone the effect is never grim, and every feature diverts the eye. A wooden gallery above the entrance conceals the old roof-top gym. The exterior is coated in gargoyles and statue niches.

The two extensions to the south are clearly afterthoughts. The farthest is a science block, to whose tower Seddon added a mosaic mural by Voysey depicting a puzzled Archimedes being offered a steam engine and a sailing ship. Seddon had to remove a downcast pope, em-bodying superstition as the enemy of reason, from his design. The landward door to the science block is flanked by two warning serpents, one marked error and the other darkness. Aberystwyth clearly felt itself at the frontier.

The interior is now scruffily academic but includes a gothic stone staircase and a central hall. The latter is a curious chamber, Anglo-Indian in character, with a heavily corbelled gallery and timber roof. It is dominated by two larger-than-life statues of Welsh worthies. That of the Welsh 19th-century politician Tom Ellis, by Goscombe John, is a plaster of the bronze standing in Bala.

CAREW CASTLE ***

Half a mile north of Carew Cheriton
Ruin of the greatest Welsh renaissance house, previously home of Princess Nest (Priv)

More than any other house in Wales, Carew embodies the power of the Marcher lords and the splendour of their successors under the Tudor ascendancy. It was an ancient Celtic site, on which an important early Welsh cross has been found. The present castle was begun *c.*1100 by Gerald of Windsor, first constable of Pembroke, under the authority of the Montgomerys, whose rampaging campaign across mid-Wales had reached Carew by 1093. The capture of Nest, daughter of the last independent king in Wales, Rhys ap Tewdwr, led to her becoming Gerald's wife (see Cilgerran). Carew is reputed to have been built for her and her family.

Most of Carew was begun two centuries later by Edward I's courtier Sir Nicholas de Carew. He raised the two mighty drum towers that look out over the river and millpond, with battered bases and tiny windows. This castle passed to the South Welsh grandee Sir Rhys ap Thomas, whose troops lent crucial support to Henry Tudor at Bosworth.

Briefly the most prominent man in Wales, Rhys adapted Carew as his principal seat (with Weobley as a lesser one). In 1507 he celebrated his elevation to the Garter with a tournament of unprecedented lavishness. Six hundred nobles were treated to hunting, feasting, jousting and, as if in atonement, a penitential ride to St David's.

Under Henry VIII, Rhys's grandson flew too near the sun and lost his head. Carew passed to the Crown and later to the Elizabethan courtier and probably illegitimate son of Henry VIII, Sir John Perrot. Rich from office in Ireland, Perrot converted Carew (and Laugharne) into grand renaissance mansions before also falling foul of the tyrannical monarch and ending his life in the Tower of London.

It is Perrot's structure that makes such a vivid impression today, albeit as a ruin. It is approached from the car park across an outer ward, presumably the site of Rhys's jousting, and entered through an inner gatehouse next to the remains of the old Norman tower (perhaps Nest's chamber).

The inner ward is instantly impressive. The ruin of Rhys's great hall runs along the south range of the ward, its porch adorned with the arms of Prince Arthur, eldest son of Henry VII, and his wife, Catherine of Aragon. This memorial to a brief union shines from the rough stone like a renaissance jewel.

The two earlier round towers at either end of the hall range were converted by Rhys as comfortable apartments, one of them supposedly to receive the king. But it is Perrot's larger structure to the right of the ward that dominates the interior, the range facing over the water. This is plainly post-medieval, three storeys high and with tall Elizabethan windows and a long gallery above.

Carew was among the greatest 16th-century buildings in Wales, still largely intact in Buck's engraving of 1740. Its appearance today, with walls rising their full height but floorless and roofless, is both sensational and tragic. This was Wales's Hampton Court and merits a more vigorous reinstatement than as a 'stabilized ruin'. If only Cardiff's Marquess of Bute had been a Pembrokeshire man.

CARREG CENNEN CASTLE **

5 miles south-east of Llandeilo
Romantic citadel with secret cave (Cadw)

This is a castle of Arthurian fantasy. It commands a 300-foot rock thrust upwards from the basin of the Tywi valley like an Albigensian redoubt. Whether floating on a mist in the early morning, or blazing at dusk in a moist Welsh sunlight, it seems unreal.

The site has yielded Roman remains. A fortress here was captured by the Normans and changed hands under the Llywelyns until rebuilt for the Crown in the late 13th century. It held out for a year against Glyndŵr and was later garrisoned to deny it 'to brigands and robbers' (or Lancastrians) until demolished by the Yorkists in 1462.

By the 18th century Carreg Cennen had been transformed from menace to magnet. Well established in the Picturesque canon, it was visited by Turner and later restored by the Earl of Cawdor, who sadly did not go further in his work than to 'create a ruin'. The view of the south front from below the cliffs is spectacular, as is the long walk up an ancient pathway from the road.

The castle proper is entered through an outer ward, now demolished, by means of a

Carreg Cennen: romantic redoubt

stepped ramp into the gatehouse. This ramp is overlooked by the entire north range of the castle and must have been impassable as a means of assault. The two northern towers, one round and the other with squared corners, still stand to half their height, as does the gatehouse. The inner ward retains the outlines of the great hall and chapel adjacent to it. The solar and some fireplaces and windows form part of Cawdor's part-restoration.

Most intriguing are the remains of a sallyport at the south-east corner of the site, leading through a cave to the cliff below. This is accessible but finishes in a wall. Like all sallyports, it risked being as useful to an attacker as to a defender.

CILGERRAN **

4 miles south of Cardigan
On crag above ravine, scene of
Nest's abduction (Cadw)

The valley of the Teifi is the most quietly beautiful in South Wales. Since the Middle Ages its fertile meadows made it rich in livestock. By the early 19th century, there were said to be over forty gentry houses in the 20 miles below Llandysul. The valley's hunt claimed to be among the oldest in Britain and refused to stand down even on the day of Queen Victoria's funeral.

Nowhere is Teifi's beauty more spectacular than from Cilgerran crag, a prominence worthy of the Dordogne. The castle is believed to have been built, like Carew, by Gerald of Windsor to protect his northern flank against the Welsh pressing down from Powys – his fort called Cenarth Bychan is assumed to be Cilgerran. It was here in 1109 that Nest's celebrated abduction by Owain ap Cadwgan supposedly occurred, earning her the title of 'Helen of Wales'.

Nest was daughter of Rhys, last king of Deheubarth. Captured by the Normans in 1093 she became mistress of the future Henry I and bore him a son, FitzHenry. Granted to Gerald as wife in the hope of placating the Welsh, Nest came to Pembroke and bore four more children. Her reputation was such that men were said to pine just for a sight of her beauty.

In 1109 her distant cousins, the Cadwgans, were raiding south from Cardigan in the neighbourhood of Cilgerran. The hot-blooded young prince Owain ap Cadwgan assaulted the castle with his friends, set fire to part of it and surrounded Nest and Gerald in their chamber. Nest pleaded with her husband to flee for his life down the latrine shoot. She and her children were carried off into the wilds of Cardiganshire. History has long debated her complicity in the venture.

No Norman was likely to accept such humiliation, let alone from the Welsh, and the outcome was predictably bloody. Nest managed to return to Carew and Owain was eventually tracked down and killed by Gerald's Flemish archers. After Gerald's death Nest married twice again, in both cases to Normans, her career symbolizing the unstable fusion of conqueror and conquered over the century after the conquest. Today's visitors to Cilgerran search in vain for Nest's chamber, but there could be no more romantic venue for her story.

The castle was rebuilt by William Marshall after the Llywelyn uprising, with two of his characteristic drum towers overlooking the entrance. With a precipice guarding the far wall they must have made Cilgerran near impregnable. It withstood an assault by Glyndŵr but soon fell into ruin. Today the view down into the woody gorge is as awesome as ever. On the river below, that peculiarly Welsh craft, the coracle, is still in use.

CILWENDEG: SHELL HOUSE *

Boncath, 7 miles south of Cardigan
Delightful folly lost in woods (Priv)

The Georgian house of the Morgan Jones family is now a nursing home, but outbuildings in Regency picturesque style survive. The Joneses inherited the Skerries lighthouse on Anglesey, entitling them to a penny a ton of all cargo going (safely we assume) in and out of Liverpool. Their seat was here at Cilwendeg in South Wales. In the woods of its grounds is a '*cottage ornée*', comprising a one-room shell house. This decayed into ruin over the years but was restored

Cilgerran: scene of Nest's abduction

and reopened by the Temple Trust in 2006.

The house is approached through thick trees like something from *Hansel and Gretel*. The exterior has a veranda, gothick windows and a stepped pediment oddly adorned with white quartz blocks. The interior is entirely coated with shells, the floor with animal bones. The principal motif is a gothick arcade formed of black mussels round a pink conch shell. Even the oil lanterns are covered in shells. On ledges are shell-coated statues of owls. The fireplace looks as if it has never been lit.

CRESSELLY **

Nr Jeffreyston, 6 miles north-east of Pembroke
Gentry house with rococo ceiling (Priv)

The Georgian house sits at the end of an impressive drive, built in 1769 in the Adam style by a local architect, William Thomas of Pembroke. The client was a local landowner, John Allen. Its five-bay villa façade would have been beauti-

Dinefwr: Rhys dynasty house

fully proportioned before the addition of Victorian wings, whose bays clumsily seek to mimic the central block.

The interior is shown to visitors by a descendant of the original owners, Hugh Harrison-Allen, and is that of a comfortable gentry house. The fittings reflect the Adam taste and walls are hung with family portraits, the ladies in the style of their period, the men in soldiering or hunting uniforms that seem not to have altered over centuries.

The house's most prominent feature is the ceiling of the drawing room, a swirling, vigorous rococo composition with tendrils radiating from the centre as if about to trail down the walls and envelop the room. The craftsmen were believed to be Italians from the Bristol area. It is a delight to find such a masterpiece hidden away in a Welsh country house. There is also an exceptional library with built-in Regency bookcases.

Church and state at Kidwelly

DINEFWR ***

1 mile west of Llandeilo
NEWTON HOUSE
Victorian exterior encasing Restoration
mansion in deer park (NT)

Dinefwr was the seat of the kings of Deheubarth and as such was capital of Celtic south-west
Wales. It was here that King Rhys ap Tewdwr's
daughter, Princess Nest, would have been born
and from here that he set out to his death at the
hands of the Normans at the battle of Brecon
in 1093. The conquerors made their base on the
coast at Pembroke and the castle, though fortified until the 16th century, fell to ruin.

Today the castle is represented by its original
keep but surmounted by a 17th-century belvedere. It sits in an 800-acre park owned by the
National Trust and embracing Newton House.
This mansion was begun by the Tudor Sir Rhys

ap Thomas of Carew Castle and remained in the
same family (Anglicized to Rice) until 1976. The
present house dates from *c.*1660 but was remodelled in a late-Georgian castellated style in the
1770s, after the fashion of Picton and Fonmon.
The old village of Dinefwr was cleared and the
grounds laid out on the advice, or under the
influence, of Capability Brown.

The house exterior was again altered in 1856,
the windows gothicized, a Venetian porch attached to the front and curious turrets added to
each corner. When in the 1970s the family could
cope no more, Newton passed through the customary purgatory as a school, arts centre and
recording studio, before passing to the Trust
in 1990.

The restoration has been superb, reviving
the 17th-century decoration and furnishing the
rooms in the style of *c.*1912. I am less persuad-
ed by the appearance of actors in the rooms.
Whereas waxworks take the present back to the
past, however artificially, actors drag the past
into the present.

We are thus led through the familiar servants' quarters of brushing room, tack room, plate room and butler's sitting room. Upstairs are the dining and drawing rooms, the former with a Victorian copy of a 17th-century ceiling and portraits of the Rice family down the ages. The drawing room looks out over the park beneath its original ceiling and is furnished in the Edwardian style.

Portraits of Talbots, into which family the Rices married in the 18th century (see Margam Castle, Glamorgan), line the hall and staircase. The latter is original to the 17th-century house and rises three storeys. Newton is emerging from a long sleep. It retains its service courtyards and outbuildings. The great deer park is host to a rare breed of white Dinefwr cattle.

KIDWELLY CASTLE **

Concentric fortress with mural gatehouse and chapel (Cadw)

Church and castle gaze at each other across the river over the roofs of a modern village. The castle sits on a low bluff on the River Gwendraeth and from the right viewpoint is one of Wales's most imposing ruins. The castle inspired one of Turner's most atmospheric watercolours.

Kidwelly was an important Norman fortress on the southern flank of 'English' Wales. It had access from the sea and guarded the Tywi estuary to Carmarthen and routes west. The first castle was rebuilt by Roger of Salisbury, appointed by Henry I to hold south Wales in 1106. The inner fortress acquired an outer ward in the 13th century and a great gatehouse in the 14th. New apartments were added as well as a chapel, jutting out of the castle wall towards the river.

This castle was later besieged by Glyndŵr, but was held with barely a dozen men. It remained in good repair throughout the Middle Ages as the local headquarters of the Duchy of Lancaster. It later passed to the earls of Cawdor, who stabilized the ruins in the 19th century.

The D-shaped castle shares with Beaumaris and Caerphilly the plan of concentric, rather than contiguous, inner and outer wards. This meant that defenders could retreat from the outer defences into what amounted to a second castle within. At Kidwelly there was a third line of defence, a formidable main gatehouse, as at Chepstow, forming part of the outer wall yet linked to the inner. It could thus be defended independently of the other two 'castles'. Before the invention of artillery this was a fortress of immense strength.

The building today is entered between the towers of the gatehouse, with twin portcullises and murder holes. The inner castle has four towers and walls intact. The masonry indicates where the inner fortifications were heightened at the time of the building of the outer wall. Little of the interior remains, though the roofless chapel with a chamber for a priest is clearly identifiable, as are the guardrooms in the towers.

LAMPETER **

ST DAVID'S COLLEGE
Earliest Welsh university buildings,
old library (Priv)

Lampeter was Wales's first university, indeed the first in Britain after Oxford and Cambridge. It was planned by Bishop Burgess in 1806 as a college for training Welsh priests under the auspices of St David's. The original location was to be Llanddewibrefi, to designs allegedly by John Nash. The offer of a site in the old Norman borough of Lampeter by a Bristol banker, J. S. Harford, led to a change of plan.

C. R. Cockerell was commissioned and produced what was, in essence, an Oxford quadrangle. The college opened in 1822. Though its students expanded beyond Anglican ordinands, it did not become a part of the University of Wales until 1971.

The old college, embraced by modern extensions, retains its Regency gothic appearance. A castellated two-storey façade has a central gatehouse and tower with two projecting wings in Tudor-gothic. Beyond lies a quadrangle with cloister (now glazed), hall and chapel, adorned with a statue of St David. The walls are partly rendered and the windows are iron-framed. The chapel was altered by T. G. Jackson, architect of

Laugharne Castle: Elizabethan picturesque

Oxford's 19th-century Jacobean revival, with later fittings by Caröe.

Lampeter is rightly proud of its library, built round 22,000 books acquired almost at random and donated in 1834 by an East India surgeon, Thomas Phillips. To this has been added a collection of early religious tracts, together with three Hebrew scrolls and eight medieval manuscripts. The ensemble forms a delightful academic backwater in this secluded part of central Wales.

LAUGHARNE CASTLE **

Seaside castle turned into Elizabethan house with ornamental garden (Cadw)

Laugharne vies with Solva and Oxwich among the scenic delights of the South Welsh coast. In the Middle Ages it attracted military attention and now attracts Dylan Thomas devotees. The castle was occupied by Lord Rhys of Deheubarth and the Llywelyns until rebuilt by the de Brian family, whose two giant round towers stand, as majestic from below today as in Turner's watercolour of the scene. The castle was granted to the Percys, Earls of Northumberland, during the Wars of the Roses.

Laugharne's present character was determined by its 16th-century rebuilding by Sir John Perrot, Elizabethan adventurer (possibly the queen's half-brother) and rebuilder of Carew. He converted it into a residential mansion complete with formal garden. The castle fell into ruin but the grounds were turned into ornamental gardens and the site today is more picturesque than military – witness its magnificent cedar.

Laugharne has received much attention from archaeologists (with nine pages in Pevsner), seeking to distinguish military from domestic work. This is near meaningless to the visitor, for whom the ancient walls seem all of a piece.

The outer gatehouse gives on to the gardens, with the ruins of the house and the inner ward ahead. Here the round towers of the medieval structure are linked by the gentler buildings of Perrot's additions, including a stately staircase turret. The inner ward is surrounded by the great hall and offices of the mansion, now reduced to bleak walls and gaping windows but with glorious views over the bay.

A tower overlooking the garden has been converted into a gazebo. Here the author, Richard Hughes, who rented the castle between the wars, wrote many of his novels. A stream and ancient bridge lie immediately below.

LAUGHARNE: DYLAN THOMAS HOUSE **

Boathouse workplace and shrine in coastal idyll (Priv)

A short walk along the coast path east of the village leads to the garage and old boathouse in which Dylan Thomas spent the four years before his death in 1953.

The boathouse was put at the 35-year-old Thomas's disposal by Margaret Taylor, wife of the historian A. J. P. Taylor. It was no small kindness as Thomas had a wife and three young children and his chronic indebtedness made it unlikely that he would leave.

Here in the gentle seaside village that he both loved and hated, Thomas found a sort of contentment, writing copiously and producing his 'voice play', *Under Milk Wood*, a satire on the daily life and gossip of Laugharne (christened Llareggub). He recorded the dark net-curtained half-secrets of people 'who you can see any day of the week, slowly, dopily wandering up and down the streets like Welsh opium-eaters'. The village wears its celebrity lightly and the pubs eschew 'Thomas drank here' signs, but it cannot shake off the magnetism of celebrity.

The 19th-century boathouse is preserved to excess as a shrine, under siege from tourists. It has been converted into a souvenir shop above and tearoom below, so that only the sitting room remains of the Thomas period. This preserves a sense of 1950s petit bourgeoisie, from which Thomas was clearly unable to detach himself. It has furniture of the period, armchairs, antimacassars, a gramophone and copies of the *Illustrated London News*. There are pictures of Thomas's all-suffering wife, Caitlin. Even this

Dylan Thomas's garage study

idyllic setting could not calm a relationship with Dylan that she called sheer hell, 'raw, red, bleeding meat'.

The setting fed Thomas's sonorous metaphors with its view over the estuary marshes and its cries of seabirds: 'Under and round him go / Flounders, gulls, on the cold, dying trails.' The house is enlivened by a tape of Thomas's rich 'old port wine' voice, reading his lines as if over an old radio. Sound is a sensation so often missing from historic buildings. It is good to have an excuse for it here.

Back along the path is the garage, a poet's study as he left it, visible only through a window. This is an inspired work of conservation. It appears that nothing has been touched. Everything is a mess. Scribbled and screwed-up paper litters the floor. Newspapers lie everywhere. A bottle of beer stands next to an inkwell. An old jacket is over the chair (added, I notice, since Peter Segar's 1990 photograph). Pictures are pinned to the walls, including one of D. H. Lawrence and another of a Modigliani. There is dust everywhere. It would give a National Trust housekeeper a fit.

LLANELLI HOUSE *

Llanelli
Rare surviving Welsh town house,
awaiting restoration (Priv)

Llanelli is trying to recover some of the personality of its industrial past. Its coastal reclamation is one of the most ambitious in Britain and efforts are being made to recover from the 1960s, when streets were demolished to make way for cars and when the roundabout was king. Little remains on which to anchor renewal, but Llanelli House survives, facing a church across a bleak roundabout. Barely noticeable in the surrounding dross, it is like a fine old lady in a prison camp.

The house dates from 1714 and is of three storeys. The seven-bay façade is enlivened by three of the bays being slightly projecting, with a heavy cornice. The sash windows are grand and their rhythm spoiled only by later alterations (correctible) on the ground floor. The

ABOVE: *Llanelli House: touch of south Welsh baroque*   RIGHT: *Nash gentility at Llanerchaeron*

down-pipes carry the crest of the Stepney family, the original builders. Urns still adorn the roofline, an eccentric touch of class. The whole composition is excellent, reminiscent of the urban baroque of Thomas Archer in London's Covent Garden.

The house is being restored at the time of writing. This has already revealed a 17th-century building behind the Georgian façade, including a stairwell rising the full height of the house, with balconies and balusters intact. Much of the panelling survives, with fitted wall cupboards and plasterwork, as well as delightful overmantel paintings.

With the proposed closure of the gyratory road system this could yet be an impressive addition to Dyfed's architectural heritage. Whether it can bring a sense of urban style to Llanelli is the real challenge.

LLANERCHAERON ***

3 miles south-east of Aberaeron
House and self-sufficient estate preserved from the early 19th century (NT)

The villa sits in a secret valley inland from Aberaeron and is an early work of John Nash, marrying architecture to landscape. Nash had just escaped bankruptcy after a career as a builder and amateur actor in Carmarthen and was struggling to reinvent himself. The result was a dozen villas in the Aberystwyth district, of which only Llanerchaeron survives in its original form.

We owe this to the house's other quality, the unfaltering continuity of a Welsh gentry family, the Lewises. They were self-sufficient, married locally, hunted, fished, remained unobtrusive and content with their lot. Their antecedents,

the Parrys, had lived in the Aeron valley since the 17th century. A Colonel William Lewis commissioned Nash in the early 1790s, by when he had already built Llanfechan (demolished) nearby. Nash produced a simple villa, now yellow pebble-dashed, that would not look out of place in London's Regent's Park.

Lewis's daughter-in-law, Mary Lewis, lived at the house until her death at 104 in 1917, presiding over the estate and permitting none of the alterations seen in most Victorian houses. It was a homely property with Georgian domestic offices round a rear courtyard. Lewis's great-nephew succeeded her and lived at Llanerchaeron as squire until 1989, after which it passed to the National Trust. By then it had seen just three conservative occupants since construction.

The Trust struggled to revive the garden, but a bequest of a million pounds rescued the house and enabled it to be opened to the public in 2004. What could be found of the family's collection was recovered and much else was acquired. That said, Llanerchaeron suffers from the Trust's difficulty in giving its properties a sense of habitation. The house needs a resident, a child, a dog, a bit of clutter, even a speck of dust.

The exterior is handsome rather than uplifting, a formal box with shallow hipped roofs and deep Regency eaves. Curved arches surmount the ground-floor windows and Doric door surround. The interior is modest but beautifully proportioned, the hall framed by shallow arches leading to a staircase with conical rooflight. Nash took great trouble over his cornices and friezes, as if eager to break out of the minimalism of the Regency villa style. The walls are covered in trophies not of the grand chase but of the wildlife of a Welsh valley, mostly foxes, badgers, stoats, otters and fish, some startlingly ferocious.

The furnishings are, by contrast, mostly early 20th century. The result is an eclectic jumble of mantelpieces, tables and chairs that can jar with their settings. The ubiquitous group portraits and hunting prints (which seem to outnumber books in the 'library') render the rooms Victorian rather than Georgian. The Lewis family may have passed on, but their faces are everywhere.

The presentation of bedrooms and bathroom upstairs is again immaculate, the main rooms being separated by oval boudoirs. A firescreen in one is adorned with early theatrical photographs. The curved dressing room is Nash at his most sophisticated, with the tables and basins fitted into niches.

Two rooms have been converted, somewhat eccentrically, to house a collection donated to the Trust by Pamela Ward, a Kensington antique dealer, in 1994. It comprises some 5,000 pieces mostly of up-market junk, referred to as of 'high decorative quality': toys, corkscrews, children's books, stickers, mugs and fans, including the 'language of the fan'.

Llanerchaeron is especially proud of its service quarters, which survived into the 1980s devoid of 19th- or 20th-century technology (other than electricity). Here are a kitchen, beer cellar, pantry, scullery, larder, laundry, dairy, cheese press, smoke house and salting room, the entire battery of rural self-sufficiency. For some reason 'the cooks were always English or Scottish'. At the end of the servants' range is a Victorian billiard room.

The house has a generous kitchen garden whose produce is on sale to visitors. Beyond is a home farm, again largely unaltered and restored by the Trust.

MANORBIER CASTLE **

Picturesque castle on bay, birthplace of Gerald of Wales (Priv)

Just as Laugharne is for ever Thomas so Manorbier is Gerald of Wales, the first British writer whose work conveys a sense of authorial personality. He was son of a Norman colonist who settled in Manorbier and of Princess Nest's daughter, Angharad. He was thus a commentator on 12th-century Wales, and acutely aware of his dual nationality – 'too Welsh to be Norman and too Norman to be Welsh', he wrote (in Latin).

Gerald deplored the Welsh custom of reducing every argument to a battle and the Welsh inclination 'to avenge not only recent but ancient affronts'. Yet he constantly pushed the Welsh,

Manorbier Castle: birthplace of Gerald

rather than the Norman, cause. Sent for his education to France, Gerald's one ambition was to become bishop of St David's and make the diocese a Welsh archbishopric, separate from Canterbury. He was unashamed in his self-promotion, describing himself as tall, handsome, a magnificent horseman and talented scholar. But Welsh autonomy of any sort was anathema to the Normans (and to Rome) and Gerald's cause was doomed to failure.

In pursuit of this ambition, in 1188 Gerald travelled the length of Wales, accompanying Archbishop Baldwin of Canterbury to raise money and troops for the Third Crusade. The journey yielded the first great work of British topography, the *Itinerary and Description of Wales*. It referred to everything from nature, the weather and the diet of the people to the (Norman) laxity of the monasteries visited.

Gerald declared that: 'You will never find anyone worse than a bad Welshman, but you will certainly never find any better than a good

one.' He added, 'When I see injustice in either race I hate it.' On one topic Gerald would brook no argument, Manorbier was 'the pleasantest spot in the country'.

He could say the same today. The castle in which he was born sits on a bluff separating the village from the beach, facing the church across a narrow valley filled with a dribble of roofs and car parks. This was the home of the Norman de Barri family and, as it seems to have held little military value, the de Barris retained it with comparative ease for two centuries. In the 1600s it was acquired from the Crown by the Philipps family, who own it to this day. It was leased by the Victorian antiquarian J. R. Cobb (see Caldicot Castle, Gwent, and Pembroke Castle), who repaired some of the floors and roofs and built a house in the inner ward.

The composition is attractive, a castle wall without a keep but lined with domestic buildings, including a gatehouse, hall and chapel. The last retains its barrel vault intact above traces of a later fireplace. There are also basements, corridors and tower chambers in which the owners have made an attempt at bringing a medieval castle to life. There is even a waxwork of Gerald. The presence of a holiday home within the walls adds a touch of humanity to the ensemble.

NANTEOS ***

3 miles south-east of Aberystwyth
Romantic house, once home of the Holy Grail, with ruined stables (Priv)

Was *Parsifal* composed in Wales? Nanteos played host to Wagner and is fabled as the home, for four centuries, of the 'Holy Grail'. Legend holds that the cup at the Last Supper was entrusted to Joseph of Arimathaea, who brought it to his alleged foundation of Glastonbury in Somerset.

With the impending dissolution of the monasteries in the 16th century the grail was carried to Strata Florida, on whose dissolution it was carried over the hills to Nanteos outside Aberystwyth, where it remained an object of wonder and pilgrimage.

The Nanteos Cup certainly exists. It is a battered wooden bowl four inches wide with many chips out of it, probably medieval. It was eagerly sought for its miraculous healing powers, and remained at Nanteos into the 1960s. It is now believed to reside in a Hereford bank vault.

The house is charmingly shabby-genteel, set in the secluded Paith valley. Seat of the Powells throughout history, it was rebuilt by them in 1739 as a result of the marriage of two families who lived on either side of the valley, the Joneses and the Powells, rich from lead-mining. In the late 19th century Nanteos was the home of George Powell, eccentric poet, Icelandic scholar and music-lover. It was he who invited Wagner to stay at the time of the composition of Parsifal, so a local inspiration is not implausible.

The house was finally sold in 1967. It was bought by the Bliss family and near ruined as a craft centre. The latest owners, the Lipscombes, are nobly seeking to restore its old glory, currently as a wedding and bed and breakfast venue. It can be seen on application. Nanteos still has an air of grandeur anticipated but not yet realized.

The building is essentially Georgian, though the façade has a later centrepiece, with a Doric porch and tall arched windows. More curious are the baroque window pediments. These ostensibly 17th-century features must have been added later as decoration. The Pevsner authors suggest that their additional use on the side walls suggests that the architect 'had unwillingly to find place for fourteen pediments and chose to use as few as possible on his main façade'.

The interior had, at the time of writing, lost much of its domestic character. The entrance hall and staircase are grand, if sparsely furnished. The former drawing room, dining room and library are allocated to conference use, but benefit from the presence of Powell portraits. The stairs rise spaciously on treads of Welsh oak to a fine upstairs gallery/corridor, lined with pillars and pediments. Stained glass depicts the arms of the Powells.

The jewel of Nanteos is the middle room on the first floor, the rococo music room. Here a local harpist, Gruffydd Evan, played the harp for sixty-nine years and here, so it is said, Wagner did some of his composing. The room is a thrilling experience. The rococo ceiling, frieze and overmantel drip with ribbons, tendrils and sprays of fruit and flowers. A screen of painted columns conceals the entrance alcove, while curtains guard the windows. Candle-lit at night and with the sound of harp and piano carried out over the valley this must have been a place of special magic.

Nanteos has stables and outhouses worthy of Vanbrugh. They are lost in vegetation, bordering on jungle, and plead for restoration. The whole Nanteos ensemble illustrates the walking-wounded character of so many Welsh houses at the end of the 20th century. Happier days must lie ahead.

PAXTON'S TOWER *

Llanarthne, 9 miles west of Llandeilo
Folly with views over Tywi valley (Priv)

The tower on the hill overlooks the valley of the River Tywi on one side and Carmarthenshire on the other. The valley is lush, with the castle

Norman fury: Pembroke keep

of Dryslwyn on a mound immediately below, one of those Welsh views that appears unaltered over two centuries. To the south lies the sleek glass roof of Wales's national botanic garden in the grounds of Middleton Hall.

The tower was built as a folly in honour of Lord Nelson, so as to be seen from Middleton by its then owner, Sir William Paxton. The architect was Samuel Pepys Cockerell and the style is Picturesque gothic, triangular with three robust round turrets and a central hexagon rising from within.

As at Kymin (Gwent), the upper storey was intended for 'banquets' or picnics. Carriages could enter through the arches below and there are closets for food preparation. The whole structure is in grey stone and not for faint hearts on a dark evening. But on a fine day the picturesque location is worth the climb. There are few places in Wales as lovely as the Tywi valley on a cool morning with the mist still lying in its depths.

PEMBROKE CASTLE ***

Grim Norman fortress with round keep (Priv)

At the time of the conquest, William I was content to leave the king of Deheubarth, Rhys ap Tewdwr, alone at Dinefwr, and the rest of Wales to its feuding princes. The policy did not outlast William's death. In 1093 Roger of Montgomery, Earl of Shrewsbury, and his son, Arnulf, crossed into Wales from their base in the central Marches and swept all before them.

Pembroke Castle soon established itself as the strongest fortress in the south-west, both asserting Norman supremacy and protecting the sea route to Ireland. In 1105 Gerald of Windsor was sent as constable, with Rhys's orphaned daughter, Princess Nest, as his wife, in earnest of the Normans' desire to forge bonds with local chieftains. From the mid-12th to the mid-13th century, Pembroke was held first by the de Clares and then by the 'king' of the Marches, William Marshall and his descendants.

Marshall's story is almost as spectacular as Nest's. A young adventurer at Henry II's court, in 1189 he unhorsed the king's rebellious son and heir, Richard (later Lionheart), in a skirmish but spared his life. Richard rewarded him with the daughter of Richard 'Strongbow' de Clare, heiress to estates in Wales and Ireland.

From 1204 Marshall rebuilt the two greatest castles in South Wales, at Chepstow and Pembroke, and secured dominance over the whole region. Pembroke, like Berwick, enjoyed semi-autonomous 'palatinate' power, so decisions could be taken quickly against an ever-threatening enemy. A line of lesser castles was built across mid-Pembrokeshire, and the southern half of the present county was colonized by English and Flemish settlers.

The castle today is most impressive from outside, since Marshall's walls appear to stand virtually intact. In the Civil War Pembroke declared for Parliament but, as at Chirk, the occupiers switched to the Royalists just when the latter faced defeat. Cromwell personally supervised the only concerted assault the castle ever faced. He cut off its water supply and promised its defenders safe passage, which they took. To ensure no further trouble he demolished the outer walls of all the towers and the great gatehouse.

What is seen today owes much to 19th- and early-20th-century reconstruction, first in the hands of the antiquarian, J. R. Cobb, who bought it in 1879, and then of the Philipps family, who own it to this day. Cobb and the Philippses were equally active at Manorbier. Towers were rebuilt and floors and chimneys inserted. A parade ground has been laid down in the vast outer ward where, on my last visit, a detachment of redcoats were preparing to do battle in the pouring rain.

The castle comprises a spacious outer ward and, at its seaward side, a mostly destroyed inner ward. The latter is dominated by Marshall's circular Norman keep of c.1204, the largest and most impressive of its period in Britain. To Jan Morris it is 'the most frightening thing in Wales

... the nastiest castle'. The keep rises 75 feet, with a battered base 20 feet thick, enclosing four storeys reached by a single spiral staircase in the wall. From its domed summit a view can be had over the Pembroke river towards Milford Haven. Although all the main floors have gone, the view upwards from within echoes to the fury of Norman power.

Next to the keep is a dungeon tower, with a waxworks prisoner visible through a glass trapdoor. The ruins of a great hall and chapel survive, while beneath lies the Wogan Cave, a large natural cavern that also served as a boathouse. Remains found inside date back to the Stone Age.

PICTON CASTLE ***

4 miles south-east of Haverfordwest
Ancestral seat with medieval remains beneath Georgian superstructure, Gibbs hall (Priv)

Picton has been the seat of the Philipps family since the time of James I, from whom John Philipps bought a baronetcy for £1,095. He himself was a descendant of Sir John Wogan, who held the castle here as early as 1301. Philippses have thus been squirearchs of Pembrokeshire for seven centuries. They were prominent in helping rescue many of the county's castles (see Pembroke and Manorbier) and still live on the estate.

The castle well illustrates the evolution of a Marcher property down the ages, from medieval fortress to Victorian mansion. The result is slightly unreal, as if each of its features were pretending to be another sort of building altogether. But real it is. Medieval Picton was a rectangle of four round towers protecting a great hall between them and fragments of this structure survive in the basement, including a medieval undercroft and the remains of the original entrance on what was formerly the ground floor.

The 18th-century conversion involved building a causeway up to the present first-floor entrance between two of the towers, enabling visitors to enter the main rooms on what is a *piano nobile*. The old ground floor thus became

the basement. Then in 1800 on the ennoble-
ment of a Philipps as Lord Milford, the building was drastically altered by the demolition of
the far end and its extension into a castellated
block with additional rooms. These included a
drawing room, dining room and bedrooms. The
whole was then rendered and painted white,
turning a dark fortress into a Regency castellated villa. The effect has since been lessened by
the removal of some of the render.

As a result of these changes, a wander round
the house is to pass back and forth in time. The
core of the house remains the hall, refashioned
in the mid-18th century to designs on which
James Gibbs was reputedly consulted. Deeply set
arched windows shed light on a classical interior,
pink-walled, warmly furnished and hung with
family portraits. At the entrance end is a balus-
traded gallery on fluted Doric columns, above
which rises one of only four Snetzler organs extant. The stone fireplace by Henry Cheere indicates Philipps's determination that nothing but
the best would do for a gentleman's house.

The Georgian domestic rooms are located
in the round towers, the delicacy of their decoration contrasting with the formidable depth
of their walls. The library is the finest of these,
with curved bookshelves, secret panels and
even a curved door, carpentry of the highest
quality by James Rich of London. Most of these
rooms have Cheere fireplaces. Behind the organ
is the entrance to the family chapel, where the
organ was previously set. It is arranged with box
pews against the side walls and a stained-glass
window behind the altar.

A corridor beyond the hall leads to the 1800s
wing, past a Philipps family tree of impressive
pedigree. The Regency dining room is boldly
painted in deep blue and white with elaborate
plasterwork over the doors. The portraits are
mostly of the family of the Victorian Sir James
Philipps, one of whose thirteen children was
able to revive the title of Lord Milford. He had
later to purchase Picton from another branch of
the family to whom it had descended.

The medieval undercroft, splendidly vaulted, now contains family impedimenta as well as
the original entrance, including arrow slits and
marks of the portcullis mountings.

ST DAVID'S, BISHOP'S PALACE **

Episcopal residence with two halls and
mural decoration (Cadw)

The palace sits downhill from the cathedral,
built by the Normans and entertaining Henry
II and Archbishop Baldwin on his tour with
Gerald of Wales. The glory days were those of
Bishop Gower in the mid-14th century. Gower's
work was so extensive – the hall is one of the biggest in Britain – that little by way of addition was
later required. St David's is thus a rare, virtually
complete palace of the pre-Perpendicular era.
After Gower's death in the plague year of 1347,
St David's had no need of further magnificence
and the palace entered a long decline.

The focal point of any medieval palace was
the hall, centre of entertainment and symbol
of earthly power. Gower was a prelate of high
standing and had already been chancellor of
Oxford. He clearly regarded the existing hall as
inadequate but, rather than expand it, he built a
separate new one. We thus see two halls on entering through the gatehouse, the earlier one on
the left and Gower's hall through a porch directly ahead. These two structures form two sides of
the grand courtyard. A third consists only of a
vaulted undercroft.

The walls are united by a peculiar signature
of Gower's work, here and at his country seat
at Lamphey. This is an arcaded parapet supporting battlements in a bravura decorative
programme visible on all the roofs. The earlier
bishop's hall on the left survives complete with
its undercrofts, solar, latrines and kitchen, suggesting that Gower continued to use the old hall
for lesser occasions.

The porch to Gower's hall is a rich work of
Decorated gothic. Steps rise beneath an ogee
arch with two gabled niches containing statues
of Edward III and Queen Philippa. The hall itself is bare and the window tracery has gone,
apart from in the rose window where it has been
restored. The whole palace has a crumbling
appearance, as if slightly out of focus.

Most remarkable is the wealth of surviving
mural decoration. On the exterior of Gower's

hall lumps of white quartz have been set into the stonework, creating a chequerboard pattern. Everywhere are carvings, mostly in the form of corbel heads. These peer down from every corner of the interior and exterior, guarding windows or lurking in vegetation. This medieval art gallery reputedly includes 170 carvings.

Churches

BAYVIL *

2 miles north-east of Nevern
Regency interior, overgrown churchyard

Half the pleasure of Wales's isolated churches lies in finding them. Though Bayvil looks like a Dissenter chapel hiding in a field, it is an Anglican church, lying off the lane to Bayvil farm. The churchyard is of overgrown ferns and grass, with not a house in sight. A tiny west bellcote crowns a single cell building, now in the care of the Friends of Friendless Churches. It lacks even candle-holders for candles.

Bayvil dates from c.1812, when Anglicans were defensively adopting Nonconformist architecture. They did not adopt its ministry, Bayvil's vicar living in Hampshire and even its curate inhabiting another village. The interior is Regency with seven box pews dominated by a three-decker pulpit, its tester crammed against the ceiling. The congregation must have craned their necks to see the preacher. For some reason a large funeral bier has been placed immediately below the pulpit.

The altar is modestly placed at the east end behind an extensive altar rail. Woodwork is painted pale cream and brown. The windows, with gothic glazing bars and plain glass, offer diverting views of the woods beyond. The interior has a pleasing glasshouse effect on a sunny day.

TENBY

TUDOR MERCHANT'S HOUSE **
Townhouse immaculately restored with herb garden (NT)

Tenby is an enchanting resort. While 19th-century esplanades crown its bluffs, tiny lanes lead down to the quayside and the boats to Caldey Island (see below). Only the ruined Victorian fort on the promontory is an eyesore, and that can be rescued.

The old merchant's house would have been one among hundreds. It is of stone and dates from the late 15th century, so small that it may once have embraced its neighbour. It has just one room to each of its three floors, with a tiny herb garden to the rear.

The house is in National Trust style, highly serious, though there is a splendid stuffed rat at the bottom of the latrine. The main ground-floor room would have been the merchant's shop and is filled with examples of the goods traded from south Wales, such as woollen cloth, leather, corn and fish. Imports were wine, spices and salt. The room contains old Welsh chests. To the rear is the kitchen and large chimney range.

The first floor acted as hall and living room, at one point connected with the house next door. In one corner is the latrine tower, illuminated, with an explanation of how it 'worked'. Clothes were hung above it so the stink could kill fleas – hence the name 'garderobe' for lavatory. The room contains more Welsh furniture. On the wall is a modern tapestry of Tenby in 1991 by Ruth Harries. The tiny herb garden has been replanted, but sadly not for visitors' use.

CALDEY ISLAND

ST ILLTUD ***
Ancient settlement, chapel with ogham stone

Caldey is one of the oldest religious settlements in Britain. It is known to have been a 6th-century Celtic *clas* under an abbot called Pyro. Samson, missionary to Brittany, came from Llantwit in c.550. Caldey did not prosper under the Normans and the ruins of its Benedictine priory are later, from the 13th and 14th centuries. Even then, there was rarely more than a handful of monks, and just one at the Dissolution. The

Mercantile prosperity at Tenby

Bayvil's Anglican austerity

island was farmed until the 19th century, when an enterprising Harrow schoolmaster named William Bushell bought it as a holiday home and restored both the village and the priory churches. Caldey was reputedly the first home of the rabbit, bred for food but escaping to populate the British Isles.

Bushell sold Caldey in 1906 to an Anglo-Catholic eccentric, Benjamin Carlyle, who installed a community of Anglican Benedictines. They built the present monastic buildings with help from other prominent Anglo-Catholics, such as Lord Halifax. The Benedictines converted to Catholicism in 1925 but later sold the monastery to Belgian Cistercians.

This foundation survives today, a dozen monks living off crafts and perfume made from the island's flowers. As an exclusive, largely silent order, they do not admit the public to the monastery (other than the gallery of the plain abbey church). The Edwardian buildings by J. Coates Carter constitute, according to the Pevsner authors, 'the largest and most complete Arts and Crafts group in Wales'. Those seeking

a counselling service offered by the monks may stay in the guesthouse.

Despite the inaccessibility of the monastery, the twenty-minute sea crossing from Tenby is worth the serene one-mile walk along a path through the woods to a 'village' tearoom and post office. The monastery towers above them like that of Lhasa in Tibet. Half a mile beyond lie farm buildings and a chocolate factory amid the ruins of the old priory and its church.

The tiny church of St Illtud claims to be the oldest place of Catholic worship in Britain (albeit unused from the Reformation to the 20th century). The nave, dating from the 13th century, has lateral pews and, near a modern south window, a stone carrying two separate inscriptions. One is in ogham and relates to Illtud (see Llantwit Major, Glam) and Samson and probably dates from the 5th or early 6th century. It is thus among Wales's earliest relics. The later Latin inscription of the 9th century asks visitors to pray for the soul of Cadogan.

The church floor is of pebbles from the beach. The tiny sanctuary, possibly the chapel of the first priory, has a doorway that once led to the monastery. The woods outside seem to sprout medieval walls, fish ponds and carvings at every turn. The place is enchanted.

EGLWYS GYMYN

1 mile north of Pendine
ST MARGARET ✶✶
Arts and Crafts restoration of
ancient foundation

The church is located inland from the caravan horrors of Pendine in a circular churchyard lying within the ramparts of an Iron Age fort. The foundation is dated to 1093 by the guidebook but a Latin and ogham stone recalls Avitoria, 'daughter of Cynin', offspring of a 5th-century Irish chief, Brychan, who gave his name to Brecon. For good measure Cynin is also spelt Gymyn, Cymyn, Cummin, Cymin and Gummin. The original Irish is spelled Chummein.

The interior was restored in 1900 under the all-seeing eye of the Society for the Protection of Ancient Buildings, and was one of their set pieces. The architect, William Weir, was told approvingly by Philip Webb that 'truly it looks more ancient than when you laid hands on it'. The vault recalls the 'nave' shape of an upturned boat. On the north wall is a framed text displaying four generations of mural. The earliest is reputedly 13th century. The later three, in English and Welsh, include the Ten Commandments.

Philip Webb's contribution is at the back of the nave, two cupboards looking like barnyard stalls surrounded by robust Arts and Crafts woodwork and benches. One of the benches conceals the ogham stone. The church is full of 1900s details, including stained glass by F. C. Eden in medieval style.

HAFOD

12 miles east of Aberystwyth
ST MICHAEL ✶
Restored Wyatt church, Chantrey monument

The destruction of Wales's most famous Georgian landscape was among the worst cases of scenic vandalism in post-war Britain. In the 1780s Thomas Johnes of Croft Castle (Herefs) and his friends, Uvedale Price and Richard Payne Knight, decided that eight square miles of the upper Ystwyth valley best replicated the glades of classical Arcadia. They duly brought Johnes close to bankruptcy by building a gothic villa, bridges, arches, lodges, cottages, follies and a church amid cascades, groves and vistas. The story was celebrated in a book by Elizabeth Inglis-Jones, *Peacocks in Paradise*.

In 1962 the house was blown up with dynamite and the buildings destroyed for those twin curses of mid-Wales, a caravan park and a conifer plantation. The church had already been gutted by fire in 1932, mostly destroying one of Francis Chantrey's greatest works, an 1812 memorial to Johnes' only child, Marianne.

Partial rescue is now on the way thanks to Richard Broyd of Bodysgallen Hotel (Gwynedd). His Hafod Trust has begun to restore Johnes's glades and walks and may yet clear the conifers. The church was restored by Caröe in 1933 and can be visited from the main road, even if its view down the valley is obscured by trees. Built for Johnes by James Wyatt in 1800, its later Victorianization and fire damage were partly reversed by Caröe to Wyatt's original.

In the church are the charred remains of Chantrey's memorial, full of the poignancy of a departed child, holding a book and a lyre and overseen by her heartbroken parents. The fittings are Wyatt revival by Caröe. Johnes's own vault lies outside in the churchyard.

HAVERFORDWEST

ST MARY ✶✶✶
Town church with stiff-leaf and
gentry memorials

This is the most English of Welsh towns, proud above its river and close to the Landsker line, a Norse term for a medieval boundary between Wales and Henry I's Norman settlement of English and Flemish immigrants. Founded round a Norman castle it was the major town of south-west Wales into the 19th century. An attractive maze of streets between the castle and the two churches of St Martin and St Mary has been devastated by road engineers, demolishing historic buildings and creating an incomprehensible traffic scheme that separates town from riverside.

St Mary's sits at the end of the High Street and was built by William Marshall (see Pembroke Castle above) in the 13th century as a symbol of the importance of the settlement. Though its spire was removed as unsafe in 1801, it still boasts its origins, with French stone and French masons believed to have been working at Wells. The early-Decorated plate tracery in most of the windows appears to be original in design. The stiff-leaf carving in the porch suggests no expense spared.

The nave is dominated by a four-bay north arcade, one of the finest Early Gothic works in Wales. The arches have multiple shafts and their capitals are a gallery of 13th-century sculpture, traced to the Wells masons. Grotesques, apes and pigs peer from the stiff-leaf vegetation, playing musical instruments and grimacing with toothache.

The nave and chancel roofs are later but no less splendid, Tudor with wooden panelling and magnificent painted bosses. A deeply splayed Perpendicular clerestory floods the furnishings with light, including two bench ends, one of St Michael killing a dragon. The 20th-century pews are by Caröe and the east window depicts the life of Christ by Kempe.

Every corner of the church carries memorials of Pembrokeshire's Anglo-Welsh gentry. Many are of the Philipps family of Picton, restorers of Pembroke Castle, and of a quality worthy of a London City church. A memorial to Sir John Philipps of 1736 is ostentatiously baroque with weeping putti. There is a battered medieval effigy of a pilgrim carrying the emblems of St James of Compostela.

KIDWELLY

ST MARY ✱✱✱
Large priory church in Decorated style

Here is a Welsh town church worthy of its castle. The tower is crowned by a stately stone spire, that of the old Benedictine priory founded in the early Norman colonization, c.1110. The tower has five stages to the foot of the spire, each given upward thrust from the angle buttresses. The broached spire is rough and unadorned.

The interior is mostly 14th-century Decorated and gives an impression of overwhelming size, there being no aisles to the nave or transepts but deeply splayed windows in north and south walls. Since the west end collapsed and was truncated, the original must have been even more impressive. The crossing area is puzzling, apparently intended to support a central tower (the present one being to the northwest). The piers are out of proportion to the triple-moulded arches. One of the corbels has a grotesque human face. There is a tomb recess behind a radiator and a half-hidden stair to a screen loft.

Kidwelly's chancel is almost as wide as the nave. Its piscina has a beautifully carved ogee arch with a triangular head above it, as do the sedilia. Next to them on the east wall is a rare 15th-century carved figure of the Virgin in a niche. The east window is Decorated, with soaring intersecting tracery, and all for a priory that seldom had more than a dozen monks.

The vestry door in the chancel is crowned with a plaster panel decorated with French fleur-de-lis. The transept houses a delightful 1762 organ case, brought for some reason from a church in Swansea and sitting well amid these limestone walls.

LLANBADARN FAWR

ST PADARN ✱✱✱
Ghost of Celtic clas with Early Gothic doorway, local museum

This impressive church lies inland from Aberystwyth, beyond a wilderness of hypermarkets, sheds, roundabouts and estates. Llanbadarn was founded in the 6th century as a clas, pre-eminent over those of Clynnog Fawr, Bangor and Meifod. For half a millennium it taught Christianity in Welsh and Latin, notably under the 11th-century monk, Sulien, whose son wrote the Llanbadarn (or Rhygyfarch) Psalter,

now at Trinity College, Dublin. Two crosses in the church museum commemorate those days of glory.

After the age of saints, Llanbadarn like all Celtic foundations went into a long decline. Despite being rebuilt, possibly by the Lord Rhys of Deheubarth in *c.*1136, a furious passage by Gerald of Wales in 1188 recorded it as secularized and degenerate.

As a good Welshman he was appalled to find this old centre of Celtic learning under a lay abbot 'grey in iniquity'. The clergy had surrendered the church and its wealth to local landowners who 'usurped full power in their impudence, appropriating all church lands … leaving the clergy nothing but their altars'. He decided to say nothing 'for fear of infuriating this wicked people'.

The celebrated lament by the 11th-century priest Rhygyfarch put the local view of things, that 'One vile Norman intimidates one hundred natives with his command / And terrifies them with his look. / You, Wales … your beard droops and your eye is sad.' Llanbadarn was soon overshadowed by the Lord Rhys's Cistercian foundation at Strata Florida.

Llandeloy: Arts and Crafts medieval

Today there is a big-boned character about the church that survived even its rebuilding in the early 13th century. The doorway is a lovely Early Gothic composition with multiple shafts and stiff-leaf capitals, a work of French sensibility in contrast with the awesome plainness of the church.

Llanbadarn's interior is lofty, aisle-less and minster-like in its proportions. The bare nave leads to faintly pointed crossing arches. The high-roofed transepts and wide chancel form a visual unity and would be cold but for the warmth of the Victorian wood ceilings.

The chancel is a contrast, a crowded 19th-century mausoleum of the families of the Ystwyth and Rheidol valleys, the Powells of Nanteos and the Pryses of Gogerddan. On one, an angel holds open a door, presumably to usher the departed to Heaven. Another, by Flaxman, depicts a man weeping on a memorial tablet to Harriet Pryse (d. 1813). Everywhere are plaques, cartouches and frames, attended by putti or angels according to period.

Seddon's late-19th century restoration is

not wholly successful, William Morris having protested that Llanbadarn was 'too precious to alter'. The glass is Morris in style but not in quality. Other windows are by Heaton and Butler.

The south transept has been converted by Peter Lord into a small museum dedicated to the history of the church and its patrons. It is immaculate, the best I have seen in any church. A wooden screen with etched lights carries words by the 14th-century poet, Dafydd ap Gwilym, another son of Llanbadarn, dividing the museum from the rest of the church and forming a calm retreat in which to tell Llanbadarn's story.

St Padarn's altar lies in an alcove, above which is a chi-rho monogram. A stained-glass window shows the life of Padarn, a contemporary of St David, in the form of a manuscript narrative. Other exhibits tell of the Powell and Pryse families and of a community that seems far detached from the neighbouring eruption of modern Aberystwyth.

LLANDELOY

4 miles north-east of Solva
ST TEILAW *
Arts and Crafts restoration, modern rood

The little church is hidden on the outskirts of this 20th-century village across a churchyard alive with wild flowers. Its long roof, low-slung over side walls and entrance, is strangely mysterious. The building was a ruin until taken in hand by J. Coates Carter, architect of Caldey Island, in the 1920s and restored with Arts and Crafts flair.

The nave is short, blocked by Carter's rood screen and loft, with a minimal view through to the transept. The effect is of an Orthodox church, or at least an early medieval one, with laity firmly separate from the office of the mass. The loft, apparently made in Cheltenham, is reached by stairs inside the wall, while other steps lead to the pulpit.

Beyond the screen we enter another world, as if indeed we were back on Caldey. A transept appears to merge into a large squint that leads to the stepped and off-centre chancel, all in rough-cast stone. The painted reredos is by Carter, the effect delightfully odd.

LLANWENOG

5 miles west of Lampeter
ST GWENOG ***
Grand tower, Great War memorial
bench-ends

Sir Rhys ap Thomas built the massive tower of Llanwenog to celebrate Henry Tudor's defeat of Richard III at Bosworth in 1485, where Rhys fought with a detachment of men from this village. To show he paid for it himself he put his arms over the door. The splayed base and battlements look more appropriate to a family tower in San Gimignano.

The interior is reached down steps from an entrance in the tower and presents a long barrel-vaulted ceiling, beautifully panelled, from nave to chancel. The vista is enjoyably broken by a modern gothic screen with tracery and sunbursts along the top. The 14th-century walls are whitewashed, their windows deeply set, carrying passages in Welsh from the Creed and the Ten Commandments, in excellent condition (or restoration).

Twentieth-century bench-ends in a medieval style commemorate local families and events. Carved during the Great War, they record deaths in peace and war and important visitors to Llanwenog, such as bishops and benefactors. They were designed by Mary Davies Evans and carved by a Belgian war refugee, rejoicing in the name of Joseph Reubens. Stained glass of the same period is less successful, commemorating the tight-knit gentry families of the Teifi valley.

Set into the reredos is a much eroded carving of the Crucifixion, imported from outside the church by Caröe. The font is 12th century and, like most Welsh fonts, a solitary echo of an earlier church on the site. It is like something from Easter Island, with no sign of Christian imagery.

Llanwenog has a most immaculate churchyard lavatory.

Manordeifi: Teifi valley decorum

MANORBIER

ST JAMES *
Detached tower, de Barri monument

Like Laugharne and Kidwelly, Manorbier is an example of the Norman genius for scenic location. Castle and church are on opposing hills, as if offering an attacker a choice of targets or a defender a choice of refuges. The plastered church tower is almost detached from the body of the building. The interior is cavernous, whitewashed to hospital standard, and might be a creation of the 20th-century modern movement.

The vaults and arcades are pointed and the transepts and chancel asymmetric. Everything is irregular and, at the crossing, looks as if the builders proceeded with no idea of plan. The reason for this appears to be the addition of nave aisles in the 15th century, involving the 'excavation' of arches in the old Norman walls, hence the complete absence of mouldings or other decoration. The south transept is out of alignment, the chancel arch is low and the chancel disappears off to the south as if escaping its tower.

During restoration, portions of the original rood loft were reused in the north transept to give complicated gallery access to the tower. The chancel contains a medieval effigy of a de Barri of Manorbier Castle, early 14th century in date and excellently preserved. De Barri was the family of Gerald of Wales (see Manorbier Castle). He has chain mail and a shield. The reredos was carved by a local lady to designs by her son, Fergusson Barclay.

MANORDEIFI

Llechryd, 6 miles south-east of Cardigan
SLT DAVID **
Riverside church, Georgian fittings

The little stone chapel sits among trees on the banks of the River Teifi with just a farm for company. It is reached across a bridge from Llechryd and a turning left opposite the Malgwyn Castle hotel. A coracle was provided inside the west door in case a visitor was cut off by a flood. The Teifi is one of the few Welsh rivers on which coracles still appear.

Such was the church's inaccessibility that a new one was built by the Victorians in the village, and Manordeifi is now in the care of the Friends of Friendless Churches. The mostly 14th-century exterior is of grey stone, a bellcote and windows the result of an 1847 restoration. The windows have gothic glazing bars. The west porch was rebuilt to embrace a prominent outside memorial to the Lewis family.

The delight of the church is the survival inside of a complete set of Georgian fittings above rough-hewn flagstones. The box pews are curious, since the grandest appear to be at the east and west ends and the lesser benches in the middle. The western pews, flanked with fluted columns, are for the owners of Ffynone and Malgwyn Castle, two fine local houses. The easternmost ones, for the Lewises of Clynfyw and the Daviesses of Pentre, have fireplaces.

The chancel is bare but for a three-sided altar rail, carved with quatrefoils. The monuments include by one to Capt. Colby of Ffynone, who was killed in Rawalpindi in 1852 by a tiger, a far cry from the gentle water meadows of the Teifi.

MARTLETWY

1 mile south-west of Martletwy
BURNETT'S HILL CHAPEL *
Raked seating, old hat pegs

This early Methodist chapel was built in 1813 in a field where open-air services were previously held. The building looks like a simple farm cottage, with windows on either side (one formerly the door). A rearrangement put the entrance at the back and the seats facing the pulpit on either side of a central aisle. These are raked as in a theatre, giving the minister and the seated elders the presence of actors on stage. The original seats are at the back, more comfortable ones at the front.

The interior is distinguished by prominent hat rails on either side. These are of different sizes as the chapel segregated men and women on opposite sides of the aisle. The former con-

gregation of shipwrights and mine workers has long vanished and new uses for these old places of worship must be found. The chapel was ruinous until restored by a trust with help from the Pembrokeshire national park. It is used for local concerts.

MWNT

3 miles north of Cardigan
HOLY CROSS *
Wild pilgrim church on cliffside

The only remarkable feature of Mwnt church is its location, which is glory enough. The lane west from the Cardigan–Aberystwyth road plunges through gullies until opening out on to a spectacular headland overlooking Cardigan Bay. A sandy beach nestles between wind-blown, moor-capped cliffs. Everywhere is wild grass and gales. This is pilgrimage Wales at its most dramatic.

Mwnt clings to the hillside in an ancient enclosure, painted bright white. The fabric is 14th century but a 12th-century font is a ghost of some predecessor, believed to commemorate a battle near here between the Norman Flemings and the Welsh in 1155. This would also have been a pilgrim church on the route from St David's north to Strata Florida and Bardsey. This coast was more frequented in the Middle Ages than today.

Inside the low single-cell church is a good 15th-century roof and deep, square-topped windows. A modern slate altar has been installed, while relics of a screen adorn the north wall. All is simple and dignified, as befits a Caröe restoration. This place belongs as much to nature as to mankind.

NEVERN

ST BRYNACH **
Pilgrimage church with yew avenue,
ogham stones

Nevern is as ancient as Britain gets. To the south lie the Preseli hills, from whose slopes the builders of Stonehenge extracted their health-giving

Isolated pilgrimage church of Mwnt

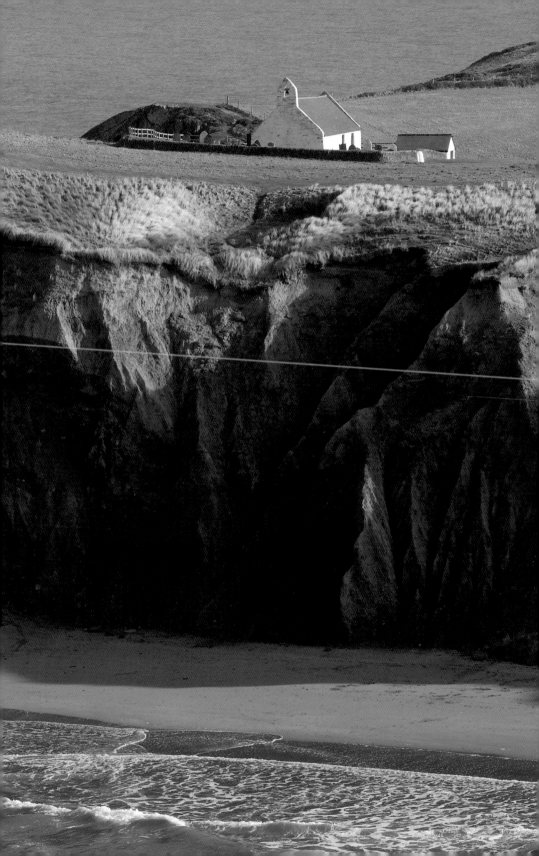

bluestones. Discarded menhirs remain among the holy wells which may make this place of religious and possibly medical resort earlier even than the Wiltshire henges. The Irish chief Brynach came here in the age of saints, and presumably stayed to found a church. Pilgrims followed along the trail to St David's. As Tim Hughes puts it, at Nevern 'the fragile light and shifting air are loaded with more weight than they can seem to bear'.

The church sits under a squat tower in a wooded churchyard, the path to the south door lined by a guard of honour of yews. One of them perpetually bleeds resin. At the end of this path, up which a million pilgrims must have walked, is Nevern's tall Celtic cross, one of the most impressive and well-preserved in Wales and a work of art to rank with the Abergavenny Jesse and the Llanrhaeadr window.

The decoration dates the cross to the early 11th century and the pattern is of weaves and knot-work, incised on durable stone. Nora Chadwick marvelled at the sculptor being able to 'repeat the same design with an unerring hand over the entire surface, arguing an astonishing control over the tools'. Next to it is a memorial cross to 'Vitalianus' inscribed in Latin script and ogham and possibly 5th century. These two stones, located in the same place, are half a millennium apart, bestraddling the Dark Ages in an extraordinary testament to Welsh cultural continuity.

The interior has been rigorously restored in Decorated gothic style. But a vaulted south chapel survives with original piscinas and choir stalls. In the windowsill is embedded a 6th-century stone inscribed in ogham. Other such stones appear to have been used as building material, both inside and out, so the past might infuse the present.

Back in the churchyard is a charming epitaph to the Griffiths children: 'They tasted of life's bitter cup, / Refused to drink the potion up, / But turned their little heads aside, / Disgusted with the taste, and died.'

Celtic cross of Nevern

PONTARGOTHI

6 miles east of Carmarthen

HOLY TRINITY ✳✳✳

Puginian chapel covered in stencil decoration

This Victorian oddity lies alone on the banks of the Cothi river a mile upstream from the village. As an essay in ecclesiastical gothic revival it has no equal in Wales. The simple exterior with wooden bargeboards and bellcote flèche looks Swiss. The large gravel car park (presumably a Cadw installation) is a mistake. None of this prepares the visitor for the interior.

The church was commissioned by a Swansea shipping tycoon, H. J. Bath, who bought a house nearby at Llanegwad. Annoyed to find local services only in Welsh, he decided to build his own church for English worship. The path from the house to the church was allegedly divided into two, one side being wide enough for Bath and his wife to walk arm-in-arm and another along which the servants had to walk single file.

Bath died when the foundation stone had only just been laid and his heir died before the church was completed. It was unrecognized by the diocese and has no burials, yet it stands as a monument to the taste of its age and to the wealth of Swansea. Bath named his ships after the letters of the Greek alphabet. One, the Zeta, was incorporated into the name of a descendant, the Welsh actress Catherine Zeta Jones.

As architect, Bath commissioned Benjamin Bucknall, a follower of Pugin. Bucknall's friend, Anthony Stansell, supplied the stencilled decoration that covers the interior. The walls were built with cavities to keep out the damp and thus preserve the murals. These comprise twenty-five panels in ochre monochrome depicting Bible stories, surrounded by abstract stencilwork. No inch is unadorned. In the chancel, the medium changes to polychrome. The decorative programme is comparable only with that in Garton-in-the-Wolds (N. Yorks).

The barrel vault is tied by colourful beams and painted with stars, which become more elaborate in the chancel and yet more so over the sanctuary. The stained glass is by Clayton and Bell, that in the west window depicting Bath holding a model of the church. The furnishings are all by Bucknall, completing his masterpiece.

ST DAVID'S CATHEDRAL

✳✳✳✳

Wales's loveliest church, Norman and Transitional gothic, Decorated bishop's throne and tomb

For over a millennium St David's was the heart of Christian Wales. Today it is Britain's most enchanting small cathedral. The best approach is from the shore up the path along which pilgrims, hermits, devotees and Irish missionaries must have walked, ecstatic at finally reaching their destination. However wild the weather, the Gulf Stream keeps St David's balmy. Timeless Wales survives here amid the spindrift, gorse, bilberries and sea birds.

Legend holds that David was born on the neighbouring cliff top, where now stands the ruined chapel of St Non, named after his mother. He was supposedly a prince of the royal house of Ceredigion and founded his monastery sometime in the mid-6th century. His asceticism was extreme, including the practice of standing in cold water for long periods and eating only bread and herbs. He is one of the few Welsh saints (among thousands of imposters) to have been formally canonized by Rome.

Despite the present-day solitude of the monastery, it was probably a key strategic location in the 6th century, easily accessible to Ireland and the Welsh coast. It was equally vulnerable to Viking raiders. No doubt as a result, nothing survives from the pre-Norman period. But David's cult was actively promoted by the Normans as a way of bringing unity and celebrity to this distant corner of their empire. William the Conqueror symbolized his sovereignty over Wales – and the supremacy of Canterbury – by visiting the shrine in 1081.

Although Gerald of Wales was still lobbying Rome a century later for Welsh ecclesiastical independence, it was not to be. Henry I appointed a Norman as bishop of St David's and induced

ABOVE: *St David's in meadow above sea*

RIGHT: *St David's: nave and pulpitum*

the papacy to make two pilgrimages to St David's worth one to Rome, an astonishing concession which did more than anything to bring the shrine prosperity. Gerald's eagerness for Welsh autonomy must at least have hastened the building of a new cathedral. The Lord Rhys, last king of Deheubarth, was buried in the new building in 1197 and may have helped finance it.

Today's normal approach is from above, down into the defile of the Alun stream, where cathedral and old bishop's palace nestle by a meadow. The building was begun in 1182 and displays the flowering of 12th-century roman-esque, commenced after the gothic style was already spreading across England. St David's shows masons aware of the new style, play-ing with the transition from round to pointed arches as work progressed. Despite additions

and restorations by Nash, Butterfield and Gil-bert Scott in the 19th century, the cathedral re-mains essentially Norman.

Nowhere is the hand of restoration more evident than in its neo-Norman west façade, designed by Scott to replace one by John Nash and forming an unnerving first impression of the cathedral from outside. (Indeed St David's is best entered at speed.) Inside, the Norman immediately reveals itself in six bays of multiple shafts carrying a wealth of chevron decoration and clustered trumpet capitals. Malcolm Thurl-by, in his essay on the cathedral, lists twenty-two different forms of chevron ornament.

Above a clerestory is St David's superb roof. Panelled and with elaborately carved Tudor pendants it is a masterpiece of openwork carv-ing, drawing the eye forward over the bulk of

the pulpitum, lightened by Butterfield's restored aisles in big-windowed Decorated gothic.

The pulpitum that divides the nave from the monastic east end of the cathedral is St David's masterpiece. The original cross-wall was built by St David's most regal bishop, Henry de Gower, in the 1340s and has his tomb built into it, framed by a Decorated arch carrying crocket and ballflower decoration. This is flanked by four saints' niches arranged by Butterfield in the 19th century. Above runs Caröe's 20th-century rood loft, with above that a soaring organ case inserted by Peter Bird in 2000. Six centuries contribute to this harmonious whole.

On either side of the pulpitum small arches lead eastwards. Through them we leave the great hall of popular pilgrimage and enter the sanctuary of the Norman clergy. Gothic vaults and secluded chapels contrast with the spaciousness of the nave. The choir and sanctuary, located under the crossing, form a church within a church. Norman arches are now pointed, their capitals a gallery of transitional Norman/gothic art.

The 15th-century choir stalls are Perpendicular, with delicate canopies, lierne vaults and ogee arches. Twenty-one surviving misericords depict commonplace scenes, including one of pilgrims being sick on board ship. Overseeing all this is the bishop's throne, again Decorated at its most ostentatious and one of the finest in Britain. A wedding-cake confection of pinnacles shoots upwards as if only the roof will stop it.

Beyond lie the sanctuary and presbytery, heavily restored by Scott in Early Gothic style. Edmund Tudor (d. 1456), first husband of Margaret Beaufort and father of Henry VII, is buried here in pride of place under a chest tomb. The brass is 19th century. Victorian too is the reinstatement of the east wall of the presbytery, with three towering blind lancets filled with mosaics by the Italian firm Salviati. The four Norman windows above are faintly pointed. The roof is a Scott restoration of a Tudor original. In the presbytery wall is the 13th-century shrine of St David, with ledges for offerings.

Behind the presbytery the cathedral has yet another surprise, the Holy Trinity chapel built by Bishop Vaughan in the 1500s as his memorial and as a tribute to the Tudors. It is a Perpendicular tour de force, complete with fan vault, an altar of medieval fragments and the original pilgrim recess with a box said to contain the bones of St David.

Most of the side chapels were ruinous and even unroofed when the Victorians arrived. Off the north transept is the 14th-century Becket chapel (with the cathedral library above). The Lady Chapel has restored sedilia and a remarkable 1920s tomb of Bishop Owen by the ubiquitous Caröe. The style is gothic but, at St David's, time and style are both extended and compressed.

ST GOVAN **

1 mile south of Bosherston
Romantic chapel in seaside ravine

This is Welsh myth fused into rocks and crashing waves. The Gulf Stream hurls itself against the Pembrokeshire coast where legend has a saint fleeing bandits towards the cliff where, as he is about to fall, the ground opens and a cleft leads down to the sea. There he builds his hermitage. If you prefer, it is here that his namesake, Sir Gawain, climbed up the cliff from the sea to meet the Green Knight, struggling against a south-westerly gale that goaded the waves to fury.

Either way the noise of wind, water and gulls is deafening. The church is reached down precipitous steps from a small car park. It is said that any count of the steps yields a different answer. The chapel must be the most spartan place of worship in Britain. It is no longer consecrated. A simple stone box is jammed into the ravine, with rough stone walls and a mud floor. The pointed roof, also of stone, suggests a post-Norman date.

A stone altar slab, on which today's visitors leave wild flowers, is said to hide the hermit's bones. Behind it, an opening leads into a tiny cave, apparently his cell. A small window gives a view of the sea below, where there is a holy well of indeterminate date. St Govan is believed to have been a 6th-century Irish saint, but this is immaterial when place is all.

The cliff chapel of St Govan

SOAR-Y-MYNYDD **
Abergwesyn, 8 miles east of Tregaron

I find it hard to convey the exhilaration of encountering this chapel off the long mountain road east from Tregaron to the Llyn Brianne reservoir. The wide expanse of the Cambrian Mountains was wretchedly ignored by the postwar creators of Wales's national parks, presumably because it was considered just too remote and unimportant. This moorland is probably now more deserted than ever. The scattered sheep farms and drovers survived until after the Second World War, when they gave up and sold their land for forestry or reservoirs.

Here down a side road (at OS reference 752533) above the river Camddwr stands a Cal-vinist chapel (doubling as a school). It was built by Ebenezer Richard of Tregaron, whose life-work was the erection of chapels across Wales to serve the needs of rural communities far from existing settlements. R. S. Thomas called it 'the chapel of the soul', which well describes it.

The building consists of a substantial hall with Regency tracery in its windows, an adjacent *tŷ'r capel* and stable, all now boldly white-washed. The interior is remarkably well-appointed, with box pews and a finely carpentered pulpit between the windows. This has double-steps and rich balusters. A few headstones lie in the field outside.

The chapel is celebrated for the recollection of preaching visits in the 1930s by the Reverend David Idris Owen. This involved a train from Aberystwyth to Llanddewibrefi and an eight-mile horse ride over the mountains. One service would be conducted in the chapel and another in the parlour of a local farm. On one occasion Owen nearly died in a snowstorm trying to get back to the train. Small wonder the chapel is reputedly 'the most isolated in Wales'.

STACKPOLE

3 miles south of Pembroke
ST JAMES AND ST ELIDYR **
Medieval and later gentry tombs

The church occupies a lovely spot, filling its own private dell with homage paid it by trees on every side. This was the home church of the Campbells, Earls of Cawdor, owners of much of south Pembrokeshire in the 19th century. Their over-restoration of local churches at least meant, in the case of Stackpole, the presence of Sir Gilbert Scott in person. While the exterior is dominated by a slender Pembrokeshire tower, the interior is Victorian.

The attraction of the church lies in its memorials, mostly of the Stackpole, Lort and Campbell families. In the chancel stands one of the best medieval tombs of Wales, that of Sir Elidyr de Stackpole of the mid-14th century. A cross-legged knight lies beneath a freestanding hexagon arch, adorned with crockets and ballflowers. On the chest beneath him are six panels containing weepers in unusually naturalistic poses. One, a swaggering youth, looks eager to burst from his arboreal frame. These must depict members of his family. Though much repaired, the chest offers a gallery of Welsh figures in the years before the Black Death. Opposite is the effigy of Lady Stackpole, much restored but again vivid, with flowing hair and garments, and weepers full of character.

The Lort chapel has memorials of all shapes and sizes. Most spectacular is the Jacobean wall tomb of Roger Lort (d. 1613), a renaissance composition with Ionic columns and elaborate entablature. Lort and his wife are naively carved at prayer, their faces painted on, with twelve children crowded along the base. Another Lort and his wife are commemorated in a marble tablet of 1712 with cherubs and skulls.

The Cawdor tombs are no less impressive. That to John Frederick of 1860 reverts to the medieval tradition of a recumbent effigy. A window in the south transept depicts a Cawdor as Solomon overseeing the building of a temple. The Lort chapel also contains an inscribed Celtic stone.

Stackpole's lychgate is an Arts and Crafts work in the style of Lutyens by Christopher Turnor, a Cawdor relative. The ridge carries a swirling Art Nouveau pattern.

STRATA FLORIDA *

Fragment of ancient Welsh abbey

This is the only entry for a single arch, but what an arch. The abbey of Strata Florida was, after St David's, the most famous church in Wales from the 12th century to the Dissolution. The Cistercian foundation came under the patronage of the Lord Rhys of Deheubarth, following a resurgence of Welsh power and the defeat of the local Norman lord in 1166. Rhys built a new abbey in 1184 and his heirs were buried here into the 13th century.

Llywelyn the Great summoned his grandees to Strata Florida in 1238 and the abbey was dubbed the 'Westminster of Wales'. It was a stopping place, and shrine in its own right, on the pilgrimage route north from St David's to Bardsey. Here the Holy Grail was reputedly brought from Glastonbury (see Nanteos). By the Dissolution only seven monks remained.

Of the great church, its plan bigger than St David's, almost nothing survives apart from a fragment of wall and the extraordinary romanesque west arch. This is adorned with five continuous roll-mouldings uninterrupted by any capitals or other ornament apart from periodic stone bands, each terminating in a tiny scroll. There is nothing quite like it anywhere else (other than at Margam Abbey, Glamorgan) and attempts to place it in the Norman canon seem quite pointless. This is 'Welsh romanesque', its relationship with English, Irish, Norse or Manx styles rightly described by Peter Lord as a 'swirling pool rather than a flowing stream'.

Strata Florida sits sublime in its valley, still recognizable from the Buck engraving of 1741.

The 14th-century Welsh poet and troubadour Dafydd ap Gwilym is buried under the yew in the adjacent churchyard. The *Companion Guide* records meadows abounding in lady's smock, purple orchid, buttercup and cow parsley.

TENBY

ST MARY ✳✳✳
Tudor town church with fine memorials to local worthies

Tenby is a charming hugger-mugger town round a small harbour, gracefully transformed in the 19th century into an agreeable resort. The church is worthy of the town. Its late-15th-century rebuilding reflected Tenby's growth as a trading port during the Wars of the Roses and the Tudor ascendancy.

As at Haverfordwest, the builders seem to have looked for inspiration to Somerset. The tall spire would have been a beacon to sailors and the double-ogee arch to the west door echoes the orientalism of the north porch of Bristol's St Mary Redcliffe. The interior is that of a spacious town church rich in memorials. The painted roof bosses would have illustrated biblical and mythical scenes.

Symmetry is not Tenby's strong suit. Even the chancel arch is off-centre. The north arcade, which continues through from the nave, is distinct from the south in both height and rhythm.

St Nicholas's (north) chapel has a wall that slopes disconcertingly inwards. The effect is of a regiment on parade but out of step.

What might seem a jumble of spaces is pulled together by the whitewashed walls and embossed wagon roofs and by the elongated chancel. Steps lead up to the sanctuary, crowned by a large Perpendicular window filled with glass by Wailes. The chancel used to carry an upper floor with a chapel of St Anne, hence the lower chancel arcading.

Most celebrated of the many memorials is the one to Thomas White, protector of the young Henry Tudor before his exile to Brittany to escape the Yorkists in 1471. He was one of many Welsh gentlemen to be richly rewarded by the future Henry VII. He lies next to the chancel, head to toe with his son, the epitome of a late-medieval entrepreneur. The two effigies are in merchant dress. Round the tomb base are informal family scenes. An effigy in the north aisle is of a female in fine 14th-century costume.

Of the Jacobean monuments the most prominent, in St Nicholas's Chapel, is to Margaret Mercer (d. 1610). The effigy lies on its side, hand on heart and head on cushion. The armoured husband kneels above in prayer, while the children kneel below. A bust erected in 1910 was to a local man, Robert Recorde, who lived in Tenby in the 16th century and invented the mathematical sign for equals.

Glamorgan

Glamorgan is Wales's home county formed of the medieval lordships of Glamorgan and Gower. It contains almost half the country's population as well as its seat of government. In the course of the reign of Queen Victoria its mineral exports made it the richest county in Britain. As a result, the decline seen in the second half of the 20th century was the more drastic, and insensitive attempts at renewal have made recovery halting. Only in the 21st century has Cardiff recovered strongly, assisted by political devolution.

St Illtud's church at Llantwit Major is accepted as the most important known link between Roman and Dark Age Christianity in mainland Britain, sending missionaries to Cornwall, Brittany and Ireland. The invading Normans built an early castle at Cardiff, which survives, and a cathedral and diocese at Llandaff, intended to rival the appeal of 'Welsh' St David's. Monasteries came to Margam, Neath and Ewenni. Margam's collection of Celtic stones is among the most remarkable of that age in Europe

While the county was distant from the medieval turbulence of the north, Llywelyn's revolt led to the construction in 1268 by Gilbert de Clare of the great castle at Caerphilly. This predated those of Edward I in the north. Lesser forts protected Gower and the fertile coast towards Carmarthen and Pembroke. Tudor domestic building can be seen at Llancaeach Fawr and St Fagans Castle, and at the occasionally open St Donat's, restored by William Randolph Hearst.

Norman church-building, following hard on the castles, is displayed in the impressive naves at Ewenni and Margam Abbey. Llandaff Cathedral was rebuilt c.1200 in the Early Gothic style. St John Baptist, Cardiff, is Perpendicular in the West Country tradition. Otherwise the county is poor in pre-Victorian architecture. The Orangery at Margam Castle and the rococo saloon at Fonmon are exceptional as works of the 18th century.

The use of coking coal rather than charcoal to work iron brought John Guest to Dowlais in 1760 and commenced a boom unlike any other in Britain, a 'black gold rush'. Workers poured into Glamorgan from the surrounding countryside and from the Midlands. Merthyr Tydfil was the only industrial town in Britain where English was not the language of the streets – 'perhaps the first properly Celtic town of modern times', wrote Marcus Tanner, though this later changed with English immigration.

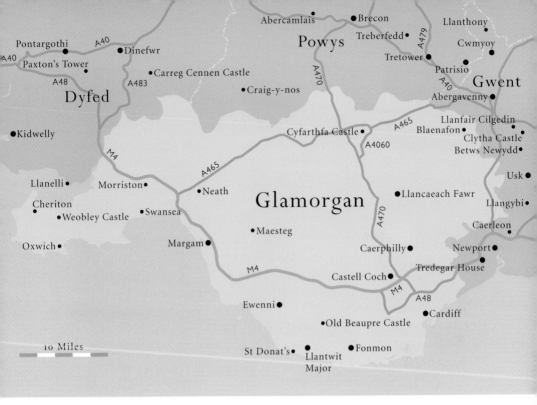

Virtually all traces of this boom have vanished, wiped off the map by politicians eager to erase signs of what they considered an alien capitalism. Today's citizens of the valleys can have little idea what brought their ancestors to these places. The best effort to remind them is at Blaenafon, where traces of the first blast furnaces (1788) and workers' cottages survive in an industrial park. Fragments of the Cyfarthfa ironworks are at Merthyr, as is the Crawshay family's Regency Cyfarthfa Castle, now an art gallery and museum. Nothing is left at Dowlais, cradle of Wales's industrial revolution, which might once have challenged Shropshire's Coalbrookdale as a tourism magnet.

Glamorgan was also the home of what Anthony Jones calls 'without question the national architecture of Wales', the Nonconformist chapel. It is certainly the defining building of every Welsh settlement. From the earliest barn conversions (see St Fagans) to the neo-baroque splendour of the valley preaching houses, chapels dominate the Glamorgan townscape. Though few are accessible, fine examples stand proud at Morriston and Maesteg. The preservation of these buildings is the more urgent given their declining congregations and the loss of the industrial monuments that gave them birth.

In Cardiff the 3rd Marquess of Bute inherited extensive Herbert land and used his wealth to build Cardiff docks and two of the most spectacular gothic revival palaces in Europe, Cardiff Castle and Castell Coch by William Burges. A

Bute relative also commissioned a polychrome church by William Butterfield at Penarth overlooking Cardiff Bay.

These patrons were challenged at least in scale by palaces of civic administration in Cardiff and Swansea, the first a culmination of the Edwardian baroque revival, the second a work of inter-war Art Deco containing Frank Brangwyn's murals. In comparison, the new Assembly building in Cardiff Bay is insipid and the adjacent Wales Millennium Centre an extraordinary beached monster, but at least unmistakably Welsh.

Houses and Castles

Blaenafon *
Caerphilly Castle ****
Cardiff:
  Castle ****
  City Hall ****
  St Fagans National History Museum ***
  Senedd/Assembly Building ***
  Wales Millennium Centre ***
Castell Coch ****

Cyfarthfa Castle *
Fonmon Castle ***
Llancaeach Fawr ***
Llanelli House *
Margam Castle and Orangery ***
Old Beaupre Castle **
Oxwich Castle *
St Donat's Castle **
Swansea Guildhall **
Weobley Castle **

Churches

Cardiff:
  Llandaff Cathedral ****
  St Augustine, Penarth **
  St German *
  St John Baptist **
Cheriton **
Ewenni Priory ***
Llantwit Major ***
Maesteg *
Margam Abbey ***
Morriston *
Neath Abbey *

Houses and Castles

BLAENAFON

ENGINE ROW *
Ironworkers' cottages from the earliest Glamorgan boom (Mus)

The rescue of traces of Blaenafon's earliest ironworks is a valiant attempt to bring the past of the valleys alive for generations that have no memory of them. So much of the blast-furnace site has been destroyed that what is left, clinging to the side of a hill, is almost beyond interpretation.

Two rows of Georgian cottages, Engine Row and Stack Square, survive and these have been restored, albeit to a surreal standard of cleanliness. Philanthropists recording these dwellings in their original state emphasized their poverty and squalor, unappealing qualities to a modern curator.

The cottages in Engine Row, dating from 1788, were apparently occupied by workers imported from the Midlands, perhaps from the earlier industrial site of Shropshire's Coalbrookdale. Hence the first cottage depicts a relatively comfortable family in the 1790s, with a scattering of Shropshire furniture and prints. A replicated leg of mutton is on the table. Upstairs is the workman's Sunday-best suit, his wife's best shoes and a Bible.

The second cottage is decorated as of 1841, for an Irish family in poorer circumstances. The main downstairs room is set up for clothes washing. Irish newspapers serve for wallpaper and the family sleep on mattresses on the floor. The Catholic faith is reflected in crucifixes and rosaries. Neither cottage has sanitation and the rooms would have been coated in grime from the adjacent blast furnaces.

In 2008 three families spent a fortnight in the cottages, working in the pits and enduring the hardships of Victorian industrial life for the benefit of a television audience. It made for a vivid documentary, an experience from which some of those involved emerged traumatized and others as celebrities.

CAERPHILLY CASTLE ****

Sensational moated castle set in a
suburban park (Cadw)

Henry III's Treaty of Montgomery of 1267 briefly acknowledged Llywelyn (the Last) as effective king of Wales after the most successful campaign against the English of any Welsh leader. Llywelyn's territory included virtually all of present-day Wales apart from the southern strip of the Marches. The Marcher lords were on the run and Henry, hard-pressed by Simon de Montfort in England, was forced to acknowledge it.

Of the still resisting Marcher lords, Gilbert de Clare of Glamorgan, did not sit and wait. A year after the Treaty of Montgomery he built at Caerphilly one of the most impressive fortresses not just in Wales but, claim its admirers, 'in the Western world'. The only explanation for its modern obscurity is that it now stands in a suburban town north of Cardiff. Its surrounding municipal park no longer besieges it, but rather bores it into submission. Since it was built on flat land, topography lends it neither distance nor romance. Yet Caerphilly's walls, moats and gatehouses form a fortress comparable in Britain only with Dover.

The castle was begun in 1268 and modelled on Kenilworth, where Simon de Montfort's forces had recently been defeated. De Clare noted that at Kenilworth lakes had been as effective as walls or contours in fending off attack. Water rendered ladders, catapults and wall-sapping ineffective, and approach across water was hard

to conceal. Caerphilly's network of concentric waterworks and walls thus presented assailants with multiple obstacles, and defenders with multiple vantage points.

De Clare lost Caerphilly briefly to Llywelyn's resurgent revolt, but it was recaptured and reinforced, later passing to Richard II's favourite, Hugh le Despenser. Only when Marcher power in Glamorgan was concentrated in Cardiff, did Caerphilly fall into decay. Its stone was used as a quarry and one of its towers subsided into the marshy ground. But its splendour did not escape the ever-attentive Marquesses of Bute. They removed houses that had invaded the site, re-roofed the great hall and rebuilt walls and towers where it was clear how they had fallen, using original masonry or, in some places, early concrete.

The approach today is as was originally intended, the drained moats being re-flooded in the 1950s. A mighty curtain wall faces the visitor across a first moat, with a fortified gatehouse reached only after crossing two drawbridges. Beyond lies a second stretch of water with a second curtain wall rising directly from it. Another drawbridge must be crossed and another gatehouse/keep confronted before the inner ward is reached.

The gatehouse to this ward contains the chambers of the constable of the castle and is in every sense the *pièce de résistance*. The gatehouse rooms are guarded by two massive doors and reached up a spiral staircase with arrow-slit windows. The interior was reconstructed by Bute, including a great chamber and chapel.

The inner ward is that of a conventional 13th-century castle, with defensive towers and turrets round the walls and a great hall to one side. Remodelled by Despenser in the 1320s, this hall has been restored close to its original form and is most impressive. The roof rests on capitals depicting Edward II and his queen. The windows are Decorated gothic with ballflower decoration.

I last saw Caerphilly on a spring evening when it was being prepared for jousting and feasting, of the sort much ridiculed by purists. If the Victorians could re-create with such care the fabric of these places, why should we not re-create the spirit in which they were used?

CARDIFF

CASTLE ★★★★
Civic Centre
Victorian masterpiece dominating city centre,
painted interiors (Cadw)

The grouping of Cardiff's civic centre is un-equalled in any British city. Formed of the cas-tle, law courts, city hall, national museum and university it is an architectural memorial to the industrial wealth once synonymous with Gla-morgan. Yet the setting of this memorial awaits rescue with increasing desperation.

In the first decade of the 21st century Car-diff decided to cut itself in two by rebuilding its national stadium, empty most of the time, in its busy commercial heart, while the Welsh Assem-bly building and a new opera and entertainment centre were dismissed two miles away to Car-diff Bay. It was an extraordinary plan. Even the chance of creating a 'Champs Elysees' between the two centres was ignored and a cheap sprawl of commercial and residential blocks permitted to reinforce the split.

Cardiff Castle itself is a building of Euro-pean stature, marooned behind a high wall by a moat of traffic like the Kremlin with a Holly-wood make-over. The outer ward, which should be Cardiff's central piazza, cannot even be seen without a ticket. The demolition of at least part of the wall should be a civic priority.

The old Norman castle survives on its mound, the military headquarters of Robert of Gloucester, first Norman lord of Glamorgan. Cardiff held the key to South Wales and thus to Ireland and its custodianship passed from one Marcher lord to another, from the Despensers to the Earls of Warwick to the Earls of Pem-broke. It became redundant under the Tudors and other buildings were erected to house con-stables and governors in more comfort along the west side of the ward.

These buildings were transformed after the marriage in 1766 of a Pembroke heiress to a Scots grandee, Lord Mountstuart, future Mar-quess of Bute. The Mountstuarts' principal seat was (and remains) on the Isle of Bute in Scotland and the then Marquess intended Cardiff as a

residence for his son. He employed Henry Hol-land and Capability Brown to reorder the castle site. The Norman castle became a picturesque ruin.

Holland's house survived until the maturity of the 3rd Marquess, who had succeeded to the title in 1848 at the age of just 1. By now the min-eral reserves of the Herbert/Bute properties in Glamorgan were soaring in value and Bute was christened 'the richest baby in Britain'. He grew up to be a retiring, aesthetic youth, obsessed with archaeology and the rituals of religion, converting to Roman Catholicism at the age of 21. He married into the family of the Catholic Dukes of Norfolk. Bute went on to study Cop-tic, translate Turgenev, promote Wagner and inspire Disraeli's novel *Lothair*. He was an echo of Bavaria's Prince Ludwig.

In 1865 when still only 18, Bute met the me-dievalist architect William Burges. Supremely confident in any style from romanesque to Is-lamic, Burges could design a palace, a stained-glass window or a set of toiletries to order. In the bonding of Bute and Burges, money met art in the most fruitful alliance in Victorian aes-thetics. Nowhere was this alliance realized with such brilliance as at Cardiff.

The castle, like Bute's summer retreat at Cas-tell Coch (see below), was unfinished on Burges' death in 1881. At no point did the family spend more than two months a year in Wales and de-scendants donated both houses to the people of Cardiff in 1947. They are admirably maintained and accessible today.

The exterior of the castle peers over the bat-tlements of the wall that separates it from the city. Corners are adorned with watch-towers, pinnacles, flags and banners. The clock-tower might be from Carcassonne. Next to the en-trance gate is the black tower, surviving from the medieval fortress.

Once inside the gate we see the Norman keep across the lawn, but it is the rambling com-position to the left that commands attention. This comprises a 15th-century façade, rich in bay windows, sandwiched between the 18th-century Holland house and the massed towers of Burges' block on the left.

Inside, these disparate exteriors are resolved

Marcher glory: Caerphilly Castle

by Burges's genius, or perhaps by a conversation between Burges and Bute. There is no domesticity to Cardiff Castle, let alone any sense of functional progression. The chambers are, rather, distinct caskets of decorative art, objects in a museum, created with money no object.

The first group of rooms, in the clock-tower, was built for Bute when a bachelor. The finest is the winter smoking room, completed in 1872 on a theme of time. Every inch is painted with images depicting signs of the zodiac, seasons of the year, days of the week and times of the day. The huge overmantel is carved with a procession of medieval characters, hunting, wooing and sitting by the fire, by Burges' master-craftsman, Thomas Nicholls. The characters are as brightly coloured as would have been their 14th-century predecessors.

The Bachelor's Bedroom is a celebration of the geology of Bute's wealth, though the geology is less mundane coal and iron and more precious stones from classical mythology. Here base metal becomes gold. Next to it is a bathroom lined with alabaster, with a bath imported from Rome, into the sides of which Burges set fishes that appear to swim when it is filled with water.

The summer smoking room at the top of the tower is intended as the climax of this suite, one of the most extraordinary rooms I know. The tiled floor is based on that of Westminster Abbey chapter house. The lower walls are lit by small windows lined with legends of the zodiac, and the chimneypiece is crowned by Cupid carrying lovebirds. Below runs a frieze of medieval lovers in a wood.

In the four corners of the room are alabaster columns disappearing into giant corbels, with below them the eight classical winds. These columns support a gallery, round which is a clerestory of windows beneath a dome representing the heavens. In the murals classical, gothic and metallurgical themes jostle for attention, ablaze in gold, red and brown. This room, indeed the whole castle, refutes any claim that Victorian gothic is a grim or humourless style.

Beyond the bachelor suite is the family or guest tower. Here a children's nursery carries a frieze of characters from fairy tales, alive with

Burges's invention and wit. The Bute governess was supplemented by Welsh and French maids instructed to speak to the children only in their native languages.

Visitors now pass into the former 15th-century wing and the last work completed under Burges' personal supervision, the Arab room. This is in blue marble with a ceiling of 'jelly-mould' vaults. It is worth trying to lie on the floor and look up at this psychedelic pattern of circles and stars. On all sides are Burges' favourite peacocks, gazing arrogantly at the fuss.

Next door is the castle's original first-floor banqueting hall, except that the Tudor original is everywhere touched with a gothic imagination. The hammerbeam roof is supported on miniature fan vaults. The murals and fireplace glorify the Norman Robert of Gloucester, depicting his castle with trumpet-blowing heralds.

The other rooms continue in the same rich theme. The stairwell has a crocodile carved on the banister, to eat any child sliding down it. The octagon tower beneath the flèche contains the lavish Chaucer room, celebrating scenes from the *Canterbury Tales* beneath a ceiling of gothic rococo. Lady Bute's contribution is said to be the eight classic heroines, 'who suffered in the cause of love'.

The Bute tower rises to the roof garden, a Pompeiian court with surrounding peristyle and bronze fountain, alive with animals at its centre. Dappled with sunlight (if we are lucky with the weather) it is as far from the spirit of Cardiff outside as could be imagined. After this the ground-floor library, still sheltering the 3rd Marquess's leather-bound volumes, might be an anticlimax. Yet over a doorway two monkeys squabble over a book. Monkeys are everywhere.

An almost humorous shock is offered across the former entrance hall in a drawing room surviving from Holland's conversion. Plain, white and Georgian it is hung with portraits of the Marquesses of Bute and appears to have been left untouched by Burges, as if in homage to his predecessor. Yet even here two monkeys lurk over a doorcase, protesting bitterly. Cardiff Castle is one long burst of exhilaration – and never without a smile.

Cardiff Castle's riotous medievalism

CITY HALL ✶✶✶✶
Civic Centre
Public palace from Wales's richest age (Mus)

The civic centre in Cathays Park is nicknamed the 'Welsh Washington', laid out as a burst of confidence at the height of Cardiff's Victorian prosperity. The 59-acre site was bought from the Marquess of Bute in 1898 and a grid created for a new town hall, law courts and national museum (see Cardiff Castle above). The architectural quality of the law courts, city hall and museum was not sustained when the rear of the site was developed for the university. But Cathays Park retains its dignity and its relationship to the rest of Cardiff is not beyond rescue.

The star of the show is unquestionably the city hall. This was begun by Lanchester, Stewart and Rickards in 1901 with baroque swagger. The style might be termed Wren Imperial. The façade is dominated by a grand central bay forming the visual base for a dome, with an enriched Venetian window rising above a *porte-cochère*. The ground-floor windows and the corner pavilions are rusticated. This composition is offset by a clock-tower surmounted by a ferocious Welsh dragon.

The exterior drips with sculpture. Groupings include Welsh music complimenting poetry, commerce paying court to industry and unity to patriotism. The building has a serene balance, echo of a lost architectural form and a lost respect for the fusion of sculpture and building. Everywhere are the Latin initials VC, trumpeting a pride in Villa Cardiff.

The interior is more than a match for the exterior. Two staircases lead up from the spacious entrance hall to a suite consisting of council chamber, marble hall and assembly room. The hall takes pride of place, flanked by paired columns in Siena marble with the chamber appearing to float between the twin stairwells. Newman in Pevsner relates this to the Residenz at Wurzburg. The wells are flanked in turn with statues, commissioned by Lord Rhondda, of Boudicca, Gerald of Wales, Llywelyn the Great, Glyndŵr, Henry Tudor and others. The walls carry paintings and busts, including of Lloyd George, James Callaghan, George Thomas and a surreal 'triple portrait' of Diana, Princess of Wales. The hall is presided over by a large statue of St David.

At each end of the hall are two baroque door-cases leading respectively to the council chamber and the assembly room. Each is surmounted by a giant scallop shell surrounded by reliefs of ships, mermaids and mermen. The assembly room has a massive barrel vault decorated with rosettes. The walls are lined with Doric columns set at an angle to emphasize the window niches. The whole scheme of niches, cartouches and scrolls is turbulent. Only the semi-circular wall panels at either end remain sadly empty of their murals, as if to mark the ebbing of Cardiff's civic pride. This splendid memorial to Welsh history should have been the seat of the National Assembly.

ST FAGANS NATIONAL HISTORY
MUSEUM ✶✶✶
Repository of 2,000 years of Welsh buildings (Mus)

St Fagans is the best architectural museum in Britain. It boasts over forty buildings brought from every corner of Wales and is marred only by the bland modernity of its entrance and museum block, more like an airport than a welcome to Wales's past. The site has the added attraction of St Fagans Castle, a well-restored Tudor manor with sumptuous garden.

The collection embraces a Celtic village, medieval cottages and rural farmsteads, together with a prefab, tollbooth, pigsty, bakehouse, smithy, cockpit, schoolhouse, bee-hive, shopping street, working farm and workmen's institute. The group is constantly expanding. A recent acquisition was Tŷ Gwyrdd, a supposedly self-sufficient modern house, using bricks and wood from the site, water from the roof and woollen insulation. I have chosen a few buildings for special mention.

St Fagans Castle
The Elizabethan house, built in the 1580s, remains on its original site. It belonged to the Lewis family who married into that of the 18th-century Earls of Plymouth. The house was re-

stored and 'Victorianized' in the 1880s as a seat for the heir to the earldom. In 1946 the then earl donated it to Cardiff as a museum, along with the surrounding estate. Much effort has gone into reassembling furniture appropriate to the Victorian restoration and portraits appropriate to the Plymouths.

The main façade displays the transition from medieval to Elizabethan architecture in its explicit symmetry, with a central porch and equal wings and with gables balancing the front and the sides. Yet the interior clings to the medieval past, with a screens passage, great hall and elaborate overmantel.

The downstairs drawing room has another Elizabethan overmantel, carved with the Lewis arms, and a tapestry copied from a Teniers painting. The sofa cover is a patchwork stitched by Victorian house guests, while the gramophone once belonged to Adelina Patti (see Craig-y-nos, Powys). The library houses a Gillow bookcase and an enticing bottle of port.

The state bedroom contains a 1710 bed of red silk damask and embroidered wall-hangings. Panelling and fireplaces have been imported, presumably from distressed houses elsewhere in Wales, to create a sense of neo-Jacobean warmth. Even the kitchen, which in most restorations is a predictable and forlorn place, looks ready to leap into life at the mention of guests.

The castle grounds include a 1900 rose garden (with 100 varieties of rose), carefully recreated from old records and photographs. There is a rose called Bardou Job, thought to be extinct until rediscovered in the garden of California's Alcatraz Prison. The Italian garden has been restored and beneath it the grounds fall away dramatically to a set of ancient fishponds in a ravine.

Rhyd-y-car Ironworkers' Houses
(from Merthyr Tydfil)
I once took my father back to his birthplace in the Merthyr suburb of Dowlais and saw him shell-shocked at the destruction of the place. Not only had streets and houses been demolished but so had most of the public buildings of his youth. It was as if Hitler had come to the

valleys, he said, to repeat the job he had begun on Cardiff Docks.

The rescue in 1987 of a row of Merthyr's Georgian terrace houses (*c*.1800) gives some sense of what has been lost. Six properties have been re-erected and displayed as each might have appeared in succeeding periods, in 1805, 1855, 1895, 1925, 1955 and 1985. Their tiny gardens too can be seen changing over time, complete with rabbit hutches, pigeon houses, privies and tool-sheds.

The display is imaginative in conception and execution. Respect has been paid to the role of clutter in ordinary life: hence sewing kits, posters, unfinished meals and old newspapers. An air-raid shelter is converted into a potting shed. Since the sites of so many of these terraces now lie empty one is tempted to ask: why not rebuild them *in situ* for Cardiff commuters now repopulating the valleys?

Pen-rhiw Chapel
(from Felindre, Carmarthenshire)
On my last visit to St Fagans, the whitewashed Unitarian chapel from Felindre in Carmarthenshire was preparing for one of its regular services in Welsh. A number of regulars were unable to get in, having been pre-empted by a group of Japanese tourists whose command of English, let alone Welsh, was minimal. They were not to be dislodged from the chance of a lifetime.

The chapel looks as if it has been at St Fagans all its life. Nestling behind a hedge up a short lane it is scarcely bigger than a drawing room, with gabled roof and simple side door. It became a chapel in 1777, possibly converted from a barn, with the present narrow gallery added in the 19th century.

The box pews were apparently erected by the families who were to sit in them, thus all being bespoke and slightly different. The high pulpit is lit by a large window in what is a dignified and simple interior. The floor is mostly of beaten earth.

Llandeilo Tal-y-bont Church
(from Pontarddulais, Swansea)
This is a most exciting project. St Teilo's was a 13th-century Swansea church, extended into a

south aisle at the turn of the 15th century and with a small chapel and porch added. Had it remained in place, it would doubtless have stayed frozen in the whitewashed state of modern conservation. A set of wall-paintings dating from *c.*1520 would have remained concealed or at best partly revealed.

Reconstruction at St Fagans enabled St Teilo's somehow to burst free of the bonds of ideology. A decision was taken not just to conserve the wall-paintings but to return them to their pre-Reformation state. Careful scholarship went into researching both their subject matter and the materials used. Nor was reinstatement confined to the walls. A rood screen and loft have been inserted, as are the icons, altars and fittings associated with Catholic worship at the time. This is the only full medieval reinstatement in Britain. The church was opened by the archbishop of Canterbury in 2007.

The mural colouring is alarmingly vivid, but that is how it would have been. There is no reason to insist that old must mean faded, dejected, dark and tumbledown. Oriental conservation does not see the past in that way – nor for that matter do picture restorers. St Teilo's justifies the restoration of fragmentary medieval structures elsewhere in Britain. Medieval art deserves to be appreciated as such. It should not require the removal and reconstruction of a building to recapture the glory of its past.

Celtic Village (from Flintshire)
A small Iron Age camp has been re-created from three dwellings excavated from actual buildings. One is stone-walled, the others made of Flintshire wattle. They are appropriately filled with smoke from fires being used both for cooking and for the firing of pots.

The village is not just an archaeological relic but is peopled with theatrical 'Celts' attempting to make the village work as it would have done, including the planting of crops and rearing of animals. It is surrounded by a simple palisade with ditch, which cannot have kept out any but the most timid of wild animals. On my visit it had not deterred a passing 'Roman platoon', clearly enjoying the human comforts of their Celtic hostesses.

SENEDD/ASSEMBLY BUILDING ✱✱✱
Cardiff Bay
Modernist forum under wooden tent facing bay

The decision to locate the Welsh Assembly on the windswept shore of Cardiff Bay beyond the Wales Millennium Centre was unfortunate. It must play second fiddle to the Centre and turns its back on its city and its country.

The structure itself, designed by Richard Rogers, intends its see-through levity to express 'a core philosophy of openness and transparency'. The effect is achieved by an absence of solid walls. Sheets of glass under an undulating roof straddle the site. This is supported by thin Festival of Britain pillars with struts.

The underside of the roof is the building's forte, made of wood in a thrilling sequence of curved planes. The effect is of tent-like impermanence, as if a group of Bedouin had just arrived and pitched camp on the shore.

The building sits on a slate acropolis approached up a sweeping rake of steps. At the top is a wall of impenetrable glass behind which are ranks of security guards, both mocking the ideal of openness. Beyond the reception area is an internal piazza for seating, meeting and eating, arranged round a large central funnel. This funnel rises to the roof like the trunk of a thick palm tree and reflects the ceiling of the Assembly chamber itself, which is located in the bowels of the building below.

The Assembly is emphatically buried. Visitors to the public gallery look down on the participants through glass windows, as if peering into a goldfish bowl, a strange sensation. The sixty-seat chamber is small and cosy, made mostly of wood. On the floor is a swirling op-art sculpture by Alexander Beleschenko, representing 'the heart of Wales'. The roof is formed from the base of the funnel, here an inverted wooden cone and at this level a bravura creation.

Compared with the City Hall, the Assembly building might be the meeting place of a modest municipal authority. It contains no manifestation of Welsh history or ceremonial, of a nation's achievements or ambitions. But I imagine that, as with all such places, Wales will grow used to it in time.

WALES MILLENNIUM CENTRE ✳✳✳
Cardiff Bay
New palace of culture in Welsh garb

Wales's national opera house turned 'Millennium Centre' was born in controversy and a sense of financial crisis. An international design by Zaha Hadid, a pile of glass sheets shooting off into the sky, failed the test of economy (and perhaps climate) and was superseded by the present structure, designed in 2001 by a Welsh architect, Jonathan Adams. It opened in 2004.

The WMC is ostensibly an ugly duckling. Built to be 'instantly recognizable', it has been likened to an armadillo, a turtle and a slug. If a nation's architecture is primarily a matter of materials, this is Wales. The main structure is coated in dun-coloured steel panels forming a giant carapace (described as of champagne-coloured oxide). This is offset on the sides by various shades of slate and other Welsh stone in the footings, walls and window surrounds. Light is allowed into the building through thick glass blocks interspersed with the slate. Unlike the 'transparent' Assembly building next door, the Centre is emphatically enclosed, inviting visitors to seek warmth and shelter inside.

The old conundrum of how to relate an auditorium to its foyer space is resolved by pushing the latter to both sides, in slate-clad extensions. The entrance is signified by the carapace swooping down to culminate in an extraordinary beetle-brow of giant letters. These spell out the obscure words 'In these stones horizons sing' by the poet Gwyneth Lewis. The Welsh words translate as 'creating truth from inspiration's furnace'. Never can architecture have paid such an obscure compliment to poetry. The façade looms over the entrance doors and foyer, containing reputedly the longest ticket counter anywhere.

The foyers wrap round the auditorium, extending outwards in swirling balconies. Fronted in Welsh hardwood they have considerable presence and towards the bay give access to an atrium of subsidiary chambers, restaurants and shops. The 2,000-seat auditorium is a success, its slate walls an ochre colour, softened by wooden facias to the circles and seating.

CASTELL COCH ✳✳✳✳
Tongwynlais
Fantasy Victorian castle in woods (Cadw)

The site is as romantic as the imagination that exploited it. Where the River Taff shakes off suburban Cardiff and disappears into a forested ravine, rises the Welsh Neuschwanstein, dream castle of Ludwig of Bavaria. On the site of a de Clare fortress, the young 3rd Marquess of Bute in 1875 erected a summer retreat, using the same architect as he employed at Cardiff Castle, William Burges. With the old ruins as his guide, Burges produced a rich variation on his Cardiff masterpiece.

Castell Coch took many years to build and was completed after Burges' death. It was used only briefly and occasionally by the Marquess's family before its contents were moved to Cardiff Castle. A vineyard planted on the slopes survived into the 1920s. (*Punch* declared its wine needed four men to drink, two to hold down the drinker and another to pour it down his throat.) The building was given to the state by the Butes in 1950 and has been well restored, with the original furniture replaced.

The walk up to the castle from the valley below is a wander back through time. Bute and Burges carefully excavated, measured and re-created what they could of de Clare's ruins. Hence the basements are mostly medieval, as is the asymmetrical entrance comprising a gatehouse with working portcullis and drawbridge flanked by two towers. These have conical roofs with Bute weathervanes and cigar-like chimneys. The keep tower on the left, with its slit-eye windows, looks almost comical.

The interior courtyard has too much the image of a Robin Hood film set. Galleries, outside stairs, windows and turrets await Douglas Fairbanks to swoop down, sword in hand. But they are an accurate medieval re-creation and Burges' gothic was never meant to create a facsimile, rather a contemporary castle in the medieval style.

Only one of the four main rooms was completed by Burges in his lifetime, the banqueting hall. It is dominated by a large fireplace

Castell Coch: gothic delight in nature

over which stands St Lucius, reputedly the first Christian king of Britain, with scenes from his life on the wall to the right. Overhead is a finely panelled ceiling.

Beyond is the finest of the castle's chambers, designed by Burges but completed after his death. The drawing room employs gothic as a joyful delight in nature, vibrating with colour, light and shade and with barely an inch undecorated. The fireplace and high vaulted ceiling (which deprived the Marquess of one bedroom) were inspired by the French medieval revivalist Viollet le Duc.

For crockets on the rib vaults, Burges designed butterflies. The spandrels are filled with birds flying in a starry sky. Over the chimneypiece is a gothic screen framing the three ages of man and their respective Greek gods. The walls are painted with murals depicting Aesop's fables (including a monkey with side-whiskers). The roof has a central boss of a radiating sun. As the guidebook exults, this is a celebration of 'earthly creation, with the rich fertility of nature and the fragility of life symbolized by butterflies'.

Bute's bedroom is positioned over the entrance, as if to monitor his visitors. Here the stone walls and bare tiled floor seem austere. The roof is high, with a heavy tie beam and a stove/fireplace that might be that of a Victorian pumping house. Burges' touch is shown in the carvings of animals and birds, in the lightness of the green and in the strange bed, half medieval, half Art Nouveau.

Lady Bute's bedroom rivals the drawing room in magnificence. The circular chamber carries stencilled blind arcading, above which rises a Moorish domed ceiling in gold and green. While the walls are medieval the ceiling is composed of panels, each decorated with flowers and animals in the Arts and Crafts style. It is as if, after Burges' death, his craftsmen felt free to keep abreast of the times.

Monkeys crawl all over the place, playing with squirrels, grasping at grapes, singing the praises of nature. Nothing is left bare, not even the twin 'towers' on the washstand, dispensing hot and cold water. The extraordinary Arabic bed is supposedly a Viollet le Duc design. 'Lady Margaret's bedroom' above is Spartan in comparison.

If there is a sadness to Castell Coch it lies in the purposelessness of the place. Designed with exhilaration and intended for pleasure, it needs to hear music and see hospitality and entertainment, not silent groups of tourists moving quietly round hallowed halls. It cries out for an injection of life.

CYFARTHFA CASTLE *

Merthyr Tydfil
Ironmaster's gothic palace now a museum
(Mus)

The mansion of the Crawshays, kings of industrial Merthyr, stands bold in its park on the flanks of the Taff valley. Visitors must use their imagination to recapture the context in which it was built in 1824–5. William Crawshay's hard, vulgarian father bitterly opposed what he regarded as the extravagant cost of £30,000. 'A great house and an expensive establishment will not fight our battle in trade,' said the old man, probably the richest industrialist in Britain at the time.

His son William was becoming an educated if flamboyant young man. On taking command of the firm he chose, unlike his father, to live in Merthyr in a house of his own creation. It was designed by Richard Lugar in a Regency castellated villa style on a terrace with views up and down the valley and directly opposite the Cyfarthfa works. The factory was based on the valley's astonishing reserves of coal, iron and limestone, aided by fast flowing water. At the time the house was built, this was the largest ironworks in the world, drawing thousands to the relative security of wages which, in Merthyr, tended to be above the Glamorgan average because of the higher skills required for ironworking.

The scene from the terrace at night, according to Crawshay, was 'truly magnificent … resembling the fabled Pandemonium, but upon which the eye may gaze with pleasure and the mind derive high satisfaction, knowing that several thousand persons are there constantly employed and fed by the active spirit, powerful enterprise and noble feeling of the highly respected owner'. To Thomas Carlyle, Cyfarthfa was somewhat different, 'a vision of hell'. Jan Morris later referred to it as 'a colossal detonation of smoke, steam and fire. Tall black chimneys, like etiolated tree-trunks, forcibly eject their smoke into an almost solid mass across the scene.'

Crawshay was to have three wives and fifteen children and they did not enjoy living so close to so much noise and pollution. By the end of the 19th century the family had revolted against any such commitment to their home town and were living in the Home Counties. In 1909 Cyfarthfa was sold to Merthyr Council.

The view from the terrace is now of modern warehouses and patches of suburban housing. The castle has been converted into a museum and gallery, but traces of its residential past remain. The castellated composition is grey and unappealing, especially when compared with such contemporaries as Penrhyn and Gwrych in the north. The most prominent feature is a round tower turning the corner between the formal and service wings.

The entrance gives on to a mock medieval hall (with mock medieval sales desk). To its right are the former reception rooms, now crowded with exhibits but refurnished with wallpaper and curtains and hung with Welsh pictures and sculptures. Those in the morning room include works by Cedric Morris and Kyffin Williams.

The round drawing room has wallpaper by Robert Adam and display cases of Wedgwood. The red drawing room is more eccentric, with a display of Egyptology and a magnificent fireplace.

The dining room concentrates on portraits of the Crawshays and their factories, and an exhibition of Merthyr's continuing cultural treasure, the Cyfarthfa Brass Band.

FONMON CASTLE ***

3 miles west of Barry
Ancestral manor with medieval and
rococo rooms (Priv)

At first view Fonmon is an ugly duckling, mis-shapen, poorly crenellated and covered in streaky grey render. Inside it is quite different, an enjoyable Glamorgan gentry house with a pedigree dating back to the Norman period, kept going against all odds by descendants of its 17th-century owners.

The original fortified tower house was sited on the fertile Barry shore and protected by a steep incline to the east. The hall was on the first floor. Having survived some four centuries, the St Johns found their loyalties divided by the Civil War, a clash vividly displayed in the family mausoleum at Lydiard Tregoze (Wiltshire), with its memorial to the Golden Cavalier. The Fonmon branch, despite siding with Cromwell, sold their Welsh property in 1650 to a Parliamentarian colonel, Philip Jones.

Jones became governor of the South Welsh castles and Cromwell's chief adviser on Wales. He made his peace with Charles II after the Restoration and added a new north wing to Fonmon, with extensive offices and bedrooms. Jones's descendants, now named Boothby, have resided in the castle and cared for it to this day.

The Joneses were Baptists but this was no impediment to their status as Welsh gentry, their sons making the grand tour, collecting Italian landscapes by Pannini and forming a charming group in a painting by Hogarth. They welcomed John Wesley on his visits to Wales in the 1740s. It was then that Wesley suggested to Robert Jones that his son attend the new Methodist school at Kingswood, where a regime of puritanical asceticism was promised. It was not a good idea. Young Jones (also Robert) revolted, ran away from school and lived the life of a Hogarthian rake in London and Bath.

On marrying a girl from Llantwit Major and inheriting the estate, the younger Jones expressed his aversion to his parents' educational taste in a most emphatic way. In 1762 he commissioned the Bristol firm of Thomas Paty to convert the old castle interior into a fashionable 18th-century residence, with plasterwork by Thomas Stocking. Windows were replaced by sashes. A handsome staircase and a gallery with rococo ceilings were created in the range linking the two main wings.

Jones next went to work on the old medieval hall. This was expanded to form a library running from front to back of the house, adorned with the finest rococo plasterwork in Wales. At each end, arches decorated with rosettes frame Venetian windows, one of them looking down on the ravine below. Mirrored girandoles reflect candlelight from the walls. The gilt fireplace surround looks up towards a ceiling that carries rococo devices radiating from a central sun into every corner.

Of a different stamp are the service rooms, including those in the stone-vaulted medieval basement. The 17th-century kitchen has a dresser filled with Jones family pewter. A photograph of a visit to the house by Queen Mary in 1938 shows the grand lady in familiarly severe mood. She is surrounded by Boothbys looking shell-shocked.

LLANCAEACH FAWR ***

Gelli-gaer, 2 miles east of Treharris
Large Tudor mansion with re-enacted
Commonwealth experiences (Mus)

Llancaeach Fawr is a spirited attempt by Rhymni Council to bring an intact Tudor house to life for visitors. It has been restored as it would

Gentry rococo at Fonmon

have been in the time of the Prichard family, 17th-century owners during the Civil War. Edward Prichard was initially a Royalist, charged with raising troops in the king's cause, but as a strong Puritan he changed sides and ended the war as Parliamentary governor of Cardiff Castle.

The present house is staffed by actors pretending to be Prichard's servants. This is no place for those who find 'sire' and 'fare ye well' irritating, let alone for those whose gorge rises on being told that the back staircase is out of bounds on account of 'God bless, but please note the health and safety features.' Sometimes I want to be left to wander through a house in peace, and do my own imagining as to how it might have been.

Llancaeach is transitional medieval/Elizabethan. It was built in the 1530s when the old plan of a side entrance into a screens passage with hall to one side was being replaced by a central door in a lesser receiving hall, with the formal chambers upstairs. Here the door is still to one side, but the principal family rooms are on the first floor, linked by a formal staircase only in 1628.

The archaeology of the house is thus curious. Most of the windows and possibly the porch are later additions and Newman in Pevsner suggests that the Elizabethan house, with its tiny windows and remarkable height, might have been designed so as to be internally defensible. The doors to the family rooms on the first floor are arranged to be heavily barred. The existence of two separate ground-floor kitchens may again be a sign of insecurity. The owner cannot have trusted even his retainers.

The house was restored and furnished in the 1980s with help from St Fagans. The furniture is either original to the period or good reproduction. The surfaces are crowded with pewter, writing implements, hourglasses, guns, pots and pans, in other words with the clutter normal to a house of the period.

The only anachronism is the insertion of a metal staircase to the top storey, another dreaded blow from the health and safety authorities. The house has a knot garden in front and a wild garden to the rear.

MARGAM CASTLE AND ORANGERY ***

Spectacular Victorian mansion on hill with park and celebrated orangery (Mus)

Christopher Rice Mansel Talbot was a larger-than-life Victorian, descendant of the medieval Mansels of Gower (and of the Talbots of Wiltshire) and owner of a Glamorgan estate to rival that of the Butes. He was also a scholar, fellow of the Royal Society, yachtsman, Lord Lieutenant and, for fifty-nine years, Liberal MP. His parliamentary career was distinguished by his never making a speech, except once to ask that a window be closed. Talbot gave his name to the docks at Port Talbot, which he largely rebuilt, and his private steamer was the first to pass through the Suez Canal.

On assuming his inheritance in 1813, Talbot considered his Georgian family seat at Penrice insufficiently grand. He therefore demolished the house at Margam which his family had previously abandoned, and in 1830 commissioned the architect of Penrhyn, Thomas Hopper, to build him something bigger, overlooking the ruins of the old abbey (see below). The view was superb, framed by thickly wooded hills with views over Port Talbot to the Bristol Channel and Somerset beyond.

This new house lasted barely a century. It was stripped by the family and its remaining contents sold with the Margam estate in 1942. Like so many Welsh houses, it was gutted by fire and taken over in 1977 as a roofed ruin by the local council. It has since been rescued as an education centre, its walls reduced to heartbreaking scalded brick but its windows and roofs repaired and intact.

Unlike his Norman at Penrhyn, Hopper gave Talbot Elizabethan at Margam, with a giant central tower and a skyline massed with battlements, chimneys and finials. The façade presents a wall of windows, adorned with every Elizabethan feature in the pattern book. Octagonal turrets have crocketed domes. Windows thrust out into oriels of varying sizes. Gables seem to rise wherever the mood takes them.

The interior, for all its dereliction, retains Hopper's sense of drama, most noticeably in the stairwell. This rises on gothic arches the height of the tower to end in a tall lantern. It would make an admirable hotel, college, house, anything.

The steps in front of Margam Castle descend theatrically to the woods surrounding the old abbey. These were laid out by Mansel Talbot's Georgian predecessor, Thomas, after the latter had left the old house for his new seat at Penrice, near Oxwich on the Gower. He designed the grounds as a free-standing arboretum. The ruins of the old property, such as gateposts and the magnificent renaissance façade of the banqueting house, were left as picturesque features, as was one of the largest Orangeries in Britain.

This structure, 330 feet long, was designed by Anthony Keck in 1780. The building is Palladian in design with a sculpture gallery intended at one end and a library at the other. The façade is articulated by subtle changes to the bays and roofline and by the rustication of the lower half of the wall. Venetian windows complete each end. Surrounded by pines and palm trees the building might be in the French Riviera. Nelson was so impressed by it he gave the custodian the then huge tip of three shillings. The building is today used for concerts.

OLD BEAUPRE CASTLE **

Nr St Hilary, 2 miles south-east of Cowbridge
Ruined mansion with renaissance porch (Priv)

The magic of Beaupre (pronounced Bewper and from the Norman for beautiful retreat) lies partly in its isolation and partly in its rarity. It is a magnificent relic of the Elizabethan renaissance lost in the Welsh countryside. The house is attached to a medieval farm, reached by a half-mile footpath from a lay-by on the A48. The old 14th-century manor is still inhabited, but not the ruinous additions of the mid-16th century, begun by Sir Rice Mansel on his marriage to the heiress to the local Bassett estate. Mansel's daughter by his second wife married another Bassett and took the property with her.

Mansel formed a ceremonial forecourt to the old manorial hall, whose own courtyard remains behind. This is entered through a large fortified gatehouse with graffiti of ships on the walls. The carved date of 1586 apparently relates to Mansel's grandson, Richard Bassett, who in 1600 added the magnificent porch over the hall door on the far side of the court.

This fine work of the Elizabethan renaissance is a complete 'tower of the orders', a classical composition of columns, Corinthian above Ionic above Doric. Coats of arms fill the panels, and the friezes and crowning gable are richly decorated. Historians debate whether the porch may have come in 'kit' form from England. It certainly looks odd next to the rough Welsh chimneybreast besides which it is squeezed, and the ruined medieval hall behind.

Round the courtyard are the ghostly apartments of the Elizabethan house, bleak but still restorable. As if to prove the point, the older buildings of pre-Tudor Beaupre are in use behind, full of the bustle of a modern farm.

OXWICH CASTLE *

Mansel castle-turned-house
overlooking bay (Cadw)

Here is a South Welsh castle that is nothing to do with Normans, Marcher lords or rebellious Welsh. It sits overlooking the sandy and picturesque Oxwich cove where it was built by the ubiquitous Sir Rice Mansel, c.1520. His family had adhered to the Lancastrian cause in the Wars of the Roses, shifting allegiance to the Tudors after Bosworth.

Sir Rice acquired Margam Abbey on the Dissolution and, through his third marriage – to a lady-in-waiting to Mary I – rose to become the royal chancellor of South Wales, with permission to keep a retinue. He died in 1559. He and his son Edward built Oxwich and later converted the dissolved Margam Abbey as a residence (see above).

Oxwich was thus not a fortress but rather, like Old Beaupre and Carew, the stylish house of a Tudor grandee, its gateway fortifications largely for show. Later generations made

Margam their home, and yet later ones Penrice. The house was tenanted and finally used as part of a farm. Mansel's arms crown the entrance, flanked by the initials RM.

The earliest part of the house is the south range, to the right inside the courtyard. This is a traditional hall house with upper great chamber, now roofed and disappointingly devoted to exhibitions. The interior is a clutter of stands and displays.

Opposite the entrance is the ruin of Sir Edward's east range, once a grand structure rising four storeys, or six in the towers and built round the time of his father's death. The house had two pillar staircases, another great hall and a long gallery. It must have been as splendid as Hardwick Old Hall. Certainly it bankrupted Sir Edward.

Today all this glory is recalled only in bare walls, gaping windows, fireplaces and the gaunt ruin of one surviving tower. Outside the house enclosure is the ruin of a massive dovecot.

ST DONAT'S CASTLE **

2 miles west of Llantwit Major
Medieval castle, much restored by
American press tycoon (Priv)

This is, or was, a precious survival of a Glamorgan fortified manor, in continuous family occupation from Norman times well into the 18th century. It is now a school, one of Kurt Hahn's United World Colleges, intermittently accessible but with the exterior visible from the car park.

The castle's most remarkable contents came with its purchase and conversion into a Welsh San Simeon by the American press tycoon William Randolph Hearst, in 1925. This was in honour of the supposed Welsh origins of his mistress, Marion Davies (her real name was Douras, from Brooklyn).

Hearst's mostly medieval imports appear to have involved the destruction of fine houses across Britain, notably Bradenstoke Priory in Wiltshire. His defenders might say he preserved at least their contents. Hearst, or his dealers, had a good eye, though he hardly ever visited the place.

The castle lies on a hillside sloping down to the Bristol Channel with a happy outlook to Exmoor in the distance. The castle has no keep or obvious defensive efficiency. There is an outer wall with a dry moat and gatehouse, behind which rises an inner wall and another gatehouse of Norman origins. There is hardly more than a passageway between the two walls.

Inside is a charming courtyard surrounded by a jumble of late-medieval façades, reminiscent of Berkeley Castle (Gloucs). These carry early renaissance medallions apparently copied from those by Giovanni da Maiano at Hampton Court, whether original or imported from elsewhere is unclear.

To the left of the court is the entrance to the great hall, the fabric of which survives, including apparently some of the roof timbers. Beyond it is mostly Hearst and, as at Berkeley, there is no clear guide as to what is medieval *in situ* and what imported.

The justly named Bradenstoke Hall fills the space between the old hall and the outer curtain wall, its roof and windows from Bradenstoke and its fireplaces from France. Its windows embrace the full view downhill to the Channel. The school dining room is also a spectacular chamber, thanks to a stone screen from a West Country church, a ceiling from Lincolnshire and a chimney from France.

SWANSEA GUILDHALL **

Art Deco civic palace with
Brangwyn murals (Mus)

Swansea in the 19th and 20th centuries was a story of urban flight, largely from pollution emanating from the tinplate works of the lower Tawe valley. The Victorian town processed half the copper in the world and at one point had a larger population than Cardiff. The resulting smoke was dreadful, driving any citizens who could afford it to move westwards along the coast and making a mockery of the town's ambition to be a port and holiday resort on a par with Weymouth.

After the war, the bombing of the docks area and the lack of imagination shown in rebuilding

Tudor dereliction at Oxwich

made any creative urban renewal a labour of Hercules. There is a new 'maritime quarter' round the docks, but few cities feel more like a small town than Swansea. The station might be that of a seaside halt.

The more astonishing is Swansea's guildhall, rebuilt in the breezy western suburbs in the 1930s on a scale appropriate to a great commercial metropolis. Designed by Percy Thomas in 1930, it displays a totalitarian Art Deco more familiar in inter-war Germany or Italy. It is not to every taste. Jan Morris calls it 'as unexciting as a cake that has failed to rise'. Perhaps it is the politics that has failed to rise.

The absence of the façade's intended porticos is a pity, leaving the white Portland exterior relieved only by a prominent tapering clock-tower 160ft high.

The interior, however, is a confident work of inter-war ceremonial architecture. Stairways rise past columns and through arches to the council chamber. Corridors lead right and left, hung with the council's art collection. One corridor leads through the George Hall, with a classical frieze depicting theatrical entertainers through history.

Beyond is the main assembly chamber. It takes its name from the murals by Frank Brangwyn, painted as a Great War memorial for the Royal Gallery in the House of Lords in 1931 but rejected by the peers as too colourful. The rejection, which devastated Brangwyn, was because he had depicted not military heroics but those the war had defended, young people set amid the natural history of the British Empire. His pastel shades of tempera compose seventeen panels of trees and flowers, mountains and rivers, inhabited by a cosmopolitan commonwealth of peoples. It is pacifist rather than militaristic.

The murals had been paid for by the Earl of Iveagh and, since Brangwyn was of Welsh parentage, were donated to the National Museum in Cardiff and to Swansea. Brangwyn was too upset to visit them in Swansea but communicated the hope that 'in years to come a few people will stand in front of my murals at Swansea and say, Hullo, there's a fellow who loved colour and nature'.

WEOBLEY CASTLE **
Fortified manor with views from Gower over bay (Cadw)

Weobley is the most evocative of the castles of the Gower. It had been a fortified residence since the Middle Ages and has few equals for location even among the finely positioned fortresses of South Wales. It sits on a grassy bluff looking north across the Llwchwr estuary to Llanelli and the mountains beyond.

Begun in the early 14th century the castle was rebuilt in the late 15th by Sir Rhys ap Thomas, later passing into the ever-expanding Gower domain of the Mansels. Today the castle is approached from a neighbouring farm with what seems half of South Wales spread out before it.

The exterior is a mix of medieval and 16th-century work, the latter intended to convert what had been a castle into an Elizabethan mansion. Weobley would not have been hard to capture from the landward side and was presumably designed to be defensible against local troublemakers rather than play a part in a major conflict.

There is a pleasant absence of marketing clutter about the entrance, with a simple arch in the wall of the main residential block. Inside, the courtyard is a cosy jumble of façades, as if the components of a fortified manor had been compressed and squeezed upwards. To the left is the two-storey porch of the great hall and solar wing. To the right are service blocks and guest quarters. Almost all lack their roofs but have further views over the estuary.

Churches

CARDIFF
LLANDAFF CATHEDRAL ****
Mix of Norman, Early Gothic and modern, Pre-Raphaelite art

Llandaff is one of Wales's more curious churches, within the boundary of the capital yet apart from it. As a cathedral it lacks the emotional

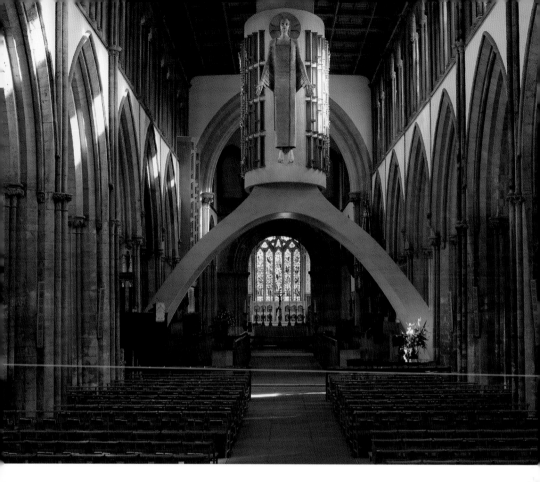

Gothic/modern fusion at Llandaff

punch of St David's, sitting, as it does, humbly at the bottom of a steep slope in a Cardiff suburb, as if it had carelessly fallen over the hillside from its close.

Heavily restored after a bruising history of decay and demolition, its dimensions are those of a large English parish church. But the nave is one the most serene works of Early Gothic in Wales, enhanced by a 20th-century arch and Epstein's *Majestas*. With good Victorian and later furnishings and glass, Llandaff is a satisfying place.

A Norman cathedral was built here in 1120 by Bishop Urban, who acknowledged the supremacy of Canterbury and was eager, as were his successors, to rival the popularity among the Welsh of St David's. Urban's masons were brought from Hereford and Gloucester. Their work survives in a north and south nave doorway and in the chancel arches.

This church was superseded *c.*1200 by an Early Gothic structure of great splendour, embracing the west front, nave and choir. The heavily restored west front exterior comprises three tall lancet windows above a round-arched door, with stepped trefoil arcading. Inside, the lancets become lofty openings with multiple shafts. With the clerestory, they fill the nave with a light more familiar in a Perpendicular interior. The capitals of the nave piers have stiff-leaf carving.

At this point the restoration story takes over. By the mid-18th century Llandaff was near-derelict. One of the two west towers had collapsed, as had the roof of the nave. John Wood of Bath was asked to build a church within a church at the chancel end, which he did in the style of Bath assembly rooms. By 1840 this 'Heathen temple' was more than the local Anglicans could bear and a quarter-century of rebuilding began.

This included a new south-west tower by the Welsh architect John Prichard, follower of Pugin, patron of Seddon and son of a vicar-choral of Llandaff. He was a leading exponent of the gothic revival and much of the character of the cathedral is due to him. Prichard's tower and spire are an Early Gothic response to the original Perpendicular north-west tower. This remains with its pierced and pinnacled crown, reminiscent of a Somerset parish church.

Equally happy was the employment in the 1950s of the ecclesiastical architect George Pace to repair bomb damage which had brought down the nave roof. He designed Llandaff's most instantly recognizable feature, the astonishing paired arches that bridge the nave in bland, cream-coloured concrete, supposedly 'conversing' with the gothic on either side and the Norman chancel arch beyond.

Above these arches rises an oval-shaped organ case, its openings adorned with imported Pre-Raphaelite angels. The west side carries Epstein's *Majestas*, seeming to float free, awesome and powerful, its hands extended towards the congregation. It is not to every taste: Peter Sager calls it 'murder in the cathedral'. Though Epstein in 'neo-romanesque' mode can be stiff and unmoving, this is a fine work, filling the building with a human presence. Its scale dominates the nave as the rood figures would once have dominated a medieval parish church.

In the north-west corner of the nave is the Illtyd Chapel with Rossetti's lovely triptych of the *Seed of David*, brought to Llandaff by Prichard's partner, Seddon. Other Pre-Raphaelites who contributed to the work included William Morris, who painted David's head, and Burne-Jones, who painted the shepherd. Jane Morris was the model for the Virgin. Reviewing the work, the *Ecclesiologist* magazine criticized her 'anxious expression' and 'tangled and dishevelled hair', which today seem charming. In the south aisle is a beautifully hung 15th-century Flemish carving of the Dormition, the falling asleep of the Virgin. Both aisles have Pre-Raphaelite glass.

East of the nave, the cathedral takes on a wholly different character. The stalls and bish-op's throne are by Prichard, as is the arch that frames the view east into the presbytery. Here it confronts the original Norman sanctuary arch with its intricate capitals, zigzag moulding and an outer arch of unusual medallions. A gallery above is suffused with the colour of an east window by John Piper.

The Lady Chapel, dating from the early 13th century, lies beyond the sanctuary arch. It is lit by a Decorated east window, its cream walls covered with early-20th-century stencils, variants on the letter M for Mary. The Perpendicular reredos niches are alive with red and gold patterns of twigs, each holding a flower named in Welsh, an imaginative way of filling niches bereft of statues. The east Jesse window is by Geoffrey Webb in 1951.

The two chapels filling the east end of Llandaff's north and south aisles are dedicated to St Dyfrig and St Teilo. Behind the altar is a glorious set of porcelain panels of the six days of creation, by Burne-Jones with Lizzy Siddal as his model.

Pace supplied the neo-classical pulpit, overlooking an exquisite medieval alabaster tomb of the Matthew family, with sleeping bedesmen under the effigies' feet.

A neo-gothic processional way leads from the north side of the nave past Pace's St David's chapel to the vestries. This chapel is a fine fusion of gothic arches on the west side and modern windows on the east, a serene retreat from a great church.

CARDIFF

ST AUGUSTINE, PENARTH **
Polychrome temple on a hill

Towering over the Cardiff suburb of Penarth was once a medieval church tower that was a beacon to shipping visible far out in the Bristol Channel. This was replaced by William Butterfield in 1865 under the patronage of a member of the Bute family, Baroness Windsor. She clearly sought a spectacular gesture overlooking the family's new docks under construction below on Cardiff Bay.

The outside is uninviting and austere –

Butterfield's exteriors need to be pristine clean – but the interior is a brilliant essay in polychrome stone. Chancel and aisles are compressed, as if to emphasize the height of the nave. The clerestory has a gallery piercing its walls. When fully lit, the place is dazzling.

Butterfield's polychrome technique relies on both colour and material, in this case cream and black brick, and Bath and local pink Radyr stone. These vitalize the piers, arches and walls with an array of bands and lozenges, trefoils and quatrefoils. The banding is particularly effective round the chancel arch.

Here is the climax of the interior, with Butterfield's reredos in white, green, red and black marble, beneath a stained-glass window by Alexander Gibbs.

CARDIFF

ST GERMAN *
Metal Street
Bodley grace and colour in a
Cardiff backstreet

Cardiff has many Victorian churches but almost all are locked. Here in the old dockland district of Splott is a masterpiece by the firm of Bodley and Garner. Like St Bartholomew, Brighton, the church evangelical towers over the surrounding working-class streets, the long ridge of the nave roof relieved by a simple flèche.

The outside offers little sense of the brooding interior. Completed in 1884 it was described by the critic Goodhart-Rendel as 'a greyhound church, strong, lithe and thin', displaying Bodley's genius at making a spectacle from a small space. The proportions are Perpendicular, almost a Dutch hall church. There is no nave clerestory, allowing the aisles to float high and the chancel arch wide, almost uniting nave and chancel in one. The thin shafts of the nave bays and the soaring window tracery point relentlessly upwards. A remarkable rood beam high over the chancel opening carries Bodley's lofty organ case.

St German is a church of colour as well as space. The nave ceiling is predominantly red and the chancel green. Both are stencilled. The folding panels of the reredos, another Bodley speciality, are turquoise. The east window is by Burlison and Grylls and a small Kempe window is in the north chapel.

CARDIFF

ST JOHN BAPTIST **
Town church with decorative tower
and Herbert monuments

St John Baptist is a curiosity. Down a side street in the commercial centre of Cardiff we might be in England, say Taunton. The Somerset-style church tower is of three stages, with a Perpendicular west window and a crown richly fashioned as if dropped from elsewhere. The battlements are pierced and each corner carries an octagonal pinnacle composed of a forest of lesser ones. It forms an rare jewel on the Cardiff skyline.

The entrance through the west door is into a typical civic church, with double aisles (added by the Victorians), ceremonial monuments, banners and emblems of parochial activity. The nave is of five bays with a pink wagon roof and coloured bosses.

The heavily screened chancel has a more involved ceiling of angels and stars. In the chancel are the remains of what appears to be a much earlier building of c.1300, visible in the south arcade. The reredos in this arcade is by Comper in memory of Lord Kitchener. What could be more English than that?

There is an enjoyable busy-ness to St John Baptist, despite a 1975 vestry by George Pace which intrudes on the spaciousness of the south aisle. The north chapel contains monuments to the early Herberts, who bequeathed to the marquesses of Bute their stupefyingly rich Glamorgan properties (see Cardiff Castle). One monument has a magnificent coloured cushion. A heraldic window records the Bute connection.

St John's glass has the usual variety of a town church, some good, some bad. The east window is by Comper, of Christ without a beard. The north aisle has works by Morris, Madox Brown and Burne-Jones.

CHERITON

2 miles west of Llanrhidian, Gower
ST CATWG ✶✶
Decorated mouldings in sylvan clearing

Nowhere does Gower seem more Arcadian than round Cheriton. The tumbling hills conceal a glade whose winding lane reveals an old church of crumbling limestone hidden among trees. The senses are overwhelmed with wild flowers and birdsong.

Cheriton is a rarity in Wales, a cruciform church mostly in the Decorated style of the early 13th century. The central tower is massive, as if intended for defence. The walls are equally robust, windowless on the north side and with only lancets on the south. The doorway is remarkable, roll-mouldings adorned with stiff-leaf carving, thought to be by carvers from Llandaff (and thus from England). Similar decoration adorns the crossing arches, one capital being a human face. Both nave and chancel have painted wagon roofs, with bosses added by the vicar in the 1870s.

Clearly someone has been looking after Cheriton. The east and west windows are modern works inserted by Celtic Studios in 1971. Two slate memorials hang behind a strangely broken font. In the churchyard is the grave of Ernest Jones, devoted acolyte and biographer of Sigmund Freud. There cannot be much call for his profession in this idyllic spot.

EWENNI PRIORY ✶✶✶

1 mile south of Bridgend
Atmospheric Norman interior celebrated by Turner

Ewenni is lost down a track beyond a farm, as if awaiting the return of the Celtic missionaries who brought it into being, or the Normans who built and fortified it against the marauding Welsh. The dedication to St Michael and the number of Celtic crosses built into the walls suggest a much earlier church, possibly an outpost of Llantwit Major.

The present priory church, begun between 1116 and 1126, is a Norman Benedictine foundation probably inspired by Bishop Urban of Llandaff, first Welsh bishop to swear allegiance to Canterbury. It appears to have declined by the 15th century and passed to Edward Carne on the Dissolution, when just three monks remained. Carne converted the monastic buildings into a house for himself and his descendants, the Turbervills, who occupy the property today. Remains of the priory survive in the adjacent farm.

Ewenni is best known as the subject of an atmospheric Turner watercolour, showing the transept and chancel with the sun piercing the gloom. The north and west sides of the church had by then collapsed and total ruin was forestalled only by a late-Victorian reconstruction of most of the nave.

In 2004 a glass screen was inserted above the old pulpitum wall between nave and chancel. While this makes the nave more intimate, it destroys the spatial integrity of the interior and does so not with stone, as in the old monastic church, but with an unsympathetic modern material, glass. The screen was designed by Alexander Beleschenko (who also did the floor of the Assembly building, see above) and depicts a cross surrounded by a rare local species of butterfly.

The nave is supported by four Norman pillars with scalloped capitals. These giant drums are crowned by rudimentary moulded arches and deep clerestory windows, all heavy and impressive. The presbytery is bare but the south transept carries much Norman decoration, mostly zigzag and chevron, with windows and arcades answering to the plan of the monastery buildings beyond. A gallery allowed sick monks to see the services below.

On the floor lies a fine 13th-century tomb slab composed of foliage surrounding a clear-cut inscription in French, dedicated to the reputed founder of the monastery, Maurice de Londres. Other memorials are to the Carne and Turbervill families, one a lovely baroque plaque to Richard Carne of 1713.

A Tudor oak screen guards the presbytery, its roof so low-slung as seeming about to collapse. Two bays of barrel vault and one of ribs

Benedictine grandeur at Ewenni

are apparently copies of ones at Gloucester, to which Ewenni once belonged. The space has a closet-like calm, lit with deep-set Norman windows.

Round the east wall are the remains of wall-paintings, relics of the colour and narrative vitality of these interiors when built. Today's limewash is familiar but insipid.

LLANTWIT MAJOR

ST ILLTUD ✱✱✱
Earliest Welsh monastic remains, Celtic crosses, Norman carvings and Jesse niche

The history of Celtic Christianity is bringing Llantwit Major ever more to centre-stage. The inhabitants of a substantial Roman villa appear to have been buried in a Christian fashion and here, possibly within living memory of the Roman retreat, emerges one of the first recognizable figures of British Christianity, St Illtud.

Illtud was probably a Breton, ordained by Germanus of Auxerre c.445 and known to have been at Llantwit c.500. By the seventh century the anonymous biographer of his pupil, Samson, regarded him as the leading scholar of the early Church, 'renowned master of the Britons, learned in the teachings of the Church, in the culture of the Latins and in the traditions of his own people'.

It was from Illtud's monastery at Llantwit that Samson set out in c.520 on his mission to Brittany, as did Paul Aurelian for Cornwall and Gildas for Ireland. Archaeological remains have been found here from as far as Bordeaux and the Mediterranean – there are even palm trees in the churchyard.

Scholars conclude there is no need to posit an Irish-Christian evangelical 'reconquest' of Britain in the 6th century. The Romano-Christian tradition lived on at least in this part of south-east Wales. To John Davies, Llantwit 'can be considered the axis of the Christianity of the Celtic speaking peoples'. It appears to have prospered from the early 7th to the late 9th century, but was almost wiped out by Norse raiders in the 10th, and declined with the subsequent

rise of Norman Llandaff. *The Guinness Book of Records* is in no doubt, recording Llantwit as Britain's earliest university.

Despite its decline, the old Celtic church was rebuilt by the Normans in c.1100, and in the 13th century was extended eastwards for a monastery with a new nave and chancel. The old Norman nave was partly rebuilt as a parish church, while the newer 13th-century end was for monastic use.

After the Reformation this arrangement was reversed, so that by the time Wesley preached here in 1777 the west end was ruinous. He supposed 'it has been abundantly the most beautiful as well as the most spacious church in Wales'. A century later a guidebook has a visitor relating, 'A thrill of horror passes through the visitor as he enters the western portion or old church … a sepulchre, a charnel, the floor unpaved, in the midst are graves … a gruesome place indeed.'

Little of this atmosphere survives, apart from the Celtic crosses casually littering the western building, now filled with Sunday-school clutter. The crosses are mostly of the 9th and 10th centuries and include the celebrated Houelt stone, a disc-headed cross covered front and back with intricate interlacing. It is inscribed for a known historical figure: 'This cross Houelt prepared for the soul of Res his father.' The reference is apparently to Hywel ap Rhys, king of Glywysing (roughly Glamorgan) in the 9th century.

Among various unmarked tombs in this oddly informal chamber is an Elizabethan effigy of a lady, richly dressed and lying in prayer. Of the former romanesque nave only a round-headed south arch inside the porch survives.

The main church now in use is, as Wesley saw, the 'new' east end, beginning with crossing arches decorated with trumpet and stiff-leaf capitals, marking the transition from romanesque to gothic at the turn of the 13th century.

The nave is stark. Its plastered and whitewashed arches are pointed but devoid of adornment, apart from revealed patches of mural on the nave walls and over the chancel arch. The effect is of a canvas left unfinished. A large rood beam and crucifixion were inserted in the 1950s.

The church has two remarkable gothic

Celtic crosses at Llantwit Major

remains. One is the reredos, an ambitious Decorated work of the mid-14th century extending across the east wall, with greater and lesser image niches under ogee canopies. The sculptures have gone, though one of the Virgin and Child was later found and stands in a south window.

The Lady Chapel has a separate image niche, known as the Jesse niche. This most unusual relic has the tree rising from Jesse's groin along the base and then dividing to enclose the sides of a trefoil arch above. It is a delightful work.

MAESTEG

BETHANIA BAPTIST CHAPEL *
Celebrated Nonconformist chapel

Maesteg chapel represents the climax of the great era of Welsh chapel-building and is being rescued from near-dereliction by the Welsh Religious Buildings Trust. Dating from 1906 it demonstrates the baroque revival confidence of the later chapel architects – in this case William Beddoe Rees – happily borrowing stylistic motifs wherever they found them.

The façade is a five-bay classical composition. The centre is composed of a screen of attached columns, with round windows below and a semi-circular window above, all held together by a bold pediment with urns and four graceful pilasters. The whole is in two tones of stone.

The interior is in the form familiar to late-Victorian chapels, vaguely related to Wren's St James, Piccadilly. It contains a panelled gallery supported on columns of cast iron. Further ironwork, some of it in the form of pierced panels, fronts the seats of the elders and the centrally placed pulpit. Above this rises the great organ, its pipes curving upwards in response to the downward curve of the arch behind. The composition appears hierarchical for a Dissenter chapel. The windows contain Art Nouveau glass.

The baptismal pool was housed in front of the elders' seats. Bethania still boasted 400 members in the 1940s and the Sunday school registered 100.

MARGAM ABBEY ***

4 miles south-east of Port Talbot
Norman abbey church, Talbot monuments, Celtic crosses

Margam is rich in architectural variety. The first Norman lord of Glamorgan, Robert of Gloucester, invited the Cistercians in 1147 to found a monastery on what was probably an established place of Celtic worship, and thus colonize the plain between the Brecon Beacons and the sea.

This abbey was extended in the early gothic period by Abbot Gilbert. It included a chapter house, which is all that survives of the monastery today, a lovely gothic chamber distantly recalling the chapter house at Wells. After the Dissolution, the property passed to the Mansel family, who later married the Talbots of Lacock Abbey in Wiltshire and prospered from adjacent Port Talbot. The family converted the abbey into a house, let it decay, then built and let decay a Georgian house, of which only a banqueting house façade and orangery remain (see Margam Castle above).

Meanwhile the abbey church became parochial, with complaints as to its dereliction from parishioners throughout the 18th and 19th centuries. Then in 1872, Theodore Mansel Talbot, an ardent Tractarian, took the church in hand and turned it into a centre of High Church worship. To him we owe excellent windows by Burne-Jones and James Powell.

The church today is the nave of the Norman abbey, once longer than Tintern. The west front exterior, with original round-arched windows, looks Tuscan thanks to the addition of Victorian side turrets, replacing a former central one. Inside is a spectacular six-bay nave arcade with Norman capitals, described by Newman in Pevsner as 'more eloquent of the original austere Cistercian ideal than anywhere else in Britain'. So assiduous was the Victorian restoration that old and new carvings are hard to distinguish, except by their sharpness.

Theodore's Tractarian influence is noticeable in the chancel, a remarkable Victorian collection composed of choir stalls, pulpit, wrought-iron gates, altar steps and screen. The east and

Morriston: 'cathedral' of Nonconformity

west windows are by Burne-Jones, who wrote of them that the work was so priceless that 'I make no charge for the genius displayed in this work, but for the trouble … £15.'

Margam's treasures are the Mansel chapel monuments, rivalling the Herbert tombs in Ab-

ergavenny as a family record in stone. Alabaster chests recall the family at the time of the Dissolution in Tudor dress. By the time of Sir Lewis Mansel (d. 1638) the effigies are still recumbent in prayer but classical motifs have supplanted medieval weepers round the base. This work was reputedly by the royal carver, Maximilian Colt. Barely accessible in the north chapel is a lavish Victorian monument to Theodore himself. He died prematurely while foxhunting in 1876 and is commemorated beneath a vaulted chest tomb copied from a 13th-century bishop's tomb in York Minster.

The Margam crosses are displayed in an old schoolhouse across the churchyard. It is the largest collection in Wales but has been stripped of atmosphere by being set in an aggressive 1990s context of modern steel and glass. I prefer Jan Morris's earlier glimpse of the stones through the window, 'among the shadows, through the dancing filigree of the leaves, immensely holy and enormously old. They are an age petrified … princes and saints themselves turned to granite and limestone.'

The collection dates from the 6th to the 11th century and was gathered by the Mansel Talbots in the 19th century. It includes the imposing Conbelin Stone of the late 9th century, among the first in the British Isles to depict St John and the Virgin supporting Christ on the cross. It is one of the most impressive relics of Celtic Britain, with hunting scenes carved round its base.

MORRISTON

2 miles north of Swansea
TABERNACL *
'Cathedral' of Nonconformity

In an otherwise unremarkable suburb of Swansea stands the proclaimed 'cathedral' of Welsh Nonconformity, Morriston's Tabernacl Congregational Chapel of 1872. It replaced earlier chapels built successively in 1796, 1831 and 1857 as the tinplate industry expanded. The chapel acquired the functions of local welfare state and education charity. The patron and financer was the Swansea entrepreneur Daniel Edwards, and the designer was a local builder, John Humphreys, who toured the country looking for designs. Cost was no object.

The chapel soars over the humble streets of Morriston, a lofty steeple, gothic in character, hugged close to a classical temple. All the arches are rounded, the paired columns of the portico Corinthian and the windows tall and slender, some of them neo-romanesque with plate tracery. The composition obeys no stylistic rule and is robustly vernacular.

The chapel is normally inaccessible – even the courtyard gates are padlocked. The interior is unaltered and retains its amphitheatre of gallery seating, grand pulpit and massive organ. Morriston remains in use and is celebrated for its choir singing.

NEATH ABBEY *

Ghostly remains with ghostly house next door

This is a sad spot. Surrounded by semi-industrial suburbs and deadened by the hand of official conservation, Neath Abbey yearns for a dash of Victorian reconstruction to jolt it to life.

The Cistercians' foundation shared with Margam a strategic role on the coastal plain of Glamorgan and became one of the order's richest houses in Wales. At the Dissolution the abbey was still considered by Leland 'the fairest in all Wales'. The buildings were partly converted by Sir Philip Hoby into a mansion, but the site was blighted by Neath's industrial prosperity, which began as early as the 17th century with the extraction of coal, copper and lead.

The abbey ruins have been stabilized in old Ministry of Works style, with bleak puddles of stone set in lawns delineating the ground plan of the church and monastic quarters. The two buttresses of the west front rise as gaunt evidence of past magnificence. The surviving undercroft is a serene space, a forest of piers and rib vaulting. A carved boss of Christ in majesty survives, deeply undercut.

Adjacent to the dormitory is the no less ghostly shell of the 16th-century mansion, built by Hoby in the ruins and from the stones of the abbey. High walls, gaping windows, exposed stairs and fireplaces remain. Some are boarded over, as if the rooms inside await reuse and nobody has a clue what to do with them.

Gwent

No Welsh county has so ugly a coast and so blessed an interior. Gwent was a 6th-century kingdom adjacent to Morgannwg, but as 'gateway to Wales' it was always vulnerable to invasion. There are Roman villas aplenty and the military base at Caerleon is still visible, with a barracks and amphitheatre in a municipal park. Gwent was swiftly subdued by the Normans, with the great castle, the first in Wales to be of stone, begun at Chepstow within a year of the battle of Hastings. It still looms over the mouth of the Wye.

The Normans built twenty-five castles in Gwent alone. They and their successors form a fine collection: White for isolation, Raglan for pomp, Caldicot for size and Usk for endearing ruination. With the castles came monasteries and churches. Extensive Norman work survives at Chepstow, Grosmont and Usk, spectacularly so in the carvings at Newport Cathedral. Benedictines and Cistercians colonized Abergavenny, Llanthony and Tintern, their deeds and misdeeds recorded by Gerald of Wales at the end of the 12th century. Later gothic is well represented at Tintern and Trelech. The foothills of the Beacons offer a setting for the delightful churches of Cwmyoy and Penallt.

The county was anglicized by Henry VIII as Monmouthshire and not 'returned' to Wales until 1974. Its medieval churches, however modest, were mostly rebuilt under the Tudor ascendancy, with numerous screens and lofts, including the most complete set in Britain at Betws Newydd. Elizabethan and Jacobean manors survive at Llanvihangel Court and Treowen and the Restoration is splendidly represented at the Morgan mansion of Tredegar, recently restored to its full glory.

The Picturesque movement fell in love with the Gwent hinterland, notably the valley of the Wye. This is represented by two follies, at the Kymin and at Clytha, set in attractive parks. The Victorian mural decoration of Llanfair Cilgedin is an unobtrusive gem.

Houses and Castles

Caerleon Roman Fortress *	Llanvihangel Court ***	Tredegar House ****
Caldicot Castle ***	Monmouth:	Treowen **
Chepstow Castle ****	the Kymin *	Usk Castle **
Clytha Castle *	Shire Hall *	White Castle ***
	Raglan Castle ****	

Churches

Abergavenny:	Grosmont ✱✱	Penallt ✱✱
St Mary ✱✱✱	Llanfair Cilgedin ✱✱	Skenfrith ✱
Our Lady and St	Llan-gwm Uchaf ✱✱	Tintern Abbey ✱✱✱
Michael ✱	Llangybi ✱	Trelech ✱
Betws Newydd ✱✱	Llanthony Priory ✱	Usk ✱✱✱
Chepstow ✱✱✱	Llantilio Crossenny ✱✱	
Cwmyoy ✱✱✱	Newport Cathedral ✱✱✱✱	

Houses and Castles

CAERLEON ROMAN FORTRESS *

Fragmentary remains of great
Roman fortress (Mus)

The extensive legionary fortress at Caerleon lays claim to being one of the largest and most important surviving Roman military sites in Britain. The fortress of Isca was capital of Roman Wales, constructed in the 1st century AD on the banks of the Usk. It consisted of a barracks round a central headquarters, hospital and bath house.

Outside its walls was and still is an amphitheatre, the best preserved in Britain in layout but with over-neat refashioned footings. The fort remained occupied for 250 years, an imperial longevity that makes the outposts of the British empire seem transient.

While the walls of Caer-went to the east are more impressive, those at Caerleon are more complete. That is about all that can be said of them. The footings of the barracks, centurion's house and baths are sandwiched between a playing field and a housing estate.

The bath house in the centre of the village has been excavated, partly restored to ground level and then covered in a giant shed with viewing gantries. Visible are the bases of the outdoor swimming pool, changing room and cold room, together with fragments of the under-floor heating system. A mosaic fragment is displayed on a wall.

This is all pretty miserable. Such ruins should either be left in the ground stabilized and open to the skies as before, or they should be rebuilt along lines known from similar sites elsewhere. The public should be able to enjoy the ruins of time or shown what a working Roman bath looked like. I see no good reason for not doing the latter.

What we are given instead is a 20th-century warehouse with shopping and education

BELOW: *Caldicot: adaptable medieval*   OVER: *Chepstow Castle: symbol of Norman supremacy*

paraphernalia erected on top of a heavily restored ruin. Museologists hate rebuilding old buildings but have no compunction in smothering them with their own work.

CALDICOT CASTLE ***

Large open-plan fortress with Victorian 'improvements' set in park (Mus)

Caldicot is a tremendous castle but little appreciated. Though its extensive park remains intact, it sits in the ugly Gwent coastal strip, neither city nor suburb. Finding it requires an act of will.

The reason for Caldicot's good condition is that it was bought and restored in 1884 by the antiquary J. R. Cobb, who also restored Pembroke and Manorbier. It passed to the county council in 1963.

Approached through thick trees, the castle from the outside looks like a film set. It was begun on a site of a Norman motte by the Bohuns, one of the three earliest Marcher families, and extended to its present size in the 14th century.

The keep, crowning the north-west of the inner bailey, is similar to those built by William Marshal at Usk and Pembroke, its masonry excellently laid. The sequence of gatehouse, keep and the late-14th century Woodstock tower (named after a later owner, Thomas of Woodstock, Duke of Gloucester) contributes to one of the most impressive circumambulations of any castle in Wales.

The inner bailey is landscaped and three of the towers and some later outbuildings are in residential use. Creeper climbs up the walls and vegetation spills over the intact battlements. Ghostly fireplaces set into the bailey walls indicate residential structures now vanished. Why not replace them?

The interiors are much as Cobb left them. The keep is in excellent condition, with domestic rooms, fireplaces and even a latrine tower. Cobb converted the gatehouse with its upper hall into a house and this is now used for entertainments, weddings and banquets. The central bailey is open for jousts. Flowers and trees are everywhere.

CHEPSTOW CASTLE ****

Greatest of Wales's Norman fortresses, with work of all periods crowning the mouth of the Wye (Cadw)

The castle is the glory of medieval south Wales, overlooking the final bend in the River Wye as it joins the Severn. It was the first of the fortresses built by the Normans to contain the Welsh, begun within a year of the battle of Hastings. Today it has lost much of its menace and spreads itself along a limestone cliff like a sleek cat resting in the sun.

Chepstow's walls, keep and gatehouse, its four baileys and great hall are everything a model castle should be. If it suffers from over-scraping – compared with Turner's romantic depiction in 1793 – there is a delightful whisper of wallflower and rosebay willow-herb on the battlements. The view from the bastions over the river is placid and sylvan.

Chepstow and the Saxon earldom of Hereford were awarded by the Conqueror to his most loyal follower, William FitzOsbern, partly in return for his fealty and partly to guard against 'the bellicose Welsh'. Begun in 1067 the square keep was one of the first stone castles in Britain, one of a line of defences (initially of earth and wood) along Offa's Dyke and including Monmouth, Hereford and Ludlow. FitzOsbern died within a decade and his son forfeited his inheritance through treachery.

The land and castle passed in c.1115 to another Marcher grandee, Walter de Clare, and later by marriage to the glamorous William Marshal. This 'flower of chivalry', soldier, jouster and Jerusalem pilgrim was premier courtier to Henry II and Eleanor of Aquitaine. He later negotiated the Magna Carta for King John and was regent of England during the minority of Henry III. He died in 1219, lord of Pembroke and Usk as well as Chepstow. His prominence in Welsh history is a measure of the threat Wales posed to the Normans.

Marshal's descendants held the castle through the 13th century, converting it from a tower on a cliff to the castle we see today. The grandest, Roger Bigod, Earl of Norfolk and Earl Marshal of England, appears to have made it his principal residence, doubling the size of the Norman tower and creating an extensive early medieval palace in the lower bailey. By the time of the Tudors, Chepstow had joined Raglan in the domain of the Earls of Pembroke and Worcester, eventually Dukes of Beaufort.

Only with the Tudor accession did these mighty castles decline, briefly returning to life during the Civil War. Even as a ruin Chepstow retained its magnificence into the 18th century, and with the celebration of the Wye as a tourist destination under the Regency, it was seen as the embodiment of romantic Wales. It was the first castle to be used as a film set, for *Ivanhoe* in 1913.

The approach is up a steep lawn above which rise the massive 13th-century Marten's Tower on the left and Marshal's Norman gatehouse. Together with their adjoining walls they form as imposing a composition as any in Britain. Immediately inside the gatehouse are Roger Bigod's later domestic buildings, including chambers for his knights and servants, the great kitchen range and the gloriette, or private wing, with dining hall and views over the Wye valley. This is in a good state of preservation in part because it was still inhabited into the 19th century. I am mystified as to why this admirable tradition cannot be continued as it is at Caldicot.

The interior of Chepstow continues with three further baileys or courtyards, each with a distinctive character and purpose. The middle bailey leads uphill to the original Norman hall or Great Tower. This was almost certainly intended as William the Conqueror's base in south Wales, even if he did not use it. There is a Norman arch and some wall-paintings, said to be the earliest domestic decoration in Britain. The upper part was rebuilt by Marshal and then by Bigod. Some of Marshal's gothic vaulting survives and is of high quality.

Beyond these domestic quarters the castle becomes a rambling series of walls, openings and obscure footings. The walls offer exhilarating walks with views towards both the town and the river.

CLYTHA CASTLE *

3 miles west of Raglan
Folly in picturesque setting on a hill (Priv)

Clytha is an artful landscape of the sort that once abounded in Wales, mostly reduced to such ghosts as Hafod (Dyfed) and Gwrych (Clwyd). As we pass up the Usk valley along the eastern flank of the Black Mountains, the landscape briefly mellows. Slopes, trees and meadows appear to come to order as if in response to the hand of man, which is what has indeed happened.

In 1790 a local landowner, William Jones, decided to commemorate his beloved but departed wife, Elizabeth, with a gothick folly on a prominent hill a mile from his seat at Clytha Park. It was to be a banqueting house dedicated, says a plaque on the exterior, to 'the purpose of relieving a mind afflicted by the loss of a most excellent wife'.

That consolation is spectacular. Castellated turrets start up from the trees (of which there are now too many) as from a fairy castle. The building is formed as two sides of a sham castle, plastered with a pink wash, with two fake towers and one inhabited. These are linked by a swooping concave parapet.

The whole is embattled and studded with arrow slits, overstated but presumably designed to be seen from a distance. It was this that caused John Loudon, historian of the Picturesque, to dismiss Clytha as 'gaudy and affectedly common'.

Guests would have enjoyed magnificent views across the valley to the Skirrid and Sugar Loaf mountains. Though the house belongs to the Landmark Trust (and can be rented) it is accessible from the surrounding National Trust parkland.

Jones's heir, also William, converted Clytha Park in the 1820s into an anything-but-gothick Greek revival house, designed by Edward Haycock of Shrewsbury.

This is visible from the main road through a jolly arch. Its Bath stone Doric portico displays a stern austerity, contrasting with the castle on the hill.

LLANVIHANGEL COURT ***

Llanfihangel Crucornau,
4 miles north of Abergavenny
Ancient Tudor house in beautiful setting
with original stables (Priv)

This is a heart-warming place, a well-restored
Elizabethan/Jacobean mansion safe in private
hands and accessible to public view. The old
stone façade of six spacious bays gazes across
the sweeping valley of the Monnow towards
the English border, backed by the slopes of the
Black Mountains. A painting depicts the house
in the 17th century with formal avenues of trees
radiating from its terraces and the Skirrid depicted as a Welsh Table Mountain. The present
owner, Julia Johnson, is replanting the avenue
with Scots pines.

The entrance front is that of a Tudor mansion built in 1559 by Rhys Morgan, a son-in-law
of the mighty Herbert family. The house was
'modernized' when it was sold, first to the Earl
of Worcester and then to Nicholas Arnold in
1627. It was then altered to give its façade a classical symmetry. A flight of steps leads from the
terrace to a relocated central doorway, behind
which the screens passage was removed and the
old great hall turned into an entrance hall. A rear
extension and new staircase were added.

The Arnolds were fierce and intolerant Prot-
estants and their fortunes ebbed and flowed with
the religious feuds of their times, eventually ebbing. The house passed through various (mostly
English) hands until bought in 1945 by Somerset
Hopkinson, a descendant of the earlier owners,
the Earls of Worcester. His descendants own it
to this day. They have removed much Edwardian fenestration, including a giant oriel window,
reinstating the original Jacobean appearance.

The interior is remarkably of a piece, that
of a 17th-century manorial residence in which
original and restored features are in harmony.
Whether the ceiling plasterwork in the hall is
old or a replica, or the beams, or the panelling,
or the dresser, seems immaterial. Ghosts of the
medieval house linger in such features as the
step of the old hall dais and the holly and ebony
frieze in the morning room.

The staircase, entirely of yew, rises through
the entire house to the attic and is so grand it
might have been imported from elsewhere.
Hound gates guard the upstairs rooms from
animal intrusion. Modern stained glass depicts
supposed visits to Llanvihangel by Elizabeth I
and Charles I.

The stair landing gives access to what would
have been the old great chamber above the
hall. Its splendid doorcase reflects this status.
The chamber is now the Queen's Room, from
Elizabeth's putative presence. The plaster ceiling
is of intertwined Tudor roses and fleurs-de-lis.
Opposite is the King's Room (for Charles). All
chambers are richly beamed and some contain
linenfold panelling. In the kitchen is a charcoal
precursor of an Aga dated 1679.

Llanvihangel still has stables built by the
Arnolds for their breeding horses. They retain
their original 17th-century stalls with handsome turned posts. Such survivals are rare
in England (see Little Peover, Cheshire) but
unique in Wales.

MONMOUTH

THE KYMIN *
1 mile east of Monmouth
Picnic folly in Wye valley (NT)

To Jan Morris the Kymin, overlooking Monmouth and the Wye valley, is a re-enactment of
an Indian hill station. Here as if in Simla, 'delec-
tably encouched in their gardens, the little villas lie, trellised, rose-embowered, with lazy fat
Labradors lying on their verandahs, reached by
nooky lanes'. The hill is owned by the National
Trust.

In July 1802 Lord Nelson came on a visit to
the increasingly fashionable Wye with Lady
Hamilton and her long-suffering husband. They
rode in a coach up the Kymin hill, where Nelson admired the small temple erected two years
earlier to British naval victories over the French
and others. He was delighted to see his name
included among earlier admirals. The visitors
returned to the town on foot and were given a
banquet, at which Lady Hamilton sang 'Rule,
Britannia'.

Gwent picturesque: Clytha Castle

Next to the temple is a Regency banqueting house, in effect a tower, built in 1794, round, rendered and with pretty windows and battlements. There is a dining room above and kitchen below. Though built for the 'Kymin club', gentlemen of Monmouth, to enjoy 'a cold collation and a dessert of fruits with wine and other liquors to a certain limitation', it was also open to the public. The charge was 6d. to the housekeeper if you brought your own food and a shilling if you wished her to serve tea.

The tower offers views over the Wye valley to the Brecon Beacons, but for some reason the Trust has allowed too many trees to obscure the full vista. There is a croquet set in the pavilion for use on the lawn below.

SHIRE HALL *
Agincourt square (Priv)

The centre of Monmouth still evokes an English Georgian town, heir to an earlier Norman colonial settlement. It sits on a hill at the confluence of the Wye and Monnow, with the church, castle and market square crowning Monnow Street, running down to Monnow Bridge with its ancient gatehouse. The effect is partly spoiled by the A40 dividing the town from the river and infesting it with car parks.

At the top of Monnow Street is Agincourt Square, named after Henry V, who was born in the castle in 1387 and whose statue (erected in 1792) adorns its façade. The shire hall was built in 1724 and is an exceptional Georgian building of an unusual six bays with a pediment over the middle two and paired pilasters at each end. Tall windows grace the façade with an open arcade beneath for the market.

Inside is a tour de force. The staircase doubles back on itself twice to arrive at a Doric screen at the top, supporting the lantern. On the first floor is the late-Georgian courtroom, still with its furniture and the magistrate's seat under a pediment. Outside in the market is a monument to Charles Stuart Rolls (d. 1910), co-founder of Rolls Royce, by Goscombe John. He is incongruously holding an aeroplane, of which he was also a pioneer. He was the first Briton to die in a plane accident.

RAGLAN CASTLE ****
Ostentatious late-medieval castle with moated great tower (Cadw)

Raglan ranks with Chepstow as a majestic fortress of the southern Marches, yet it is an oddity among Welsh castles. It dates neither from the Norman era nor from the rebellions of the Llywelyns or Glyndŵr. It was built later in the mid-15th century when Wales was more or less at peace, and by a Welsh adventurer, Sir William ap Thomas, the 'blue knight of Gwent'. He founded the great Welsh dynasty of the Herberts and lies in effigy in Abergavenny church with his wife, Gwladus. He had done well fighting the French and returned to build himself a Welsh Bodiam (Sussex), a castle as much for show as for defence.

William began the great tower on the model of a French citadel in 1434. Building continued under his son, who became 1st Earl of Pembroke, halting briefly with Pembroke's beheading as a Yorkist in 1469 during the brief Lancastrian revival. Work continued under successive members of that family. Raglan then passed by marriage in 1508 to the ubiquitous Somersets, Earls of Worcester and cousins of Henry Tudor. They converted the domestic ranges into a full Tudor palace, as at Carew and Laugharne.

A feature of the Tudor ascendancy in Wales is that its leading figures had shared exile with Henry Tudor on the Continent, returning after Bosworth in 1485 steeped in the culture of Europe's most developed renaissance courts in Burgundy and the Low Countries. A similar injection of French and Dutch taste occurred with the return of the Stuarts after the Commonwealth in the 1660s. Wales was never a closed civilization.

In its prime in the early 16th century, Raglan was one of the great renaissance houses of Britain. Its approach, through a gate flanked by prominent hexagonal towers, was apparently modelled on the Duke of Orleans' chateau at Aisne. The great hall and ceremonial chambers were adorned with tapestries and Flemish manuscript books. The scale of entertainment was

The Kymin: Nelsonian delight

lavish. Wales under Henry VII was awakening from a long sleep.

Little of this period survives, apart from architectural fragments of the hall and long gallery. In the 17th century, with the Marches at peace and the Royalist Worcesters becoming Dukes of Beaufort, the castle was abandoned and its fittings and its glory moved to the family's more accessible seat of Badminton (Wilts). The great parlour chimneypiece at Badminton is said to have come from Raglan, which is still owned by the Beauforts.

The castle was later re-fashioned to the requirements of the Regency Picturesque. Ivy grew and covered the wounds of age. Ghosts flirted with owls in the turrets and crumbling windows. The 20th century brought 'stabilization' and Raglan now sits immaculate amid lawns. The dramatically slighted great tower looks like the design for an opera set.

The approach to the castle remains impressive, with the gatehouse, flared machicolations and great tower forming a composition visible from a distance and unlike any other in Wales. This is no gaunt Norman keep but the citadel of a grandee in the Marcher tradition, but more intent on impressing than suppressing the surrounding populace.

The moated great tower to the left is the earliest part of the castle, built by William ap Thomas as a self-contained residential stronghold surrounded by water and reached by a bridge. Its slighted wall tilts alarmingly – or now picturesquely – outwards, revealing hanging fireplaces and window-frames.

The main gatehouse leads into Pitched Stone Court, so named after its cobbled surface. Large fireplaces survive in the kitchen tower, while the buttery range leads to the great hall. This has a spacious oriel window and the arms of the Earls of Worcester over the dais and would once have been a scene of great magnificence.

Beyond lies the Fountain Court and the private family chambers, including a chapel and long gallery with views north-west towards the Brecon Beacons. Immediately below the Fountain Court wall remain buried some of the most remarkable renaissance terraces and water gardens in Britain. We await their reinstatement.

TREDEGAR HOUSE ★★★★

Nr Newport
Restoration mansion with
17th-century interiors (Mus)

The house of the Morgans at Tredegar is equal only to Powis among the great houses of Wales. The land was owned by the same family from the 14th century to the 20th. A substantial medieval house on the site was first rebuilt as a result of John ap Morgan's support for Henry Tudor at Bosworth and was grand enough to receive Charles I after Naseby in 1645. Some of this house survives behind the new one built at the Restoration.

Rebuilding began c.1670 with the judicious marriage of a Royalist Morgan, who had joined the Stuart court in Continental exile, to the daughter of a wealthy lawyer. The Dutch style was much admired by returning exiles. Tredegar is, says Newman in Pevsner, 'one of the outstanding houses of the Restoration period in the whole of Britain ... a great statement of dynastic wealth and self-confidence'. Two Warwickshire brothers named Hurlbutt are believed to have been the architects.

The house survived into the 18th century when it passed through the female line to the entrepreneur Sir Charles Gould, who changed his name to Gould Morgan. Like the Butes of Cardiff and the Talbots of Margam, Morgan (1726–1806) capitalized on the growth of industrial south Wales. A tramway through the park was nicknamed 'the golden mile' for the tolls charged on vehicles using it to reach the docks.

A later Morgan took part in (and survived) the Charge of the Light Brigade, an incident commemorated in a monument to his horse, Sir Brigg, in the garden to the east of the house. In 1859 the Morgans became Barons Tredegar.

The one thing the family did not do, unlike many of their contemporaries, was apply their new wealth to rebuilding their ancestral home. A modest Victorian reordering of the interior moved the entrance from one Restoration range to the other, but any changes had to be approved by the 1st Baron Tredegar's brother, Octavius

Raglan: Renaissance magnificence

Morgan, an antiquarian and ardent enthusiast for 17th-century architecture.

The lords of Tredegar limped on into the 1930s when Evan Tredegar entertained Charlie Chaplin, Nancy Cunard and Evelyn Waugh, together with a menagerie of assorted parrots and boxing kangaroos. He was a darling of the gossip columns. His extravagance, followed by three bouts of death duties, led the last of the Morgans to sell the house in 1951 and flee to the casinos of Monte Carlo.

After the family's departure, Tredegar entered the familiar purgatory. It was a school for twenty-three years and was then sold to Newport council, under whose inadequate charge it was described in the 1977 *Companion Guide* as 'in a kind of limbo, with vandals smashing everything they can lay their hands on'. A programme of restoration ensued and Newport eventually redeemed itself. The house is now superbly repaired, furnished and displayed – though little marketed.

Key to understanding the exterior is that there are two remarkably similar façades at right angles to each other, both enriched. The original intention was to build four ranges, but money ran out and the two lesser sides of the internal court survive from the pre-Restoration house. This gives Tredegar a pleasing sense of evolving over time.

The main façade (on the far side of the present entrance) is guarded by iron gates made by William Edney in 1714. The eleven bays are of two storeys plus an attic with a hipped roof, a customary Restoration composition. The roof was altered and a central lantern removed under the Regency, to give it a lower and perhaps more fashionable pitch. It still seems perfectly in balance.

The windows are unusually adorned with 'broken' pediments surmounted by a lion and a gryphon, supporters of the Morgan arms. The effect is of a sculpted garland thrown round the entire exterior. The front door is similarly decorated with Italianate barley-sugar columns, emblems of Royalist sympathy. To the left is the secondary façade of nine bays with similarly enriched windows. The two façades, both of which serve as entrances, might be essays on a common theme.

The interior is astonishing not just for its decoration but for remaining largely as it would have appeared in the 17th century, thanks to the care shown in its Victorian restoration by Octavius Morgan.

The new side entrance hall is in dark wood with family portraits and a seated statue of Sir Charles Morgan (1760–1846). Off one side is the morning room, furnished as a ladies' sitting room, and off the other is the dining room. Here the panelling is original, though the ceiling is a Victorian re-creation. The windows contain armorial stained glass and the dinner service is in the family colours of blue and gold. A secret panel leads to the kitchen.

The former entrance hall, or 'new hall' to distinguish it from that in the old Tudor house, has its original panelling. The two other ground-floor rooms are Tredegar's stars. The Brown Room retains its 1680s panelling, alive with deeply undercut foliage on panels, pilasters, roundels, swags and bolection mouldings. The doors are crowned with scroll pediments filled with classical busts. They include the emperor Augustus and his wife Livia, perfectly at home in Restoration Gwent.

The Gilt Room is one of the great rooms of Wales. The ceiling surrounds a painting copied from the Palazzo Barberini, illustrating Pope Urban's glorification of Rome by his improbable conquest of Lust and Intemperance. The chimneypiece with overmantel drips with gilding and frames a picture of William Morgan, *c*.1650, whose grandson built the new house. Barley-sugar columns salute fat cherubs climbing swags heavy with fruit. The walls are covered in paintings built into the panelling, grained to look like walnut. The panels are adorned with swags and drops.

The sumptuousness continues upstairs with bedrooms and dressing rooms appropriate to various stages in the house's history, including Evan Tredegar's dabbling in the occult. The service wing has been restored in all its particulars, down to the jars of spices in the housekeeper's room.

The Gilt Room, Tredegar House

TREOWEN **

Wonastow, 3 miles south-west of Monmouth
Isolated Jacobean mansion with screen and
staircase (Priv)

North Monmouthshire turns its back on the
world and loses itself in the foothills of the Beacons. Near the village of Jingle Street is the tiny
hamlet of Wonastow, from where a lane leads
north into a wilderness of dark woods and tumbling contours. Suddenly an old Jacobean pile
comes into view on top of a hill, with no sign of
other habitation.

The house had been in the same family since
its construction in the 17th century when in 1954
it was sold to the present owners, the Wheel-
ocks. It has been carefully restored, if sparsely
furnished, and let out for weekends and marriage parties. I can imagine no wilder spot from
which to set out on the journey of matrimony.

The exterior is austere for 1627, when it was
built for a family named Jones on a grand scale,
doubled pile with façades front and back. Only
a later front porch is enriched, with two tiers of
doubled columns, crowned by a coat of arms in
the pediment. For some reason the top storey
of this range was removed in the 18th century,
giving the side elevations a lopsided look. The
stone-mullioned windows are regular and severe. When the front was a full three storeys, the
house must have looked like a fortress.

The interior has been much altered, but the
beautifully composed classical screen was restored in 2001. The ground floor, apart from the
hall, is mostly kitchens and services. The chief
feature of the house is one of the most spectacular staircases of any house of this period. It fills
an open stairwell the entire three storeys to the
attic. Even the servants were beneficiaries of
the owner's ostentation. The work is crafted of
turned newel posts with pendants and finials.
The view up from below is breathtaking.

On the first floor the old great chamber survives, with what appears to be its original frieze
and plasterwork ceiling. The present owners are
trying to reinstate as much as they can of the
original fittings, and acquire maps and portraits
of the estate. It is a valiant endeavour.

USK CASTLE **

Marshal castle settled into herbaceous
old age (Priv)

Usk Castle is privately owned and everything a
Cadw castle is not. It is wild, unmanicured and
idiosyncratic. Vegetation is everywhere. Where
a government castle is scrubbed and tidy, Usk
respects the dishevelment of age. The car park is
lost in the woods.

The approach is past the owner's family
home, fashioned from the medieval gatehouse
(*c.*1375), and the stables still have horses. The
outer ward of the castle is now the garden of the
house, with paddock and herbaceous border.
Visitors are asked to put a pebble in a basket ('we
are told we must count numbers') and entrance
money in a dish, the most casual and economical
unmanned entry control I know.

The castle was built by the de Clares during their sovereignty of the southern Marches
in the 12th century. The walled inner ward is
reached up a path enclosed by fuchsia and Virginia creeper past the foot of a massive Norman keep of 1170. This was built by the Norman
warlord Richard 'Strongbow' de Clare, and the
castle took its present form under the equally
ferocious William Marshal, who won de Clare's
daughter for unseating the future Richard I in a
joust in 1189.

Marshal added his distinctive innovation, a
round 'garrison' tower, at the time of the castle's
fortification against Llywelyn the Great in the
13th century. It then passed to the Mortimers
and, in the 18th century, to the Beauforts. It has
been in private ownership ever since.

The pleasure of Usk lies in the present rather
than the past. If ruins must be ruins, let them be
like this, as if playing a game with the surrounding rocks and enveloping vegetation. The centre
of the ward is rough grass with roses and creeper clinging to the walls. Round the perimeter
are the remains of turrets, a chapel and a great
hall. Marshal's garrison tower rises four storeys.
More recent features include geese and a yew
peacock. The treasure tower, still inhabited, was
once occupied by 'a dog called coker', believed
to be the first reference to a cocker spaniel.

Jacobean vernacular at Treowen

Moated White on its hilltop

WHITE CASTLE ***

Nr Llantilio Crossenny,
5 miles east of Abergavenny
Lonely fortress with view of the
Beacons (Cadw)

White is my favourite among the castles of the
Marches. It is both the wildest and the most
complete, with sensational views over the Usk
valley to the Brecon Beacons. The original Norman fortress was substantially altered in the
mid-13th century against Llywelyn ap Gruffudd
but there was no adjacent village or church.

The castle appears to have been abandoned by
the 16th century, sparing it Civil War slighting.
The name comes from its old lime-wash, sadly
vanished.

The outer ward is a spacious parade ground,
now grassy, surrounded by a dry ditch, wall and
towers. To the left the main castle and inner
ward rise across a deep moat, a remarkable engineering feat on top of a hill. The castle walls rise
on a steep mound and from below look wholly
impregnable. The gatehouse across what would
have been a drawbridge is massive, flanked by
drum towers from which can be enjoyed a 360-
degree view. From here south Wales might be a
deserted landscape, composed only of woods,
fields and mountains.

Churches

ABERGAVENNY

ST MARY ✳✳✳
Priory foundation with monuments and
Jesse relic

Abergavenny is what show business would call
a slow burn. Its outward appearance is dull, but
the interior gradually unfolds to reveal one of
the finest groups of monuments in Wales and a
medieval relic of international importance, the
Jesse carving.

Founded within two decades of the Conquest in 1087, the old Benedictine priory church
was reordered by Thomas Nicholson in the
1880s. This reordering dominates the interior,
whose walls are marred by Victorian scraping.
Abergavenny is an urgent candidate for lime-
washing, as at Newport. Nicholson converted
the nave and north aisle into a large preaching
space, divided only by a slender Perpendicular
arcade.

Eastwards the interior becomes a more complex arrangement. The earlier choir and crossing (here lime-washed) lead to the sanctuary
beyond, its roof with gothick decoration. The
choir stalls date from the final days of the priory
in the late 15th century and carry poppy-heads
and animals beneath a fretwork canopy.

All eyes now turn to the monuments. The
15th-century Jesse carving is north of the crossing. The old man lies majestically on his side (as
in the Llanrhaeadr window in Clwyd) with an
angel behind his head and the beginnings of a
tree emerging from his stomach. The garments
flow with energy.

Most remarkable is the size. Almost no Jesse
trees survive, other than in stained glass. Given
the dimensions of the Jesse windowframe (of
stone) in Dorchester Abbey (Oxon), the tree
of which this Jesse is the base must have risen
almost as high as the roof. It would have been
painted and probably jewelled, a work of overwhelming majesty. Here is a taste of the quality
of British art at the close of the Middle Ages on a
scale to be found nowhere else in Britain.

Near the Jesse stands the monument to Sir
John de Hastings (d. 1325), in wood on a reconstructed base of gothic arcading. The effigy is a
masterpiece of English 14th-century carving,
elongated, serene and well preserved. To Claude
Blair it is 'one of the most beautiful pieces of
medieval sculpture in Britain' and ranks in my
experience with that of Blanche Mortimer in
Much Marcle (Herefs). In the north chapel is
an earlier memorial to Eva de Broase (d. 1257),
unusual in that a woman's effigy is covered with
a large shield.

The principal monuments are in the Herbert
chapel to the south of the crossing. Most would
have been imported from England, of Pains-
wick marble from the Cotswolds or alabaster
from Derbyshire. Pride of place in front of the
altar is the tomb of Sir William ap Thomas, the
'blue knight of Gwent', and of his wife, Gwladus.
William was the leading Yorkist in South Wales
and progenitor of the Herbert dynasty, embracing the Powis and Pembroke lines. He was
builder of the earliest stages of Raglan Castle,
dying in 1445.

The effigies still have traces of paint, as do
the imitation vaults above their heads. Twelve
robed figures fill the ornamented niches on the
chest with, at its east end, a tableau of the Annunciation. This tableau, though mutilated, is
exquisite, the figures in flowing robes with Mary
shielded by a canopy. Gabriel holds a lily crucifix,
a rare survival of this icon in alabaster.

Lying to the north is Sir William's son, Sir
Richard Herbert (d. 1459), again in alabaster and with angels holding shields round the
base. Against the wall is the tomb of Sir Richard
Herbert of Ewyas (d. 1510), bare-headed under
a painted ogee arch. A panel of weepers has at
their centre a carving of the coronation of the
Virgin, with patrons kneeling at her feet. The
'sleeping bedesman' has been removed from the
chest and placed on the wall.

On the north side of the chapel is a complete
contrast, the Jacobean tomb of William Baker
(d. 1648), a work of renaissance swagger erected
after the Restoration and commemorating a devout Roman Catholic. It seems as far removed
from the medieval work as is the modern altar
by Keith Jameson (1998).

ABERGAVENNY

OUR LADY AND ST MICHAEL *
Victorian neo-gothic reredos

Roman Catholics were present in Wales contin-
uously from the Middle Ages. The tradition was
particularly strong in Abergavenny, sustained
by Franciscans and Benedictines and even supplying two martyrs, St Davis Lewis and St Philip
Evans. When the priory became the post-Reformation parish church, Catholics had to worship
in a barn and then an attic. A reredos of the period survives in the local museum. In the mid-
18th century, half the Catholics in Wales were
said to be located in the Abergavenny district.

By 1857 they were strong enough for a local
benefactor to buy a site for a new church at Pen-y-
pound. The architect chosen was the young Benjamin Bucknall, who had taken over from Pugin
and then Charles Hansom at the doomed Woodchester House project near Stroud. Bucknall
also designed Pontargothi (Dyfed).

Here he built a bold composition of church
and presbytery, with a fine Decorated window
overlooking the road. The interior is that of a
conventional Victorian Catholic church, worth
seeing for its exceptional reredos added twenty-
five years after the completion of the church.
The designer was Edmund Kirby of Liverpool.
It is an astonishing work of neo-Decorated
gothic, filling the east end of the chancel. Six
nodding ogee niches contain angels and musicians, attending a central baldachino. Above
erupts a forest of pinnacles whose crockets seem
to sprout before one's eyes.

The reredos is complemented by an east
window by Hardman. The decline in ecclesiastical patronage is demonstrated in the dreadful
pietism of the Stations of the Cross.

BETWS NEWYDD **

3 miles north of Usk
Rare set of screen, loft and tympanum

Betws is isolated, tiny and simple. It lies on a
hillside on the outskirts of its village, dwarfed
by a grove of billowing yews. One yew is among
the oldest in Wales and has grown into a work
of natural sculpture, with a new tree appearing
to grow within the casing of the old.

The church contains a remarkable work of
craftsmanship, a rood screen with stairs, loft
and tympanum, among the most complete such
arrangements anywhere. The screen itself is
conventional Perpendicular, its beam adorned
with the familiar trail of vine leaves, crudely
carved, as well as a less usual trail of oak. Above
is a pierced balustrade to the loft, decorated
with what seem small Christmas trees. Above
this rises a tympanum partition, dividing nave
from chancel by filling the arch space below the
wagon roof.

The partition is pierced by windows enabling
the players in the loft to see the service in the
chancel. It is supported by large beams formed
into a cross. Whether this was structural or was
intended to represent the crucifix in place of the
rood figures is a matter of conjecture. The Betws
screen has a rough self-confidence, as if made
by local carpenters and with pride.

A font at the rear of the church is Norman,
based on a rope pattern. Sunlight and a view
of trees flood in through clear-glass windows.
Betws is a clock stopped at the right moment
in time.

CHEPSTOW

ST MARY ***
Norman church in shadow of castle,
carefully restored

Chepstow church is a match for its castle and
town, from both of which it stands aloof. Few
churches can have suffered so much from change
and decay and recovered so well. A Benedictine
priory was established here in 1070, just four
years after the conquest and at the same time
as the castle. God and the sword were to guard
entry to Wales.

The impressive west front is a Georgian reconstruction of the original Norman doors and
windows, with dogtooth and zigzag below an
18th-century tower. Inside, Victorian restoration has not marred the high Benedictine austerity of the nave. A plain clerestory surmounts

Cwmyoy: tranquillity in Ewyas

...hen pul...he died y e
19 th day of July 1781
Aged 3 years

GILES DUKE

TO THE MEMORY OF JOAN WIFE OF JOHN WILLIAMS
late of the Sharphall
in this Parish who died the 11 th of
August 1813 aged 67 Yrs

Near this place lies buried here
The mother and her children dear

a triforium of doubled openings divided by columns. Beyond, light streams into the crossing from the transepts, leaving the distant Victorian chancel dark.

Both the crossing and transepts were rebuilt after the collapse of the central tower in 1700 and the chancel was built in 1891 by Seddon and Carter. These sections are near impossible to read since the Victorians used old materials where possible, notably stiff-leaf capitals and, in the south transept, excellent corbel heads. The chancel is sombre but noble, lit with tall arched windows and capitals, again making re-use of that most engaging Early Gothic device, stiff-leaf.

The monuments include two contrasting tombs. One at the west end of the nave is of the Earl of Worcester (d. 1549), lord of Chepstow – Elizabethan and severely classical in style. He and his wife are in coronation robes. The other, to Margaret Cleyton, is in the south transept and dated 1620, a crude Jacobean baroque. It depicts Cleyton and her two husbands in effigy, while beneath kneel two sons and ten daughters.

CWMYOY

2 miles north-west of Llanfihangel Crucornau
ST MARTIN ✳✳✳
Tilting church with Brute memorials

Cwmyoy is the jewel of the Vale of Ewyas. Even the distant view from across the valley indicates something eccentric. The church tower tilts downhill at an angle that makes Pisa seem upright. In the churchyard headstones tumble in all directions, as if some calamity had upset the dead. Inside the church, Alice in Wonderland continues. Visitors might be on the deck of a galleon in a storm, with the chancel about to slide overboard. A local joke holds that Cwmyoy is only for those 'so inclined'.

The cause of this merriment was a landslide sometime after the church's Norman construction, which successive generations have combated not by rebuilding but by erecting buttresses, beams and struts. The massive open-beamed roof is original, dating from the late 13th century and firmly bonded to the walls. The simple chancel arch has been so often repaired as to retain no dressing or adornment.

All this besides, Cwmyoy is a church full of character. The walls are of soft yellow plaster and the floor is of Welsh flagstones. Only the modern gothic pulpit is out of place, but perhaps it will one day sink through the floor. The memorials are of high quality, mostly by the 18th-century Brutes of Llanbedr, whose coloured baroque monuments are found throughout the border country. An earlier tablet commemorates Thomas Price (d. 1682), who 'takes his nap in our Common Mother's lap, / Waiting to hear the Bridegroom say, / "Wake, my dear, and come away."'

The church contains one exquisite treasure, an ancient cross found in a neighbouring farm showing Christ upright, not twisted in agony. Peter Lord suggests that the strange head-dress derives from the Holy Roman Empire, though it is also found on Irish crosses of the 16th century. Cwmyoy is blessed with one of the loveliest photographic cards in my collection. It is by Nick Jenkins of a memorial to Joan Williams (d. 1813) above an open hymnal on a window ledge, with sun streaming in from the Black Mountains beyond.

GROSMONT

ST NICHOLAS ✳✳
Norman garrison church with
Early Gothic carving

The church is on the English border, its name and castle both relics of a Norman settlement. Dating from the 12th century and rare among Welsh churches, Grosmont is French in plan, cruciform with an octagonal tower and long sweeping nave roof enclosing the aisles. When Seddon restored it in the 19th century, he pre-empted the 20th by moving the congregation into the crossing, screening off the old nave and clearing it of furniture. On my visit a harvest festival was being arranged in the chancel while noisy children played games in the nave.

The size of the nave is attributed to the needs of the adjacent castle garrison and is

O·YE·WINDS·OF·GOD·BLESS·YE·THE·LORD
PRAISE·HIM·&·MAGNIFY·HIM·FOR·EVER

Llanfair Cilgedin: sgraffito murals

appropriately barn-like. Muscular arcades and late-Norman arches are barely pointed. A Decorated west window carries reticulated tracery. In the south aisle is a 13th-century effigy and a 16th-century chest or 'hutch', with four handmade locks.

The crossing and chancel display Seddon's respectful 1870 restoration. The church was close to collapse and he rebuilt it with as much deference to the old as possible. The piers carry Early Gothic stiff-leaf, some original, some new. In the chancel Seddon restored the asymmetrical lancets and traceried windows and reset a double piscina with cusped tracery.

In the south window is a charming Virgin and Child in unusual pose, the Virgin with her hair loose in what might be Rastafarian braids and the child with its arm extended in awkward benediction.

LLANFAIR CILGEDIN

5 miles north of Usk
ST MARY **
Complete set of Art Nouveau murals

The church is a mile north of the village and half a mile east at the end of a farm track. It sits forlorn in a field overgrown with grass, guarded by a giant oak. A scatter of tombstones is nearly consumed by vegetation. The Friends of Friendless Churches have laboured valiantly to prevent the church from collapse and restore the remarkable murals inside.

The building is Victorian, in soft pink and grey stone with two bells hanging in a bellcote. It was reconstructed by a wealthy 19th-century rector rejoicing in the name of the Reverend W. J. Coussmaker Lindsay.

In 1873 he had J. D. Sedding design him a new, if modest, structure. It is architecturally unexciting but the furnishings are of the richest Arts and Crafts work, notably the altar rails and reredos. Sedding re-used or re-created whatever he could find on the site, incorporating windows, stained glass and the tracery of the elegant screen.

The interest of the church lies in Lindsay's scheme of wall decoration, a memorial to his wife executed by Heywood Sumner in 1891–3. The pictures are in sgraffito, five layers of plaster colours etched when damp and framed, to illustrate the Benedictus of the Mass. Each is a swirling composition of Art Nouveau lines depicting young people and winged creatures amid lush landscapes. One is entitled 'O Ye Mountains and Hills' and shows the Usk valley and Sugarloaf mountain. Their appearance is sometimes Pre-Raphaelite and sometimes startlingly modern, as in the picture of children playing with hoops. It is all a wonderful discovery in so isolated a church.

LLAN-GWM UCHAF

3 miles east of Usk
ST JEROME **
Restored screen, green men

The church was comprehensively restored in the 19th century (by Seddon) as a setting for its screen and loft. The church is located at the end of a farm track on the sloping banks of a stream and should not be confused with another church passed on the same track. It contains the usual Seddon richness of fittings, including pulpit, lectern, choir stalls and floor tiles.

The screen's history is hard to disentangle given the care of Seddon's reconstruction. Dating from 1500, it is a dignified work with features similar to that at Patrisio (Powys), including surviving Tudor paint. The work is of eighteen bays with linenfold in the panels and fretwork in the lights. I counted eleven distinct bands of decoration below the loft and six above. The loft panels have openwork with ogee niches for absent saints. The composition is grand for so small a space, as if awaiting the arrival of the enveloping woods to creep in and colonize it.

Behind the screen are its genies, green men appearing at the base of the chancel arch with verdure sprouting from their mouths. Near the door is an inexplicable object, obviously of great antiquity with trellis work round its middle. It may be a stoup, a standing lamp or pillar piscina. Visitors are asked to write down their suggestions.

LLANGYBI

4 miles south of Usk
ST CYBI *
Surviving wall-paintings

The church lies in the flood plain of the Usk, with a masterly interior restoration by Caröe. Perpendicular tower and windows have been added to what is clearly an older structure, the windows set in deep reveals.

The inside is atmospheric, lime-washed and with post-Reformation fittings, the pulpit a large 17th-century piece with tester. The nave carries wall-paintings, some medieval, some over-painted after the Reformation. The former includes a rare Christ of the Trades in the chancel, depicting Jesus wounded by the tools of workers disobeying the commandments by working on the Sabbath.

There is also an indistinct Virgin with scales as well as post-Reformation biblical texts, including a Creed and Ten Commandments within frames.

LLANTHONY PRIORY **

5 miles north-west of Llanfihangel Crucornau
Romantic ruin in secluded valley

Is Llanthony more sublime than Tintern? The latter has the Wye but the former has seclusion. This is a vale, as Peter Sager puts it, 'of recluses and drop-outs, monks and artists, legends, dreams and ruins … where every path is a Welsh knot'.

The valley is that of the river Honddu, where William de Lacy, Norman Earl of Hereford in *c*.1100, founded the first Augustinian abbey in Wales. He had been hunting in the area and was captivated by a ruined chapel to St David. He promptly abandoned his position at court and, so it is said, became a hermit. Llanthony is a corruption of Llanddewi Nant Hodni or the church of David.

The monastery was so secluded that the monks did not even clear trees from their chosen site, and some soon fled to a new foundation at Gloucester. This great cathedral began life as

Llanthony Secundo, 'having no mind to sing to wolves'. Some returned fifty years later and a stone building was begun in 1175, which was visited by Gerald of Wales in 1188. He found 'the rains frequent, the winds boisterous but generally the climate temperate and healthy. The air though heavy is mild and soothing and diseases rare'.

His visit was the occasion of a lengthy and vivid outburst against the decline in Welsh monastic life under Anglo-Norman influence, with the earlier, ascetic Llanthony used as a favourable comparison. The Cistercians were greedy, said Gerald, the Benedictines rich, the Cluniacs feckless. And here were the Gloucester Augustinians stripping old Llanthony of its tithes and treasures to feed to gluttony of England. As is often the case, Gerald was probably exaggerating to make his proto-nationalist point. Llanthony was to be one of the richest and most comfortable monasteries in Wales.

After the Dissolution the abbey drifted into untroubled ruin. It was used as a hunting lodge before being discovered by the Regency romantic Walter Savage Landor, and converted into a picturesque retreat. He occupied the abbot's residence but soon moved to Italy, which he found warmer. Turner's depiction of the neighbouring river was considered by Ruskin 'the most perfect piece of painting of running water in existence'.

Here Kilvert came on a visit from Clyro and was appalled to find someone else also visiting. He expostulated: 'Of all noxious animals the most noxious is a tourist; and of all tourists the most vulgar, illbred, offensive and loathsome is the British tourist.' What was he?

The abbot's residence is now a small hotel and the abbey ruins are accessible from its front garden. Enough of the old abbey church remains to evoke its grandeur. The west front is spectacular, two towers rising to roof level with graceful blind arcading. The nave arcade is transitional Norman to Early Gothic. A vault of the same period survives south of the south transept.

The whole composition, in private ownership, is charmingly casual. The hotel bar serves delicious soup on a cold day.

LLANTILIO CROSSENNY

ST TEILO **

Green man, Kempe windows

The church cuts a proud figure when approached from the west, with a porch symmetrically framed by the nave gable and sloping aisle roofs. A broad spire rises over the crossing. The size of the building is attributed to the patronage of the lords of neighbouring White Castle. From the churchyard are views to the Brecon Beacons.

The interior is curious. The handsome Early gothic nave seems an afterthought to the large crossing arch, through which there is little view of the chancel beyond. The fiercely scraped chancel, restored by Prichard and Seddon, gives on to a north chapel through a Decorated gothic arch. Its corbel carries a green man with leaves in his nose and tongue lolling out. The chapel is lit with three Kempe windows, rich in reds and greens.

Most odd are the crude floor slabs of c.1620 in the chancel. One has a man, John Walderne, his wife and three apparently whiskered sons, carved in low relief and childish for their period, unless they have been damaged by the passage of time. A contrast is the adjacent, supremely sentimental wall memorial to Mary Ann Bosanquet (d. 1819) by Flaxman, in which she is attended by distraught mourners, with her dead infant returning to her as a cherub.

NEWPORT CATHEDRAL

ST WOOLOS ****

Norman interior with carved arch,
1960s Caröe chancel

Newport is a planning disaster. The bleakly isolated castle and wretched waterfront overlooking the Usk could have been imaginatively restored but have been ruined by ugly and ill-sited modern buildings. The more merciful is the great church on the hill, now a cathedral.

The original church was dedicated to St Gwynllyw (Woolos in English) who was allegedly told by God to found it where he might see a white ox with a black spot on its face. The exterior is heavily restored and uninteresting. The interior is a different matter, one of Wales's best Norman naves encased in a Perpendicular box.

The earliest work is the unusual galilee chapel inside the west entrance. This contains a Norman font with grotesque heads and swirling ribbons suggesting an affinity with the Herefordshire carvers. A trumpet-blowing green man leers from one corner. The main church extends to the east through a magnificent romanesque arch, with vigorous chevron and zigzag decoration.

The capitals on this arch are exceptionally interesting and subject of much scholarly debate. They are in a bastardized Ionic/Corinthian order with scrolls and leaves intermingled with human faces, birds and dolphins. It is as if the carver were seeking to free the Middle Ages from the rigours of classicism. Figures have their arms upraised like the titan Atlas carrying the world. Some have wondered if these capitals were Roman originals re-cut by the Normans. Peter Lord opts for French carvers of c.1100 arriving at the new monastery at Gloucester, to which St Woolos belonged.

The nave is noble, of five regular bays with aisles and clerestory. Each capital is slightly different and the walls are brightly whitewashed. At the back of the south aisle is a battered but beautiful renaissance tomb of Sir Walter Herbert (d. 1568). The lofty gothic arch at the east end of the same aisle is modern, though the glass in the distant window and some of the side windows is by Pugin's assistant, Hardman.

The chancel of St Woolos is a comprehensive rebuild by A. D. R. Caröe, son of W. D., in 1964, deferential to surviving Norman and gothic fragments, light but bland. The space is redeemed by Thompson of Kilburn's modern choir stalls, with many appearances of his mouse.

The chancel's east wall is intentionally dramatic: a giant rounded arch in mauve on a white wall enclosing a rose window by John Piper, executed by Patrick Reyntiens, of blazing reds and yellows. Below is a swirling reredos wall, painted to look like marbling and allegedly 'Roman in spirit'. The effect is Lord of the Rings, but seen from a distance the composition has presence and dignity.

Llanthony Priory: Gwent sublime

PENALLT

3 miles south-east of Monmouth
OLD CHURCH **
Pilgrimage church with chi-rho altar

The little churches of the upper Wye are particularly charming. Penallt sits on the old pilgrimage route to St David's amid rolling wooded hills. With a thick mist rising from the valley beneath, we might be anywhere between Wales and Santiago de Compostela. The church is isolated in a spacious churchyard at the end of an avenue of limes and tumbling gravestones. The outline of saddleback tower, nave, aisle and porch forms a picturesque composition.

The interior suggests a rebuild at the turn of the 16th century, with a date on the door of 1539. The arcade piers between nave and aisle are curious, as if intended for a grander superstructure. Barrel roofs are restored with coloured bosses throughout.

A wide arch leads down into an intimate chancel, with an altar table carved in 1916 by a Belgian war refugee, apparently the chief woodcarver of Malines cathedral. His pattern was said to be a church in Ravenna. The original stone altar with a chi-rho symbol stands in the south aisle. A tapestry depicts various cathedrals along the pilgrims' route to Santiago.

SKENFRITH

ST BRIDGET *
Dovecote tower, tombs and Virgin cope

This is a big, jolly church associated, like Grosmont, with a Norman castle and blessedly under-restored. The exterior is of deep red sandstone with a double-lantern on the tower. The tower walls are massive, five feet thick, while the lantern served as a dovecote should the villagers take refuge here in an emergency and need food.

The interior is bright, with Perpendicular windows, a fine arch and white-painted barrel vault to the chancel. The floor is of flagstone. Skenfrith's chief interest lies in its furniture. In the north aisle is a chest tomb of John Morgan

(d. 1557), last governor of the 'three castles' of the Monmouth Marches, White, Skenfrith and Grosmont. It is a fine work, simple but bold, with sons and daughters squeezed into the side panels as weepers, looking like students trying to cram into a phone box. Next door is the Morgan pew with, above it, a framed Ten Commandments.

The south aisle boasts a Jacobean pew for minstrels, presumably evicted by Puritans from the former loft. The modern lectern is of 1909 (by George Jack) showing St Bridget reading at her desk. Skenfrith's greatest treasure is a 15th-century velvet cope still in good condition and depicting the Virgin. The survival of such pre-Reformation objects is rare and especially valued in a parish church.

TINTERN ABBEY ***

Picturesque ruin in beautiful Wye valley

There are three Tinterns. One was the great Cistercian foundation, the first of ten in Wales, built on the banks of the Wye in 1131. Few locations could have better honoured St Bernard's admonition to 'find among the woods something you never found in books'. It remained a premier British monastery until the suppression of 1536, patronized by the Marcher lords William Marshal and Roger Bigod. They initiated a major rebuilding in the 13th century. Tintern was, and even as a ruin still is, a masterpiece of English gothic.

The second Tintern arrived in the 18th and 19th centuries. The monastic quarters had mostly collapsed and their stones been reused. Only the great church stood, roofless and exhilarating. Creeper clambered over its walls and the aisles and cloisters yielded to vegetation. First came the Buck brothers, whose prints of Tintern and the Wye first appeared in 1732 and were popular. Gilpin's publicizing of the Wye after a visit in 1770 further transformed the place, with trippers voyaging down from Ross to Tintern. His view of the ruins was partial: 'A number of the gable-ends hurt the eye with their regularity ... a mallet judiciously used might be of service in fracturing some of them.'

Newport Cathedral: chancel by Caröe

Perhaps with this in mind the then owner, the Duke of Beaufort, cleared the site of 'rubbish', mostly fallen carvings. Turner arrived in 1792 and Samuel Palmer later declared, 'Such an abbey! The lightest gothic – trellised with ivy and rising from a wilderness of orchards – and set like a gem amongst the folding of woody hills.'

Finally came Wordsworth, with his definitive poem of the Romantic movement composed on the Wye above Tintern: 'Once again / Do I behold these steep and lofty cliffs / That on a wild secluded scene impress / Thoughts of more deep seclusion.'

Today we have a third Tintern, product of late-20th-century conservation ideology. The ivy has gone and with it the image of ancient stones and gothic arches rising above rolling waves of green. Gone too is the sense of communion with the steeply wooded Wye hills. In its place are stabilized footings, scrubbed stonework and ubiquitous government lawns set about with visitor centres. Why grass rather than stones or gravel is considered the correct flooring for an abbey is beyond me.

Of the abbey's domestic buildings the footings and wall fragments remain, but only the porch, monks' day room and refectory rise to any height. Pride of place goes to the abbey church, built between 1270 and 1300. Despite losing its roof and much of its window tracery, the building retains its walls and gable ends. It is their proportion and slender verticality that display the gothic style at its most serene and stylish, so-called Decorated.

This is best seen in the west window, where seven lancets rise to a filigree of cusping, crowned by three circles with bar tracery. Below is a double doorway with blind arcading. The interior survives to roof height, the nave of six bays leading to two giant crossing arches and the presbytery beyond, a balanced rhythm. The piers in the nave south aisle are shortened to allow for a wall that defined the area reserved for lay brothers.

The view west from the presbytery at Tintern offers the most sublime evocation of gothic art in Wales. It yearns for judicious restoration, as of the vanished window tracery. The Victo-

rians would have done it and we would have respected their skill. Tintern can still recapture some of its lost glory.

TRELECH

ST NICHOLAS ∗
Decorated church, 17th-century tourist guide

Trelech was once an industrial town larger than Cardiff or Swansea, the centre of medieval iron-making and an important Marcher borough. The church was rebuilt after a fire in 1296 and, like Tintern, is a work of Decorated gothic. It is impressive for its lofty nave and steeple, a rarity in Wales, impressive even where red sandstone has been so coated in lichen as to seem almost leprous.

The interior is handsome but curiously cold, in a county where church interiors make a practice of cosiness. The nave arcades are of a stately five bays, on octagonal piers with clerestory. A stone arch under the tower reveals a reticulated tracery window. The aisle windows are uniformly of opaque glass, thus depriving the interior of the pleasure of the trees waving outside. The chancel has a three-sided Laudian altar rail and east window by Heaton and Butler.

In the south aisle is a sundial of 1689 inscribed with Trelech's three tourist sites – Bronze Age stones, a castle motte and a well. The stones, in a field south-west of the village, appear aligned to the top of a hill but are tilted by age into a nodding conspiracy. Jan Morris claims that occultists have found them so potent that, on one divination, the investigator was knocked to the ground.

USK

ST MARY ∗∗∗
Gothic priory porches, cathedral organ

The church belongs to a Norman priory founded in the 1160s by Richard 'Strongbow' de Clare, illegitimate son of Henry I. He married an Irish princess and killed his son for cowardice in battle. He was, says Tim Hughes, 'just the kind of man to found a nunnery', in this case for 'vir-

Decorated arcades at Tintern Abbey

gins of noble birth'. Whatever else the Normans brought to Wales it was good intentions.

In the 13th century the priory nave was given a north aisle for the use of the town. The transepts were later demolished and a chancel inserted under the tower. This and the screen give the church an enjoyably domestic character. In the 15th century the Herbert family added two porches to the north aisle. These became centres of civic business, including law, education and charity administration. The Usk porches are handsomely vaulted, the arch to the west one carrying a slender ogee arch bearing crockets. Clearly the 'town side' was intended to outshine the nuns' side.

The interior reflects the church's history, with four bays replacing what would have been a wall dividing nuns from citizens. The Perpen-dicular screen is painted in fairground colours. A plaque fixed to it commemorates Adam of Usk (d. 1430), with what is said to be the oldest Welsh epitaph.

Beyond the screen, the original Norman church survives as a chancel with scalloped capitals. It is a calm composition lit by three lancet windows. Here too is an extraordinary organ moved from Llandaff Cathedral in 1900. Most of the painted pipes stand upright but a battery of the largest point horizontally into the choir (the technical term is *en chamade*). They look like the guns of a passing cruiser crashing through the wall and are even painted with dragons' teeth.

The west wall carries impressive neo-classical memorials with the usual shrouded urns, weeping willows and descending doves.

Gwynedd

[*Merioneth, Caernarfonshire, Conwy*]

Gwynedd is the heart, if not always the head, of Wales. It is the most remote, most mountainous, least conquered and most 'pure' province. From Rhodri Fawr in the 9th century to the Llywelyns in the 13th its rulers presumed the leadership of free Wales, as a result of which they were almost always at loggerheads with both their neighbours and the English. The tradition is a habit of mind to this day. From Cardiff, Gwynedd can still seem a law unto itself.

Traces of pre-Celtic and Celtic civilization remain all over the peninsula known as Llŷn, to the north of Cardigan Bay. Hardly a hilltop is not adorned

with a hut circle or fortified encampment, most spectacularly at Tre'r Ceiri, the lofty Iron Age fortress-town with views over half of Wales. Early Christian settlements are likewise plentiful, especially along the pilgrimage coasts north and south to the shrine at Bardsey. They are best illustrated in the two Llangelynnins, one on the shore near Tywyn and the other in the hills above the Conwy valley. The wealth brought by pilgrimage is evident in the oversized churches at Clynnog Fawr and Llanengan. Much-rebuilt Bangor claims to be the earliest cathedral foundation in Britain.

Gwynedd formed the backbone of the rebellions of Llywelyn and Glyndŵr in the late 13th and early 15th centuries, with Llywelyn's own castles surviving at Bere and Dolwyddelan. These are overshadowed by the English castles, most of them Edward I's compliment to the power of Gwynedd at the end of the 13th century. The best are at Caernarfon, Harlech and Conwy, works of Edward's master-builder, James of St George, who retired to become constable of Harlech. Edward settled English boroughs or colonies round his castles, of which Conwy is today the most complete, its medieval walls intact.

The Tudor ascendancy is represented in two of the finest 16th-century town houses in Britain, Plas Mawr and Aberconwy, both in Conwy. Gwydir Castle outside Llanrwst is a medieval mansion, successively altered and extended to form a textbook sequence of early British architecture. To the Tudors Gwynedd also owes its church screens, most exquisitely carved at Llanegryn and Llanrwst.

The religious conflicts of the 17th century are better illustrated in Gwynedd than anywhere in Wales in two private chapels committed to the Old Religion, Gwydir Uchaf and Rug (now in Clwyd). They were followed by equally inconspicuous Dissenting chapels, often hidden in woods and farms, as at Nanhoron (Capel Newydd) and Llanbedr (Salem). The latter offered a setting for Sydney Curnow Vosper's famous Sunlight soap painting.

The county's prosperity from slate and minerals is displayed in the grandee houses built along the north coast in the 19th century. Pre-eminent is the massive pile of neo-Norman Penrhyn by Thomas Hopper, overlooking Menai outside Bangor. Less ostentatious is the model Regency town of Tremadog and its innovative Peniel Chapel.

Herbert North's Wern Isaf is a rare Welsh example of the Arts and Crafts movement, matched by a remarkable church in the same style by Henry Wilson at Brithdir near Dolgellau. Finally, glowing on the north shore of Cardigan Bay is Portmeirion, a delightful essay in 20th-century Welsh picturesque by Clough Williams-Ellis.

Houses and Castles

Bodysgallen Hall *
Bryn Bras Castle **
Caernarfon Castle ****
Castell y Bere *
Cloddaeth Hall *
Cochwillan *
Conwy:
  Castle ****
  Aberconwy House **
  Plas Mawr ****
  Smallest House *

Dinorwig Quarry
  Hospital *
Dolwyddelan Castle **
Gwydir Castle ****
Harlech Castle ****
Llanrwst Almshouses *
Llanystumdwy *
Pennal *
Penrhyn Castle ****
Plas yn Rhiw **

Portmeirion:
  Village ****
  Town Hall *
Tre'r Ceiri **
Tŷ Hyll *
Tŷ Mawr **
Wern Isaf **

Churches

Aberdaron **
Bangor Cathedral ***
Beddgelert *
Betws-y-coed **
Bontddu *
Brithdir ****
Capel Curig *
Carnguwch *
Clynnog Fawr ****
Dolwyddelan ***
Gwydir Uchaf ***

Llanaber ***
Llanbedr *
Llandanwg *
Llanegryn **
Llanengan **
Llanfaglan *
Llangelynnin (Conwy)
  **
Llangelynnin (Tywyn)
  ***
Llangwnnadl **

Llanrhychwyn **
Llanrwst ***
Maentwrog *
Mallwyd *
Nanhoron **
Penllech *
Pennal *
Penygwryd *
Pistyll *
Tremadog **
Tywyn **

Houses and Castles

BODYSGALLEN HALL *

2 miles south-east of Llandudno
Jacobean mansion restored as hotel (Priv)

The old medieval-cum-Jacobean hall of the prominent Mostyn family is now a luxury hotel, proud of its past and careful of its present. The core of the building is an old tower house, similar to the pele towers of the Scottish borders. This was probably built in the late 13th century as watchtower for Conwy Castle, located in the tumbling hills of Pydew behind Llandudno.

Here we must imagine Norman soldiers far from home manning its roof-top and signalling to Conwy of an approaching Welsh horde. There is a fine view (accessible on polite request).

The property passed by marriage from the Mostyns to the no less ubiquitous Wynns. It was Robert Wynn who built the present house c.1620, essentially medieval in form, with a hall on the ground floor (now the reception area) and a great chamber above (now the drawing room). Both have overmantels with extrovert heraldry, depicting the Wynn and Mostyn pedigrees, similar to those in the Wynns' Plas Mawr in Conwy.

The Victorians took Bodysgallen in hand in the 1890s, adding a new dining room and a neo-Jacobean staircase enclosing the ancient tower, as at another former Mostyn property, Cloddaeth Hall, across the valley. Most remarkable was the restoration of the 17th-century garden, which appears not to have suffered from Regency romanticization and whose terraces and walks have been well-restored by the hotel's owner, Richard Broyd.

BRYN BRAS CASTLE **

3 miles east of Caernarfon
Neo-Norman mansion by Hopper, tower rooms and chapel (Priv)

The owner of Bryn Bras was appalled to hear that I had come hotfoot from mighty Penrhyn. I should have seen his first, he said. Bryn Bras was the work of Penrhyn's creator, Thomas Hopper, apparently a sketch in the margin of the great castle. It is more than a doodle, rather a rare neo-Norman country house displaying all Hopper's dexterity.

Bryn Bras is owned and lived in by Mr and Mrs Gray-Parry, with some holiday apartments available for rent. Originally a farm it was converted in the 1820s for Thomas Williams into a towered keep and residence. This has four turrets, rising two storeys above an arcade of wide Norman arches. The house is beautifully set in 30 acres of ornamental gardens on a knoll overlooking the meadows towards Caernarfon and Anglesey.

The interior is stately but not grand. A Norman doorway gives on to a hall alive with patterned decoration, dark and lit with coloured decorative glass. Steps to the left rise to a round flag tower, whose two circular chambers are filled with Hopper's favourite motifs, intersecting blind arcading and zigzag. The heads of the arches are all different and even the door is curved. The upper room has a slate fireplace.

In the main body of the house, the drawing room, dining room and sitting room are more sparing in their Norman decoration. One has an Art Nouveau frieze beneath a Norman cornice. On the stairs a 20th-century owner, Duncan Alves, inserted heraldic stained glass on the basis of a promised knighthood that never arrived.

The library is a workaday room but with a surprise, an arched window bay in the form of a Catholic chapel, adorned with three windows depicting faith, hope and charity. It was used when the house was a school during the war and former girls still return to gaze on the revered spot.

CAERNARFON CASTLE ****

Greatest of Welsh castles set in Edwardian settlement town (Cadw)

Caernarfon, fortress, palace and emblem of alien rule 'is one of the most striking buildings the middle ages have left to us', or so claims the guidebook with some justice. Legend holds that Constantine the Great, first Christian emperor of Rome in the 4th century AD, was born here to the wife of a Welsh noble, Macsen Wledig. Later in life the emperor is said to have dreamt of a castle at the mouth of a fair river among high mountains, its turrets crowned with golden Roman eagles.

The site was indeed a Roman colony and the town's mother church is on the old Roman camp outside the town at Segontium. The Normans recognized the strategic value of the location and built a motte and bailey on the present castle promontory. Gwynedd princes lived here through the 12th and 13th centuries, including Llewelyn the Great. It was the final suppression of his grandson's revolt in 1282 that led to Edward I's colossal rebuilding.

Caernarfon was the greatest of the fortifications begun that year by the king's builder, Master James of St George. It was intended to evoke the spirit of Welsh history, the Roman occupation and the walls of Constantinople – a pan-European display of kingship. Into its walls were built bands of red sandstone imitating bands on the walls of Constantinople.

When Edward and Queen Eleanor arrived from Conwy in July 1283 they stayed in timber apartments, but when they returned the following Easter the Eagle Tower was sufficiently habitable, so it was said, to see the birth of the future Prince of Wales, Edward. Both the castle and the town walls were complete within five years

Caernarfon Castle: the interior wards

and accounts for fitting out cease after 1292. The final outlay was a vast sum, c.£25,000.

Despite this expense, Caernarfon proved vulnerable to Welsh insurgency. In 1294 Madog ap Llywelyn's forces overwhelmed the castle and town and burned anything that could be destroyed. Edward promptly ordered the castle repaired and strengthened, a task continuing until 1304. Turrets were added to the Eagle Tower and the great hall was brought from Conwy and re-erected in the inner ward.

Caernarfon remained a closed English settlement for two centuries and Edward's reinforcement enabled it to withstand Glyndŵr's rebellion with just twenty-eight armed men in 1403–4. After 1485 the Tudor ascendancy reduced the need for such bastions of English power and the buildings fell into decay. Only the Eagle Tower was re-roofed in 1620. The castle was garrisoned by Royalists during the Civil War but not seriously damaged afterwards, despite orders for its slighting. Caernarfon was thus able to survive into the picturesque age externally intact. A late-Victorian deputy-constable restored it

with a vigour that would be deplored today, but prevented further ruination. It saw investitures of Princes of Wales in 1911 and, amid much-ridiculed solemnity, in 1969.

In the 20th century the castle suffered its most ignominious assault, from a car park directly under its south wall. This ruined the view of its walls rising from the River Seiont, as painted by Turner and Wilson. The zigzag wall with its towers and battlements is made to look like a film backdrop. The approach from the town is more impressive, where the castle forms the focus of almost every street vista.

The interior is set round two great wards or courts, one leading out of the other and defined by five towers. The entrance is through the King's Gate, as fiercely defended as that at Beaumaris. The guide offers half a dozen ways in which a hostile visitor might be painfully eliminated. The gate included a chapel and potentially a hall, never completed. On the exterior is an eroded but original (1321) statue of Edward II, first Prince of Wales.

Most of the interior of the castle now has the familiar form of 'ruins in a lawn', round which visitors tend to wander in a daze. Understanding what each block of stone, arch or dank chamber once meant is left to the imagination. The Eagle Tower was supposedly the fortified palace of whoever represented the king in Wales, initially the lieutenant, Sir Otto de Grandison. Three storeys of grand chambers have smaller rooms off them in turrets, including latrines. They are now used for exhibitions and other museology. There is still an excellent view from the battlements.

The Queen's and Chamberlain Towers contain a regimental museum, with between them the footings of the old great hall, centre of hospitality for the English settlement. The remaining towers are composed of passages and chambers, chiefly for defence. The upper ward of the castle was completed only in part and much was restored in the 19th century.

CASTELL Y BERE *

Dysynni valley, 7 miles north-east of Towyn
Heroic Welsh fortress on dramatic rock
(Cadw)

Bere was the iconic castle of the Welsh resistance under Llywelyn. It sits wild and proud under the Cadair Idris massif, looking down past Bird Rock to Cardigan Bay. The Dysynni river at its foot once offered a route for ships from the sea, where now lazy cormorants come inland to nest.

When I was a boy the castle's location was unknown. After the discovery of carved masonry by a local farmer, archaeologists from Aberystwyth instructed masons on its partial reinstatement. When I now read learned Cadw references to its 'complex building history' and 'bewildering joins', I wonder how much is Llywelyn and how much some modern stonemason. What the visitor now sees is not what I first saw, which is why I cannot understand why it was not built higher to grant Bere its due 13th-century magnificence.

The castle was the last redoubt of the greatest of Welsh uprisings, by Llywelyn the Great in *c.*1221. It was defended through the century but finally fell in 1283 to a siege by Edward's mid-Wales supporter Sir Otto de Grandison,

operating from Montgomery. Though Edward refortified it, unlike Cricieth and other Welsh-built castles the alterations were minor. A castle somewhere so wild and hard to defend was soon abandoned. So too was the putative borough in the valley at its foot. Bere is thus the most authentically 'Welsh' surviving castle in Wales.

The defences are based on the steep rocks on all sides, reinforced where needed by ditches and ramparts. The form is of four keeps, two of them in characteristic Llywelyn D-shapes, linked by a wall curving round a courtyard where the rock permitted. In the yard is a well. The south tower is regarded as the most probable location of Llywelyn's apartments.

Access is by a circuitous route over two bridges beneath one of the towers. Since the masonry is mostly new and insubstantial, the chief appeal of the place is its location and view, though John Hilling finds in 'the sinuous lines of banks and ditches' of Bere an echo of the 'sensuous interweaving of the decorative arts' of these Celtic descendants.

CLODDAETH HALL *

2 miles south-east of Llandudno
Medieval hall within 'Jacobethan' school (Priv)

The old hall house of the Mostyns is now buried within a boarding school, St David's. Victorian and modern buildings tower over the old hall and near squeeze it out of existence. But we can still envisage old Cloddaeth (or Gloddaeth) clinging to its hillside, gazing across the valley at its rival, Bodysgallen. It must have been a toss-up which survived as a school and which as a luxury hotel.

The medieval hall, accessible on application, is entered up steps to the old door and has two Perpendicular gothic windows. It is rare in having its original decorative scheme intact. The fireplace is a precious survival, of carved stone, mid-16th century, with an unusual gothic stone fender. The inscriptions painted into the stone arch are in Welsh and Latin, the Mostyn motto, 'Without God nothing, with God plenty'.

The dais end is a virtuoso performance, its

Cloddaeth's Elizabethan splendour

Elizabethan decorations described by Cadw as 'among the largest, best-preserved and most magnificent domestic survivals anywhere in Britain'.

It is raised and adorned with an expansive coved canopy entirely covered in heraldry and grotesques in yellow and red on a mostly grey background. The central arms are of Elizabeth I and, unlike the fireplace, the inscription is in English. It was restored in the 19th century but apparently on the basis of the original design. The wood panelling, beautifully arcaded and crested, survives.

The 16th-century solar wing contained the family room or parlour. It too has an elaborately decorated fireplace, but is now the headmaster's study and offices. Behind what would have been the screens passage at the other end of the hall is the much-restored Jacobean wing, with a magnificent staircase and stained glass inserted by W. E. Nesfield for the Mostyns in 1876.

A bold 1889 façade by John Douglas has been applied to the front, with mullioned windows in red sandstone, some as oriels to take in the view south towards Snowdonia. With its asymmetrical black-and-white gables and lofty chimneys, Cloddaeth is 'Jacobethan' at its most extravagant.

COCHWILLAN *

Tal-y-bont, 2 miles south-east of Bangor
Medieval hall restored as drawing room (Priv)

Cochwillan is the freestanding hall of a medieval courtyard house, built in the 1450s for William ap Gruffydd. He was a supporter of Henry Tudor at Bosworth and was rewarded with the sheriffship of Caernarfon for life. The hall fell into ruin after being abandoned in 1870 but was restored in 1970 by the Penrhyn estate as the drawing room of an adjacent private house. It is used for charity events and is open by appointment.

The hall is a superb relic of its period. The approach is from what would have been the outside of the old courtyard, the original entrance being from within. The dais end is thus to the left of the present door and the great fireplace is on the present entrance side. Restoration

moved back a timbered wall, which had been partitioned for extra accommodation, to allow the Perpendicular window to serve its original purpose of lighting the dais. The other windows are simple trefoils.

The roof is a hammerbeam construction with shields on the terminals. The timbers are dressed with chamfering and there is an intricate carved frieze, all signs of prosperous ownership. The room is furnished for contemporary living, with sofas, heaters, shelves and clutter. While it cannot always be warm – the owner's most reliable heating system, she says, is a trampoline – Cochwillan shows that any historic building can serve a use.

CONWY

CASTLE ★★★★
Edwardian fortress with town walls standing, Victorian bridges (Cadw)

Conwy is another of Edward I's fortresses, masculine to Caernarfon's feminine. Both have suffered grievous assault not from war but from subsequent engineering.

In Conwy's case the offence is near unbelievable, not one but three bridges driven over the river head-on as if in assault on its walls, veering to either side at the last minute to leave the castle marooned as if on a motorway round-

LEFT: *Cochwillan: the great hall*   ABOVE: *Conwy and its three bridges*

about. Since pictures of the castle cannot avoid featuring these bridges they have become part of the castle composition.

Conwy, with its castle, sloping streets and quayside, is the most spectacular of the Edwardian boroughs. Thomas Telford's box girder bridge (1848) at least deferred to it in erecting castellated gateways at each end, while the adjacent footbridge has embattled suspension towers.

The 1950s road bridge – rendered superfluous by a 1991 tunnel – should be removed and an attempt made to recapture Turner's 'sublime and overwhelming emotion' on seeing and painting the castle in 1798.

The castle was begun at the same time as Caernarfon, in 1283, and took ten years to complete. The builder was again Master James of St George, assisted on site by Richard of Chester, using as base a bare rock surrounded by water and marsh.

The castle remains intact to outward view, its walls and eight fortified towers undamaged, as are the twenty-one towers that line the town's walls. Turrets, passageways, windows, arrow slits and battlements are all in good repair. The 'slighting' of a wall during the Commonwealth was, ironically, rectified by the railway company when driving its track past the gap. It did what nobody would let it do today and simply rebuilt the castle wall. Conwy is one of the great achievements of medieval military architecture in Europe.

The interior has none of Caernarfon's lax spaciousness though St George divided it similarly into inner and outer wards. The outer ward, the first approached from the entrance, contains the curved outline of the great hall partitioned by arches, only one of which survives. The towers were used as barracks, kitchens and a prison. A middle gate in a separate wall leads to the inner ward where the royal apartments were located.

These survive, albeit roofless, built into the castle wall, with bedrooms and a great chamber for receiving guests. They were occupied only twice, by Edward himself on his return to Wales in 1295 and by Richard II before disastrously confronting Bolingbroke at Flint in 1399.

Though they appear bleak and the windows have lost their tracery, they are rare examples of fortress accommodation of this period. There is a small vaulted chapel in the chapel tower, with lovely lancet windows.

CONWY

ABERCONWY HOUSE **
Medieval townhouse with later
furnishings (NT)

Aberconwy House is a survivor of a medieval merchant's house of a type that all but vanished for post-war street widening. The house was built in the mid-16th century, though parts date from the 13th. The latter may be the work of English masons travelling in Edward I's retinue.

The house has a stone-walled ground floor with basement, above which rises a timber-framed upper floor. The occupants were initially merchants but later included a coffee shop, temperance hotel, museum and antique shop. When threatened with removal to America, where these buildings were more appreciated, the house was bought and donated to the National Trust in 1934.

The ground floor is reached by an external staircase so distinctive that one resident, Samuel Williams, was nicknamed 'Sam Pen y Grisiau' or 'Sam Top-of-Stairs'. The downstairs comprises just two rooms, a kitchen and living room.

The former carries robust carpentry in the form of two magnificent dressers with appropriate pewter, and a rare hanging bread crate to keep the bread away from vermin. The parlour is simply furnished in 18th-century style, which seems anachronistic.

Anachronistic too is a modern staircase inserted at the insistence of health and safety, spoiling the approach to the great chamber upstairs. This has now been partitioned into a living room and bedroom, the latter with 19th-century furniture. A storeroom contains a dreaded video screen.

Aberconwy House

Tudor nudity at Plas Mawr

CONWY

PLAS MAWR ★★★★
Elizabethan house with restored plasterwork
and courtyards (Cadw)

The house of Robert Wynn, son of John Wynn
of Gwydir, is the most splendid town mansion
of the Tudor period remaining in Britain. Built
in 1576, it shows the pride of the new Welsh mercantile class in being at last permitted to own
property in an English settlement. The house
is filled with motifs indicating Wynn's ancestry
and commercial interests, as well as his loyalty to
the Tudors. The initials RW occur everywhere.

Robert had served in the retinue of the British ambassador to Bruges and returned to Conwy at the age of 50, marrying Dorothy Griffith
of Penrhyn and buying a plot of land to erect a
new house within the town walls. After Robert's
death the property was saved from destruction

by being the subject of a long legal dispute. It
was variously a school, a tenement and a business, partitioned, quartered and multi-occu-
pied but never destroyed. Taken on by the Royal
Cambrian Academy of Art in 1908, it featured in
an early edition of *Country Life*.

The house exemplifies the European merchant house of the late Middle Ages. The street
frontage was designed defensively and for
business. The main house sits retiring beyond
a courtyard surrounded by domestic offices. It
has the traditional 16th-century plan of hall on
the ground floor and great chamber on the first.
However, the house was later expanded and its
orientation turned to present an entrance front
to the side street.

This reorientation gives Plas Mawr much of
its interest. The house is approached through its
south wing with kitchens, pantries and brewhouse beyond. The entrance hall is airy with a
vividly colourful overmantel of 1580, proclaiming the Wynns' princely ancestry to all visitors.
It carries coats of arms, Tudor roses, pilasters

and, most bizarre, bare-breasted caryatids with baskets of strawberries on their heads. I am told the painting of the nipples caused much debate among the conservationists.

The ceilings and walls of most of the formal rooms are coated in swirling ribs into which are set heraldic and hunting motifs. The family parlour is downstairs among the domestic offices, on the site of what would have been the earlier hall. It carries the richest of plasterwork and must have been a warm and cosy retreat on a winter's day. Upstairs are three plastered rooms, two of them principal bedrooms with a servants' room between.

Most spectacular is the great chamber, reached by two spiral staircases and overlooking the side street. The plasterwork here contains more family references and those of local worthies. The overmantel celebrates Queen Elizabeth. The caryatids which line the walls look appropriately overawed. Ceiling bosses have been repainted and the floor laid with rush matting.

My only quarrel with Plas Mawr is that museologists have colonized every corner that is not part of the main suite of rooms. Visitors emerging from an Elizabethan environment are assailed with audio-visual displays, noticeboards and computer screens. Atmosphere is replaced by education monotone. The red-and-white bedrooms are lost to this cause, as is the brewhouse. The attic, which should be a crammed, busy, squalid warren of stores and servants quarters, looks like something from a BBC makeover programme.

CONWY

SMALLEST HOUSE *
… is what it says (Priv)

Is this Britain's smallest house? It is exceedingly small. Its owner and measurer, Margaret Williams, claims its 122 inches by 72 inches as a record, and so does the *Guinness Book of Records.*

The house is authentic and stands on the harbour front with an attendant in old Welsh costume. The last inhabitant, in 1900, was a fish-

erman named Robert Jones who stood (when he could) 6ft 3ins, higher than the ceiling. Known previous inhabitants included a married couple, whose life in the living room and tiny upstairs bedroom defies imagination.

The house was reputedly built in the 16th century on what must have been a peculiar plot of land. The downstairs door occupies half the house's width. Inside is a corner stove and a settee under which the coal for the stove was stored. A ladder leads upstairs where there is a single window and a small bed in which only one person could conceivably sleep. A few Victorian pictures adorn the wall and the owner makes a good living from tourists. Good luck to her.

DINORWIG QUARRY HOSPITAL *

Llanberis
Earliest industrial hospital,
still equipped (Mus)

Facing the north flank of Snowdon across Llanberis is the mighty gash of the Dinorwig slate quarry. Various schemes to landscape it have achieved little, leaving the works of man to return to nature of their own accord. A slate museum stands on the site of the old workshops, run by the National Museum of Wales. But the best impression of work in the quarries is gained by walking along the lake and up to a house built as a hospital for injured miners.

The building dates from 1840 and was an innovation in industrial medicine. There were some 3,000 miners at the time and accidents occurred daily. The hospital was supported by a small subscription taken from their wages. The treatment today looks primitive and mechanical, since the chief injuries were broken and crushed limbs, but the hospital remained in use into the 1950s, and offered first aid for another ten years.

The original wards are in place, together with the dispensary, operating theatre, kitchen and the earliest X-ray machines to be used in Britain (1898). The terrace offers a magnificent view over Lake Padarn towards Snowdon.

DOLWYDDELAN CASTLE **

1 mile west of Dolwyddelan
Surviving fortress of the Llywelyns
on a wild pass (Cadw)

Here is the best place in Gwynedd to sit and imagine the embattled princes of Wales retreating
to defend their land from the invading English.
Dolwyddelan is, like Castell y Bere and Cricieth,
a Welsh castle built by the Welsh. The old keep
stands high on the pass from Betws-y-coed into
the Ffestiniog valley under the shadow of Moel
Siabod. On all sides rise bleak, untrammelled
mountains, almost free of forestry and with
little habitation in sight. Under a dark sky, this
place cries out its Welshness.

Dolwyddelan was built sometime after 1200
by Llywelyn the Great, though legend has him
born in or near it in 1173. It was defended by his
grandson, Llywelyn the Last, against Edward
I, but it fell in 1283, one of the last redoubts of
independence in the Principality. The keep was
supplemented by a curtain wall and, by the end
of the 13th century, a second tower. This stands
ruined on the far side of the courtyard. The
castle was later acquired by Maredudd ap Ieuan,
founder of the Tudor Wynn dynasty and a
descendant of Llywelyn.

The keep is entered by steps to the original
raised entrance, inside which is a roofed great
chamber, with living quarters above. The upper
storey dates from the 15th century. There are
no furnishings. At Dolwyddelan the view, and
history, is all.

GWYDIR CASTLE ****

Half a mile south-west of Llanrwst
Medieval mansion on banks of the Conwy,
panelled Jacobean chamber (Priv)

The story of the rescue of the Wynn seat of
Gwydir is told in Judy Corbett's *Castles in the
Air*, one of ceaseless struggle against adversity.
Stripped of later accretions, the house has been
returned to its medieval and later splendour by
Corbett and her husband, Peter Welford. Cosily
sited in a small park on the banks of the River

Conwy, it is open to visitors and for bed and
breakfast.

The house was the seat of Hywel Coetmor,
who served the Black Prince in France as com-
mander of the celebrated Welsh bowmen. It was
sold to Maredudd ap Ieuan of Dolwyddelan,
who rebuilt the core of the present hall, and
added the adjacent tower. He died here in 1525
and is buried at Dolwyddelan church (see below) after fathering over thirty children. His son
John (d. 1559) took the Anglicized surname of
Wynn (the fair) and benefited from the dissolution of Maenan Abbey, fragments of which start
like ghosts from the walls of Gwydir.

John was father of Robert Wynn of Plas
Mawr in Conwy and grandfather of Sir John
Wynn, late-Elizabethan landowner, business-
man, scholar and politician. He extended
Gwydir by building two ranges of outbuildings
(now vanished) to form an enclosed courtyard.
All that remains of this work is the splendid
porch.

Gwydir, like many Welsh houses of its time,
benefited from ceasing to be the chief residence
of its proprietor and thus escaping demolition.
It suffered an opposite fate in escaping repair.
After this branch of the Wynns died out in the
1670s, the house was owned by various English aristocrats until coming into the hands of
the Victorian Marquess of Lincolnshire, under
whom it saw a visit from the future George V
and Queen Mary. It was sold in 1921 and disaster
followed, the solar tower and west wing being
gutted in separate fires. The place was abandoned until 1944 when it was bought by a well-
meaning bank manager, Arthur Clegg.

While Clegg's renovation saved the building from certain ruin, its 'medievalization'
damaged much of the original house. The superb 1640s panelling in the dining room was
sold in 1921 to William Randolph Hearst (see
St Donat's, Glamorgan), who bequeathed it to
the Metropolitan Museum in New York. There
it was discovered by Welford and Corbett in its
original packing cases, reacquired and brought
back to Gwydir in 1998. The solar hall panelling,
also sold in 1921, is still missing.

So complex is the architectural history of
the house that a walk round it soon dissolves

Gwydir Castle: Jacobean doorcase

into detective work. Most confusing is that the medieval hall on the left of the courtyard, with the later 'hall of Maredudd' inserted above, was supplanted in importance by the solar tower, with its own Elizabethan first-floor great chamber.

The old hall is moodily medieval, with rough stone walls, flagged floor and heavily beamed ceiling. This would once have been open to the rafters and is a remarkable survival of a form altered beyond recognition in most houses of the period.

The 'hall of Maredudd' above was inserted around 1500 and is reached by a spiral staircase of c.1540, encrusted with stone brought from Maenan Abbey, including gothic features in its top lantern. This hall has a wind-braced roof, gothic trefoil windows, two fireplaces and tapestries. Its screen is like the timber-framed outer wall of an old house, while behind is a massive fireplace that looks as if carved from native rock, awesomely vernacular.

To the east of these older halls are a garderobe tower and linking passage to the solar wing. Here is the solar reception room, still naked of its panelling, with a great chamber above, reached by another of Gwydir's many staircases studded with Maenan fragments. A pretty Elizabethan oriel window looks down into the courtyard from over the porch.

The dining room with its restored Jacobean panelling lies to the rear of the linking block. This is among the finest rooms of its period in Wales, c.1640, precursor of the great Gilt Room at Tredegar (Gwent). Dark and glowing in any light, the walls are of rectangular panels with geometric dado decoration, below a frieze of embossed and silvered leather. At one end is a fireplace, at the other a doorcase, both grandly baroque and reminiscent of a similar set in Wolfeton (Dorset). Each is flanked by twinned spiral columns in the style of Bernini, said to indicate support for the Royalist cause.

The fireplace columns form a cornucopia from which tumble putti and birds. Heraldry and zoology drip from every corner. The door has a panel depicting a gryphon whose components – an eagle (front end) and lion (rear end) – mischievously quote the Wynn quarterings.

Gwydir is gradually being refurnished with Elizabethan and Jacobean pieces. Medieval rooms with velvet hangings are already peopled with the ghosts of families long dead. Long tables and benches await wedding guests, their cries echoed by ubiquitous peacocks. Across the Conwy rolls a valley mist, above water meadows that present Gwydir with the menace of an occasional flood.

HARLECH CASTLE ****
Edwardian stronghold on cliff,
Glyndŵr's headquarters (Cadw)

Harlech is the definitive Welsh castle. It stands 200 feet high on an outcrop of the Rhinogs above Tremadog Bay, long painted and photographed with the bay and Snowdon in the distance. It suggests, wrote Jan Morris, 'such a gay glitter of flags and pageantry that the angriest Welsh separatist can hardly resist its charm'. Here we expect to find bards in full cry and damsels in distress. The difficulty with this view today is that politicians have allowed the Morfa dunes at the foot of the castle to be coated in a sprawl of bungalows, sheds and caravans. The humiliation of fortress Wales knows no bounds.

Harlech was built by the ubiquitous James of St George at the same time as Caernarfon and Conwy in the epic year of 1283. To the Welsh its claim to fame is in falling to Glyndŵr in 1404 and becoming his military headquarters for the five years of his uprising. It was also held for the Lancastrians in the Wars of the Roses, enduring the longest siege (eight years) of those wars, the occasion of the song 'Men of Harlech'. It was also the last Royalist castle to surrender in the Civil War.

Harlech has a raw power less evident in other St George castles because it was crammed tight on to a crag. While technically a concentric plan on the Beaumaris pattern, the outer ward is merely a low wall hugging the cliff edge. The main castle thus appears to rise straight from the rock, with an impression of soaring impregnability rare even in Welsh castles. It is also in good condition.

Harlech: definitive Welsh fortress

Like other Edwardian castles, Harlech had to double as a house and garrison. The tight square of walls and corner towers embraced a fortified gatehouse that was both a keep and private chambers.

The inner ward beyond contained the great hall, services and barracks. Guardianship of Harlech was conferred on St George as reward for his royal service. He was constable from 1290–93, a rare instance of an architect living in a building which he created for others. The inner parts of the castle apart from the gatehouse are mere footings.

LLANRWST ALMSHOUSES *

Old charity rooms on show (Mus)

A lane runs from Ancaster Square in the centre of Llanrwst to the church, lined on the right-hand side by a whitewashed Jacobean building with an enclosed courtyard behind. The almshouses were founded, with a free school, in 1610 by Sir Richard Wynn of Gwydir, a characteristic gesture of 17th-century philanthropy.

The charity was to maintain twelve men of the town (and women after 1843). It survived into the 19th century when, like many such foundations, it was ruined by corruption and mismanagement.

Re-founded in 1851, the charity lasted until the death in 1976 of the final inhabitant, Mary Delyn, widow of one of Llanrwst's many harpists. Of gypsy descent she spoke Romany as well as Welsh and would play the harp in the town square. The council declared the building unfit for habitation and was only just prevented from pulling it down.

Restoration as a museum began in 1996 and was completed in 2002. At first every room had been crammed with furniture, but museology took over and rendered the place immaculate. One room has been restored to its 17th-century appearance and another to the 19th century.

Since the almshouses were the eventual home of so many Llanrwst harpists, it is a pity that such music cannot be heard in them today. Is there not a Mary Delyn left in Llanrwst? Or a simple recording would suffice.

LLANYSTUMDWY

LLOYD GEORGE'S CHILDHOOD HOME *
Memorabilia of the great man with
uncle's cobbler's shop (Mus)

The museum dedicated to the famous son of Llanystumdwy sits in the centre of the village opposite a smart chapel, Moriah, designed by Clough Williams-Ellis in 1936. It is filled with the customary paraphernalia of 20th-century history and statesmanship. More atmospheric is the neighbouring house where Lloyd George was raised.

After the death of his father, the young David Lloyd George and his siblings came to live at the simple two-up, two-down cottage named Highgate. It was owned by his mother's brother, Richard George, a cobbler, whose workshop is preserved downstairs.

George was more than a cobbler. He was chapel elder, reader and intellectual, and his conversation while working on his boots was music to the young David's ears. A portrait of him in old age was commissioned by Lloyd George as a tribute. Such men are the unsung artisans of greatness.

Apart from the workshop, downstairs consisted of a kitchen/living room and formal parlour which became the children's study and contained the books left to them by their father. These books, revered by Lloyd George, are sadly now in the museum next door. The kitchen is as it was, with fire and range, cutlery and the usual contents of historic homes rearranged for 'education'.

The family moved to Cricieth in 1880 and the house was sub-let until 1969 when it was recovered and converted into the museum. A delightful cottage garden has been created to the rear, with a path to the garden privy or 'throne room'. On his death in 1945 Lloyd George chose to be buried not in Westminster Abbey but under the rock on which he used to sit and dream by the local stream, the Dwyfor. Here he could see the village bridge and his old school. He refused to allow even an inscription on the tomb. To this day we too can sit by the rock and dream.

PENNAL *

Cefn Caer
Medieval farmhouse with gothic fireplace,
Glyndŵr association (Priv)

Whether or not Owain Glyndŵr 'lived here' is,
like most stories attaching to the man, moot.
He would have passed this way from Harlech
to the parliament believed to have been held at
Machynlleth in 1404.

More significant, a letter written two years
later by his clerical aide, Gruffydd Young, re-
questing help from the king of France was dated
from Pennal on 31 March 1406, and is preserved
in the French national archive. It offered to bring
the Welsh church under the authority of the
Avignon pope in return for papal recognition of
such a church as distinct from that of England.
The bid proved abortive, but gave plausibility to
Pennal as a royal bed and breakfast.

Further evidence is adduced in the white
farmhouse still standing on a hillock to the
south of the village. The site is within the walls of
a Roman camp and many Roman objects have
surfaced over the years. The acquisition of the
farm by the Rowlands family in the 1960s has
led to its restoration, including the discovery
of a 14th-century fireplace. It is here that the er-
rant Glyndŵr is supposed to have warmed his
bones.

The enterprising owner, Elfyn Rowlands,
has gone to great lengths to restore and uncover
the history of the house. He is proud to show
visitors round and holds medieval banquets in
the hall, with guests in period costume. Pennal's equally enterprising vicar has less plau-
sibly accorded the local church the status of
'chapel royal of the princes of Gwynedd' (see
below).

Cefn Caer is certainly an old Welsh hall
house. The hall appears to have been divided
in the Tudor period and given a new chimney,
dated by the beams to *c.*1525. What is remarkable is the survival behind it of the fireplace and
chimney of the original house, with a double-
arched opening dated *c.*1490, and an old bread
oven. The walls have Roman tiles presumably
gathered from the fields outside. A dais screen

is decorated with an owl, a kestrel and human
figures.

The house is filled with furniture and objects of the period, including dressers, pewter
and a reproduction table with benches. Outside
are splendid views over the Dyfi valley, familiar to me from regular visits to this village since
childhood.

PENRHYN CASTLE ****

1 mile east of Bangor
Grand Victorian extravaganza, painting
collection and railway museum (NT)

Penrhyn is one of the greatest Victorian houses,
and surely the least known. As a work of architectural romanticism it stands comparison with
Windsor, Arundel and Eastnor. As a work of
Norman revival it is in a class of its own. The creator, Lord Penrhyn, spent half a million pounds
on its construction, yet he appears not to have
batted an eyelid. His was the greatest slate mine
in the world, at neighbouring Bethesda, with
sugar estates in the West Indies to match. Two
Penrhyn daughters were nicknamed Sugar and
Slate in honour of the family's wealth.

The original estate belonged to the Griffiths
of Anglesey, with a medieval manor house set
on a promontory overlooking the Menai Straits
opposite Beaumaris. This was sold in 1622 and
passed to an Englishman, John Williams, who
was a descendant of an earlier owner named
Gwilym, from whom it passed by marriage to
a family of wealthy merchants, the Pennants of
Flintshire.

The 18th-century Richard Pennant, later 1st
Baron Penrhyn (1739–1808), was Wales's answer
to Coke of Norfolk, an improver, entrepreneur
and politician. His slate quarry benefited from
his salesmanship of 'slates' as a standard school
writing material. He also championed the sugar industry and defended the slave trade as a
Liverpool MP.

Pennant was so rich that when slate went
into recession he redirected his workforce from
quarrying to construction to await an upturn,
building an early tramway from Bethesda to
Port Penrhyn. With the boom in domestic

tourism during the French wars, he also built hotels for visitors to Snowdonia at Capel Curig and Bethesda.

Pennant employed the ubiquitous Wyatt family as managers and architects. Samuel Wyatt built estate villas and extended the old castle on the cliff, while his brother Benjamin designed villages, avenues and bathing pools. By the time Pennant died in 1808 he had transformed north Caernarfonshire from a wild hill-farming community to a prosperous landscape of slate quarries, factories, surfaced roads, villages and resorts. His memorial is in Llandygái church, a sarcophagus attended by a quarryman and a farm girl.

Pennant was childless and bequeathed his estate to a distant cousin, George Dawkins (1764–1840), on condition that he add Pennant to his name. Dawkins was MP for Newark and though he had to wait until 1816 and the death of Pennant's wife to assume his inheritance, he did so in style. Wyatt's old gothick house he considered out of date, not to mention too small. Gwrych Castle had already been completed for another Lancashire plutocrat, Bamford-Hesketh, along the coast at Abergele. This had to be outdone.

Why Dawkins-Pennant chose Thomas Hopper as architect, and romantic neo-Norman as the style, remains obscure. Hopper had worked for the Prince Regent but had designed little of substance. Conscious of Welsh history, he avoided Edward I gothic, choosing instead the style of Wales's earlier invaders, the Normans. Building began about 1820 and continued to 1835.

Penrhyn is gigantically Norman, a fairy-tale composition of keep, towers, turrets, wings and service ranges. The old medieval manor was not demolished but rather engulfed, surviving ghost-like in fragments of the state rooms. The service ranges constitute a castle in themselves. Most remarkable, Dawkins-Pennant insisted that the building materials and craftsmen (apart from stained glass) be local.

The design was not castellated pastiche but properly defensive, defying Pugin's complaint that most Regency castles were so domestic that an assailant could 'kick his way in through the

conservatory'. The castle came complete with arrow slits and murder holes. There were also hot-air ducts, oil and later gas lights, lavatories and an early system of hot and cold running water to the bathrooms.

The creator of this splendour lived barely four years after its completion and was buried in Oxfordshire. The house passed through a daughter to another English family, the Douglases (perforce becoming Douglas-Pennants). They continued to expand the estate, acquired a major art collection and lived in the castle, where they entertained Queen Victoria, the Prince of Wales and Gladstone. Penrhyn passed to the National Trust in 1951.

The interior might be an epic movie set, except that Hopper never seems to lose stylistic control. The quality of carving and craftsmanship renders every corner a museum piece. Norman is everywhere, from window openings and vaults to fireplaces and chair-backs.

An entrance gallery leads into the grand hall. Stone-vaulted and aisled, it is like the chancel of a 12th-century cathedral, rich in shafted columns and dogtooth carving. Like much of Penrhyn, it is not to every taste. One visitor described it as 'about as homely as a great railway terminus … or an exhibition of locomotives or dinosaurs'. Lofty windows are filled with Willement's finest neo-medieval glass.

From here the plan of the house is clear. A passage to the left leads to the family bedrooms in the great keep while to the right stretch the state rooms, expanded from those of the former manor. The latter are formed of the library, drawing room and ebony room.

Here Hopper struggled to domesticate his Norman tendencies. Arches are flattened, windows expanded and not an inch is free of swirls, dogtooth, nail-head and geometrical carving. The ceiling bosses declare Dawkins-Pennant's (distant) ancestral title to the place. Each doorcase, fireplace, table and settee is an individual creation, carved with mummers, animals and heraldic beasts. Axminster carpets cover the floors and the curtains and furnishings are of silk.

Between the drawing room (on the site of the manorial hall) and the ebony room is an

Penrhyn Castle: plutocracy of state

entrance to a medieval spiral staircase to a lost tower. The ebony room, used as the ladies' drawing room, takes its name from the veneered and fake ebony of the arches and furniture, their rich brown/black enhanced by velvet upholstery.

The main staircase is Hopper's virtuoso piece, a vertical shaft of interlaced Norman arches, real and blind, rising to an oriental lantern. The walls display motifs taken from pattern books of ancient architecture and medieval sports and pastimes. Each capital appears different, even in its stone.

Upstairs a ghostly passage leads back to the keep, modelled on Hedingham Castle in Essex. Here are the family rooms, arranged as a suite on each floor. In one is the slate bed in which Queen Victoria famously refused to sleep on her first visit. Wallpapers are by William Morris. The state bedroom has heavy coffered ceilings yet delicate furnishings, including Chinese wallpaper. The furniture and pictures are all in place, remarkably intact after the vicissitudes of the 20th century. The wallpaper in the lower India room is glorious Regency chinoiserie.

Two spectaculars remain. In the chapel Hopper risks exaggeration. The dogtooth vaulting comes down to shoulder-height to join piers coated in zigzag. Not an inch is left flat and the room is suffused with light from stained glass by David Evans of Shrewsbury. The dining room is near indigestible in its richness. The ceiling might be that of a medieval Florentine palazzo enhanced, says the guide, 'by the study of West Indian botanical forms'. The walls carry stencilled Norman motifs while the dado is carved of wood with intersecting arcading.

Walls throughout are hung with paintings from the Penrhyn collection, by Teniers, van der Neer, Gainsborough, Ramsay and a large group portrait of the Dawkins family, with the builder of the castle as a boy. In the breakfast room next door are works by Holbein, Rembrandt, Palma Vecchio, Canaletto and van der Velde. Penrhyn is the Welsh national gallery of the north, yet how many know it?

The familiar offices of a great house are at Penrhyn doubled in scale. To the normal services are added an ice tower, a dung tower and, for good measure, a railway museum. These now form an attraction separate from the house.

For all the demands of conservation, Penrhyn's rooms are kept excessively dark, making the pictures hard to see and preventing views of the majestic setting over the Menai Straits.

PLAS YN RHIW **

5 miles west of Aber-soch
Picturesque retreat restored by
Clough Williams-Ellis (NT)

Former owners of Plas yn Rhiw claimed continuous descent from the 9th-century kings of Powys to 1874. The house was then abandoned until acquired by the three Keating sisters of Nottingham in 1938. They restored it, re-created the Victorian garden and gave everything to the National Trust in 1946, one sister living here until 1981.

The most prominent feature of the house is its location, near the tip of Llŷn overlooking Hell's Mouth Bay. Like all views on Llŷn, on a fine day it is beyond compare, sweeping the full extent of Cardigan Bay to Strumble Head. Open to the Gulf Stream and shielded from the north and east it is an ideal place for the shrubs and flowers that fill the garden to bursting.

The Keatings engaged Clough Williams-Ellis to help them acquire the house and restore it. They also set up the Council for the Protection of Rural Wales, much needed in these parts. Williams-Ellis's minor work on the interior offers the chief interest in what is a modest home.

The entrance is into a small hall dating back to the house's 17th-century origins. Williams-Ellis adorned it with oak columns, plaster capitals and a gothic doorcase, all known as 'Cloughing it up'. The parlour, staircase and upstairs rooms are filled with Keating *objets trouvés*. These include family portraits, pewter, furniture, paintings and watercolours of Wales. There is an early Teasmaid in the bedroom.

From the upstairs sitting room is a view out over box, yew and rhododendron to the deep blue of Hell's Mouth Bay. Here as often as not can be seen the reason for its name, the foaming anger of a storm that brought many ships to ruin.

PORTMEIRION

VILLAGE ✳✳✳✳
Supreme work of 20th-century picturesque,
with houses, streets and tourists (Mus)

The view north across Cardigan Bay from Harlech embraces a harmony of water, wood and mountain with, on the distant shore, what appears a Mediterranean mirage of village campanile.

This is Portmeirion, creation of the 20th-century architect Clough Williams-Ellis and never free of controversy. Portmeirion has been variously dismissed as un-Welsh, Continental, tropical, pastiche, a stylistic junk-yard and, worst of all, popular.

The settlement was begun in 1926 and mostly completed by 1976. It thus straddled the modernist era, at which it thumbed its nose. Most visitors regard it as no more than enjoyably festive. To Williams-Ellis it was a serious exercise in both planning and architecture.

The site was bought in 1925 for £5,000. It consisted of a forest of semi-ornamental trees behind a Victorian villa on the shore, with a steep rocky ravine next to it. Here Williams-Ellis planned his township. He was not intending a joke, nor was he trying to import an Italian language to jolly up a Welsh resort. He understood that the jumbled settlements of the Mediterranean derived their communal quality from deferring buildings to context and contour. Modern architecture might be averse to colonnades, arches, terraces, gazebos, towers and intimate public spaces, but that did not make these things foreign.

Each Portmeirion house, many saved from demolition elsewhere in Wales, has its personal rock or defile, linked to others by steps and terraces. Movement round the village is on foot, cars being unusable in these spaces. There is elegance to Portmeirion and a constant visual surprise, well captured by its use as the set for the TV series *The Prisoner* (whose cult is honoured in a small museum).

Williams-Ellis intended Portmeirion as a holiday village. He restored the waterfront villa as a hotel (with Art Deco restaurant interior)

and continued with cottages to let, each with some foible reflected in its name: Battery, Toll House, Prior's Lodging, Government House, Watch House and Lady's Lodge. Each was embellished with an architectural distinction, such as a Dutch gable, pantiles, a baroque doorcase, a Regency window.

Of the early buildings the one obviously Italianate structure was the bell tower, intended by Williams-Ellis to 'open my performance with a dramatic gesture'. While it clearly echoes Portofino in Italy it also echoes an English church. The buildings are almost all coloured in a bright, cheerful stucco, an East Anglian touch that is undeniably unusual among the grey slate villages of Snowdonia. This again was considered 'un-Welsh'.

After the Second World War, Williams-Ellis became more ambitious, deciding to extend Portmeirion into 'a home for fallen buildings'. The Town Hall (see below) came from Emral in Flintshire. The Gloriette, Gothic Pavilion, Bristol Colonnade and Pantheon were all salvages. Williams-Ellis's genius was in marrying these elements into a theatrical whole by relating them to a series of public spaces, as in any informal village. I have seen Portmeirion in all weathers and elements and it never fails to delight the eye.

Portmeirion's tragedy was to be so ridiculed by professional architects as to render repetition anathema. Its use of sculpture and murals, mosaics, plaques, and even a statue of Shakespeare on a balcony, seemed to reduce architecture to whimsy. The Prince of Wales's mild homage to Portmeirion at his Poundbury estate outside Dorchester suffered similar obloquy. 'Another Portmeirion' became a term of abuse.

While the village is an amusing variation on architectural themes, it reflects a sophisticated aesthetic eye and the hand of a craftsman. Williams-Ellis professed to 'a natural instinct for responding to a site or a building's requirements appropriately … an unerring judgment for proportion and a weakness for splendour and display'.

The proof is in the eating. Portmeirion must be the only 20th-century town in Europe which 200,000 people a year pay just to visit.

TOWN HALL *

The most remarkable of the 'salvage' buildings stands on the far side of the village where the road runs down to the hotel. It was Williams-Ellis's most developed creation, round the rescued great hall of 17th-century Emral Hall in Flintshire.

Its treasure is the most glorious Jacobean ceiling surviving in Wales, barrel-vaulted and depicting the labours of Hercules in plaster. This was on the brink of destruction in 1937 when Williams-Ellis rescued it for £13. He had to dismantle and remove not just the ceiling but much of the house with it, including mullioned windows reused for the opera house-cum-community centre.

While the building's appeal is in these imports, it remains a Williams-Ellis building. The ground floor is of stone, the upper floors a pale terracotta wash. Windows and doors are reminiscent of Frank Lloyd Wright (who admired Portmeirion), yet the roof lantern with a crown on top of a pig boiler is pure Williams-Ellis. Inside is his bust by Jonah Jones, a Durham sculptor who settled in Wales and went on to become principal of Dublin school of art. He contributed many of the plaques and statues at Portmeirion.

The Town Hall, like all of Portmeirion, embodies qualities that should move all architecture: a respect for the creations of the past and an ability to set those creations in a new context.

TRE'R CEIRI **

Llanaelhaearn, 1.5 miles south of Trefor
Iron Age town on mountain top (Cadw)

The image of prehistoric settlements as scattered family enclosures in woods and on hillsides is shattered by the experience of this, the most spectacular fortified township in Britain. Dating from the Iron Age, Tre'r Ceiri spreads like a Celtic Machu Picchu atop Yr Eifl near Trefor on Llŷn, a half hour climb from the nearest road (B4417). The view is breathtaking in all directions, out to Anglesey and back into Snowdonia and the sweep of Cardigan Bay. The site would have been ideally defensive, despite being exposed on open scree with just one spring for water. Its name, meaning town of the giants, must have meant it.

The enclosure is the size of a large but compact village, covering five acres and surrounded by a wall to an average height of 6 feet (in some parts 15) with two clearly discernible defended gates. There is a cairn at the east end (possibly Bronze Age) and an outer rampart to the north, probably guarding a cattle enclosure. In between are arranged some 150 hut footings, mostly circular and so closely packed as to touch each other in rows. They vary in diameter from 6 feet to 18 feet. Larger rectangular structures lay along the north side, as if this were the aristocratic quarter. There appears to be an open courtyard in the middle.

Finds indicate that the settlement was occupied into the Roman era. Much of the ruination of the site was caused in the 19th century when a local woman dreamed of a crock of gold buried somewhere beneath it, causing a minor gold rush. It must once have presented an astonishing sight.

TŶ HYLL *

2 miles west of Betws-y-coed
THE UGLY HOUSE
Rare medieval 'house of the night'
in romantic dell (Mus)

This extraordinary structure is an example of Darwin's survival of the fittest. Ancient law stated that anyone who could build a house in a night and have smoke coming from its chimney by morning would enjoy squatters' rights. Hence the nickname *tŷ unnos* or house of one night. The builder could also claim a smallholding to the extent that he could throw an axe from each corner of the building.

There were once many such buildings in Wales but this is the only one to survive in recognizable form. Unreliable tradition has it built in 1475 by two outlaw brothers. It cannot have been built in a night, but it may have been constructed of turf and then rebuilt, and there was often goodwill from manorial authorities eager for immigrants.

Portmeirion: north Welsh picturesque

The wall stones are undressed slabs from the mountain outside, positioned so the rain would run off outwards. For mortar there would have been moss, traces of which have been found in the walls. The roof would initially have been of logs covered in heather thatch. The lack of any 'finish' is what gives the house its name, curiosity and charm. Only the later slate roof indicates modernity.

The story of the house is lost. It was abandoned when workers on Telford's Holyhead road came upon it in 1815 and stayed in it for the duration of their work. There was no census reference but a Victorian guide of 1853 mentions it as 'one of the most picturesque cottages imaginable … giving additional beauty to this romantic dell'.

The house was later visited by tourists to Snowdonia, occupied first by a shepherd and then by a Great War veteran named Riley, who invented himself as 'the little crooked man in the little crooked house' of the children's rhyme. He and his wife died in the 1960s. The house fell on hard times until taken over by the Snowdonia Society in 1988 as part office and shop, part Welsh cottage museum. The garden is still mercifully wild.

TŶ MAWR **

3 miles south-west of Betws-y-coed
Lonely farmhouse, birthplace of
Bible translator (NT)

Tŷ Mawr was the birthplace of William Morgan, translator of the Bible into Welsh. It is an old farmhouse beautifully situated in an isolated corner of the Wybrnant valley, tributary of the Conwy three miles south of Betws-y-coed.

Morgan's life typified the Tudor Welsh ascendancy. He was born the second son of a farmer in 1545 and brought up conversant with the verse and song of Wales. Showing early promise he came under the patronage of the Wynns of Gwydir and made his way to St John's College, Cambridge, returning as vicar of Llanbadarn Fawr and Welshpool, a classic case of upward social mobility. It is a measure of the decline of Anglicanism in Tudor Wales that, in 1587, only three of the 134 parishes in St Asaph diocese had resident incumbents. One reason was Henry VIII's decree that only English be used in church, a language few worshippers would have understood.

Morgan's work on the Bible was preceded by that of William Salesbury and others who translated the Prayer Book and New Testament into antique Welsh. Morgan preferred a more contemporary language, only marred, says the guide, 'by occasional traces of North Wales dialect'. He completed his translation in 1587 and went to London to supervise the printing (and proof-reading). Some 1,000 of his Bibles were printed.

The Morgan Bible was astonishingly popular. Despite editing and revision it has survived unaltered, while the English Bible was being 'authorized and revised'. Not until 1988 was a new text published, and Morgan's creation still lies massive and majestic on lecterns, tables and dressers across Wales. He rose to become Bishop of St Asaph and died in 1604.

Tŷ Mawr is a conventional Tudor farmhouse, but more substantial than that in which Morgan was born, which would have been of just one storey with a hall open to the roof. In the rebuilding of the late-Elizabethan period a fireplace and upper chambers were inserted. Later alterations were removed when the house passed to the National Trust and was restored to its early-17th-century state.

The house has a screens passage, hall and upper bedroom. The furniture is contemporary with, but not original to, the house. Part of the upstairs is devoted to a museum of Welsh Bibles. The flowers round the outside are of the 16th century and an old byre has been left on the other bank of the stream. The site, indeed the entire valley, is idyllic.

WERN ISAF **

Nr Bangor, 1 mile south-east of Llanfairfechan
Art nouveau 'butterfly' house (Priv)

This rare example of a 'butterfly' house sits on a hillside outside Bangor, looking across the Menai Straits to Anglesey. It is inhabited by the granddaughter of its architect, Herbert North, an English immigrant to Wales who worked for Lutyens and was a pupil of the Arts and Crafts master Henry Wilson. He co-authored pioneering works on the churches and cottages of Snowdonia.

The house is charmingly set in woods above a meadow. It was built in 1900 and has been preserved to convey the self-conscious ideology of its period. The concept of the butterfly was to emphasize the line from the entrance through a staircase lobby and out on the far side into nature. The rooms were set at an angle to this axis, like the wings of an insect. It is architecture as metaphysics.

Such a house was meant, said the architectural theorist William Lethaby, to derive a *genius loci* from this arrangement. North's house even has a crystal ball hanging in the hall to carry its spirit from the front door through the French windows at the back to a pool on the far terrace. He said it needed 'the element of beauty and poetry which gives it individuality … the relations of window to wall, of chimneys to roof, of mass to contour – a beauty for which many of the old cottages are so conspicuous.' Would that all builders were so sensitive.

The entrance hall is in white wood, dominated by stairs which rise to a landing giving access to all bedrooms. There is thus no need of a space-wasting corridor. The downstairs is composed of a curved sequence of living rooms looking out into the garden. They can be combined as one volume or divided by partitions into four. The window-seats are repeated in the seats of the terrace outside. Delightful wooden shutters carry patterned cut-outs, declining in number as they approach the kitchen.

Everything original has been retained, cupboards, furniture, tables and fireplace surrounds, some decorated with lozenge patterns, others with ceramic or mother-of-pearl. North's wife, Ida, was a keen needlewoman and her work is displayed everywhere, along with alcoves containing pots and other objects of the period.

North designed Wern Isaf when he was just 28 and died in 1941. It retains the atmosphere of a young man's fancy.

Churches

ABERDARON

ST HYWYN ✱✱
Pilgrimage point for Bardsey, Norman arch, seaside botany

In 1190 the papacy, eager to build on Henry II's reconciliation with the Church after the murder of Thomas Becket, granted St David's in Pembrokeshire and Bardsey Island off Llŷn the same pilgrimage status as Santiago de Compostela in Spain. A visit to both equalled one to Rome. The effect was to give medieval Welsh tourism a sensational boost. Pilgrims poured across Wales to the favoured sites and many travelled between the two along the shores of Cardigan Bay, with a detour to the monastery of Strata Florida in the middle.

The monastery on Bardsey (or Enlli) was founded in AD 615 by monks from Bangor Iscoed near Wrexham, retreating from their defeat by a Northumbrian army. They fled to Bardsey, which may or may not have been an existing Celtic settlement, and there sustained a Christianity independent of Rome into the Norman period. There were still a dozen inhabitants on the island in the 1950s, now reduced to a single couple of custodians.

Aberdaron was both a *clas* in its own right and the point of embarkation for pilgrims to Bardsey, already reputed resting place of 10,000 (or possibly 20,000) saints and enticingly visible from the entire sweep of Cardigan Bay. It was formally the sister church of Enlli on the island, lying sheltered in an anchorage behind a headland. Today it still evokes both destination and point of departure. There is next door an ancient hostelry, Y Gegin Fawr or great kitchen. The Norman door to the church overlooks the beach, with a triple moulded arch. Through this door would have passed hundreds of thousands, perhaps millions, seeking salvation from the ills of the world and convinced of the imminence of salvation.

Nothing else survives of the Norman church. Such was the popularity of Bardsey that

Aberdaron: pilgrimage departure point

Aberdaron's nave was extended in the 13th or 14th century and a south aisle, eventually a second nave, was added in the 16th, with a fine hammerbeam roof. With the decline in pilgrimage after the Reformation, the church too declined and in 1841 the encroaching sea consumed part of the churchyard and threatened the church itself.

A new building was erected on the hill above the village, but this proved so unpopular that the Welsh restorer Henry Kennedy repaired the old one for reuse in 1860. In the north wall are set two monks' headstones from neighbouring Tudweiliog, probably predating the church, allegedly from the 5th century.

The churchyard is remarkable in remaining wholly wild. It slopes towards the Gulf Stream and the south-westerlies and is protected from north and east, creating a natural Kew Gardens of salt-tolerant wild flowers. The common names of the plants recorded are a delight: thrift, mayweed, sea beet, rest harrow, kidney vetch, yarrow, wild carrot, lady's bedstraw and bird's foot trefoil.

Aberdaron was the last of the Welsh churches of which the poet R. S. Thomas was vicar, from 1967–78. On this weather-beaten shore he found inspiration for his pessimistic naturalism, as if reassured in his doubt by the spirits of the departing faithful:

I lie in the lean hours awake
Listening to the swell boom somewhere in the
    Atlantic,
Rising and falling, rising and falling,
Wave on wave on the long shore
By the village that is without light,
And compassionless.

BANGOR CATHEDRAL

ST DEINIOL ✱✱✱
Ancient foundation, much restored by Scott,
modern murals

Given the mess that is central Bangor, the survival of its cathedral in what remains of a close
is remarkable. It was formed in AD 546 as a
diocese by Maelgwn, son of King Cadwallon
and great grandson of Cunedda, first ruler of
Gwynedd.

The church was based on St Deiniol's monastic cell of c.525. This puts it as among the oldest churches in Britain. Whatever remained of
early buildings on the site was destroyed by the
Vikings, and a Norman successor church was
burned by King John in 1210, during the rrev-
volt of Llewellyn the Great. The present structure is predominantly Decorated gothic of the
13th and 14th centuries.

Though not much bigger than a large parish church, Bangor Cathedral is big-boned and
confident. 'It thrills but does not overawe', writes
the dean sensibly in the guide. The Perpendicular west tower looks incongruous, as if tacked
on to a parish church in Suffolk. Lack of funds
prevented the completion of a steeple intended
to rise above the central crossing. The grey exterior is heavily restored.

The whitewashed interior was created or
repaired by Sir Gilbert Scott in the 19th century, using such fragments as he could find of
the ruined 14th-century crossing and choir.
Scott's attention to detail is well displayed in
the coloured vault and episcopal furnishings
of the choir or presbytery, including a fine set
of choir stalls and bishop's throne. The medieval floor tiles were meticulously copied and
relaid, while the reredos is of 1881 by Scott's son,
Oldrid.

The Lady Chapel reveals a delicately chamfered 13th-century arch framing a modern mural by Brian Thomas (1955) above a reredos by
Caröe. The Thomas mural is of Christ on the
road to Emmaus in the style of Caravaggio. Another mural by Thomas at the west end of the
cathedral depicts too plentiful cathedrals of
Wales.

Next to it stands the Mostyn Christ, a late-
15th-century life-sized statue in wood with a
face of poignant suffering. Belonging to the
Mostyn family, it is one of those exquisite medieval works, presumably created in Wales, that
so enhance a visit to churches un-raided by
museum curators.

Bangor's guidebook constantly incants that
the cathedral 'is not a museum', yet that is just
what it is, and a fine one too. It should be proud
of it.

BEDDGELERT

ST MARY ✱
Early English arcade and window

The church is beautifully located amid the
foothills of Snowdonia. In rain its grey-black
stone adds to the enveloping gloom yet it leaps
to life when the mountains turn Alpine under blue skies. Here was a Celtic *clas* still independent when visited by Gerald in the 12th
century. It later became an Augustinian priory
with extensive land in Gwynedd and therefore under the patronage of the princes of
Gwynedd. The legend of it being the grave of
Llewelyn's dog is an 18th-century invention.

The church sits between the village and the
river in a carefully tended garden with flowers
allegedly coloured to the emotions of the seasons. Fragments of a 12th-century structure
survive in the walls but this is mostly a Victorian
rebuild. There is no tower, just a bellcote.

Inside the scene is dominated by a remarkable Early Gothic north arcade and east window
of c.1230, superlative architecture for these remote parts. The arches and triple lancet window
over the altar must have seemed revolutionary
after the rough Norman style. Panelling and
furnishings are all Victorian or modern, the
screen and rood inserted in 1921.

The font is an antiquarian curio. It was restored in 1882 and carries two inscriptions. One
is in the Nennius alphabet, 'said to have been
devised by the supposed 8th-century monk,
Nennius', the other is in a different alphabet devised by the eccentric Welsh bard Iolo
Morganwg (1747–1826).

BETWS-Y-COED

ST MARY **
Robust tourist church by Lancashire
architects

After the wealth of single-cell Gwynedd boxes
it is a relief to come across a great shout of a
building. By 1873 the medieval church at Betws
had become too small for the booming gateway
resort to Snowdonia. This is locked, sadly so
as it was the setting for David Cox's *The Welsh
Funeral*, a celebrated image of Welsh life.

Cox brought artists to Betws in the 1840s,
based at the Royal Oak and forming one of the
first artists' colonies in Britain, in contrast to the
peripatetic habits of his predecessors.

The village felt it needed something not just
bigger but more appropriate for a prosperous
clientele largely from the north-west of England.
The parish sought out the most fashionable Lancashire architects of the day, Paley and Austin,
who supplied a church in robust Norman/Gothic
transitional style, as if Betws were Preston or
Stockport.

The cruciform structure looks from the outside like a cliff hewn from the adjacent Welsh
mountains, designed to withstand driving
Snowdonia rain and miserable in sunshine. The
surface is two-tone within and without, grey
local bluestone dressed with pink Lincolnshire
sandstone.

The tower, not completed until the 20th century, contains a set of tubular bells which can be
played on a keyboard in the vestry. At its base
is a curious door in what appears to be a neo-
Egyptian style.

The interior begins with a vigorous Victorian nave with elaborately carved scallop-and-
wave arcade capitals. At the crossing, ornate
stepped arches rise to a stone-ribbed vault, repeated in the chancel and giving the church a
formal grandeur.

An unusual arrangement of five lancets and
two rose windows fills the east wall above an
alabaster reredos. The choir stalls are Arts and
Crafts, and Burne-Jones glass fills the north
aisle lancets. The whole composition is smart
and confident.

BONTDDU

Caerdeon, 2 miles west of Bontddu
ST PHILIP *
French-style Victorian church
with large porch

This extraordinary building is perched on a
steep hillside west of Bontddu with a view over
the Mawddach estuary towards Cadair Idris. In
style it might have been transported from the
Pyrenees. The chapel was built in 1860 by a cler-
gyman retired from Christchurch, Oxford, W.
E. Jelf, for use by undergraduates studying clas-
sics at his neighbouring house. They were reluctant to travel three miles to Barmouth where, in
addition, the services were in Welsh.

A licence granted by the Anglican bishop of
Bangor for the chapel to worship in the English
language incensed the Welsh clergy, not least
the rector of Barmouth, and became a cause
célèbre. There were appeals to the courts and
the archbishop of Canterbury, and 'unfriendly
and un-christian letters' were sent between the
participants. Sadly this is not recorded in the
guides. This typically Anglican dispute died
with Jelf in 1875, but meanwhile another church
had opened in Bontddu itself, as the guide says
with 'more than a hint of being regarded as a
mission church for the poor of the village while
the gentry attended St Philip's'.

The building is chiefly remarkable for its site
and outward appearance. It was designed by
Jelf's brother-in-law in the style of his favourite Pyrenees. The original was a large chamber
whose most prominent feature is a parvise
porch of rough-cast stone big enough to hold
a French market, the only one I have seen in
Britain. The bellcote has four external bells
with carillon hammers. Beneath the west wall
a steep and picturesque dell runs down to the
Mawddach.

The interior is exceedingly plain but has two
fine windows in the colourful abstract style of
Wailes. There is also a so-called Positive Organ,
apparently a simplified instrument designed to
be played by any pianist.

The church has enthusiastic support and is
kept open.

Brithdir: Arts and Crafts in Mawddach valley

BRITHDIR

3 miles east of Dolgellau

ST MARK ★★★★

Arts and Crafts masterpiece in Dolgellau woods

Apparently lost in the woods to the east of Dolgellau is one of the most remarkable Arts and Crafts churches in Britain. Where we might expect a modest rural chapel is a looming structure of Transylvanian gloom. It owes its existence to the marriage of the Reverend Charles Tooth, chaplain to the English community in Florence, to Louisa, widow of a member of the local Richards family. On Tooth's death Louisa honoured his wish for his fortune to be devoted to advancing Christ's cause with a church in Wales. She asked the Arts and Crafts architect J. D. Sedding and his assistant, Henry Wilson, to build something that reflected Tooth's Italian interest.

Sedding died soon after, but Wilson completed the church, declaring that it would look 'as if sprung out of the soil instead of being planted on it'. It was to be of local stone and slate, forming 'a subtle connection between the look of a scene and the geology of it … The art of the place must be of the place, not imported into it.' The church was completed in 1898. The exterior, surrounded by dark evergreen and thick with rhododendron, is severe. Cruciform with a small bellcote over the crossing, its most prominent feature is the west wall, where a gable juts on giant brackets and the roof sweeps down over the doorway and porch. The windows are tiny.

The interior is extraordinary, Italian romanesque in style yet modern in atmosphere. The bright cream of the nave contrasts with the red ochre and sky blue of the chancel and apse walls. Rounded arches and niches form a dramatic setting for the fittings, either executed or planned by Wilson and all of outstanding quality. The altar is particularly fine, given by Charles Tooth's brother, Arthur, who was best known for having stones thrown at him while taking Holy Communion, for alleged popery. The beaten copper front depicts the Annunciation among roses, with two angels in attendance, one portraying Charles and other his guardian angel. The reredos, also of copper, shows a vine emerging from a chalice. Round it are set candle-holders and wall brackets.

The choir stalls are pure Arts and Crafts, of chestnut and adorned with rabbits, squirrels, mice and an owl. The pulpit is covered in beaten copper depicting bunches of grapes in relief. The font is of lead and the north and south doors are of teak inlaid with sparkling abalone shells. The modern seats are a disappointment. Brithdir is with the Friends of Friendless Churches.

CAPEL CURIG

ST JULITTA ★

Unrestored Snowdonia chapel

Along the Snowdon road from Capel Curig is a tiny church near the river in the Nant y Gwryd valley. Curig was a Welsh bishop of the 6th century but the dedication was changed by the invading Normans to a Latinized saint of a similar name. Curig thus became Cyricus, a 3-year-old son of a 4th-century Turkish Christian named Julitta. When his mother was being led away for torture and execution, the presiding governor attempted to pacify the screaming infant. The child kicked and scratched him and was dashed to death on the ground for his pains. He and his mother were duly canonized – and are bizarrely commemorated in this wild place.

The church has a double square plan, probably of the 14th century, with a small south chapel. It was the church for the village of Capel Curig but, following the Victorian tourist boom, a new church was built in the centre of the village in 1883. The old chapel, already rebuilt in 1839, was rededicated to Julitta, supposedly Curig's 'mother', and was thus saved from stripping. Box pews and an 18th-century pulpit survive as does the plastered ceiling. St Julitta's thus appears like hundreds of Welsh churches would have been before Victorian restoration. It is deconsecrated but the tourism which saw its demise is reviving its fortunes. A group of friends has opened it for information about Snowdonia and exhibitions of local art.

CARNGUWCH

4 miles east of Nefyn
ST CUWCH *
Mountainside enclosure with
crowded graveyard

The mystic solitude of this place engulfs the
visitor. It sits alone on a grassy platform on the
slopes of Mynydd Carn Guwch, a breast-shaped
mountain at the far extremity of Llŷn. Its saint is
unknown, variously Ciwg or Cuwch.

What can have induced anyone to locate a
llan here? The early hermit churches of Llŷn are
almost all on the pilgrimage routes along the
coast while this is on a mountainside. There is
no evidence of any settlement, only the muddy
farm of Penfras Uchaf below, through which
the church is reached on foot. Was it perhaps
a prehistoric site, a lookout affording the security of a view out to Cardigan Bay and inland
to Snowdonia? Certainly if there is holiness in
a view it is here.

The church stands within an extensive
stone-walled enclosure crowded with old slate
headstones, suggesting loyal parishioners from
some distance. Tim Hughes points out that the
Welsh inscriptions are remarkably detailed and
explicit, apparently reflecting a local obituary
tradition. A few hawthorn trees battle with the
wind. The building is undistinguished, a simple
cell with larger tower than is usual. The walls
are painted green and white. Simple benches fill
the interior with a two-decker pulpit. Oil lamps
must have supplied an eerie light in winter.

CLYNNOG FAWR

ST BEUNO ★★★★
Pilgrimage church with original fittings
and saint's shrine

This was the main assembly point for pilgrims
travelling along the north coast of Llŷn from
Caernarfon to Bardsey. St Beuno, uncle of St
Winefrid of Holywell and patron saint of North

Pilgrim prosperity at Clynnog Fawr

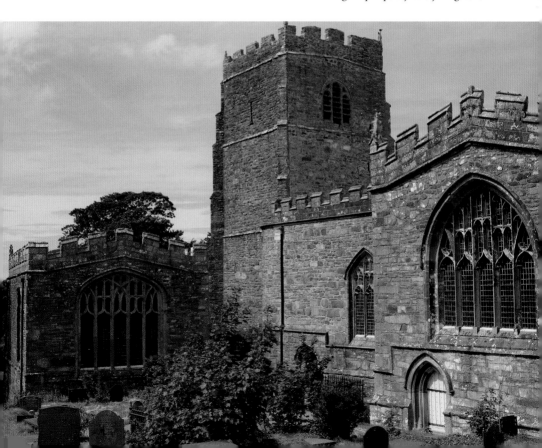

Wales, founded a *clas* here in the 7th century, dying in 642. This was rebuilt in the 15th century to handle the crush of pilgrims on a scale wholly unusual for this part of Wales. A holy well is still located near the church.

Clynnog Fawr is immediately noticeable from the main road for its robust three-stage perpendicular tower and separate, battlemented chapel containing the shrine of St Beuno. A similar arrangement can be seen at Llaneilian (Anglesey). The interior, now stripped of Victorian pews, is big and bright, lit by wide windows. It has a spacious carved and panelled tie-beam roof and a splendid seven-light east window. The plain chancel screen seems too big for its arch, but the chancel retains its choir stalls and is pleasantly intimate compared to the nave. The sedilia with ogival arches are also 15th century.

The church is crowded with objects of interest. There are dog tongs for removing obstreperous animals and a dug-out medieval chest, improbably claimed to belong to St Beuno himself. The latter was so strong that a local saying for impregnable was 'You may as well break St Beuno's chest.' Clynnog's mazer, an ornamental 15th-century drinking bowl, has been removed to the national museum in Cardiff, a deplorable practice. An exhibition of the church's role in the Bardsey pilgrimage is in the north transept.

A short enclosed passage leads to St Beuno's chapel, under whose floor was found the presumed remains of the original church. The chapel was used in the 18th century as the parish lock-up and is a light, perpendicular chamber with a reputedly pre-Norman sundial outside its south-west corner. Sick pilgrims would be laid here on rushes overnight. From here Beuno is said to have travelled each week to preach in Anglesey. One day his precious book of sermons was mislaid on a sandbank and threatened by the tide. A helpful curlew picked it up and brought it to the saint's feet, as a result of which he asked God to make the curlew's nest the hardest of all to find, which duly occurred. One good turn deserved another.

In homage to the early pilgrims, bishops of Bangor led pilgrimages from Clynnog to Bardsey in 1950 and again in 1992. Hundreds attended.

DOLWYDDELAN

ST GWYDDELAN ✳✳✳
Picturesque interior, original screens
and fittings

I entered this church in its Snowdonia glade late on a spring day and found a priest in jeans and an elderly lady deep in worship. They prayed for the village and for various of its residents by name, for its sister churches, for the archbishop of Canterbury (a Welshman) and for the war in Iraq. They recited some of the prayers in English and some in Welsh. It was a ritual of quiet dignity, truly *urbe et orbe*. When they had finished they welcomed me and showed me round.

While its saint is old – Gwyddelan means little Irishman and was presumably one of the Irish diaspora said to have arrived in Wales *c*.600 – the church was rebuilt *c*.1500 by the local lord, Maredudd, founder of the Wynn dynasty, later of Gwydir. It is a single-cell structure with south chapel built by Robert Wynn of Plas Mawr in Conwy.

Inside, the cell is divided by a two-bay arcade and what appear to be Saxon arches and a bulbous Saxon pillar. The theory that these are anything to do with Romans, let alone Saxons, is implausible, attributed to a Wynn antiquarian conceit. Dolwyddelan has intact furnishings. The vernacular screen, apparently from an earlier church, is crudely carved, with a parapet decorated with S-shaped balusters. It is lined with candles. The pulpit, lectern and altar rail are all pre-Victorian and an old ceiling survives over the chancel. The pews have wooden 'sleigh' sides to protect the occupants presumably from a former mud floor. The church has an ancient hand-bell, allegedly used by the early monks to ward off the devil.

On the north wall are the memorials to Wynn and his family. Maredudd is depicted in a brass and in a fine baroque monument, at prayer but fully armed, a necessary precaution in these parts. Outside is a 3,000-year-old yew.

Peace in Snowdonia: Dolwyddelan

GWYDIR UCHAF ✱✱✱

1 mile south-west of Llanrwst
Private chapel with painted ceiling

Gwydir, like Rug (Clwyd), is the chapel of a wealthy Welsh family built on their estate away from the religious and physical plagues of the local parish church. It was an aloofness disapproved of by the established Church, eager to strengthen parochial unity and discourage dissent of all kinds. In the 17th century, private worship was also a safety valve for those whose loyalty to the 'Old Religion' conflicted with their loyalty to the state.

The chapel was built in 1673 by Sir Richard Wynn, descendant of Maredudd (see Dolwyddelan) and nephew of the Sir Richard who, half a century earlier, had built the gothic family chapel alongside the parish church in Llanrwst.

Gwydir Uchaf: High Church jollity

The two chapels illustrate many things – the growth of gentry exclusivity and the transition in religious preference and architectural style over the course of the 17th century.

Gwydir Uchaf (Upper Gwydir) was a new house built by Wynn uphill from the ancient, presumably damp and unhealthy, house in the valley. Its surviving parts are forestry offices. The chapel is in what was the garden, a complex of exotic terracing now lost in the woods. The exterior is a plain rectangular box, with a bellcote and gothic tracery in the east window, as if to camouflage the interior in Protestant garb. The side windows have little hearts carved into their surrounds.

The exterior is no preparation for the interior. This was unashamedly High Church, so much so that a letter to Wynn from a local Jesuit regrets his inability to find a cross for the new chapel since 'ye art is now wholeye lost, and non durable to be gott unlesse out of some old church windowe'. The dedication was

to the once-forbidden cult of the Holy Trinity. The evolution in style from William Salusbury's earlier but equally High Church Rug of 1637 could not be greater. Medieval gloom has given way to Restoration lightness.

Round the walls are box pews arranged collegiate style, with built-in pulpit and lectern. In the centre of the church are magnificent Jacobean chairs, as if the congregation were assembled to listen to the reading of a will. The altar, slightly raised, is severe. A gallery to the west would have been for the musicians.

All eyes turn to the painted ceiling, an arch-braced structure covered in figures in pastiche baroque, on a blue background to indicate sky. In the east bay the theme is Christ, in the middle bay God and in the west the Holy Ghost as a dove, with two angels trumpeting the Day of Judgment over the musicians' gallery. There is much gold paint and many charming cut-out angels on the springers. The work does not bear much scrutiny – childlike and 'miserably ex-ecuted' wrote an 1800 visitor – but the effect is delightful. Here are none of the skeletons and memento mori of Rug. Wynn died soon after its construction, but the chapel was used for services until 1920. It is now in the care of Cadw.

LLANABER

1 mile north of Barmouth
ST BODFAN ✳✳✳
Early Gothic arches, Cardigan Bay headland

This is a charming place. So sweeping is the large churchyard sloping towards the sea that the church looks at first like an afterthought, a graveyard chapel. It is not. Llanaber is a rich and virtually unaltered work of Early Gothic, built in the early 13th century by Hywel ap Gruffudd, lord of Merioneth. The chancel may be a relic of an earlier Celtic foundation on the site.

Llanaber: Early Gothic perfection

The much-restored exterior is uninteresting except for the porch, with an Early Gothic arch of four roll-mouldings. The interior is a casket of beauty, the nave of five bays with pointed arches on circular drum piers. The capitals carry rudimentary stiff-leaf in a variety of patterns, progressing towards a tall chancel arch with mock Ionic capitals, sophisticated, almost stately for so small a space. Everywhere are lancet windows, in the west wall, the aisles and the clerestory, overfilled with Victorian stained glass.

The narrow chancel seems to clamber up the slope to escape the sea, turning a few degrees north in doing so. It is unusually long, divided into a small choir and raised sanctuary. Mouldings again surround the east lancet, below which is a 20th-century Arts and Crafts reredos of c.1911 by John and Mary Batten. This is of foliage with a wheatsheaf motif. The roof is open, with much-needed wind braces. At the back of the church is an eight-sided font. Against the north wall are two stones with Roman inscriptions, one of them found on the beach.

LLANBEDR

Pentre Gwynfryn, 1 mile east of Llanbedr
CAPEL SALEM ✻
Baptist chapel, subject of celebrated painting

To many English (and even more Welsh) this is the most famous place in Wales, if they did but know it. A Welsh watercolour of 1908 by Sydney Curnow Vosper, entitled 'Salem', depicted an elderly lady with stovepipe hat and shawl taking her seat among villagers in this chapel. Embodying the dignified piety of rural Welsh Nonconformity, it was used to sell Sunlight soap. In reality only one of the worshippers portrayed was from Salem and the woman, Siân Owen, had to borrow the costume for the sittings. It was said that the Devil could be seen in the folds of the shawl. The picture hangs in the Lever Gallery at Port Sunlight.

The chapel sits in a wooded Merionethshire lane near the hamlet of Pentre Gwynfryn, inland from Llanbedr. It is of the Baptist persuasion, baptisms being conducted in a pool of the Artro stream at the bottom of the graveyard.

Outside it looks like a row of cottages, with a *tŷ'r capel* (chapel house) at one end. On my visit the latter had a welcome plume of chimney-smoke and a barking dog.

Inside, the chapel is spacious, lit by four clear windows. A central pulpit at one end has box pews for elders in front and then raked seating, as in a theatre, for the congregation. Hat-pegs line every wall.

As indicated by the Vosper painting – and often denied by Welsh historians – these communities were not grindingly poor. Welsh farming was diversified into livestock and wool, and the hills were mined for slate, tin and manganese. The woods prepared timber for the slate industry. Hence the many rural chapels on these hillsides. A reproduction of Vosper's painting hangs on the wall. On the shore south of Llanbedr is a rare Welsh nudist beach. What would Salem have said?

LLANDANWG

2 miles south of Harlech
ST TANWG ✻
Ancient foundation half buried in sand

This is the lost church of the dunes. It lies at the end of a cul-de-sac from the village of Llanfair and must have been supremely atmospheric before someone permitted bungalows and a car park to spread to the edge of the churchyard. It remains a lovely spot, with the sound of waves crashing beyond ramparts of sand, which blows against the walls and into the nave.

Llandanwg claims to have been founded in AD 435, which makes it among the earliest churches in Wales (indeed in Britain). It would appear, like Gunwallow in Cornwall, to have begun life as a hermit cell. Another theory is that these coastal churches were embarkation points for boats taking corpses across the bay to Bardsey, Llandanwg being adjacent to an old harbour. E. G. Bowen, in his study of Celtic church sites, makes the point that Llandanwg would almost certainly have been some way inland at the time of its foundation, though this clashes with the medieval presence of the sea under the walls of Harlech Castle. The church was unroofed by

Llandanwg: half-buried dunes church

the 19th century but restored by the Society for the Protection of Ancient Buildings in 1884.

The building is now some two feet below the level of the sand outside, and six feet below the dune crest. Steps lead down to the west door as if into a basement. A former south door is no more than a walled-up aperture, half underground. The walls contain many smooth-edged stones gathered from the beach. The nave has just one small south window while a window in the chancel boasts elaborate Perpendicular tracery. A ghost of a gothic east window can be seen outside, adorned with king and queen carvings. A small bellcote contains a working bell.

The interior is dark, flag-stoned, open-roofed and with bare whitewashed walls and a painted celure over the east end. A large beam runs across the chamber as if struggling to keep the walls apart. Oil lamps and candles are the only light. The seating is of simple benches with the aisle at the side, a rare arrangement. The font looks impossibly old, as if fashioned from a piece of pumice. Against a wall lies a pillar stone believed to be of Roman origin. A sign in the churchyard porch invites visitors to a candle-lit Christmas carol service, but 'bring your own torch'.

LLANEGRYN

ST MARY **
Loveliest Welsh screen carving

The church sits in a circular churchyard on a hillside overlooking the Dysynni valley towards Cadair Idris. An ancient foundation was rebuilt in the 13th century and again by the Victorians. There is no tower, just a bellcote and a rough porch. The church's celebrity lies in its magnificent screen and loft, reputedly moved from the dissolved Cymer Abbey outside Dol-gellau. Much legend surrounds the story of this screen. Some hold that it came by boat down the Mawddach river and up the Dysynni, others that it was carried in pieces over the hills to escape the iconoclasts.

The guidebook fiercely demands a third theory, that authorship be granted to the 'genius craftsmen' of Llanegryn itself, since 'it is probably the most famous screen in the world ... the most beautiful and most perfect piece of carving seen anywhere'. Located under a wide and low-arched beam it is unquestionably a masterpiece, but appears much too large to have been designed for this space. In addition, the loft panels are blind to the nave but open trellis-work to the chancel, which suggests a design deferring to the monastic side.

The screen itself has no lower panels, or has lost them, and enrichment is confined to the coving and loft. Here the carving is exquisite, by a hand familiar with motifs in use elsewhere in mid-Wales, notably at Llananno and Llan-wnnog. While the niches have lost their saints, the surrounds are crowded with customary foliage and fruit. The east side panels are rich with animals and leaves, the trellis of variegated filigree. This is church furnishing at its most sophisticated and surely the work of an institution, such as a monastery, with time and money on its hands. The memorials are mostly to the Wynnes of Peniarth, whose estate adjoins this enchanted spot.

LLANENGAN

2 miles west of Aber-soch
ST ENGAN (or EINION) ✱✱
Pilgrimage church, screens and choir stalls

This is close to Aberdaron and thus Bardsey and the pilgrim's journey is nearing its end. A sense of impending climax is reflected in a big church on the south Llŷn coast, matching Clyn-nog Fawr on the north. Llanengan was an out-post of the abbey of Bardsey itself, which owned extensive properties on the mainland. Many of its fittings may have come from the old abbey after its dissolution. The tower was built in

1534, just two years before the English Reformation and thus at the (official) end of the age of pilgrimage.

The interior is composed of an original nave and Tudor south aisle, virtually two naves with a graceful arcade dividing them. As at Clynnog such capacity can only have been required for a constant through-put of pilgrims. The windows are Tudor, as are the wonderful roofs, steep-pitched and arch-braced. Over the nave sanctuary is a blue celure.

These features are overwhelmed by the remarkable carpentry of the two screens and attached choir stalls, presumably (though not certainly) from Bardsey. The screen to the nave has lost its loft, but the aisle screen retains one, and both carry characteristic Welsh tracery, rich in vine leaves. The chancel side is more adorned than the nave side, possibly a sign of monastic origin. Below are roughly carved monks' stalls, looking earlier than the screens themselves, decorated with carved monsters and other devices.

At the rear of the church is a large medieval wooden chest, possibly from Bardsey, used for donations from pilgrims. It is still used for this purpose today.

LLANFAGLAN

ST BAGLAN ✱
Holy well in field

The church is a wild, lonely place near the shore of Foryd Bay just south of Caernarfon. It can be seen from the coast track across a field, its circular *llan* enclosing a grove of trees evoking the spirit of a druidical past. There are traces of prehistoric settlements in the area and over the door is a large incised stone of the 6th century recalling, in Latin, 'Fili Lovernus'.

The present church is medieval, with an imposing north porch and Tudor south chapel. The roof appears to be of original beams and the interior is whitewashed. Unmodernized furnishings date from the 18th century, with the customary mix of box pews and benches. One belonged to the 19th-century Jones family, who had eight children of whom three fought in the

Seaside calm: Llanfaglan

Napoleonic Wars for the Royal Caernarvonshire Militia.

The church is now in the care of the Friends of Friendless Churches. An ancient holy well can be found in the field, filled in but with its stone seat intact.

LLANGELYNNIN

Y Rowen, 4 miles south of Conwy
ST CELYNNIN ✶✶
Mountain church with mud-floored chapel

High over the Conwy valley a scatter of farms eventually gives way to a track over the moors. Past the 1,000-ft contour, the view opens out to reveal in the distance a steeply walled enclosure, like a miniature Great Wall of China, over which a bellcote peers incongruously. The enclosure is penetrable only through a small gate to the right of the approach. Round about are the remains of prehistoric settlements, suggesting that this was once a well-populated route. Like neighbouring Llanrhychwyn, Llangelynnin church

was both ruined and saved by being replaced in the 19th century by another in the valley.

It is hard to imagine this place as it must once have been, bustling with herdsmen, pilgrims, invalids and perhaps a mendicant friar. Inside the enclosure is still an old well with its stone seat intact, with even the remains of a pilgrims' hostel and stable. There are no trees. The graves are flat chest tombs, as if any headstone would be blown away by the wind.

The church is just 12 feet wide with thick walls, parts of which are 14th century. A tiny mud-floored transept was added in the 15th century, supposedly for male worshippers. This may have referred to passing drovers, whose demeanour (and possible disease) the parishioners would want to keep at a distance. Door hinges survive from the 14th century.

The unaltered interior retains Jacobean fittings, a three-sided altar rail and fragments of the Lord's Prayer and Ten Commandments in Welsh over the altar. The 'men's chapel' still has a mud floor. Though the screen has gone, a panel remains by the lectern, with two holes supposedly drilled to spy on the priest when the screen was shrouded during Lent.

LEFT: *Hillside glory at Llangelynnin (Conwy)* ABOVE: *Proprietory seat at Llangelynnin (Tywyn)*

LLANGELYNNIN

4 miles north of Tywyn
ST CELYNNIN ✳✳✳
Coastal church with named pews, gypsy grave

I have loved this church since childhood. Neither the railway line beneath its wall nor the neighbouring Lwyngwril caravan camp can destroy its serenity. Here we can imagine the early Welsh priests erecting a hermitage and preaching their gospel to the hill people with a view of distant Bardsey across Cardigan Bay. A bench has recently been placed in honour of this view.

The church crouches below the coast road (which offers the only parking). Services are rare yet the place is well-supported and favoured for weddings. A woman visitor from Australia, dying of cancer, pronounced it the most beautiful spot on earth and pleaded to be buried here looking out to sea. She lies near another grave, that of the Welsh gypsy king Abram Wood (d. 1799). Father of a family of harpists, he was born in Somerset and died in a local cowshed.

The church is a single cell with 17th-century porch crowned with a bellcote. The exterior is said to have remains of 9th-century work, but most of the fabric is *c.*1200, with thick walls and slit windows. The inside is dark and barn-like, with no electric light and a rugged flagstone floor. The roof of *c.*1500 is king-and-queen post with hanging brass candelabra.

Most remarkable are the Georgian pews, not boxed but narrow benches with backs, sixteen still with their names on them. These show six esquires, six gents and five clergymen, most with associated farms and dated 1823. The names are mostly of local landowners, such as Williams Vaughan and Nanney-Wynn, who would not have lived or worshipped here, but owned pews for the use of their tenants.

Pilgrimage capacity at Llangwnnadl

On the north wall are post-Reformation paintings, including a vivid if partial memento mori. The south wall houses a horse bier, used for getting coffins down from hill farms.

LLANGWNNADL

7 miles south-west of Morfa Nefyn
ST GWYNHOEDL **
Tudor pilgrim church, pier inscriptions

This Llŷn pilgrimage church lies in a sheltered cleft in an otherwise wild and windy landscape. On a sunny spring day it is an oasis of bliss, the graveyard bursting with wild flowers and the birdsong overwhelming. Its saint, Gwynhoedl, was son of a chieftain called Seithenyn, reputedly responsible for the inundation of Cantre'r Gwaelod, the lost land of Cardigan Bay. This he may have achieved by breaching a dyke. As a saint (or preacher) he was regarded as junior to

Deiniol of Bangor but senior to Beuno of Clynnog Fawr. A stone set in the south wall of the church has been dated to *c.* AD 600.

A romanesque church rebuilt in the early Tudor period comprises what are in effect three naves, like some Cornish churches, reflecting the prosperity of the Bardsey pilgrimage. The neighbouring meadow is even called Cae Eisteddfa, a resting place for pilgrims. The two handsome arcades divide the church into three chambers of equal width, all lit by new Perpendicular windows. The church is wider than it is long.

Two piers of the northern arcade are decorated with incised letters recording the burial of St Gwynhoedl and the building of the arcade in 1520. The inscription is in Latin but the date is written IHRO, in accordance with what proved a passing fashion for using archaic script for numerals.

This north arcade was later a school room. The font includes a king's head, said to be meant as a likeness of Henry VIII.

LLANRHYCHWYN

Trefriw, 3 miles north-west of Llanrwst
ST RHYCHWYN ✶✶
Unaltered Tudor interior, medieval glass

The first task is to find the church, unsigned next to a farm in the hills above the Conwy valley south of Trefriw. Llywelyn the Great in *c.*1200 is said to have had the same problem, and built a new church at Trefriw in *c.*1230 to save himself (and his protesting wife) the journey. Yet the old church survived and was considered worth rebuilding in the 15th century. It was spared by the Victorians and thus offers an unaltered interior of serenity and light. Entry is by a door hung on a pole which, as the *Companion Guide* puts it, 'groans horribly'.

The interior is double-naved, divided by a simple arcade, its piers square in section with rough abaci. The roof is partly ceiled over the altar, the walls roughcast and whitewashed. Old pews remain, with small benches at the back for children. The two-decker pulpit is dated 1691.

The church's most remarkable feature is fragments of 15th- and early-16th-century glass. One window depicts the Holy Trinity, a subject that seldom escaped the iconoclasts. God, the Holy Spirit as a plunging dove and Christ on the Cross are painted on glass in childlike simplicity, mirrored by three acorns and an oak tree.

LLANRWST

ST GWRWST ✶✶✶
Screen and loft, grandee chapel with memorials

Though the small town on the Conwy has lost much of its character, it retains a 17th-century bridge which some claim was designed by Inigo Jones, whose family had local connections. The old church was destroyed in both the Glyndŵr uprising and the Wars of the Roses, to be rebuilt in the Perpendicular style in 1470. It was comprehensively restored by the Lancashire architects, Paley and Austin, in 1884.

Llanrwst is chiefly notable for the 17th-century Gwydir chapel. Its exterior dominates the approach to the church, with heavy gothic buttresses and a battlemented roof, to which the main church seems an extension. Inside, the nave is differentiated from the chancel only by a screen and loft.

This work may have been brought – like some features of Gwydir Castle – from the dissolved Maenan Abbey. While the musicians' loft suffers from having lost its saints, the vaulting of the canopy and the filigree openwork in the screen panels are exceptional. The carving includes a pomegranate, symbol of Catherine of Aragon, dating the work to the final years before the Dissolution. Woven into the gothic tracery are symbols of the Passion, a rare depiction of the cock crowing atop a pillar at St Peter's betrayal, and a representation of the flagellation of Christ. In one of the panels swirling tracery is replaced by vine tendrils and bunches of grapes, nature usurping art.

The Gwydir chapel is a church in itself, built in 1634 by Sir Richard Wynn of Gwydir, treasurer to Queen Henrietta Maria (and thus a link to Inigo Jones if link there is). The roof is almost flat, known as camber-beam. The Jacobean panelling and decoration display the transition from gothic to renaissance in 17th-century British churches, with gothic considered more true to the Catholic tradition. In the chapel is an empty coffin, said to be for Llywelyn the Great, surrounded by deep quatrefoils. A knight in armour of *c.*1440 is complete with cushion, sword and lion.

The chapel is home to a remarkable set of 17th-century monuments to the Wynn family. A marble tablet to Wynn himself is by the court carver Nicholas Stone (1636). That to Sir John (d. 1627) is a 'barbaric exuberance' says Hubbard in Pevsner. The walls are adorned with an outstanding set of memorial brasses of the same period. Peter Lord traces a link between Wynn and the London engraver Robert Vaughan, who 'broke with the medieval tradition … and approached much more closely the form of the painted portrait'. The brass to Mary Mostyn is by the Wrexham goldsmith Sylvanus Crue.

MAENTWROG

ST TWROG *
Arts and Crafts rebuild with timber arcades

I am spooked by Maentwrog. This ghostly village lies on the hillside of the wooded Ffestiniog valley with Snowdonia's mountains massing to the north. Slate-grey, handsome and stern, its cottages are like a Strict Baptist family on its way to chapel. It was here that St Twrog hurled a stone to demolish a pagan altar, a stone that survives in the churchyard. I have no doubt the altar stayed demolished.

The church sits off the main street through a lychgate made of wood and slate with a clock in its gable. The path leads between back gardens to the churchyard, guarded by a large yew and crowded with slate headstones, arranged in immaculate rows.

The building itself contrasts with its surroundings, an almost jolly affair largely thanks to a rebuild of 1896, by which time Victorian restoration had acquired Arts and Crafts personality. The architect was John Douglas, who also designed Gladstone's memorial chapel at Hawarden (Clwyd).

Douglas took what was apparently an 1814 barn of a building and added an attractive shingled spire, visible across the valley. Inside he inserted timber arcades to make side aisles and added, in place of a clerestory, colourful stencilled panels. He then designed wooden screens to surround the vestry and organ case and a handsome panelled pulpit.

The floor is of wood blocks. This is truly a church of the forest.

MALLWYD

ST TYDECHO *
Theatrical interior of raked seating

When walking in this neighbourhood on a dark winter's afternoon I was in need of shelter from a sudden downpour. Mallwyd church emerged from the gloom, enveloped in dripping evergreens like the set for a horror film. It was open and won my heart.

Though medieval in origin, with a blocked south door and lancet window, the building derives its character from the long incumbency of John Davies, scholar and author of an early Welsh/Latin dictionary. He was reputedly appointed to the post by King James personally in 1604 – we do not know why he was blessed or cursed with so distant a posting – and stayed for the rest of his life. He was clearly a man of means and built three bridges in the parish while converting his church into one appropriate to the Protestant mood of the time.

Davis erected a wooden tower containing three bells, and a substantial porch, also of wood. Over this he set a whalebone, said to have been washed up in the estuary of the local River Dyfi.

Inside, Davies extended the church to the east, with what is now a panelled ceiling and crude east window. A gallery was added in the 18th century and in the 19th came the most remarkable feature, rising tiers of seats at the west end in front of the old gallery. These, together with the dormer windows set into the deeply sweeping roof, give the church the appearance of a village theatre.

On my visit it was more like the poop deck of a ship at sea.

NANHORON

3 miles north-west of Aber-soch
CAPEL NEWYDD **
Early chapel with high pews

This ancient Dissenting chapel is near impossible to find without an Ordnance Survey map (ref. 285309). The sign is overgrown. Hidden

Secretive Nanhoron

Nanhoron: rustic interior

down a green lane, through a wood and across a field to the right, the chapel might be an old cowshed lost in the undergrowth. The key is 'with the double-gabled house' or 'at the farm', as if that were any help. Yet even without the key, Capel Newydd is worth the search. The windows are low and afford a good view of the interior.

The chapel was built in 1769 by Independents who had split from those in Pwllheli. The origin of these disputes, whether doctrinal or personal, is lost in time. Either way, the worshippers must have had a long walk. The building was abandoned at the end of the 19th century and survives as an unaltered 18th-century interior, with a floor of compacted mud. The box pews with raised wooden bases are roughly joined, as if by a carpenter of cattle stalls. I half expected to see a horse peering over the top of them. One end has tiered benches, presumably for children.

The pulpit is illuminated by an adjacent window, casting the preacher's face in perpetual shadow, the better to emphasize his voice. His desk has two candlesticks while a candelabra on a pulley supplies additional light. A funeral bier hangs over the doorway. There is a shovel used as a collecting plate to reach over the backs of the pews.

Capel Newydd is similar in style to the Anglican churches of Llŷn, suggesting that by the Hanoverian era the Established and Dissenting traditions had, in this part of Wales, begun to converge, before the rise of Victorian evangelism.

The box pews maintained a measure of social segregation while the dominance of pulpit over sanctuary stressed the importance of preaching over ritual. This chapel was lost to nature until restored in the 1950s. The gravestones are still tumbled among the brambles and nettles. The only sounds amid the peace are of birds and sheep.

PENLLECH

6 miles south-west of Morfa Nefyn
ST MARY *
Pilgrim church, bat droppings

Never has a church seemed more in need of the Friends of Friendless Churches, who are now custodians of Penllech. The single cell lies down a farm track towards the sea from the Tudweiliog to Llangwnnadl road. The approach is unprepossessing, the churchyard so overgrown and the door so scruffy and cobwebby that at first I did not bother to open it. It is, as the FFC itself remarks, 'utterly devoid of architectural pretension. The God worshipped here was content with simple devotion.'

Yet the church is open and with welcoming literature inside. It was a pilgrim station along the north Llŷn coast, sited on heathland with fine views over the sea to the west. The churchyard is full of wild flowers, overwhelming tumbling gravestones. The interior is essentially medieval but rebuilt in the 1840s, whitewashed with clear-glazed Y-tracery windows and complete Georgian fittings.

The box pews still have their faded mushroom paint. The pulpit even has a sounding board with a baroque star-burst on its underside. Not one but two funeral biers adorn the wall. The only light is from candles. The altar cloth was, on my visit, piled with bat droppings. The Friends should not over-restore this place.

PENNAL

ST PETER *
Fake royal chapel, themed churchyard

Pennal church is a testament to the power of myth. Though undoubtedly based on a Celtic site, it is a Victorian structure of 1873 in the centre of the village, where it forces the traffic into a speed-crushing S-bend. Its interest lies chiefly in wall memorials to the remarkable number of Anglo-Welsh gentry families whose Victorian 'second homes' dotted the valley of the Dyfi, whose names I tried to memorize as I sat here

as a boy during Easter and summer holidays in this village.

The arrival in the 1980s of an eccentric but enterprising vicar, Geraint ap Iorwerth, transformed Pennal church into 'Owain Glyndŵr's Chapel Royal, 1406', a claim for which there is no shred of evidence and which was quite unknown in my youth. Glyndŵr, on his way to Machynlleth in 1404 and again in 1406, may have rested in the neighbourhood (see Cefn Caer, p. 213 above). That Glyndŵr may have worshipped in a church on this spot is pure surmise. That it was his 'chapel royal' is invention.

Undaunted, ap Iorwerth has re-created the church as a Welsh chauvinist theme park, and with some panache. The churchyard and its gravestones have been rearranged to create a heritage garden. Flags and proclamations of the fake 'Court of Pendragon' abound. The interior contains a facsimile of Glyndŵr's Pennal Letter and a painting by Aneurin Jones purporting to depict 'the Welsh Assembly, 1406', taking place in Pennal. Legend acquires its own authenticity in time.

PENYGWRYD

Nr Capel Curig, 6 miles east of Llanberis
HOTEL CHAPEL *
Memorial to climbers on Snowdon and Everest

The celebrated Snowdon hotel sits amid wild pines in the valley between the main peak and the Glyders. Here the team that conquered Everest came to train and the hotel bar is a shrine to their achievement. Here too the inn's owners, Brian and Jane Pullee, decided in 2000 to celebrate the millennium with a small chapel tucked in among the outhouses (key from reception). The pebble-dash exterior might be that of a storehouse.

The diminutive interior is serene, with whitewashed walls and a slate floor, lit only by candles. There are three rows of seats, for ten worshippers at most. The tiny east window depicts Snowdon in the distance, engraved with 'I will lift up mine eyes unto the hills', while a small west window shows St Christopher crossing a lake. On the walls are the names of mountaineers

who knew Penygwryd and Snowdon, including some who died on its slopes. There is no more appropriate shrine to one of Europe's most beautiful mountains.

PISTYLL

3 miles east of Morfa Nefyn
ST BEUNO ✶
Herbal remedies, St Christopher mural

The 12th-century church is a model Bardsey pilgrimage chapel. It sits on a shelf 200 feet above the sea, looking north to Holyhead and Anglesey. It is a cell with thick walls and a single bellcote. Yet Pistyll lives and is cared for, proclaiming a dedication to natural remedies. On my visit the floor was covered in straw and smelled delightful. The walls were adorned with medical herbs, apparently a long-standing local tradition relating to the needs of pilgrims.

The unfortunate scraping of the church walls

Pistyll: pilgrim's retreat

at least revealed an early mural of St Christopher, appropriate to pilgrimage, barely discernible but for a frame of herbs round it. The font belongs to a group widespread in Anglesey, decorated with a Manx-influenced ring-chain pattern. At Christmas the church is filled with branches of evergreen. A plant called danesberry grows in the churchyard, and was revered for assisting 'the transmigration of the soul', a sure seller to pilgrims.

TREMADOG

PENIEL CHAPEL ✶✶
Novel chapel design in model town

Peniel is a handsome chapel built in 1811 for William Madocks for his new town of Tremadog on the shores of Traeth Mawr. Here he projected a new port for the slate trade, named after Madog, the legendary Welsh discoverer of America (or at least Alabama) in the 12th century. He built a dull gothic church in the town for Anglicans, and a radiant Roman temple across the road for Calvinist Methodists. The design was roughly based on Inigo Jones's St Paul's, Covent Garden in London.

Peniel was as much a departure from the norm as was Madocks. The bold Tuscan design transformed Welsh chapel design from that of an apologetic barn or cottage into an emphatic feature of the townscape, as were Anglican churches. In particular it harnessed classicism to the purpose of Nonconformity, as had the French and American revolutionaries. It was a style many Anglicans regarded as pagan.

Other than minor variations in the positioning of doors and a bold oculus in the pediment, Peniel is a copy of St Paul's. When the bishop of Bangor complained to Madocks at its splendour in comparison with the church, Madocks replied tactfully that the church was 'on solid rock and the chapel built only on sand'. It is painted bright white.

The interior was equally novel. Most chapels respected the altar table at the east end but rearranged the seating to face the pulpit, usually placed against the north wall. At Peniel (and in later chapels) the pulpit supplanted the altar altogether and the congregation sat on raked seats facing it, as if in the theatre. It is the Word triumphant.

TYWYN

ST CADFAN **
Romanesque arcades, earliest Welsh inscriptions

Tywyn is a sad place. An ancient settlement on the flood plain of the Dysynni was chosen by the Victorian salt king John Corbett as the site of a new seaside resort, Wales's Torquay. Having employed 3,000 workers to build his palace at Chateau Impney outside Droitwich, Corbett must have thought Tywyn an easy task. A grand esplanade with a row of boarding houses was built in the 1870s, matched by a new market and hotel in the town centre. But fashion ignored Corbett and Tywyn. The seafront buildings now look stark and incongruous, surrounded by the ugliest bungalow and caravan sprawl in Cardigan Bay. Tywyn is an unplanned architectural disaster area.

The centre of the old village is more appealing. Here lies a church in a street, College Green, that recalls its early life as a *clas* founded by Cadfan in the 6th century. It was Cadfan who also allegedly founded the monastery of Enlli on Bardsey, visible across Cardigan Bay.

Tywyn's central tower, aisles, chancel and stonework are mostly Victorian, paid for by Corbett. But the old romanesque arcades survive, raised on drum piers and whitewashed, wide, bold and simple. Peter Lord suggests that, like Penmon (Anglesey), they reflect a Welsh/Irish style possibly dating back to the 11th century.

The church contains two treasures. The first is a pair of battered medieval effigies, one of an unusually hooded priest. The other treasure is an inscribed stone found in the 18th century serving as a local gatepost. Probably from the 8th century, it is purported to carry the first known writing in the Welsh language. The inscriptions are near impossible to decipher today and Cadw refers to 'at least two significantly different readings'. The writing runs up as well as down and includes reversed brackets, of some defunct grammatical significance. It records the names of departed families on four sides and the phrases 'loss and grief remain' and 'here lie four (or three)'. They show Welsh as dropping the case endings familiar in Latin.

Powys
[Breconshire, Radnorshire, Montgomeryshire]

The kingdom of Powys emerged as the advancing Saxons pushed the Welsh back over the River Severn and into the Cambrian mountains. The rulers of Powys lost their capital at Shrewsbury and set up court near Meifod. Towards the end of the 8th century, the Saxon king Offa of Mercia erected a dyke to mark what has formed the roughly agreed boundary between England and Wales to this day.

The Normans showed no such tact. In 1086 Roger of Montgomery, Earl of Shrewsbury, invaded Powys and built a castle named after his home town of Montgomerie in Normandy. He pushed on west towards the sea, dividing north from south Wales, which is why present-day Powys still meets tidal water at Machynlleth. Throughout the Middle Ages, Powys was torn between Welsh and English loyalty, given its border status and the intermarriage of its families with the Marcher lords. A witness of this is how relatively few castles were built to keep it in order.

The modern county is called by Richard Haslam in Pevsner 'a region of the happy mean', a soft landscape of hills, old villages and small churches. The Normans left a monastery at Brecon, rebuilt in a serene French Early Gothic. Later English settlements are represented in big town churches at Guilsfield, Montgomery and Welshpool. In between, the Celtic *llans* lie thicker on the ground in Powys than anywhere else, from Pennant Melangell in the north to popular Patrisio in the south.

The Tudors brought Powys what is today the grandest house in Wales, the refashioned Powis Castle, and the most endearing church fittings, the screens at Llananno, Llanfilo, Llanwnnog and Patrisio. Domestic buildings of the period survive in the remarkable complex at Tretower and in the 'border black-and-white' of Trewern and Maes-mawr. Powys has a rich crop of early Dissenter chapels and meeting-houses, at Maesyronnen, Dolobran, Pales and Llandrindod Wells.

The Georgians are thinner on the ground, evidenced at Abercamlais and the judge's lodgings, courthouse and prison at Presteigne. The Victorians were riotous at Adeline Patti's Craig-y-nos retreat and sober at the model country estates at Leighton and Treberfedd. Since then, Powys has quietly retired.

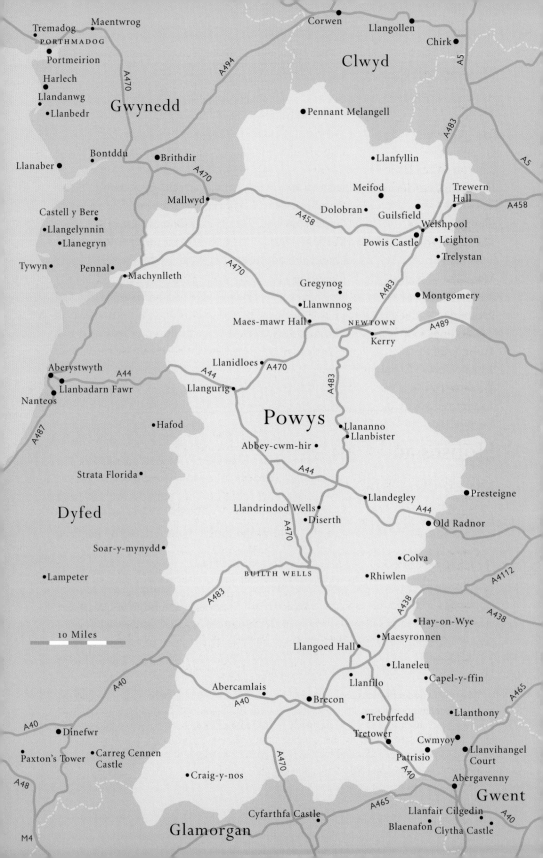

Houses and Castles

Abbey-cwm-hir ∗∗
Abercamlais ∗∗
Craig-y-nos ∗∗
Gregynog ∗∗
Hay-on-Wye Castle ∗∗
Llanfyllin, Farrier's
  House ∗
Llangoed Hall ∗
Machynlleth, Royal
  House ∗
Maes-mawr Hall ∗
Powis Castle ∗∗∗∗
Presteigne, Judge's
  Lodgings ∗∗∗
Treberfedd ∗∗
Tretower ∗∗∗
Trewern Hall ∗

Churches

Brecon:
  Cathedral ∗∗∗∗
  Plough Chapel ∗∗
Capel-y-ffin ∗
Colva ∗
Diserth ∗∗
Dolobran ∗∗
Guilsfield ∗∗∗
Kerry ∗
Leighton ∗∗
Llananno ∗
Llanbister ∗
Llandegley ∗
Llandrindod Wells ∗
Llaneleu ∗∗

Llanfilo ∗∗
Llangasty ∗
Llangurig ∗∗
Llanidloes ∗∗
Llanwnnog ∗∗
Maesyronnen ∗∗
Meifod ∗∗∗
Montgomery ∗∗∗
Old Radnor ∗∗∗
Patrisio ∗∗∗∗
Pennant Melangell ∗∗∗
Presteigne ∗∗
Rhiwlen ∗
Trelystan ∗∗
Welshpool ∗∗

Houses and Castles

ABBEY-CWM-HIR ∗∗

5 miles north-east of Rhaeadr
Restored Victorian house gone
enjoyably mad (Priv)

The only way to approach the new Abbey-cwm-hir is on its own terms. A Victorian mansion of Alpine/Transylvanian demeanour sits among the trees in one of the most entrancing valleys of mid-Wales. Here the Cistercians built what was intended to be their largest and most isolated abbey, larger even than Tintern. Today all that remains are some cursory ruins along the valley floor.

Over this presides the house bought by Paul and Victoria Humpherson in 1997, restored as a home and museum of Victoriana, though museum hardly does justice to the growing hysteria I felt as I was guided round its fifty-two rooms. The place is crammed with impedi-

menta until, in the basement and conservatory, it explodes into rampant kitsch. The place is astonishing. Abbey-cwm-hir is a Victorian version of the Dennis Severs house in London's Spitalfields.

The old farmhouse was built for a family named Philips in 1869 by the architects Poundley and Walker. The style reflects the transition from early Victorian formality to the freer eclecticism of Burges and then Art Nouveau. The Humphersons have restored the plasterwork, fireplaces, floor tiles and staircase, with decorative additions to the doors, woodwork and wallpaper by Victoria Humpherson. Modern paintings of the house in all weathers start from the walls. Everywhere is Paul Humpherson's Staffordshire pottery, he being from Stoke-on-Trent.

After the formal rooms, the magpies let rip. The library is of early editions of children's adventure books, a wonderful collection. The billiard room is stencilled with the names of Arthur's knights – Abbey-cwm-hir being a candidate for Camelot – and full of stuffed animals.

One kitchen laden with paraphernalia leads to another likewise. Bedrooms are perfectly laid out as if awaiting guests, with pyjamas folded and ready.

Rooms are variously 'themed' to ocean liners, armies, planes, motorbikes. Cupboards are full of clothes. Cabinets and bars are full of drink. There is a traffic sign here, a wall of whisky bottles there and a mass of early advertising placards. Everything is spotless, not least the walled garden which stretches up the hillside to the rear.

ABERCAMLAIS **

5 miles west of Brecon
Georgian gentry house with unaltered interiors (Priv)

The Williams house sits on the banks of the River Usk at its loveliest, upstream of Brecon. Next door is the mansion of another branch of the Williams family at Penpont. The latter is a severely classical Regency composition, possibly by Smirke, but inaccessible. Abercamlais is early Georgian and carries its years well. The house has been occupied by Williamses since Tudor times, all but one of whom from 1570 to 1935 were in holy orders. The exception became high sheriff. The house is still occupied by a Williams, Susan Balance.

What had been a farmhouse was given a three-storey Georgian front when the family came into money in 1710. Apart from the addition of dormers in the roof, the house is much as built. Identical windows spread across seven bays, unrelieved by string courses or pilasters and undeniably severe. The Victorian porch was designed by a family friend, the youthful George Gilbert Scott. The effect is of subdued tranquillity.

The interior is contemporary with the house, a series of Georgian rooms round a central hall with the staircase tucked behind. The drawing-room fireplace is said to have come from the sale of Fonthill Abbey in 1823. The baroque plasterwork in the ceiling here and in the hall is probably also imported.

An intriguing Georgian pigeon house stands in the grounds directly over a stream. The upper part is a dovecot but the lower is a latrine which gives directly into the water. It is not clear how this related to the house plumbing. The environs of Abercamlais, its bridge, kitchen garden, woods and drive suggest centuries of careful husbandry. Until the railway closed in 1962, the house even had its own request stop.

CRAIG-Y-NOS **

4 miles north of Aber-craf
Diva's baronial bolt-hole in the Brecon Beacons (H)

The Italian Adelina Patti (1843–1919) was the most famous opera singer of her age. She performed before emperors, tsars, monarchs and tycoons and was paid 5,000 gold dollars for one performance of *La Traviata* in Boston. In St Petersburg she was carried by six generals on a seat of flowers to her hotel after a show. The daughter of a Sicilian and a Roman, she first married Ernest Nicolini, Napoleon's equerry, then a French tenor, then, at the age of 56, a 30-year-old Swedish 'nobleman and masseur'.

So how did this remarkable woman come to live in a dark and wet corner of the Brecon Beacons, in a house with the Wagnerian name of the 'rock of the night'?

The answer appears to lie with another wealthy admirer, Lord Swansea. He took Patti on a tour of the Beacons and showed her an old manor clinging to the edge of a ravine. He suggested it as a refuge from her tours and love affairs.

In addition, Patti, then aged 35, needed relief from polluted city air that was upsetting her lungs. Here she could walk for hours and breathe the zephyrs of the Beacons. She fell for the place, arriving in 1878 with her lover and second husband-to-be, the French tenor.

The house had been built by T. H. Wyatt in the 1840s, but his work was drastically extended by Patti in a Scots baronial style, with towers, turrets and gables, by Bucknall and Jennings of Swansea. Ten years later she added a small concert hall in the style of a London opera house, in gold, cream and peach. The walls of this Welsh

Concrete fantasy at Gregynog

Bayreuth are adorned with classical pilasters, the auditorium is raked and a backdrop shows Patti in her favourite role, on a chariot as Handel's Semiramis.

Patti gave free performances here to anyone who could make their way up the mountain. They flocked, including the Prince of Wales and impresarios eager to sign her for their theatres. She had her own waiting room at Penwyllt station. When she arrived local people would form a guard of honour for her carriage up to Craig-y-nos. She died here in 1919 but was buried in Père Lachaise in Paris. The house fell on hard times and was for a long time a geriatric hospital.

Craig-y-nos is now a wedding hotel, crudely publicized and with few echoes of its past. Bucknall and Jennings' work appears devoid of merit, being rich and vulgar, though this may be later alterations. The rooms still have pictures and mementos of Patti, and the theatre survives, used occasionally by Patti fans for operatic revivals.

The reception rooms offer spectacular views over the ravine of the River Tawe. The place is certainly within the bounds of architectural redemption.

GREGYNOG **

Tregynon
Victorian black-and-white house made of concrete, home of philanthropic Davies sisters (Priv)

Ramparts of trees line the drive to the big house, which lies hidden in a dripping Welsh jungle. It was reconstructed from a 17th-century original by Charles Hanbury-Tracy, later 1st Baron Sudeley, in 1837 and completed by his son in the 1860s. The house was one of the first anywhere to be made of the new building material of concrete (un-reinforced), as were many cottages on the estate. It is a Victorian grandee's pastiche of how a Midlands black-and-white mansion might look, if double the normal size. The cottages are concrete *cottages ornées*.

The house had various owners until bought by Gwendoline and Margaret Davies, from the Montgomeryshire village of Llandinam and heiresses to one of Wales's greatest fortunes, that of the coal and railway town of Barry. They became champions of French art and Welsh culture, and lobbied on behalf of the Glamorganshire poor during the Depression.

The Davies sisters were among the first Britons to appreciate the Impressionists, notably Cézanne. Their collection, mostly amassed during the Great War, now graces the National Museum of Wales in Cardiff. The sisters intended Gregynog to be a Welsh centre of the Arts and Crafts movement, setting up a music room, art gallery and printing press. The last is still in being. The house was bequeathed to the University of Wales in 1960 as a residential centre, where the Davies tradition is maintained.

Gregynog is chiefly magnificent for its setting. A dip lies in front of the main terrace, once destined as a lake and now a parterre of yews. Beyond rises a stupendous wall of rhododendron and pine, which in the right light can seem like a tidal wave of green surf advancing on the house.

From the terrace, Gregynog looks like a cardboard stage set, or at least a concrete one. Painted black-and-white strips are intended to make the concrete walls look like wood and plaster, close-studded and with decorative quatrefoils. The three storeys are all of the same proportion and the gables are too small. Haslam in Pevsner concludes that 'the result does not quite escape absurdity or even plain awfulness, yet it is masculine and in a way logical'.

One room of the former Jacobean house survives as the Blayney Room, named after the original owners, its panelling and fireplace dated 1636. The rest of the interior is Victorian and institutionalized, though some works from the Davies collection remain on display.

HAY-ON-WYE CASTLE **
'Kingdom' castle of celebrated bookseller (Priv)

Hay and its castle are in every sense eccentric. The old town sits astride the English border and in 1977 was declared an autonomous 'kingdom' by its presiding genius, Richard Booth, admittedly on April Fool's Day in 1977. From the castle he ruled both his kingdom and, more important, the evolution of Hay into the world's first book town. He awarded dukedoms, earldoms

and peerages and fought (and still fights) battles against bureaucracy. His booklets have such titles as 'Bring back Horses' and 'God Save us from the Development Board for Wales'.

The old castle still dominates the town, with fine views up and down the spacious Wye valley beneath Hay Bluff. This was unusually turbulent Powys, with seven castles within two miles. The original structure of Hay replaced a motte and bailey on a knoll and was regularly burned or sacked in Anglo-Welsh conflicts. It succumbed to ruination in the Wars of the Roses but the keep survives, with Norman windows, a Norman door and later Tudor insertions.

The most prominent feature of the castle, and of Hay, is the Jacobean mansion built on to the side of the keep in the 1660s. Its tall brick chimneys and Dutch-gabled roof rise above the old mound. After frequent changes of ownership it was extensively restored by Caröe in 1910 but the interior was destroyed by a fire in 1939, including the Jacobean staircase and fittings.

Booth bought the castle as a ruin in the 1960s, restored it and then saw it again gutted by fire in 1978. Restoration is proceeding, but only the main rooms are accessible and they are full of books. Indeed wherever you look in Hay are books. The terraces of the castle during the annual Hay Festival take on the form of a literary souk, adding greatly to the scruffy charm of the place.

LLANFYLLIN
FARRIER'S HOUSE *
Murals surviving from Napoleonic imprisonment (Priv)

The Georgian property is adjacent to Llanfyllin's chemist's shop. The house, built in the 1740s, was used to incarcerate captured French officers during the Napoleonic Wars in 1811–13, their arrival causing a stir among the ladies of the village. The captives were confined to a mile radius and could attend a local dance only by the discreet moving of an offending milepost.

The inmate of the farrier's house, Lieutenant Pierre Augeraud, duly fell in love with the daughter of the rector of the church opposite. The alarmed rector secured Augeraud's immediate release and he was sent back to France. But love conquered freedom and when hostilities were over he returned and eloped with the girl. They lived happily in France ever after. Their Augeraud descendants still return to see the house.

It was during his initial stay that Augeraud painted murals over the walls of his upstairs room. Using sheep marker dye and formalin, he evoked a romantic landscape of mountains and lakes in various shades of blue. The work is of mediocre quality but charming and well preserved. The room contains cases of old chemicals. It is Llanfyllin's most remarkable war memorial.

LLANGOED HALL *

Llys-wen, 5 miles south-west of Hay-on-Wye
Arts and Crafts interior to Jacobean manor (H)

The old house of the Williams family is now a smart hotel much patronized during the Hay Festival. Built in 1632 (or rebuilt on the site of a reputed Welsh parliament) it has been remodelled inside but retains the appearance of a Jacobean E-plan house outside. Over the door is a stone depicting the Williams's three cocks. The present owner is Sir Bernard Ashley, husband of the late Laura Ashley, who rescued the house from demolition in 1987.

The appeal of the hall derives from its rebuilding in 1913 by Clough Williams-Ellis. It was his first major work in the Lutyens/*Country Life* tradition of manorial restoration. Hence the steep hipped roofs and dormer windows, as if the architect had taken a 17th-century mansion and clapped an Arts and Crafts one on top of it. This act of architectural millinery required steel girders to support it. The façade is now covered in Virginia creeper.

The interior displays more of Williams-Ellis's Lutyens humour, with only the library remaining from the Jacobean house. The dining room has Doric pilasters and a frieze. The grand staircase is Ionic in style with a fine mural of peacocks. The walls are adorned with pictures by Whistler, Sickert and Augustus John. More 'Cloughery' can be detected in the stables and outhouses, notably a cottage with a cupola, foretaste of his Portmeirion (Gwynedd).

MACHYNLLETH

PARLIAMENT HOUSE/ROYAL HOUSE *
Old town house with merchant's store (Mus)

Every self-respecting Welsh town boasts 'reputedly the oldest house in Wales', though dendrochronology has spoiled much of this fun. Machynlleth's so-called Parliament House in Maengwyn Street was heavily restored in the 20th century and historians have discredited its claim to be the seat of a Glyndŵr assembly.

The one-time draper's shop on Heol Penrallt is older and, as 'reputedly' the resting place of Charles I, is royal enough, even if the royalty is English. Its beams were felled in 1560–61 and in 1576, so this is a conventional Elizabethan townhouse, probably a hall with central fireplace and chimney over a merchant's store below. The entry to the latter is visible in the side elevation. The front was later extended towards the road, which is not original but admirably quaint.

The building is now the local tourist office and contains a jumble of antiquarian features. The old fireplace has a linen cupboard next to it. A door to a rear chamber has a carved ogee transom. The roof beams and basement area are clearly original.

Legend has it that Dafydd Gam, Henry IV's reckless Welsh supporter against Glyndŵr, infiltrated the Machynlleth parliament, tried to assassinate Glyndŵr, was caught and imprisoned in this building in 1404. This is apocryphal. But Dafydd existed, and went on to fight and die at Agincourt. His daughter, Gwladys, married William Herbert and co-founded the Pembroke/Beaufort and Stuart/Bute families.

MAES-MAWR HALL *

1 mile east of Caersŵs
Mid-Welsh black-and-white house with central chimney (H)

The hall has been a small hotel since the 1950s, its main rooms altered to form a pub and restaurant. But Maes-mawr retains the layout of a Montgomeryshire manor of the unusual cruciform type, with a central chimney stack set on the diagonal to serve fireplaces in all rooms. The house was burned out in the 18th century and rebuilt, then extended by Eden Nesfield in the late 19th. The appearance is ostensibly original and looks picturesque at the end of the avenue from the Newtown road, enveloped in rambling roses and backed by woods on the banks of the Severn.

The exterior timbering is rich, the members 'close-studded' on the ground floor, rising to a local motif of baluster studding above. There are square panels with curved quadrants round the windows and in the gable. This is not repeated on the side wings. The interior is still divided into parlour and hall, with large fireplaces. The stairs retain their 18th-century balusters. It is a jolly place.

POWIS CASTLE ****

Restoration mansion inside medieval/
Elizabethan castle, rich state rooms and long gallery, extensive terraced gardens (NT)

Powis is a pocket battleship among great houses. Its rose-red walls, half as old as Wales, rise in shimmering medieval apparition over the fertile slopes of the Severn above Welshpool. Here the princes of Powys dreamed of a glory which their border geography denied them, their loyalties divided between rebellious Gwynedd and the Marches. The 13th-century prince of Powys, Gruffudd, backed Edward I against Llywelyn, and his descendants backed the English against Glyndŵr, even when the Powis tenantry rose in Glyndŵr's favour. Just five miles from the English border, Powis embodies Anglo-Welsh ambivalence.

In 1578 the castle passed to a junior branch of the Herberts of Wilton, who created its present mostly Tudor exterior. Catholics and Royalists, they prospered and suffered for their cause. The 1st Marquess of Powis went into exile with James II in 1688. Yet despite two centuries of imprisonment, ostracism, debt and debauchery the family contrived to improve Powis, helped by the discovery of lead on their property. The grand staircase and state rooms date from the Restoration, while the baroque gardens brought a Continental swagger to soft Welsh contours.

By the 19th century the property had passed by marriage to the Clives of Shropshire, who changed their name to Herbert to merit the recreation (for the third time) of the earldom of Powis. The castle was extensively restored by Smirke in 1815 and, in a comprehensive reversion to the Jacobean style, by Bodley at the turn of the 20th century. The castle passed to the National Trust in 1952 but the family occupy part of the house to this day.

Powis is like Haddon (Derbys) or Alnwick (Northumb), a grand house packed inside a medieval box. The approach is dominated by yews, descendants of ornamental shrubs that would have defined the terraces beneath the castle walls. Now they erupt like giant ice-cream cones, spilling over walls and balustrades beyond all discipline.

The castle retains what must have been its Norman layout. An outer bailey is surrounded by high walls and service ranges, while a shell keep sits round an inner courtyard guarded by double drum towers. The exterior remains entirely of the 14th–16th centuries. In sunlight its rich sandstone glows a gloriously vivid red.

The outer bailey opens over the upper Severn valley and is dominated by a spectacular statue of Fame perched perilously on a winged horse, metaphor for the family's fortunes down the ages. A curved stairway rises to the castle entrance, tucked uncomfortably between the two drum towers. On my last visit a young visitor described them as like a pair of giant buttocks 'mooning' towards darkest Wales.

Powis's interior is both palatial and yet domestic. There are no cavernous chambers or distant corridors. The Herberts were never rich enough to rebuild their house and had to pack what they could into the space available. Thus the entrance leads without ceremony straight to the foot of the grand staircase.

While modest in proportion this is elevated by a ceiling by Verrio, royal artist of Kensington Palace. It supposedly celebrates the coronation of Charles II's Queen Catherine. Below are murals of mythological scenes by Verrio's pupil, Gerard Lanscroon, some in grisaille. These have

The Tudor gallery at Powis Castle

been given back their original colours, which some may find fierce, but they respond voluptuously to the dark wood of the stairs and the baroque doorcases of the landing above. It is annoying that the National Trust will not let visitors ascend these stairs, forcing them to use the servants' access and thus detracting from the impact of a visit to Powis.

Next to the stairs on the ground floor is the dining room inserted by Bodley in place of the old medieval hall. This is Jacobean revival (1902) at its richest. Carved chimneypieces replicate ones in the Victoria and Albert Museum, while family portraits by Romney and Reynolds look down from the walls. The smaller private dining room opposite was still used by the family in the 1980s.

The first floor is sensational. The state rooms were inserted from the 1660s to the 1680s, mostly by the Stuart architect William Winde, while the family was in exile in France. They are arranged round an inner courtyard flanked on two sides by the earlier T-shaped Tudor gallery, which Winde wisely retained: Elizabethan domesticity at the service of Restoration bravura.

A lofty library contains a miniature of Lord Herbert by Isaac Oliver. The oak drawing room is mostly Bodley, rich in linenfold panelling and plaster ceiling pendants (copied from Aston Hall in Birmingham). An extraordinary Victorian firescreen is composed of exotic stuffed birds, which could not survive long near any fire.

Off the gallery is the state bedroom, the most theatrical chamber in the castle. The decoration is French classical with a gilt-laden proscenium framing the great bed, secluded behind a rail to restrain courtiers during the levee. The ceiling depicts an appropriate Catholic theme, the apotheosis of the Virgin. The initials CR are ubiquitous, though no Stuart king ever slept here. Powis was a favourite haunt of the present Prince of Wales.

The long gallery is a charming reversion to the 16th century. Brightly lit panels and plasterwork celebrate the origins of the Herbert dynasty. Adam and Eve are invoked round the fireplace to emphasize antiquity, while the frieze is crowded with heraldry interspersed with mythical beasts. The walls are lined with Greek and Roman statuary, acquired by Clive of India, including a lovely carving of a cat playing with a snake. At the far end is a superb *pietra dura* table from Florence. Overseeing all is a mannerist doorcase.

After the lush interiors of the bedroom suite, the blue drawing room is calmly classical in style. It is hung with Belgian tapestries and graced with lacquerwork commodes adorned with oriental scenes. From here visitors are suddenly and unceremoniously booted down the servants' stairs, past the billiard room and out into the courtyard.

This is flanked by the old ballroom, once a picture gallery and surely too narrow for dancing. It has been divided to form the Clive of India museum, though Clive himself had nothing to do with Powis. Redesigned in 1774 in the Adam style by the Shrewsbury architect T. F. Pritchard, it is lined with bookcases and pictures from the Clive collection.

To one side is displayed the tent of the governor's great foe, Tipu Sultan. For all the splendour of the display, there is something odd in this oriental presence in the soft hills of Montgomeryshire.

PRESTEIGNE

JUDGE'S LODGINGS AND
SHIRE HALL ∗∗∗
Complete municipal museum in
restored Victorian lodgings (Mus)

Shire halls were centres of county government and a focus of central authority. Here presided local magistrates and assize judges on tour. The buildings embraced courts, prisons, a police station and ceremonial reception rooms. They formed a governmental one-stop shop of a sort much missed today.

In Wales, and especially here in the Radnorshire border country, this meant cross-cutting loyalties between Welsh and English. Justice might have to be done through a translator. Radnorshire was one of the most secluded counties in Britain, created after the union of England and Wales in 1536. Presteigne was made the county town after a judge was murdered in the original 'capital' of Rhaeadr.

The assize judges expected to be housed and entertained in some splendour, but since this was a charge on the town, the state of the lodgings was source of constant complaint. The previous house at Presteigne was considered 'insufficient, inconvenient, insecure and dangerous', while the prison next door was virtually open to the town. This state of affairs led in 1826 to the rebuilding of both the courthouse and the judge's lodgings, to plans by Edward Haycock of Shrewsbury.

The new building was handsome, presenting a classical façade to the street in the style of Nash. A central pilastered and pedimented block is flanked by three-bay colonnades, one for the lodgings, the other for the courthouse. Holding cells were built underneath. The new court opened in 1829, celebrated by sentencing a horse thief to death, commuted to transportation for life to Australia.

To allay the cost of the lodgings (which were irregularly used) they were sub-let or used by the local militia, by magistrates or even tenanted by a court official. In 1865 they also became a territorial army mess and de facto town hall. The 20th-century growth of Llandrindod Wells eroded Presteigne's status and the assizes were often cancelled for want of trials, the last being held in 1970.

Rather than dispose of the building, the county restored it as Wales's best museum of municipal history. The lodgings re-create a late-Victorian domestic interior. There are not too many signs and each room is furnished as if a visiting judge was in residence, complete with portraits of county worthies. The lighting is by gas and oil, with appropriate smells, and the fittings are original, including the lavatories. There are even bottles of wine, sadly not shared with end-of-the-day visitors.

The old courtroom has been restored, as have the police cells. Presteigne retains what is claimed to be the only working gasolier left in Britain, with eighteen open flame burners. The stalls and partitions are intact. But why not restore the magistrates' court to use, as in Beaumaris?

TREBERFEDD **

Llangasty Tal-y-llyn, 6 miles east of Brecon
Victorian moralist's house and estate,
Pearson design (Priv)

The house was built from scratch by a Hull banker, Robert Raikes, inspired in 1848 to found a centre of Anglo-Catholic Tractarianism in the Welsh hills. He had been told that such worship was in serious decline in these parts, as if Wales was a lapsed outpost of empire.

Raikes commissioned the young J. L. Pearson to design a building in a demure Victorian Tudor. A church (see below) and school were also erected on the shores of neighbouring Tal-y-llyn, the largest natural lake in south Wales. Nesfield was commissioned to lay out the gardens. This was a typical Victorian estate in the round, combining modern farming methods with religious rectitude. Treberfedd remains proudly in the Raikes family to this day.

The house appears from the front courtyard a characteristic early Victorian composition in the Pugin style. The façade is asymmetrical, with an entrance tower, a forest of gables and chimneys in soft pink/grey stone. The windows are heavily mullioned. To the right is a second tower rising over the service courtyard, decorated with excellent gargoyles.

The interior might be that of any spacious Victorian rectory, large rooms with even larger fireplaces, a library with its original shelving, a fine billiards room and a warm conservatory. The staircase is particularly grand with ornate finials and Raikes portraits. All is nicely cluttered. Treberfedd proves that not all Tractarian interiors need be severe.

TRETOWER ***

3 miles north-west of Crickhowell
Ancient castle and medieval courtyard
house with hall and galleries (Cadw)

Tretower is the most extensive medieval house in Wales, displaying the history of the form from the Norman conquest through the Middle Ages to rebuilding in the 15th and 16th centuries. The

Medieval hall at Tretower

outhouses of a modern farm have rather spoilt the setting of its adjacent castle ruin.

This ruin is remarkable. A motte and bailey was followed by a shell keep in the 12th century, within which the Norman Picard family built a hall and solar. A century later this inner courtyard was almost completely filled with a round keep, leaving the former 'shell' as an outer defensive wall. The old hall and solar were demolished where they impeded the new structure.

Each of the four floors of the new keep formed a room, with fireplaces and windows and a field of fire over the shell walls. Much of this survives, along with the post-holes of bridges and links to the outer wall. The castle was defended by Lord Berkeley for the king against the Glyndŵr uprising in 1403, the last time it saw active service.

A 14th-century hall house some distance from the castle was extended in the mid-15th century by Sir Roger Vaughan, a relative of the Herberts of Raglan, whose family held the property into the 18th century. They gradually improved it but were never rich enough to demolish and start again. Tretower became a farm until acquired for restoration by the Brecknock Society, passing to the state in 1930.

Four ranges now enclose a courtyard entered by a gatehouse and entirely surrounded by medieval walls. The gatehouse has an impressive chamfered doorway, with a lesser postern gate to one side. A passage leads into the courtyard, with the great hall opposite. This is given some renaissance flair by the insertion of a classical doorway and large Jacobean windows, repeated on the far side of the hall facing the meadow and castle. An oriel window survives.

The interior of the main hall, built by Vaughan to replace the earlier one in the north range, is spacious, divided by screens rising to the roof with trefoil and quatrefoil openings. At one end is the solar with latrines built into the wall and a kitchen beyond, at the other are service rooms and a servants' mess. That this arrangement should have survived across the centuries is remarkable.

In the 1460s Vaughan divided the rest of the building into residential apartments on the first floor. This involved inserting a floor in what had been the old 14th-century hall in the north range, with a new upper hall complete with fireplace and partitions for bedrooms. This suggests that the range was for a separate family, or at least for Vaughan's much extended one. The long upper chamber is a magnificent medieval room, rich in woodwork. Restoration has revealed early leaf and 'teardrop' painted decoration on the rendered partitions. Outside, a balcony runs round two sides of the courtyard and offers sheltered access to the upstairs rooms under the roof eaves. It is all most picturesque.

Tretower demonstrates the conundrum of historic house presentation. The exposure of the service end of the hall, with open floors and removed walls, conveys no sense either of what the old house looked like or of a modern reinstatement. It is as if an archaeologist had enjoyed himself tearing the place apart and gone off to write a thesis. The residential quarters are completely bare, despite being fully roofed and thus usable. This place needs urgent attention.

TREWERN HALL *

Welshpool
Yeoman black-and-white in Severn valley
(Priv)

Mid-Wales must once have been thick with houses such as Trewern. Of those that survive, few are accessible and Trewern is the more precious. It sits as it has for centuries, a piano keyboard of black and white rising to four patterned gables. The original house has been dated to the

1560s, but this probably consisted of the present kitchen wing, to which the main house was a cross wing.

Dating is confused by the richness of the later alteration, undertaken by Robert Francis with a date of 1610 over the porch. This was clearly designed to reflect a Jacobean desire for symmetry, no easy thing in a medieval hall house. The later work includes a jettied upper storey carrying excellent if battered carvings of heads and vegetation in the corbels. The gable brickwork is herringbone.

The house was again altered in the Victorian era, with the aim of creating a grander, less 'yeoman', house. The present owner, Murray Chapman, whose family acquired the property in 1918, has laboured hard to reinstate the previous Jacobean form. This has involved drastic intervention, notably new woodwork in the windows, which inevitably detracts from the appearance of antiquity. But all wooden houses need renewal, and all look old in time.

Churches

BRECON

CATHEDRAL ★★★★
Early English chancel, restored guild chapel, Zulu Wars memorial

The priory church at Brecon, like St Woolos, Newport, benefited from the episcopal inflation that accompanied the formation of the Church in Wales in 1920. It was joined in name with Swansea. Why another cathedral was needed so near Llandaff and Newport is unclear, but at least it drew attention to a handsome work of gothic architecture. Despite – or perhaps thanks to – careful restorations by George Gilbert Scott and Caröe, Brecon's crossing and east end are a harmonious composition in Early Gothic, created by French masons in the 13th century. The nave is in the Decorated style.

Norman Brecon was founded by Bernard de Neufmarche, after the first defeat of the Welsh in 1093. It was a cell of Battle Abbey in

Sussex (of which Neufmarche was also patron). Nothing of the original fabric remains but in 1201 the church whose east end we see today emerged, compact, unadorned outside and militarily defensible within its close. The interior is serenely beautiful.

On entering, the eye is immediately drawn to the far end, where five slender lancet windows gaze down the length of the interior. They are flanked by further lancets in the side walls, with clustered shafts bringing gothic verticality and light into what would have previously been a dark Norman chancel. Sedilia are arranged beneath. The vault was not completed until Scott's restoration, but this respected the elegance of the composition, as does Caröe's reredos of 1937, the latest manifestation of the gothic revival. On the north wall of the chancel is a battered Crucifixion of stone, probably 14th century, with figures strangely dissociated from each other.

The chancel is flanked by chapels. The Havard chapel to the north is dedicated to the South Wales Borderers and includes banners carried during the Zulu Wars. It contains a rare medieval treasure, a single stone of 1312 depicting in childish relief the effigies of Walter and Christina Awbrey, lying either side of a crucifix. Their necks are elongated and their arms are in ungainly prayer. To Peter Lord this is 'among the most moving manifestations in Wales of the public display of secular piety'. The south transept is dominated by a collection of wall memorials, including one by Flaxman.

Back in the nave, the 13th century moves into the 14th. The arcades seem solid and beefy after the delicacy of the chancel, with deep-set clerestory windows. The doorways have multiple clusters of shafts, their cool pink/grey local stone contrasting with the lime-wash of the crossing and chancel. The north aisle contains a surviving guild chapel, that of the cordwainers (otherwise corvizors or shoemakers), with parts of the original screen and the roof bosses reused for its partition. It is now dedicated to St Keyne. Inside is a wall tomb with florid ogee canopy.

Brecon's west end is enjoyably cluttered with curiosities. In the centre is a superb Norman font of the Herefordshire school, alive with birds, beasts, masks and decorative beading. There are two excellent tombs, a rare wooden effigy of a woman of the Games family (1555) and a chest tomb of Sir David and Lady Williams (1613), of alabaster and still in the medieval recumbent style. A cresset stone is said to have more holes for candles than any other in existence.

BRECON

PLOUGH CHAPEL **
Neo-baroque interior, carved pew-ends

At last a Welsh chapel it is possible to see inside or, if locked, which is visible through clear windows by the entrance. The Plough was founded as an Independent chapel in 1699, taking its name from a pub in which early meetings were held. It also carries the Welsh name of Y Drindod, the Trinity. The handsome porticoed building was erected in 1841 but its interior dates from the high point of Welsh chapel baroque, the 1890s. To worshippers used to the gloomy naves of Anglican churches or the simple preaching boxes of early Nonconformity, the style must have seemed exotic.

The plan took its cue from Wesleyan preachers and musicians, emphasizing the centrality of word and song. Hence the theatrical positioning of the pulpit as the focus of attention, reached up curving stairs as if to a belvedere. Arranged round it is a hierarchy of seats for clerks and elders. Behind rises the massive cliff of an organ and pews for the choir, to which deference is paid by raked galleries and pews. The carpentry is Wales's finest, by a local man, Benjamin Jenkins, of oak, pine and costly ebony. Pew-ends and lecterns are dressed with naturalistic carvings.

CAPEL-Y-FFIN *

Llanthony valley, 7 miles south of Hay-on-Wye
Isolated location with Georgian interior

This is a kindly place, called a 'brooding owl' by the diarist Francis Kilvert. I would describe it as a mischievous child tended by disapproving spinster aunts in the form of old yews. This must long have been a holy spot.

Early Gothic serenity: Brecon Cathedral

The church is 25ft by 13ft and stands at the head of the lovely Vale of Ewyas below Hay Bluff. Capel-y-ffin should be approached from the south to sense its glorious isolation, which must have been all the more glorious before the Gospel Pass to Hay became a paved road. The name translates as boundary chapel.

The church is a simple chamber with white walls, shingle roof, wooden bellcote and small porch. It was rebuilt in 1762, and furnished with five settles, apparently original to the church, and an octagonal pulpit of 1780. The front row was occupied by two teddy bears on my visit. A gallery occupies not just the west wall but runs the length of the north wall to the altar. The font is clearly much older.

The windows are clear, the east one engraved, 'I will lift up mine eyes unto the hills.' Sure enough, the Black Mountains are visible beyond. Up a side lane is the (inaccessible) remnant of Capel-y-ffin monastery, a Victorian Benedictine venture that was taken over by Eric Gill as a commune of sorts in 1924. Gill carved two headstones in the church graveyard.

COLVA

2 miles north-west of Newchurch
ST DAVID *
Cell church on hillside, slate monuments

Colva is the highest church in Wales (1,250 feet) and its view over the deep-cut Radnorshire valleys is superb. It is hard to believe that we are just nine miles from the soft farmland of England.

The church probably dates from the 13th century, but ancient yews and a 12th-century font indicate, as often in Wales, an earlier foundation. A battered wooden belfry and porch adorn the exterior.

The interior is lit by sunny Tudor windows, illuminating extensive medieval murals and Reformation over-painting. A vivid skull-and-crossbones graces the north wall facing the door, with a leper window to the east. The far wall is dominated by beautiful 18th-century slate memorials. A Hanoverian coat of arms carries the date 1733.

Colva has a vigorous friends group determined to keep it alive. As the guide says, it has been spared 'the Victorian gothic fantastication that imposed a dreadful sameness on so many churches'. In that case it is a pity about the new refectory seating.

DISERTH

3 miles south-west of Llandrindod Wells
ST CEWYDD **
Tudor roof and 17th-century pews

The church cuts a dash from the opposite side of the valley in which its village sits. Its dedication is to Cewydd, a little-known saint reputedly a bringer of rain, no great miracle in these parts. A bold stone tower guards a long, whitewashed nave/chancel set in a ring of yews. The substantial porch is filled with stone seats and unusual carved wooden panels.

The interior of Diserth is a monument to the craft of carpentry. The roof might be that of a great medieval barn, probably 16th century with rough cross beams and massive wind-braces. The chancel is ceiled and there is a ghostly upright of an old rood screen, still with its mortise holes. The windows are Georgian but set within deep earlier openings.

The most prominent survivals from a 17th-century restoration are the family box pews in the nave and chancel, dating from the 1660s and running on either side of the altar. Clearly Diserth was overstocked with prosperous, or status-conscious, parishioners. One was owned by James Watts, inventor of the steam engine, who came here to live in 1805.

The fine three-decker pulpit is of 1687. I cannot resist repeating Kilvert's story of the rector of Diserth who delivered surely the most simply concise sermon on record. He had apparently forgotten his text of whatever it was he meant to say. He ascended the pulpit and began: 'Ha, yes, here we are. And it is a fine day. I congratulate you on a fine day, and glad to see so many of you here. Yes indeed. Ha, yes indeed. Now then I shall take for my text … Yes, let me see. You are all sinners and so am I. Yes indeed.' And he sat down.

Nonconformist baroque: the Plough Chapel, Brecon

Radnorshire isolation: Colva

DOLOBRAN **

Nr Pontrobert, 3 miles south-west of Meifod
Historic Quaker meeting-house in woods

Here in the mountain redoubt of the Celtic kings of Powys is a most historic place of worship. The meeting-house in the hills behind Meifod is one of Wales's oldest Nonconformist buildings and in my experience certainly its most inaccessible.

Dolobran is the rustic equivalent of a recusant priest's hole, a place so wild and invisible that, despite the passing of the Toleration Acts a decade before its construction in 1700, it was hoped no Anglican assailants could find it.

More puzzling is why even today not one sign indicates its presence. The only villager in neighbouring Pontrobert who had heard of it assured me it was accessible by car. It is not, or rather it took me an hour to extricate mine from

the mud. The building lies in a wood across a field, a mile down the first lane east from the Pontrobert–Meifod road. It is unmarked and alone. There is nowhere quite so utterly lost in all Wales.

The owners of the house and farm of Dolobran were Lloyds back to the Middle Ages. The 17th-century Lloyds yielded two sons, Charles and Thomas, who went to Oxford and were inspired by George Fox's Quakerism. The family, much persecuted as a result, moved to the Midlands where they founded an iron business and what became a well-known bank. Charles was a follower of William Penn and signed Pennsylvania's early constitution, while Thomas emigrated to the colony and became its deputy governor from 1684–93.

In 1850, with Quakerism declining in the face of evangelical Nonconformity, the entire interior of the chapel was stripped and sent to Pennsylvania. For 180 years the building became a cattle shed. It was rediscovered by local Quakers in 1955 and re-leased from the

Lloyds for meetings. It is still in use by visiting enthusiasts.

The chapel retains the appearance of a late-17th-century woodland cottage. Built of red bricks, its façade presents two windows and two doors, with finely worked brick drip-stones. It was clearly built with care and pride. One side was for the meeting-room, the other for a schoolmaster who, at one point, had fifty pupils in his charge. This countryside was once populated to a density unimaginable today. The present interior, restored in 1975, is exceedingly simple. A small gallery has also been reinstated.

GUILSFIELD

ST AELHAEARN ✳✳✳
Street restoration of gothic interior,
Georgian monuments

Guilsfield is the sort of Welsh church people call English, despite being dedicated to a little-known son of an early prince of Powys. It reflects prosperous border country and prosperous border people. The village is pretty and the environs crowded with Georgian houses. The muscular building grew from the early 14th to the early 16th century, being sensitively restored by Street in 1879 at the expense of the local Mytton family.

The church is set in a generous churchyard filled with yews. The off-centre nave roof ridge and irregular clerestory suggest that a tower was once detached from the church. A ghost of an earlier tower can be seen on the north side of the existing one. The clock warns, 'Be Diligent: Night Beckons'.

Inside is a rich museum of fittings, memorials and curiosities, almost all rearranged by Street. The nave has a bold 14th-century arcade of three bays above which rises a later roof, a forest of tie-beams and cusped wind-braces running the length of nave and chancel. This is supplemented by a canopy ceiling over the latter. It is panelled and has 140 bosses, claimed in the guide to embrace 120 patterns. Street's new screen has an innovative whirl of flamboyant tracery describing what appear to be giant sunflowers.

Street's most regrettable move was to take out what had been a celebrated array of private box pews. He was appalled to find 'each family penned in folds like sheep'. The pews were littered about the nave, reached by a maze of aisles. Some were cramped and tiny, others lavish enough to have private fireplaces. They would doubtless have caused modern worshippers no end of trouble. But they have been replaced by severe rows of machined Victorian pews, which I imagine are now considered equally inconvenient.

The church has memorials to the Mytton and Egerton families. That to James Egerton (d. 1772) is an exquisite Georgian design by John Nelson, a chest above a plaque with mourning putto. Other adornments include Heaton and Butler glass, a carved corner cupboard and old hinges on the door. Outside under the yew by the gate is a tomb epitaph to Richard Jones:

Under this yew tree
Buried would hee bee
For his father and hee
Planted this yew tree.

KERRY

ST MICHAEL ✳
Norman tower/keep

Much-restored Kerry is known as the site of a battle in 1176 between Bishop Adam of St Asaph and the ubiquitous Gerald of Wales, representing St David's. Each claimed the parish for his diocese and each excommunicated the other on the spot. Gerald told Adam 'not to thrust your sickle into another man's corn', and had the mob drive him out of the village in a hail of stones and clods of earth. St David's won and this part of Powys looked south for seven centuries, until it moved to St Asaph in 1849.

The most distinctive feature of Kerry reflects the insecurity of the medieval Marches, its massive keep/tower. This was originally 13th century and was clearly capable of defying not just the English and the bishop of St Asaph but Victorian restoration by Street.

The interior has four bays to its chancel and

four to its nave, both of heavy Norman piers, conveying a sense of 12th-century power and robustness. The roof is 14th century, much restored, while the chancel wagon roof is in two parts, one plain and one ornamental. The pulpit is made of panels removed from the roof, while the east window is by Kempe. An excellently preserved 15th-century font is decorated with the symbols of the Passion, including fierce-looking pincers.

An engaging memorial at the back of the church is to Richard Jones, a naval purser who left money to the local poor and apprentices. It was to be invested in government stocks. A note below says that when 'the £1,000 5 Per cent Consols were redeemed by the government' the money was spent on roads instead. Thus passed the glory of the ancient welfare state.

LEIGHTON

2 miles south-east of Welshpool
HOLY TRINITY ✱✱
Victorian estate church with green man and mausoleum

Suddenly Montgomeryshire might be North-amptonshire. On the hillside overlooking the upper reaches of the Severn is the ostentatious steeple of a Victorian estate church. It was built by John Naylor, descendant by marriage of the Liverpool banking family, the Leylands, to adorn his Leighton Hall estate. This comprised a rectory, schoolhouse and model farm as a complete 19th-century project. In the grounds is reputedly the finest stand of redwoods in Britain. It was here that the notorious leylandii cypress was first hybridized.

The church was commissioned from a Liverpool architect, W. H. Gee, in 1851. While the style is conventionally gothic, the size and splendour of the building is startling in a country of tiny box churches.

The spire is of the East Midlands type, a stone steeple rising from broaches to two tiers of lucarnes or gabled openings. Crockets climb the base, as if the steeple were besieged by snails. Over the north porch is a green man, a pagan symbol rare for a Victorian church. It is 'pre-

Christian but not necessarily un-Christian', says the guide apologetically.

The interior is dominated by the steepest of hammerbeam roofs. Never did the gothicists' much-vaunted 'hands in prayer' point so emphatically to God. The spandrels of the hammerbeams are decorated with tracery and the chancel arch is spectacularly high. Blind arcading adorns the chancel.

The church is floored with Minton tiles and the pews are set in a curious zigzag arrangement with no central aisle, surely impeding any wedding ceremony. The windows contain diamond insets with the initial J & G, for John Naylor and his wife, Georgiana.

In the south-east corner is an octagonal mausoleum (technically a cenotaph as it contains no tomb) for members of the Naylor family. In its centre is a large statue of an angel carved by a Naylor daughter, Georgina, top-lit in pink and eerie.

LLANANNO

9 miles north of Llandrindod Wells
ST ANNO ✱
Fine Welsh screen

The A483 south from Newtown climbs from the valley of the Severn over the watershed of the River Ithon. On the banks of the latter, nestling in a field beneath the road, is a tiny church rebuilt in 1867 and surrounded by a hedge. The church is dedicated to St Anno (*c.*780) and is of little account except for one of Wales's finest screens, more ornate even than Llanwnnog (see below) as a work of the Newtown school of carvers.

The screen lights contain lace-like tracery, particularly splendid in the central arch. The main beams are covered in foliage and fruit, the stems emerging from the mouths of serpents. The forte of the work is the panelling of the loft, with triangular pinnacled canopies. These were admirably filled in 1880 with a replacement gallery of twenty-five patriarchs and apostles flanking Christ. It juts over deep coving, so top-heavy that it must have staggered under the weight of musicians.

Congregational ogees at Cae Bach

LLANBISTER

8 miles north of Llandrindod Wells
ST CYNLLO *
Caröe restoration, musicians' gallery

This is a tough, feisty mountain church, forced to make the best of a steeply sloping site. The east end is buried in the hillside while the west looms over the village three storeys high. The sloping graveyard means that every burial spot requires a small terrace to itself. Entry to the church is equally dramatic, up a steep flight of steps, rendered more so by Caröe's restoration. Inside the door is a baptistery designed for total immersion.

The interior is a large barn-like structure, a single chamber with massive wagon roof and thick walls, into which deep Norman openings are cut. It is like a church inside a fortress and must have been impossibly dark before two Perpendicular windows were let into the south wall. More steps are needed to ascend the chancel. An excellent screen, with carving as good as Llanwnnog's, suffers from having lost its gallery. The reredos is excellent, again by Caröe.

At the west end is an 18th-century musicians' gallery, while on the north wall is a sad exhibit of the remains of some of its instruments, including a bassoon and a bass. Could they not be repaired and used?

LLANDEGLEY

6 miles east of Llandrindod Wells
PALES MEETING-HOUSE *
Secluded Quaker house with
former schoolroom

One of Wales's favourite Quaker meeting-houses lies a mile uphill north of Llandegley with a superb view over the tumbling hills of the Ithon and Edw valleys, shamefully without national park protection. The meeting-house began life as nothing more than a burial ground in 1673, isolated far from its village for seclusion, on land donated by a friendly farmer. The Quaker George Fox is known to have preached in the valley in 1657.

The present building was erected in 1717 and takes its name from 'pale', meaning an enclosure. Local Quakerism hardly flourished, since in 1860 just one 'infirm, lame old man still crosses the hills at the hour of worship to sit there alone with God'. This soon changed when in 1867 half the building became a local school, with fifty children in attendance. As at Dolobran (see above), education was to be the salvation of the Quakers.

The Pales room is still thatched and divided into two, forming a meeting room and a schoolroom with a fireplace. The former is of extreme simplicity and is heavily varnished. Its old benches and a table are in place. On the walls are bookcases, wall charts and drawings. One has the self at the centre, with an arrow pointing up to God and down to the world. Trees wave restlessly through the windows.

LLANDRINDOD WELLS

CAE BACH, UNITED REFORM CHAPEL *
Complete Georgian interior

The chapel, named 'little field', stands next to a suburban estate north of Llandrindod Wells. From the road it looks like something on a chocolate box.

A wicket gate leads into a churchyard where two yews and two box bushes symmetrically flank a doorway, with two ogival gothic windows on either side. These must post-date the chapel's foundation in 1715. The single-cell rectangular building is whitewashed outside and within and looks very clean.

The furnishings are virtually unaltered since the 18th century, a complete set of box pews arranged to face the pulpit. The pews are painted a faded mushroom colour and are stepped up at the back under a gallery. There are candlesticks everywhere, and a sense of peace.

In the churchyard stands a row of extraordinarily tall 19th-century gravestones, wholly out of proportion to both chapel and yard. They are like stern church elders keeping watch over this bunch of Nonconformists. They are covered in lichen and slowly crumbling. Stables for resting horses during the service survive across the lane.

LLANELEU **

9 miles north-east of Brecon
Isolated hill church, ancient screen

This church is a prize to all who find it. The easiest way is on foot down from the crest of Gader Ridge on the Black Mountains above it. The building sits in a circular churchyard alone in a large meadow east of Bronllys.

In the care of the Friends of Friendless Churches, this might be the most forlorn of all places of worship, were it not for its mountainside and its accompaniment of wild flowers, birdsong and sheep. On a sunny spring afternoon it is a blissful spot, entombing the drover spirits, the brief ecstasies of life and agonies of death among the mountains. Here Wales's past is very present.

Llaneleu's walls are roughly whitewashed, its flagstones damp and cold. It is lit by candles, adding atmosphere to the church's occasional concerts. The roof is wind-braced. Medieval murals survive, while others have been overpainted with Puritan texts and a coat of arms. An old harmonium is still playable.

Most remarkable is the screen and rood loft, believed to be of the 14th century and thus one of the oldest in Wales. While the loft panels and tympanum survive, rising to the roof, the screen is no more than a rough-hewn wooden frame, at some time painted blood red with white roses. The impression of a former cross stands out from the paintwork, as if it was torn down only after the painting had been done.

Jan Morris describes the Llaneleu screen as seeming 'to stand there between the nave and the altar … not to keep secrets or amaze the superstitious but simply in mystic demarcation, between the earth, stone and sweat at one

Ecclesiastical vernacular: screen at Llaneleu

end of the church, the fire and holy water at the other'.

This is a church shipwrecked on the rock of the Reformation, its screen half-destroyed, its icons half-eliminated, its parishioners daubing paint and inserting a pulpit. Monuments recall generations of the local Aubrey family, imposing continuity and order on this lonely, lovely corner of Wales.

LLANFILO **

Restored screen and loft, millennial hassocks

The church with its prominent broach spire is visible on a hillside overlooking the Dulas valley. Entirely whitewashed, from the outside it looks at first sight like a 'done-up' Welsh farmhouse, stepping down the slope of a well-tended churchyard.

Llanfilo is a textbook of careful restoration. Its chunky steeple came in the 1850s but its greatest blessing was the attention of Caröe in the 1920s. He restored the plaster ceiling to the chancel, retained the 1630s pews, inserted new windows to brighten the nave and, above all, repaired the superb screen. To this he gave new niche sculptures by Nathaniel Hitch.

Though the Llanfilo screen lacks the pyrotechnics of Llananno and others, as restored I find it among the most satisfying. It fills the church without overpowering it and its robust details fit into the church round it. The bressummer trails are of vine and pomegranate, one emerging from the mouth of a wyvern. Caröe had to copy the panel tracery and supplied new pilasters to the loft front, but the effect is to bring alive a work of devotional sculpture, a minor masterpiece.

Beyond in the chancel is a collection of wall memorials, including two in the baroque vernacular of the Brutes of Llanbedr. The font in the nave is of the misshapen Norman form that looks almost prehistoric. The parishioners celebrated the millennium by each contributing at least a few stitches to new hassocks, their motifs taken from the screen. Needlepoint is a vernacular tradition to survive in modern churches.

LLANGASTY

6 miles east of Brecon
ST GASTAYN *
Tractarian mission to Brecon Beacons

The story of Llangasty is told under Treberfedd house, above. Raikes gave up his Yorkshire banking career to take his Tractarian mission to the shores of the largest natural lake in South Wales. Here he had the young J. L. Pearson rebuild the old church in 1848, with school and rectory next door. Here they remain, an unaltered monument to the zeal of the Oxford Movement amid the sweeping slopes of the Brecon Beacons.

The nave is simple and undecorated, in the Early Gothic style. The chancel is a total contrast. Careful restoration has left it vividly coloured, a sanctuary of faith. It has richly painted roof beams, three lancet east windows, an ornate ironwork screen to a side chapel and, most distinctive of all, coloured stencil-work covering the walls and roof beams. Surviving fragments of the screen from the old church were reused in a low chancel screen.

Mrs Raikes trained the local children to sing in the choir and dressed them in surplices. Services were held in Welsh on Sundays.

LLANGURIG

ST CURIG **
Good Victorian restoration,
genealogical windows

This was a dull church which, for once, the Victorians made interesting. It is on the site of an ancient *clas* founded by St Curig in the 6th century. The church had, by the Reformation, become neglected and derelict. A local squire claiming the name of Chevalier Lloyd of Clochfaen became an Anglican priest, then converting to Rome and back again. He emerged from the experience an enthusiastic Welsh genealogist and financed Llangurig's restoration in 1878 by George Gilbert Scott.

Lloyd was insistent that what had vanished over the centuries be restored, including, curiously, a broach spire that is most un-Welsh. It was first shingled but is now copper-covered. Scott re-created the old rood screen from surviving fragments and drawings made by an antiquarian cleric, John Parker, in 1828. Three-bay arcades to the nave and chancel were also restored and the superb angels in the roof copied from those at Cilcain (Clwyd). Those in the nave carry musical instruments and in the chancel emblems of the Passion.

The collaboration of Lloyd and Scott makes Llangurig a modest Welsh echo of the work of Sutton and Bodley at Brant Broughton in Lincolnshire, reminding us how much the modern church can owe to the Victorians. Lloyd designed windows depicting the story of St Curig, the princely families of mid-Wales and Lloyd's own antecedents. They were made by Burlison and Grylls.

The church occasioned R. S. Thomas's lines from 'Border Blues', 'Hush, not a word. When we've finished the milking/ And the stars are quiet, we'll get out the car/ And go to Llangurig.'

LLANIDLOES

ST IDLOES **
Imported Decorated arcade, angel roof

Connoisseurs of small Welsh towns rank Llanidloes high, with its focus of a quaint half-timbered market hall. Though not as picturesque as Ruthin or Beaumaris, Llanidloes is sterner and more Welsh. It hosted Chartist riots in the 1830s and visits by John Wesley. Its setting on the upper Severn, enveloped by the Cambrian mountains, is particularly charming.

Of the 7th-century saint Idloes little is known beyond a saying, 'goreu cynneddf yw cadw moes', roughly translated as 'morality is the best policy'. His church is near the river and surreally big. This is because the old church had to be heightened to accommodate an entire nave arcade imported from the demolished abbey of Cwm-Hir in Radnorshire in 1542. This five-bay structure is the treasure of Llanidloes, Early Gothic with undulating chamfers and stiff-leaf capitals. The roof was thought also to come from Cwm-Hir but ring-dating now ascribes it to the 16th-century rebuilding. It carries twenty

bays of angels and claims to be one of last angel roofs ever made (prior to the Victorians).

Stained glass is by Clayton and Bell and rather dark, but a new millennium window, donated by the Hamer family, light-heartedly depicts the Creation with the owners' dog and Chaos at its centre. Outside, even the gravestones and the yews seem oversized.

LLANWNNOG **

Nr Newtown, 1 mile north of Caersŵs
Original screen and loft

The dark little church was heavily restored by the architect P. K. Penson in 1863, but retains its rood screen and loft and some of the roof bosses. The screen is among the finest in Wales, dating from c.1500 and of the Newtown school (see Llananno).

The intricacy of the tracery in the screen lights and the depth of the coving suggest a wealthy patron. The common assumption that these Welsh screens are invariably imported from dissolved monasteries is nowadays challenged. The deep undercutting certainly indicates a skilful hand eager to show its dexterity.

The loft is secluded behind panelling. In the frieze thick foliage emanates from the mouth of a tremendous dragon. The whole composition is a virtuoso performance, delightfully aged amid the surrounding hard Victorian woodwork.

The north wall has a kaleidoscope window of 15th-century fragments awaiting a jigsaw-puzzle solver. The chancel contains a wall memorial to Matthew Price (d. 1699), complete with broken pediment, putti and a bat-like skull beneath. The red sandstone of the walls is attributed to the Roman fort at Caersŵs.

MAESYRONNEN

Glasbury, 4 miles south-west of Hay-on-Wye
INDEPENDENT CHAPEL **
Complete Georgian interior

Maesyronnen, the 'field of ash', is a rare survivor of the earliest period of chapel building after the Act of Toleration of 1689. High on a hill overlooking the Wye at Glasbury it was formed in 1697, probably from an old barn – hence references to 'granary of God' chapels. There is still an adjacent minister's house or *tŷr capel*, now a Landmark Trust property, from which the chapel is divided by a 15th-century cruck beam. In other words, this is a medieval grouping of considerable interest in its own right.

Maesyronnen retains its cluttered 18th-century fittings and aura of confident Dissent. It is not, writes Anthony Jones, 'a tantalising reflection of the glory of Heaven-to-come … but an architecture of intuition, improvisation and ordinariness'. There are no fireplaces inside, the frozen worshippers allegedly told to rely on 'the fire of faith'. At no point in its later history has anyone dared rectify this.

Support for the 18th-century roof comes from a network of masts and spars reminiscent of the lower deck of a sailing ship. The pulpit is in the centre of the far wall with a window behind the preacher's shoulder, to help him read and give his outline a 'halo' effect when preaching.

In front is a table, not an altar, with seats round it for the deacons. These were hierarchical institutions, with the community elders as notional protectors of the preacher against occasional assault by Anglican militants.

The interior is crammed with seating, each bench with its status and its regular occupant. Independent this might be, but not egalitarian, with hard benches for the lower orders. Once there would also have been floor hay to warm feet on the damp mud floor. The pulpit lists the names of ministers back to 1645, when worshippers met in secret barns or in the open.

On the walls are memorial tablets similar to those in parish churches. An oil lamp hangs overhead, an old harmonium stands to one side. The church is still in use. Peter Sager visited Maesyronnen shortly after Margaret Thatcher's re-election in 1983 and heard the preacher asking for prayers 'even for those for whom we may not have voted'. Tim Hughes points out that Maesyronnen must have been the 'Maesyfelin' of Bruce Chatwin's *On the Black Hill*, where men worshipped 'earthed by the power of this old place'.

MEIFOD

ST TYSILIO AND ST MARY ✳✳✳
Historic *clas* of Powys princes,
Celtic memorial stone

On a cool evening with a mist rising from the waters of the Vyrnwy, the ghosts of old Wales are as vivid here as anywhere I know. Meifod lies in a valley settled by the Romans, which later afforded wooded seclusion to the rulers of Powys. Here they established an ecclesiastical base near their castle at Mathrafal. The mission church, begun by St Gwyddfarch c.550, was said by Pennant to be 'as old as Christianity in these islands'.

Gwyddfarch's pupil, Tysilio, was reputedly son of the then king of Powys, Brochfael Ysgithrog, founding a church at Llandysilio in the Menai Straits (see Anglesey) before founding the *clas* at Meifod in the 7th century. It was here that the kings were buried, steeped in the ghosts of the Welsh borders.

The old village – once called a city – is still dominated by a magnificent churchyard, according to Peter Lord 'the only one in Wales where the enclosure survives on a scale comparable to that of contemporary Irish monasteries'. The remains of extensive monastic ruins are assumed to lie beneath the turf, as yet unexcavated. Great beeches, limes and yews make it less the setting for a church than the park of a mansion.

Whatever had gone before was replaced by a large romanesque church, built in 1156 by the then prince of Powys, Madog ap Maredudd, who died in 1160. Its importance was signified by the use of red sandstone, which is not a local material. Traces of the Norman church can still be seen on the outside of the tower and in the arch round the main door. It was altered in the 14th century and rebuilt c.1500 under the Tudor ascendancy.

The interior of Meifod reflects its evolution. The west end was clearly adapted piecemeal rather than demolished for rebuilding. The south arcade is in a gentle Perpendicular, as is a sturdy, unceiled oak roof, raised when Benjamin Ferry restored the church in 1871. The reredos appears to have been pieced together from old fragments, as does the vestry door. Victorian

Maesyronnen: granary of God

glass is ubiquitous but not overwhelming, the east window of the south aisle being an early composition (1838) by David Evans, depicting the church's patron saints under ogee arches.

Meifod's greatest treasure is a carved slab stone of controversial origin. Previously assumed to be a Celtic coffin lid it is now thought to be Viking in influence if not creation, dating from the 9th century. It has a Maltese cross as well as a Latin one, and the knots and small animals are in the Celtic-Norse tradition. It has a prehistoric simplicity, its jumble of motifs lacking plan or symmetry. Others have proposed it as the tombstone of a Powys prince.

MONTGOMERY

ST NICHOLAS ✳✳✳
French-influenced town church, medieval misericords, Herbert tombs

Montgomery is pure Norman, its castle begun by Roger de Montgomerie of Calvados soon after the Conquest. It was built to command the upper Severn and guard access to central Wales and the ever-hostile kingdom of Gwynedd. The church is located in the Norman fashion on a hill facing its castle across a valley, with glorious views towards the Severn valley and England. The eccentric location of the tower over the north transept is due to the old one becoming unsafe.

The interior is a complete work of the 13th century, the arcades robust sandstone to the north and pinker to the south. The roof is a fine work of Borders carpentry, with alternate arches and hammerbeams dividing bold quatrefoil panels. A wagon roof adorns the chancel, with coloured bosses.

The screen is remarkable in appearing to be two in one. The portion facing the nave is original to the church. The other side facing the chancel is of a piece with the stalls and misericords and was probably imported from the dissolved priory of Chirbury. The Elizabethan gates are of a most delicate Perpendicular, finely complementing the seven-light east window. The misericords are much battered, but one appears to be a most explicit sheela-na-gig (woman with legs apart).

Memorials of Montgomery descendants fill the aisles, while the south transept is virtually a mausoleum. On the floor are two medieval effigies of great interest. One, part-alabaster and part-sandstone restoration, is believed to represent Sir Edmund Mortimer (died *c*.1408). This scion of the great Marcher family was son-in-law of Glyndŵr and brother-in-law of Henry Hotspur.

The other effigy is believed to be of Sir Richard Herbert and probably dates from *c*.1500. He was grandfather of the Herbert commemorated in the immense Elizabethan tomb next to it, of the late 16th century. Richard lies under a magnificent canopy, in armour with his wife in an embroidered dress. Their eight children attend them and beneath is a memento mori cadaver. The tomb is virtually a chamber in itself, vaulted and with a confection of motifs piled high above.

In Montgomery churchyard is the grave of a robber unjustly hanged in 1821, swearing beforehand that where he lay nothing would grow for a generation. This proved to be the case. The spot was later marked by a rose bush and is attended by tourists and mystics.

OLD RADNOR

5 miles south-west of Presteigne
ST STEPHEN ✶✶✶
Tudor interior with original organ and ancient font

The church is within the diocese of Hereford, surrounded by an ancient earthwork on a mound looking out to the English border, as if wanting to go home. Everything here is late medieval, possibly the result of the church having been burned by Glyndŵr in 1401.

The nave roof is flat with panels and floral bosses depicting the arms of the lords of Radnor. Light floods through south-aisle windows on to restrained Perpendicular arcades, those in the chancel the work of Victorian restorers. The large east window is by Pugin's assistant, Hardman.

The screen extends the full width of the church and is so well restored as to belie its 15th century date. The pilasters rise, English-style, from floor to graceful vaulting. A gallery is meticulously carved, while the lights, panels and central arch are pierced with graceful open-work. The screen continues round to enclose the choir. Given the blame for iconoclasm so often attached to the Reformation, it is worth noting that an 1818 visitor recorded paint, gilding and 'saints and religious persons placed in ranges, compartments or niches'. These were lost not to iconoclasm but to Anglican neglect.

On the west wall are three large hatchments and other memorials to the Lewis family. The exquisite organ case of *c*.1500 is apparently the oldest in Britain, a soaring façade of linenfold and openwork, rising to a flurry of inventive motifs. The pipes seem afterthoughts. The tub font is said to date from the 8th century, a mis-shapen lump of rock, yet eerily sculptural like a work by Henry Moore.

PATRISIO

4 miles west of Llanfihangel Crucornau
ST ISSUI or ISIO ✶✶✶✶
Picture-book church in valley, screen and wall-paintings

Of all the hill churches of Wales, Patrisio is most celebrated, despite its myriad spellings. The approach is from the Abergavenny road, up a side road, then a lane, then a farmyard, across a stream, up hill, down dale and up again somewhere to the right. The building clings to a hillside overlooking the Grwyne Fawr valley amid what Wynford Vaughan-Thomas called, 'a soul-consoling view'. Patrisio should be saved for a warm autumn evening when the Welsh leaves turn golden and the spirits of the gloaming rise from the valley below.

The church lay near the medieval route north from Abergavenny into mid-Wales. It commemorated Issui, a holy man of these parts who lived by a well below the church. This was recently restored and, on Peter Sager's visit in the 1980s, thank-offerings littered the spot. Issui was reputedly murdered by a traveller to whom he had given shelter.

Pilgrims began to arrive and a Continental

The screen at Patrisio

visitor is said to have left enough gold to build a new church, the date of 1060 being associated with this foundation. The font in the main church bears a Latin inscription declaring that 'Menhir made me in the time of Genillin', similarly dated to the mid-11th century. The original shrine may be the tiny chamber to the west of the church, with its own entrance and altar. This chapel has been restored and reconsecrated, and contains a modern statue of St Issui.

It is said that Gerald of Wales preached in the churchyard in 1188, when escorting Archbishop Baldwin of Canterbury on his fundraising tour for the Third Crusade. Gerald was then eager to curry the favour of Rome for his episcopal ambitions. Why they took this high road from Brecon to Abergavenny is not clear, though Gerald implies that safety from bandits may have been a consideration. How the Welsh peasantry responded to his concern for the fate of Jerusalem is not recorded.

The present un-aisled interior remains Norman, with a windowless north wall, but with Tudor windows inserted in the south. The walls display murals of different periods. A skeleton depicts Time, with an hourglass and spade. Elsewhere are biblical texts and a faded coat of arms, apparently pre-Georgian. The roof is barrel-vaulted.

All eyes turn to the famous screen. While lacking the richness of Llananno or Llanwnnog, Patrisio is supremely elegant. The heads of the lights and the openwork on the loft panels are filigree, while the frieze tracery of dragons spewing ubiquitous vines is exquisitely wrought. The work is *c*.1500 and set behind two stone altars, survivals of subsidiary altars supposedly outlawed in 1550. The whole composition is light in design and hovers in the air between nave and chancel. It longs for music.

Many of the memorial tablets, like those at Llanfilo and Cwmyoy (Gwent), are by the Brute family of Llanbedr, masters of Welsh baroque.

Like many Welsh churches that escaped

make one line in this entry, for the next page

the Victorians, Partrisio was even luckier to be restored by the ever-sensitive Caröe in 1909. It deserves to stand as his memorial.

PENNANT MELANGELL

3 miles west of Llangynog
ST MELANGELL ✱✱✱
Romanesque saint's shrine, medieval frieze

The church sits amid rolling hills beneath the Aran Fawddwy massif. A lane leads up from Llangynog on the Bala road and disappears into a steep wooded valley. At the time of its foundation in the 8th century, Pennant must have seemed wild indeed, on the borders between Powys and the kingdom of Gwynedd. Its celebrity depended on pilgrims to the shrine of St Melangell, which remains in the church to this day and is one of Britain's great romanesque treasures.

St Melangell's (or Monacella's) claim to fame is as a daughter of an Irish prince who, in 604, caught the attention of a hunting chieftain, Prince Brochwel, when he was chasing a hare. As she prayed in a thicket, the animal took refuge in her skirts.

The chieftain approached but he and his dogs were struck with paralysis, his hunting horn stuck dumb to his lips. Impressed by the young woman's piety – she had been living as a hermit in the valley – he gave it to her as a sanctuary for nuns and hares.

Melangell stayed for a further thirty-seven years and became the patron saint of all hunted things, including refugees. Hares were duly known as Melangell's lambs. The guidebook points out that Melangell is not alone in having this legend attributed to her. Poets from Southey to R. S. Thomas have been inspired by the legend, and by the church's solitude in its private valley.

The building is Norman in origin, a series of un-aisled chambers with a tower at one end, much rebuilt over the centuries. The saint's shrine, dated *c*.1160, has been scattered and even immured in the church walls. In the 1950s an archaeologist, Robert Heaton, pieced it together and rebuilt it in the 12th-century apse.

Following a threat to remove the entire church to St Fagans, the shrine was in 1988 re-sited in the chancel. The apse is now a chapel and the chancel a 'feretory' or shrine room.

A shrine surviving in this form is unique in Britain and rare in Europe. Roughly half is renewed, such surfaces being left blank rather than covered with interlacing, honouring archaeology rather than aesthetics. The chest supposedly containing the saint's relics is raised on round columns and arches, crowned by a steep gable with dramatically drooping crockets. The motifs are strangely primitive, as if drawing on some lost pre-Christian inspiration.

The church retains a 15th-century screen in somewhat battered state. The lights are ogee-headed with foliate tracery. Part was reused in the vestry, including a delightful frieze depicting St Melangell, the prince with his horn, and the hare. A 14th-century effigy also represents the saint with hares, depicted in abundance in the church. There are prayer cards for those convinced of the saint's restorative powers, though they were surely confined to hares.

PRESTEIGNE

ST ANDREW ✱✱
Classical memorials, Flemish tapestry

The Welsh borders are blessed with a chain of small country towns, neglected by English visitors if on the 'wrong side of the track'. One such is Presteigne, former county town of Radnorshire (see Judge's Lodgings, above). The church is solid and its tower squat, the south aspect enlivened by three grand Perpendicular windows with triangular arches and panel tracery.

Though ghosts of a Norman structure remain in the north aisle, the interior was extended in the 14th century to accommodate a rugged six-bay arcade. This is divided from the chancel by a Victorian screen by Pearson, a finely detailed work with an ogee central arch. The old chancel ceiling was revealed in a restoration of the 1920s, but the walls were unfortunately scraped.

In the chancel is a collection of Georgian memorials to the Owen and Parsons families,

Romanesque shrine at Pennant Melangell

sophisticated works with broken pediments, apparently intended as a set. The north aisle houses the church's proudest possession, a Flemish tapestry of the entry into Jerusalem, dating from the early 16th century. It was presented by Richard Owen in 1737 and, thankfully, has remained in the church ever since. Long may it do so.

RHIWLEN

6 miles east of Builth Wells
ST DAVID *
Tiny hill church, altar rood

The region immediately north of the Brecon Beacons is wild country. The road over the hills from Rhiwlen to Painscastle must, on a fine day, be one of the loveliest in Wales. Streams cut through tight valleys and side lanes lead nowhere. A few sheep farms struggle manfully to survive. Nothing moves but the birds, ever restless overhead.

Here is the archetypal Welsh-Welsh church, relic of hillside worship on an old mountain trail where drovers would avoid the valleys with their mud, bandits and tolls. On such a spot, sometimes already marked by pagan yews, a holy man would plant his cross, pile stones into a hut and open for business.

In these parts he would often dedicate it to Wales's own saint, David. The structure might be repaired and a window driven through solid walls, but mostly it was too poor to merit later alteration.

Such is Rhiwlen. The church is tiny and Norman, a cell with battered wooden belfry and an uncommonly large porch. The outside walls are bright with whitewash.

The inside is a simple chamber lit by a large 18th-century window. The sanctuary appears to have had its rood over the altar, formed of a recess in the east wall. This is crowned with a triangular or shouldered arch, a simple architectural form repeated over the doorway. A strange triple-arched window pierces the north wall. The church is floored with slate, lit with candles and adorned with two simple wall memorials.

TRELYSTAN

4 miles south-east of Welshpool
ALL SAINTS *
Wood-framed church, ancient organ

Trelystan sits on a hilltop in an enclosure of ancient yews nodding at each other like a group of druids in pagan conclave. We are on the east flank of the Long Mountain above Welshpool, where lush fields sweep down to the English border.

The church is reached by a footpath over a meadow and is celebrated for being largely wooden and medieval. It was encased in brick in 1856 and looks from the outside like a village hall, black and white, of timber and painted brick. The inside is panelled in pitch pine, still with its 15th-century roof. A fragment of the old screen survives and the altar rails are Jacobean.

Near the altar is a restored barrel organ of 1827 designed as a miniature version of a full church organ. It can play twenty hymn tunes: I conjured a rendering of Rock of Ages. A fierce east window of Munich-painted glass depicts the Agony in the Garden. The Welsh naturalist William Condry noted outside such delightful wild flowers as golden saxifrage, herb paris, masterwort and bittercress. From one of the yews the Devil is said to have hanged his mother.

WELSHPOOL

ST MARY **
Town church restored by Street,
Powis memorials

The town is four miles from the English border and is capital of the mid-Welsh cattle and sheep trade. It still holds the biggest cattle market in Wales. The church is that of neighbouring Powis Castle and is filled with Herbert family memorials.

The west tower dominates a slope at some distance from the main street and market area, where its three Decorated windows with reticulated tracery, rare in Wales, beam down on the

Breconshire sublime: Rhiwlen

passing traffic. These date from the extension of the church in the 14th century, but it is a later re-building in the early 16th century that gives the interior its airy character. Further building took place in the 18th and 19th centuries, including a restoration by Street in 1870.

The interior is spacious, with asymmetric aisles and an off-centre chancel. The south windows are gloomy with stained glass, and Street's deep wooden roof is gloomier still. But the chancel has a remarkable set of Tractarian furnishings, with altar rails, chairs and sedilia. The colourful roof may have come from Strata Marcella abbey after the Dissolution.

To the south of the chancel is a small chapel with a Flemish 16th-century triptych donated by a former curate. It depicts either Christ taking leave of his mother or, more obviously, appearing to her after the Crucifixion (note the wounds). Above is a window by Wailes. Round the walls are mostly effigies of the Herberts, earls of Powis. The Victorian 2nd Earl is depicted in rich alabaster in his Garter robes with angels at his head and an elephant at his feet.

The west wall carries a display of 18th-century charity boards that once formed the front of a gallery. No one could be in any doubt to whom the poor of this parish owed their thanks.

The timbered interior at Trelystan

Glossary of Architectural Terms and Common Welsh Words

abacus (pl. **abaci**): a tablet on the capital of a column, supporting the entablature.
aber: river mouth.
aedicule: classical frame for a niche.
afon: river.
Anglo-Catholic: Victorian High Church movement within Anglicanism but stressing latter's Catholic past.
apse: semi-circular east end extension of church, typically Norman and rare in Wales.
Arts and Crafts: movement of 1870–1914, following Ruskin and Morris, stressing traditional materials and craftsmanship.
ashlar: any block of masonry fashioned into a wall, either load-bearing or covering brick.
bach/fach: little, small.
bailey: inner and outer courts of a castle, usually moated and surrounded by battlemented curtain walls, containing a motte on which stands a keep.
baldacchino: free-standing canopy over altar, supported by columns. Also called ciborium.
ballflower: rich Decorated gothic ornament of *c.*1300, formed of three petals enclosing a ball.
baluster: upright supporting handrail on stairs.
barrel vault see **vault**.
bay: space of a wall between any vertical feature, such as a window or pillar.
bedd: grave.
belvedere: a pavilion or raised turret or lantern on the top of a house, open for the view, or to admit the breeze.
betws: oratory.
bolection moulding: moulding concealing the join of vertical and horizontal surfaces, shaped like an S in cross-section.

boss: knob or projection, often richly carved, at the intersection of a roof vault rib.
boulle: elaborate inlay work on the surface of furniture, customary in 17th- and 18th-century work.
bressummer (or **breastsummer**): a summer or beam supporting the whole, or a great part, of the front of a building or a screen loft.
broach: the triangular face whereby a square tower is converted into an octagonal spire.
bryn: hill.
cae: field.
caer: castle.
capital: the top of a column or pier below the entablature, its carving typically indicating its style and date. The commonest medieval capitals were cushion, scallop or trumpet, water-leaf, stiff-leaf or moulded.
cartouche: moulded frame of a picture or statue, often oval and surrounded by a scroll.
celure: bay or bays of roof directly over the sanctuary/chancel, usually enriched to depict sky over the Crucifixion.
chamfer: surface of arch formed by cutting off the square edge, typical of Early Gothic building.
chancel: eastern end of church traditionally reserved for clergy, containing altar and usually sanctuary and choir.
chinoiserie: style of advanced rococo with Chinese motifs, often associated with gothick.
clas (pl. *clasau*): early Welsh religious community, customarily a base for teaching and missionary work.
clerestory: row of windows above arcade in nave to add light.
collar beams see **roof timbers**.
corbel: stone bracket, often carved with angels or human heads.

cornice: ledge on upper part of classical entablature, usually near the join of wall and ceiling.

cottage ornée: late Georgian/Victorian picturesque cottage, usually with thatched roof and gothic windows.

credence table: a shelf over a piscina.

crocket: decorative leafy knob usually on outside of an arch.

croes: cross.

crossing: central space of church where nave divides into transepts and chancel.

cwm: small valley, dell.

dado: lower part of wall or screen.

Decorated gothic: mid-gothic period, *c.*1250–1350, characterized by intricate window tracery, naturalistic carving and complex shafting of pillars and arches.

drip-stone: a projecting moulding over doorways, etc., serving to throw off the rain.

du: black.

dyffryn: valley.

Early Gothic: immediate post-Norman style, *c.*1190–1250, characterized by introduction of pointed arch and simple lancet windows, sometimes called Early English.

eglwys: church.

finial: the bunch of foliage, etc., on the top of a pinnacle, gable, spire, etc.

flèche: slender spire carried on ridge of church roof.

frontispiece: decorative bay above a doorway in a Tudor or Jacobean building, customarily composed of renaissance motifs.

gable: triangular end of roof or crown of projecting window.

galilee chapel: a chapel at the west end of some churches, in which penitents were placed.

garderobe: medieval lavatory, usually discharging into a ditch or moat outside medieval house or castle.

gothick: decorative gothic revival style of the late-Georgian/Regency period, distinct from the ecclesiastical gothic revival of Pugin and the Victorians.

green man: strange naturalistic figure with green fronds emanating from mouth, ears

and even eyes, found in medieval churches and assumed to be related to pre-Christian (possibly druid) fertility rite.

grisaille: monochrome painting, usually a mural and in shades of grey.

gwyn: white.

hafod: summer or upland farm.

half-timbering: term for wood-framed houses, after practice of splitting logs in two to provide beams.

hammerbeam: a horizontal piece of timber in place of a tie-beam at or near the feet of a pair of rafters.

hen: old.

hipped roof: sloping end to a roof instead of end gable.

isaf: lower.

Jesse window: church window showing Christ's genealogy in stained glass or carved on the mullions.

keep: round or square fort forming the most secure central feature of a castle.

king-and-queen post see **roof timbers.**

lancet: Early Gothic window of a single light under a pointed arch with no tracery.

lierne: see **vault.**

linenfold panelling: the pattern on wall panels imitating folded linen.

llan: strictly a holy enclosure, not a church as such, normally followed by the name of a saint or founder or local chief.

llyn: lake.

lucarne: small window opening in spire, usually decorative but perhaps to reduce wind resistance.

machicolations: floor openings through which missiles can be fired down on attackers.

maen: stone.

maes: meadow, field.

mansard: a roof with two separate pitches of slope.

mawr/fawr: great.

misericord: tiny shelf carved under hinged choir-stall to support occupant when standing. Often elaborately carved.

moel: bare hill.

morfa: sea-marsh.

motte: earth mound forming base of keep in early castles.

mullions: vertical stone or metal divides between glass panes (or lights) of a window.

mynydd: mountain.

nant: brook, dell containing brook.

neuadd: hall.

newydd: new.

oculus: a round window.

ogee: double, S-shaped curve, composed of convex and concave lines, forming late-Gothic arch. When thrust forward from the wall, the shape is a 'nodding ogee'.

ogham: an ancient Celtic alphabet of straight lines meeting or crossing the edge of a stone.

oriel: projecting upper window.

parvise: room, usually for the occupation of a priest, above a porch.

pen: head or top.

Perpendicular gothic: last period of gothic, *c*.1350–1540, characterized by spacious interiors, large windows, flattened arches and embattled walls. Represented in Wales by the 'Stanley churches' of the borders and the modernization of almost all small parish churches with seats, screens and new windows.

piano nobile: main ceremonial floor of classical building, sitting on basement or 'Rustic' lower floor.

pier-glass: wall mirror supported by small table, bracket or console.

pietra dura: inlaid work with hard stones – jasper, agate, etc.

pilaster: flattened column projecting slightly from wall.

piscina: small recess with basin and drain for washing holy vessels, usually in south wall of chancel, but also found in chapels and chantries.

plas: large house.

pont: bridge.

porte-cochère: grand porch with driveway passing through it, allowing passengers to alight from carriages under cover.

prodigy house: ostentatious grand house in early renaissance style dating from the Elizabethan era.

pulpitum: early medieval stone division between nave and east end of church, succeeded by wooden screen.

putto (pl. **putti**): very young boy, often winged, in renaissance or baroque art.

quatrefoil see **trefoil**.

quoins: dressed (worked) corner stones.

rendering: covering of an exterior wall in stucco, cement or limewash.

reredos: painted or sculpted screen behind and above altar.

rib see **vault**.

roll-moulding: rounded moulding feature in Norman arches and doorways.

rood: Crucifixion group of Christ with Virgin and St John, traditionally located above screen and facing towards the congregation. Destroyed in 16th-century Reformation but often replaced by Victorians.

roof timbers: a tie-beam runs horizontally across roof-space. A king post rises vertically from it to the apex of the roof. Queen posts rise not to the apex but to subsidiary beams known as collars. Wind-braces strengthen the roof rafters.

rustication: working of stone on a wall with indentations to look more natural.

sallyport: a gateway for making a sally from a fortified place.

sant: saint.

screen: inserted in medieval churches to divide nave from chancel, richly carved in 15th/16th centuries and usually carrying musicians' loft and rood group.

screens passage: corridor inside the entrance of a medieval hall house divided on one side by a screen to exclude drafts from the hall and on the other by kitchen range.

sedilia: group of (usually three) recessed seats in the south wall of the chancel, for the priest, deacon and sub-deacon who officiated in the High Mass, often richly decorated.

sheela-na-gig: form of exterior carving, female and apparently obscene, believed to be associated with fertility.

slighted: the deliberate part-demolition of a castle after the Civil War to prevent re-use.

solar: upstairs room at family end of medieval hall house (opposite to the screens passage).

Originally accessed by a ladder, this was usually replaced by a staircase in the Tudor period.

squint: an opening cut through an internal wall to enable priests at side altars to see the sanctuary and thus synchronize the ceremonies of the Mass.

spandrel: space between arches, roughly triangular in shape.

springer: the point at which an arch or a rib departs from the vertical line of a wall or pier.

stiff-leaf see **capital**.

string course: a band of projecting stonework on a wall surface.

stucco: plaster, usually protective covering for brick, sometimes fashioned to imitate stone.

studding: vertical timbers on exterior of timber-framed house, divided by plaster. Close studding indicated wealth.

swag: ornament like suspended cloth.

tester: flat canopy over pulpit to project sound outwards.

tie-beam see **roof timbers**.

tracery: decorative division of gothic window, variously described as plate, geometrical, intersecting, reticulated, cusped or panel.

transepts: extensions north and south from crossing, usually containing chapels and memorials.

tre, tref: home, town.

trefoil: most common gothic decorative form of three leaves, normally found in tracery. Likewise quatrefoil, cinquefoil, octofoil, etc.

triforium: middle tier in a three-tier church interior, with the nave arcade below and clerestory above, characteristic of Decorated period.

triple-decker pulpit: composition of pulpit, reading desk and clerk's desk, term sometimes used even if only two of these components are present.

trumpet see **capital**.

tŷ: house.

tympanum: space above doorway or above screen in church, filling vault area, sometimes carried rood figures and later royal arms.

tŷ'r capel: house attached to side of chapel.

uchelwr (pl. *uchelwyr*): Welsh administrative class emerging at end of Middle Ages, beneficiary of Tudor ascendancy.

undercroft: a crypt, vault.

vault: stone roof. Complete vaults are rare in parish churches, being usually confined to cathedrals, but they are found in porches, chapels and chancels. A barrel vault (also called, if ceiled, a wagon roof) comprises a simple semi-circular roof running the length of a nave or chancel. A rib is a projecting feature of a vault, sometimes structural and sometimes decorative. Lierne ribs join and cross other ribs and do not rise from piers. Burial chambers are also sometimes called vaults.

Venetian window: classical feature composed of three openings, the centre one higher and arched.

wagon roof see **vault**.

water-leaf see **capital**.

weepers: small figures set round medieval chest tombs, representing grieving relatives, priests or angels.

wind-braces see **roof timbers**.

Y Gair: the Word.

ynys: island.

Bibliography

Baker, Mark, *History of Plas Teg*

Bell, David, *The Artist in Wales*, London, 1957

Blue Guide to Wales, Benn, 1979

Borrow, George, *Wild Wales*, Glasgow, 1980

Bowen, E. G., *The Settlement of the Celtic Saints in Wales*, Cardiff, 1954

Buildings of Wales (formerly Pevsner guides), Yale Univ Press, 1979–2006:
Carmarthenshire and Ceredigion, Thomas Lloyd, Julian Orbach, Robert Scourfield
Clwyd, Edward Hubbard
Glamorgan, John Newman
Gwent/Monmouthshire, John Newman
Gwynedd (not yet published)
Pembrokeshire, Thomas Lloyd, Julian Orbach, Robert Scourfield
Powys, Richard Haslam

Cadw, *A Mirror of Medieval Wales*, Cardiff, 1988

—, *Wales, Castles and Historic Places*, Cardiff, 1990

Chadwick, Nora, *The Celts*, Penguin, 1970

Companion Guides, North and South Wales, by Peter Beazley, Elisabeth Howell, Collins, 1971, 1975

Crook, J. Mordaunt, *William Burges*, Murray, 1981

Davies, Geraint Talfan, *At Arm's Length*, Seren, 2008

Davies, John, *A History of Wales*, Penguin, 1993

—, *The Making of Wales*, Cadw, 1996

Davies, Rees, *The Revolt of Owain Glyndwr*, Cardiff, 1995

Fishlock, Trevor, *Talking of Wales*, London, 1976

Gerald of Wales, *The Journey through Wales/ Description of Wales*, Penguin, 1978

Green, Jim, *The Holy Ways of Wales*, Talybont, 2000

Harvey, John, *The Art of Piety*, University of Wales, 1995

Hilling, John, *The Historic Architecture of Wales*, University of Wales, 1975

Holder, Christopher, *Wales: An Archaeological Guide*, Faber, 1974

Hughes, Harold, *The Old Churches of Snowdonia*, National Park Society, 1924

Hughes, T. J., *Wales's Best One Hundred Churches*, Seren, 2007

Jones, Anthony, *Welsh Chapels*, National Museum of Wales, 1984

Kightly, Charles, *A Mirror of Medieval Wales: Gerald of Wales*, Cadw, 1988

Kinross, John, *Discovering the Smallest Churches in Wales*, Tempus, 2007

Lloyd, Thomas, *The Lost Houses of Wales*, SAVE, 1986

Lord, Peter, *The Aesthetics of Relevance*, Gomer, 1993

—, *The Visual Culture of Wales*, University of Wales, 2000

Morris, Jan, *The Matter of Wales*, Penguin, 1986

—, *Our First Leader*, Gomer, 2000

— and Twm Morys, *A Machynlleth Triad*, Penguin, 1993

Parker, Will, *The Four Branches of the Mabinogi*, Bardic, 2005

Peate, Iorwerth, *The Welsh House*, Cymmrodorion, 1940

Powys, John Cowper, *Obstinate Cymric*, London 1973

Rough Guide to Wales, 2006

Sager, Peter, *Wales*, Pallas Guide, 1991

Soden, R. W., *Welsh Parish Churches*, Gomer 1984

Stephens, Meic, *Wales in Quotation*, Wales, 1999

Tanner, Marcus, *The Last of the Celts*, Yale, 2004

Thurlby, Malcolm, *Romanesque Architecture and Sculpture in Wales*, Logaston, 2006

Vaughan-Thomas, Wynford, *Wales: A History*,
  Michael Joseph, 1985
—, *Shell Guide to Wales*, Shell, 1987
Walker, David, *Medieval Wales*, Cambridge,
  1990
Welsh Academy, *Encyclopaedia of Wales*,
  University of Wales, 2008
Wheeler, Richard, *The Medieval Screens of the
  Southern Marches*, Logaston, 2006
Williams, Glanmore, *The Welsh Church from
  Conquest to Reformation*, Cardiff, 1962
Williams, Gwyn, *The Welsh in their History*,
  London, 1982
Winn, Christopher, *I Never Knew That About
  Wales*, Ebury, 2007

Index

Picture Acknowledgements

Grateful acknowledgement is given to the following for permission to reproduce photographs:

Cadw (crown copyright): pp. ii, 3, 9, 11, 13, 31, 43, 45, 71, 75, 77, 81, 83, 85, 86, 97, 101, 103, 106, 109, 127, 136, 145, 147, 157, 159, 161, 166–7, 175, 180, 189, 193, 199, 201, 202, 203, 206, 209, 211, 230, 249, 253, 256, 271, 273, 275

Paul Barker/Country Life: pp. 15, 19, 27, 52, 53, 65, 78, 88, 91, 95, 111, 123, 124, 126, 151, 153, 179, 183, 190, 222, 227, 229, 231, 233, 236, 237, 238, 240, 241, 243, 259, 260, 262, 265, 267, 277, 278

NTPL/Christopher Gallagher: p. 24

Portmeirion Ltd: pp. 33, 219

NTPL/Andreas von Einsiedel: pp. 46, 60, 63, 107, 215

Ray Edgar/Ancient Monument Society: pp. 51, 116, 121

Mark Fiennes/Country Life: p. 58

Alex Ramsey/Country Life: pp. 69, 139

NTPL/Joe Cornish: p. 99

NTPL/John Hammond: p. 100

Ralph Carpenter/Carmarthenshire County Council: p. 105

NTPL/Erik Pelham: p. 114

Alex Ramsay/Ancient Monument Society: pp. 119, 235

Robert Harding Picture Library/Alamy: p. 129

John Parker: pp. 165, 177

David Dawson/Landmark Trust: p. 171

NTPL/Rupert Truman: p. 173

Richard Wheeler/Ancient Monument Society: p. 185

NTPL/Matthew Antrobus: p. 205

Ffotograff Photolibrary & Agency: p. 225